ANDREW

STORMTROOPER
FAMILIES

HARRINGTON PARK PRESS

NEW YORK, NY • USA   YORK, NORTH YORKSHIRE • UK

ANDREW WACKERFUSS

STORMTROOPER FAMILIES

HOMOSEXUALITY AND COMMUNITY IN THE EARLY NAZI MOVEMENT

Harrington Park Press
Box #350
511 Avenue of the Americas
New York, NY 10011-8436

Library of Congress Cataloging-in-Publication Data

Wackerfuss, Andrew, 1975–
    Stormtrooper families : homosexuality and community in the early Nazi movement / Andrew Wackerfuss, PhD.
        pages cm
    Includes index.
    ISBN 978-1-939594-05-1 (pbk. : alk. paper)—ISBN 978-1-939594-04-4 (hardcover : alk. paper)—ISBN 978-1-939594-06-8 (e-book)
1. National socialism and homosexuality. 2. Germany—Social conditions—1933–1945. 3. Violence—Germany—History—20th century.
I. Title.
    HQ76.3.G3W33 2015
    306.6094309′04—dc23   2015008467

Manufactured in the United States of America

10 9 8 7 6 5 4 3 2

To my family

CONTENTS

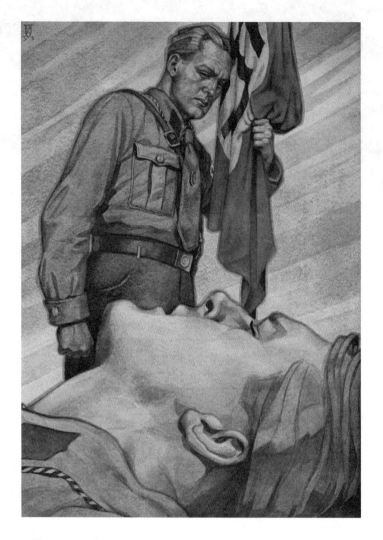

Fallen Comrade

In this image from a 1933 commemorative book of propaganda cigarette vouchers celebrating the Nazi victory, a stormtrooper gazes down in grim resolution on a fallen comrade, portrayed in the Nazis' usual idealized style. The original caption, *"There is no greater honor than to continue fighting for the Germany you died for,"* shows how Nazi media created martyrs by interpreting stormtrooper casualties as blood sacrifices, who strengthened the remaining members and paved the way to political victory.

Source: *Deutschland erwacht:Werden, Kampf und Sieg der NSDAP* [Germany, Awake! Origins, struggle, and victory of the NSDAP] (Hamburg-Bahrenfeld: Cigaretten-Bilderdienst, 1933). Personal collection, Geoffrey Giles.

INTRODUCTION

Enough time has passed that, to younger generations, telling someone that you study the stormtroopers makes them think not of Germany in the 1930s, but of a galaxy long ago and far away.

As ever fewer people who remember the Nazis' murderous regime first-hand are still living, disparate elements of their authoritarian system have become blurred in the public mind. Images of brown shirts fighting in the streets mix with scenes of gray-clad soldiers swarming across European borders, then mingle with apparitions of black-suited SS men guarding death camps. Over time, the various perpetrators of Nazi violence have been melded into a broad stereotype of unquestioned villainy, a case study for the rise of demonic forces in political realms.

For decades now, whenever a book, television show, or film has needed a bad guy that audiences will immediately and unquestionably accept as evil, the Nazis again pull on their boots and begin their goose-stepping march. In the public mind, Nazi depravity has reached the level of a Platonic ideal, as if it still exists somewhere as an embodiment of pure evil, waiting to be conjured again into the real world. But within this seemingly unified authoritarian ideal there existed a wide array of factions, rivalries, and social networks—all of which cooperated, and competed, to create the violent history that the world has found impossible to forget.

Of the various Nazi factions, the stormtroopers persist as a uniquely compelling group. As the first Nazis, they embodied the worst excesses of the early movement, but they did so in a way that was closely connected to pre-Nazi structures of political and family life. In other words, the stormtroopers show the Nazis as they emerged from normal interactions of politics, culture, neighborhood, and family.

The stormtroopers also command enduring interest because of a series of strange associations with sexuality, homosexuality, and the political meaning of sexual orientation. From the start, significant numbers of both fascist and antifascist observers of Nazi politics believed that sexual energies fueled the stormtroopers' rise, brought them political victory, and then caused their downfall in a massacre that forever cemented a link between sexuality and violence in Nazi politics.

The stormtrooper story thus offers a strange and compelling drama in which public debates over human sexuality mixed with violent political conflict, creating and ultimately destroying the men who birthed the Nazi beast. The story has fascinated and confused the public ever since.

While many historians complain that the public misreads their subject, in this field public misconceptions pair with the Nazis' very high profile to create dangerous misunderstandings. Indeed, every few years images of gay Nazis recur: as a weapon to be wielded against fascism, as a misguided argument against gay rights, or in the service of otherwise unrelated political conflicts of the day.

This book explains the truth behind the connection between sexuality and Nazism, going beyond typical formulations that merely seek to explain political evil through personal pathology. Instead, *Stormtrooper Families* demonstrates how Nazi sexuality combined with political forms connected to larger structures of family, locality, and society that crossed all sexual and political orientations.

You will read how the stormtroopers' first forays into politics came through exploiting natural social alliances, close personal relationships, and authentic local connections. You will learn how the early Nazis built political structures based on emotional bonds, and how they mobilized these otherwise positive emotional experiences to distract attention from their negative goals.

Stormtrooper Families presents the daily life experiences of a political paramilitary, and it conveys what it meant to live as a member of an all-consuming political fraternity. Finally, it shows how political movements gain strength from their interaction with human sexuality, as well as the challenges they face once they begin to exploit this powerful dynamic. In the end, these lessons will illuminate not only the Nazi past but also our political present.

Stormtroopers: A Primer

To navigate the coming narrative, it can be useful to understand a series of basic facts concerning the stormtroopers, their role in the Nazi state, and the general way historians have interpreted their specific function within the National Socialist movement. As readers follow the story to come, they should bear in mind the following six important aspects of the stormtroopers:

1. The stormtroopers took their name from the *Sturmabteilung*, a shock unit of the German Army used in World War I's later stages to penetrate enemy trenches and open the way for massed assault. The choice of name, usually abbreviated SA, thus highlighted the connection between the early Nazis and the communities of war veterans that had formed during the Great War, and which during the subsequent Weimar years influenced politics of the right, left, and center. The Nazi stormtroopers also saw tactical similarities between themselves and their wartime namesakes, as both saw themselves as an elite vanguard whose service in the literal or political trenches would prepare the way for later national triumph.

2. The stormtroopers served as the Nazi Party's paramilitary militia. They began as a protection squad that guarded Party speakers at that era's volatile political meetings, and they later attempted to build a mass political army to seize power. After Hitler's failed attempt at revolution in 1923, he reconceived the stormtroopers into a political rather than a revolutionary force. In other words, the masses of stormtroopers marching through the streets did so not to overthrow the state directly, but to promote electoral campaigns that could bring a Nazi victory through political channels. The SA thus represents the mix of legal and illegal means through which the Nazis eventually took power.

3. While the stormtroopers tactically attempted to claim legality, ideologically they represented the Nazi movement's radical and revolutionary side. They voiced the Party's social and economic demands, loudly advocated for structural economic changes and material assistance for the impoverished masses, and sought maximalist political solutions that would end democracy once and for all. The SA embodied this ideological stance as the organizational home within the Party for the young, the radical, and the unemployed, and for those who hoped to promote the Nazis' otherwise specious claim to socialism. This radicalism at times threatened the SA's relationship to the larger Party, which in general sought to cooperate with the established economic interests it would need to fight its future wars.

4. Stormtroopers embraced the use of direct personal violence against their enemies. In later years, the Nazi state became famous for inflicting violence through systemic, pseudo-legal, and bureaucratized means. This allowed the state to increase the scale of its persecution while lessening the psychological impact on the perpetrators. The SA, in contrast, inflicted violence spontaneously rather than calculatedly, locally rather than nationally, and passionately rather than aloofly. Historians have called this violence "artisanal," a tactic of the early Nazi movement that eventually evolved into the infamous, "industrial" mass murder the regime later conducted.

5. In daily life, the SA represented the social side of the Nazi movement. The SA tried to care for its members, provide social services to its allies, and build networks of support that would enhance its appeal to neighbors while converting its enemies. Over time the SA built an effective network of social spaces in which stormtroopers could live, eat, and sleep together in political and personal harmony. This unity of personal and political life became one of the movement's greatest strengths.

6. The SA combined its social and emotional claims into an all-consuming lifestyle of daily activity, common living, and close bonds between fighting comrades. While the intense emotions of same-sex camaraderie had long been a powerful political force in European history, by this point modern concepts of homosexuality had reached the public's consciousness. It now seemed that those seeking camaraderie also sought sexual relations—and, indeed, a series of public revelations established that open homosexuals existed comfortably within the SA. The presence of homosexuals in the SA, as we will see, was never as pervasive or influential as opponents claimed. However, the association between homosexuality and fascism became a consistent theme of antifascist politics and an enduring smear against generations of gay men.

If these six traits described the daily life of the SA as it strove for power between 1923 and 1933, they also caused its death after 1933. Most historians of the SA's fate agree that its downfall was all but inevitable. After all, as a revolutionary, paramilitary, oppositional fraternity, the SA existed to cause chaos rather than to impose order. Once the victorious Nazi movement gained control of the state, the SA identities and practices that it had once exploited became drawbacks. The Nazi Party would no longer encourage revolutionary attitudes, paramilitary agitation, or other disruptive behaviors that could reveal a lack of control and alienate key military and industrial elites. It would no longer encourage spontaneous personal violence, moving instead to systemic and bureaucratized persecution. Social programs would also move beyond the personal and toward the universal, demonstrating the movement's need to transcend the local social networks that had created the SA in favor of creating the unified ethnic identity that it claimed all Germans possessed.

All these elements made the stormtroopers' cliquishness and close attachments—mythologized in the image of the homosexual—into a threatening identity that Hitler eventually decided to extirpate. Thus did the stormtroopers, particularly the homosexual ones whose small numbers had belied their symbolic importance, discover that they would be among the first victims of the persecutory state they had helped to create.

Organization of the Book

The story will proceed as follows:

CHAPTER 1, "Fathers and Forefathers," introduces readers to the Free and Hanseatic City of Hamburg as it existed in the imaginations of the boys who later became stormtroopers. The stormtroopers are present in this chapter only as children. However, their childhoods first introduced them to several themes critical to their later political journeys: their city's contested heritage of democratic governance, its vibrant economic and political life, and the first debates over political homosexuality. This grand and worldly imperial *Vaterstadt*—the "father city" of their childhood—endured throughout their lives as a symbol of a vanished golden age that had been tarnished and betrayed.

IN CHAPTER 2, "Shattered Sons," the war generation marches off to fight and returns to a changed city. Their fear of political and economic crisis often intensified existing social panic about increasing rates of divorce, unwed motherhood, abortion, venereal disease, homosexuality, and other alleged symptoms of degeneracy. These youths joined the nascent Nazi movement, which had positioned itself as a self-consciously pro-family party whose earliest meetings and events showcased marriage, family, and respectable domestic life. Yet the stormtroopers also loudly proclaimed their allegiance to an all-male lifestyle, which they had honed during the Great War and now continued to rely on for emotional stability in an unstable world. They therefore existed uncomfortably between two competing kinship networks—one familial, one comradely. The tension between the two became one of the most important characteristics of the movement.

CHAPTER 3, "Stormtroopers Confront the Criminal," cuts to the heart of the stormtroopers' paradoxical family lifestyles. On the one hand, they married, they founded their own families, and they claimed to be entering politics in order to protect the traditional nuclear family. On the other hand, they actively sought to live as soldiers, disconnecting from their families in favor of their comrades, embracing violence and combat, and at times demonstrating so much affection with one another as to call their sexuality into question. The conflict came to a head in 1928, when a murder trial outed a stormtrooper as homosexual. The SA then sought absolution through a public homophobic protest against a play, The Criminal, whose tolerant stance toward homosexuality became a flashpoint the SA could use to unite the radical right's squabbling factions under the stormtrooper banner.

The next three chapters represent the SA at its fighting peak, from the beginning of the Depression in 1929 to the Nazis' takeover of the state in 1933.

CHAPTER 4, "The Battle of Sternschanze," describes a notorious battle in which an ill-planned SA march erupted into a widespread riot. This highly publicized media event established heroic masculinity and spectacular martyrdom as the stormtroopers' best political weapons.

CHAPTER 5, "Community and Violence," shows how the stormtroopers created an all-consuming daily lifestyle of intense political and personal associations. Through a network of hostels, barracks, and kitchens, they drew recruits and mobilized comrades for political violence. The stormtroopers' communal living spaces tried to root them in neighborhood and family life, but the homoeroticism, drunkenness, and debauchery found there bred conflict with more socially traditional and family-oriented wings of the Nazi movement. The tensions increased as a small number of homosexuals within the SA leadership became known, which led to the political left's increasing eagerness to challenge the Nazis' sexual self-image.

CHAPTER 6, "Bloody Sundays," describes events of 1932, the Weimar Republic's final year. A series of violent encounters that took place on Sundays culminated in Bloody Sunday, when an SA march through the suburb of Altona so provoked local Communists that it set off an epic confrontation between Communists and police. The resulting riot seemingly gave evidence to Nazi claims of Communist criminality versus Nazi righteousness. It helped align the forces of order on the Nazi side and set off a national chain reaction that began the Republic's final descent.

CHAPTER 7, "The Stormtroopers Take Power," relates how SA men used violence to secure authority that they immediately abused. The SA drove its enemies from public life, arrested them without warrants, and consigned them to "wild" concentration camps that it ruled with brutality. However, the SA simultaneously integrated itself into the community in new ways. SA men now took jobs with the police and in city government, seized patronage positions, enjoyed the fruits of corruption, and claimed psychological ownership of taverns, pubs, and restaurants that had formerly resisted their presence. These actions increased tensions between the SA's two communities, because they highlighted the conflict between two opposing goals. On the one hand, the SA sought to establish the stormtroopers as responsible young men, while on the other it hoped to strengthen the brawling same-sex society that had brought the movement this far. At the same time, the rush of victory attracted a new wave of self-interested recruits who knew little of the emotional and spiritual foundations of the stormtrooper lifestyle and instead sought only their own advantage. Victory therefore brought more grief than solace to many SA men, who now faced the irreconcilability of their two families as never before.

CHAPTER 8, "The Night of the Long Knives," shows how tensions between same-sex camaraderie, revolutionary demands, and the SA's new pretension to legitimate authority reached a head by mid-1934. By then, Hamburg had had enough of the bullying SA. The stormtroopers' loud insistence on their honor and privileges, their rampant corruption and excess, and their continued use of violence in public spaces now threatened to undermine the Nazi movement. Hitler and his cronies took action, purging the SA of its leaders and settling old scores in a national massacre that lasted for days. Hitler then mobilized political homophobia as his prime justification for the purge, arguing that he had acted to extirpate the rot of homosexuality from SA and party ranks. Now that the group was cleansed, he said, every German mother could again feel safe with the party in charge. The stormtroopers had thus fallen victim to sexualized political paradigms that they themselves had strengthened, as in their homophobic protest against The Criminal. After June 1934, not only were homosexual stormtroopers chased out of the organization, all SA men were now under the scrutiny of a Nazi Party able and eager to police its citizens' sexual morality and family circumstances. In other words, the authoritarian family policies the Nazis later imposed on all Germany came first to the stormtroopers.

THE EPILOGUE, "From Sodom to Gomorrah: Hamburg in Ruins" traces the final decline of an SA that had little purpose in the Nazi state. This concluding chapter tells how war came home to the stormtroopers, either as soldiers on the front lines of the battlefield or as old men on the home front trying to defend their neighborhoods from a rain of Allied bombs. The stormtroopers' efforts to protect their families during the destruction of Operation Gomorrah often brought them into conflict with the Party, their neighbors, and their former comrades. The SA men had always been caught between family and party. Now, at the very end, those who chose their families over their public responsibilities were purged yet again. In any case, all stormtroopers were helpless to prevent the destruction of their beloved "father city." This chapter relates the final fates of the stormtrooper leaders whom readers have met in the preceding chapters: their death, or exile, or imprisonment as broken men who had lost both their same-sex and traditional families. The book ends by tracing the enduring legacy of the sinister figure of the gay Nazi. The legend of this figure, while based on reality, has been mobilized out of all proportion to its actual authority in the Nazi system, with very real political consequences that reach into the 21st century.

A Note on Terminology

The Weimar Republic is notorious for its multitude of squabbling political parties. The number of factions and their often unclear relationships can perplex modern English-speaking readers, who are used to political systems that feature two major factions and no more than a few minor parties on the margins. In the Weimar system, however, major political orientations often generated several competing parties, and these parties cooperated, argued, fractured, and re-integrated with remarkable frequency. Readers may therefore find useful the following brief definitions of the major political factions, the parties that carried their messages, and the paramilitary armies that fought for them.

Political Factions

CONSERVATIVE

The term *conservative* as a catch-all for the parties of the center-right is defined as resistance to the social, economic, and cultural changes wrought by the French Revolution and its imitators, in this case the German revolution of 1918. Weimar conservatives admitted that the possible return of monarchy was slim, but even so they hoped to steer German politics toward the values that monarchy had enshrined: nationalism, militarism, religious traditionalism, and, all too often, antisemitism. In general, conservative parties promoted values of authority, hierarchy, and obedience as forces for national good.

Of the many small and short-lived parties of the center-right, the most important conservative party was the German National People's Party (DNVP). Formed during the 1918 revolution from the remnants of imperial conservative and nationalist parties, the DNVP united a coalition of monarchists, wealthy merchants, and rural landowners in opposition to both liberal democracy and socialism. It drew its strength from a combination of respectable and populist nationalism in the Protestant north, but this combination proved difficult to manage. From the start, the DNVP displayed a strong tendency toward radicalization in both the content and conduct of conservative politics. This trend led to eventual cooperation with its upstart cousins, the Nazis, who for their part never fully trusted the "reactionaries" of traditional conservatism.

CENTRIST

Centrist political factions in Weimar Germany supported the republican form of government that the revolution had created. This broad agreement, however, concealed a wide spectrum of political beliefs, including liberalism, political Catholicism, and socialism—the three major factions that cooperated as the "Weimar Coalition." These groups supported and ran the government. The Coalition's power, however, steadily weakened as economic depression pushed voters toward increasingly radical parties that rejected democracy from both left and right.

Within the centrist coalition, the three major factions were:

Liberal

Liberalism in 19th- and early 20th-century Europe functioned as the ideology of business, of progress, and of personal and economic liberty. In its early stages, it often fought against established states and promoted new values of freedom and personal choice, arguing that these values would bring economic gains to all. Over time, as businessmen and industrialists converted economic influence into political power, liberal parties increasingly became the establishment. In the united Germany of the 19th century, the National Liberal Party allied with the crown to support nationalism, militarism, and an expansionist foreign policy, especially in the naval and colonial realms. National Liberals cited Britain and America as examples of this model's success in promoting and protecting international trade, as well as national prosperity. In 1918, National Liberal support for the Great War destroyed the party along with the monarchy, and two new parties emerged to continue the liberal tradition:

The German People's Party (DVP) was formed in 1918 to represent the National Liberals' right wing, a role quite close to what the party had performed during the imperial period. It represented big-business interests, argued for limited government, and opposed socialism as a threat to the established economic system (which, of course, the liberals led). While initially quite hostile to the socialist-led revolution, the DVP grew increasingly cooperative over time and eventually became a reliable governing partner.

The German Democratic Party (DDP) was formed in 1918 to represent the National Liberals' smaller left wing. It combined the former insistence on national economic might with an acceptance of democracy as the best way to promote a strong nation. The DDP also embodied the side of liberalism

that sought to protect ethnic and religious minorities. While initially popular and always influential among the governing classes, it steadily lost votes
throughout the Weimar period.

Catholic

German Catholics during the imperial era had been represented by their
own political party, the Catholic Center Party (Zentrum). The Zentrum argued for Catholic reliability as loyal citizens of the German state—once a
contested issue—and it continued into the Weimar era reasonably intact. As a
Catholic party in the Protestant city of Hamburg, the Zentrum played almost
no role in local elections. Its national importance, however, was immense.
Its political pragmatism led it to accept both monarchy and democracy as
acceptable forms of government, and it therefore proved a reliable partner
for a variety of governing coalitions. During Weimar's strongest years, the
left-wing faction of Christian trade unionists cooperated effectively with the
socialists and other parties of the Weimar Coalition. During the Republic's
final crises, however, the Zentrum's authoritarian faction gained the upper
hand and forged the fatal deal that cemented Hitler's power.

Socialist

Those who assume that socialism is left wing forget that such descriptors
are always relative. Socialism originally appeared in European history as an
oppositional and revolutionary movement that sought increased political
power and economic equality for the working class. Socialism was particularly strong in Germany, especially in the large cities like Hamburg, where
it appealed to those working for the newly powerful industrial and trading firms. Eventually the movement united under the banner of the Social
Democratic Party (SPD), which, despite being banned for many years, grew
in popularity until it became Germany's largest party in 1912. In 1918, the
same socialist movement that was often oppositional and revolutionary in
the imperial era took leadership of the new republic. In the Weimar context,
therefore, we can consider socialism to be centrist, even if doing so locates
the center further left than many English-speaking readers generally expect.
Thinking of the socialists as both centrist and leftist also helps to properly
define their role in the Weimar Republic as the party most interested in the
political values centrists always claim: good governance, productive compromise, and the rule of law. Social Democrats combined these technocratic

approaches with the old socialist values of economic justice and poverty mitigation to bind working- and middle-class supporters of democracy together in support of the hard-won republic. They also mobilized their own paramilitary group, the Reichsbanner, to vigorously defend democracy against the radical paramilitary bands that sought its destruction.

COMMUNIST

When war seemed imminent in 1914, the SPD chose to demonstrate its national loyalty by supporting government credit for war expenses. This decision sowed bitter seeds within the party, especially as famine and war exhaustion soured the national mood. When the SPD expelled several key members of its antiwar wing in 1917, the exiles focused left-wing anger into a new socialist movement, the German Communist Party (KPD). As the revolution of 1918 turned into the troubled years of the Weimar Republic, the KPD embodied the radical left flank of the socialist movement. Angry at the compromises the SPD made in governing, bitter at the lack of a full social and economic revolution, and eager to take inspiration, support, and even direct orders from Moscow's violent Soviet regime, the KPD became one of two great existential threats to the Republic. The Communist paramilitary, the Red Front Fighting Brigade (RFB), protected Communist political meetings, staged massive protests and riots, attacked symbols of capitalism, fought with police, and battled enemy paramilitaries of the center and right.

NATIONAL SOCIALIST

The other great threat came from the right, from the party of rightist revolutionary violence: the National Socialist German Workers Party (NSDAP), or Nazi Party. At first the NSDAP was just one of many parties calling themselves national socialists (lower case—to the early Nazis, national socialism was a faction to which many parties could belong). As this book's opening chapters reveal, the national socialist faction emerged after 1918 as the successors to the discredited conservatism of the imperial era. The Nazis retained and often amplified many of conservatism's ideological traits—nationalism, militarism, and racist antisemitism being the most important—but the Party had none of conservatism's redeeming characteristics of respect for tradition, restraint, or continuity. Nazism's often youthful supporters sought instead to create a newly violent style of rightist politics, one that matched what the Communists had developed on the left. In other words, the national socialists matched the conservatives in ideology and the Communists in tactics. Although the Nazis still considered both of these groups to be enemies, they also cooperated with them in turn. They attacked liberalism and socialism alongside the conservatives, furthering rightist ideology and political goals.

Meanwhile, they founded the paramilitary stormtroopers, whose tactics paralleled those of their Communist enemies: mixing protection duties with protest, and electoral actions with outright attempts at revolution. Although the SA and RFB proclaimed their undying enmity, they also cooperated in actions to ensure that violent and revolutionary means of political conflict became more common than peaceful compromise. Both Nazis and Communists took to the streets to stage violent encounters that destabilized the republican system, and both paramilitaries were perfectly happy to shatter the young democracy because both believed that they would be the one to reassemble democracy's shattered pieces into the preferred utopian state.

Other Terms

HANSESTADT

Citizens of Hamburg historically have used the term *Hansestadt* to memorialize their city's long heritage as an independent, worldly, liberal democracy focused on seaborne international trade. It comes from Hamburg's historical membership in the medieval Hanseatic League, a trading federation of city-states whose importance to Hamburg's modern political culture is discussed in chapter 1.

HOMOSOCIAL

Homosocial refers to living spaces and environments that feature interactions among members of a single gender. These spaces are quite common in history, and in many ways grew stronger in the late 19th century wherever Victorian concepts of gender separation took hold. Homosocial is not in itself a loaded term; it is a neutral descriptor of the gender balance of a group, location, or organization. It refers to social, not sexual, relationships.

HOMOEROTIC

Homoerotic refers to a certain charge of attraction that may exist within homosocial spaces or between members of the same sex. Homoeroticism often represents an unacknowledged thrill or unexamined sexual energy that some may find in same-sex associations, without expressing these feelings in sexual acts. As readers will discover in the following pages, some men of the late 19th and early 20th centuries saw homoeroticism as a productive political force, while others feared that it masked hidden homosexual depravity that would undermine political systems.

HOMOSEXUAL

The perhaps logical expression of homoeroticism in same-sex acts, or homosexuality, is the final side of this triangle. The term *homosexual,* as is explained in chapter 1, emerged only near the end of the 19th century. Although the word's meaning was intensely contested, it became the key term in an emerging understanding of same-sex orientation as a component of identity, rather than as a discrete and passing act without deeper psychological relevance. As such, it marks the transition in European thinking about sexuality from a religious view, which sees the act itself as a sin, to a psychological view, which sees the act as an expression of a larger identity or inner self. While the medical-psychological view could be just as stigmatizing as religious condemnation, increasing attention to the concept brought the first stirrings of a movement for decriminalization and tolerance of homosexuality.

Today the label "homosexual" is considered a retrograde term that reveals how medicine and psychology once stigmatized same-sex orientations as disordered and abnormal. Since the 1970s, the terms "gay" and "lesbian" have largely replaced it. However, for historical purposes it would be inappropriate to refer to men who inclined toward the same sex in the 1920s as "gay." The German equivalent term, *Schwul,* had indeed already emerged within the homosexual subculture, but in neither Germany nor the English-speaking world had it yet come to represent the identity itself. Since "gay" or *Schwul* represents a certain type of gay and lesbian identity that emerged only in recent decades, this book will use the historically appropriate term *homosexual.* It does so not to stigmatize, but, rather, to acknowledge how linguistic and cultural frames of reference limited the ways people of the time could conceive their sexual identity.

PARAGRAPH 175

This paragraph of the imperial German legal code came from existing legislation in the North German Confederation led by Prussia, which in essence exported much of its law to the other German states after unification in 1871. Paragraph 175 outlawed "unnatural sex acts" between men, as well as bestiality, but it explicitly did not apply to women. Despite attempts to both extend and abolish this law, it remained on the books into the 20th century, by which time it had taken on a cultural life of its own. Common use and popular imagery used Paragraph 175 as a code to discuss the still-uncomfortable topic of homosexuality, eventually functioning as a linguistic shorthand or slang for sex acts between men.

STURMABTEILUNG/STORMTROOPERS/SA

As mentioned earlier, the name Sturmabteilung, or SA, comes from a German army unit of the same name. This work will use "SA" for the Nazi organization and "stormtroopers" for the individuals. The stormtroopers most often called themselves "SA men," a term I use in a generic sense, despite the fact that it was also an official title for the lowest rank of stormtrooper. I have generally avoided using specific ranks and titles, either for individuals or for the group, because ranks and titles changed frequently and in any case hold little meaning for 21st-century readers not already familiar with the SA's organizational minutiae.

SS

Many people confuse the SA and SS. The *Schutzstaffel*, or SS, originally grew out of the SA as an elite protection squad for party speakers, a role the SA had been created to fill but which it necessarily abandoned as it grew into a paramilitary army. The SS thus represents a mirror image of the SA: exclusive rather than universal, secretive rather than showy, calculated rather than clumsy, and scheming rather than spontaneous. The conflict between the SA and SS is a running motif in several chapters, and it reaches its climax in the deadly confrontation described in chapter 8—a resolution that had great meaning for the character and practice of institutionalized violence in the Nazi state.

VOLK/VÖLKISCH

The German word *Volk* is easy to understand, once you know to pronounce the "v" as an "f"—Volk, therefore, means folk. On one level, this easy translation conveys its meaning as an organic community of uncomplicated, earnest people living in harmony with the land and with one another. However, this translation alone does not capture the more grandiose political meaning the term came to acquire in the 19th and early 20th centuries. In that sense, the term conveys the way many nations and political movements have invoked "the people" as a powerful source of political and cultural authority.

German nationalist politics grew increasingly focused on the Volk in the late 19th century, and many political movements indeed came to be known as *völkisch*. These movements blended politics, folklore, history, and mysticism into a political project that sought power by and for a unified ethnic German people—what today we would call a militant and authoritarian form of ethnic nationalism. Völkisch politics, ironically, was never unified. Its many parties and groups often fought and argued with each other over the proper interpretation of their racial doctrines, and they constantly competed for members, attention, and political influence.

The Nazi Party was born into this competitive ecosystem of völkisch politics, which it eventually took over and dominated. The Nazis were not the only völkisch party, and indeed they were relative latecomers to völkisch politics. But their skillful deployment of the movement's symbols, their repeated emphasis on ethnicity as the basis of politics, and their aggressive persecution of their perceived enemies made them in the end the preeminent representatives of this political style. Their claim to the concept of the Volk, and the abuses they perpetrated in its supposed service, were so total as to discredit it after their defeat. Today the term is rarely used, except when referring to the historical period in which it wielded great political influence.

FATHERS AND FOREFATHERS

1

On a crisp late-summer morning in 1898, ten-year-old Franz Tügel accompanied his father on a Sunday walk through the city of Hamburg. It was one of the first times that Franz's father, a man with the kingly name of August Christian Wilhelm Ludwig Tügel, had allowed the boy to accompany him to church, and on his weekly rounds after the service. Before then Franz's father had deemed the boy too young to grasp the intellectual and spiritual implications of a church service, or to appreciate the combination of pleasure and purpose that a successful merchant's walk through his city could serve.[1] Now, however, Franz's father had finally seen fit to include his oldest son in his Sunday rituals. In time the second son would join them, but for now just the two of them shared this special ritual.

Father and son began their journey in their home neighborhood of Hamm, one of several small towns that lay within Hamburg's eastern border along the broad Elbe River.[2] Hamm, Horn, and the other city districts to the east and north of Hamburg's urban core were part of the great metropolis, but they still had a small-town feel that lent them a slower, calmer atmosphere. In his memoirs, a much older Franz Tügel looked back on Hamm as a "garden district" and a "vision of small-town life within a big city."[3] Hamm featured broad, tree-lined streets, through which trains of horse carts regularly carried goods and people from the countryside to the city center. Many of the local passenger carts featured a surprising and delightful innovation: electric meters that automatically monitored a rider's fare and charged an appropriate and precise amount.[4] Bridges large and small spanned the many canals that branched off the Elbe, allowing all of Hamburg's neighborhoods access to this essential river.

From the upper stories of Hamm's modest and widely spaced four-story apartment blocks, a childlike Franz could sit in a window and gaze westward toward the high towers of Hamburg's five main churches, whose steeples called out to adventurous boys and weary sailors alike. The tallest was an impressive gothic cathedral named for the patron saint of sailors, St. Nicholas. Until 1876 it was the tallest building in the world. In the 1890s, Hamburg's quiet eastern and northern towns were the perfect place for rising bourgeois merchants like August Christian to raise their families. August Christian's own father had come to Hamburg from provincial Mecklenburg—driven, as were so many others in that era, to leave the countryside to seek their fortune in the big city.[5]

On their Sunday walks, Franz and his father traced a path down the main avenues toward the city center. August Christian looked on indulgently as his son peered into the windows of shops stuffed with toys, bakeries that emitted delicious smells, and, later in the season, Christmas markets that combined both delights.[6] Father and son soon passed through the old Berliner Tor, once a gate in the city walls that had monitored Hamburg's commerce with Brandenburg and Lower Saxony to the east. The similar Lübecker Tor had connected Hamburg with the other great Hanseatic trading cities to the north. The walls, however, were no more: Hamburg's city fathers had ordered them demolished in 1820 as a way of proclaiming that the city, in the aftermath of Napoleon's haughty occupation and compulsory fortification, would continue to assert its traditional neutrality in armed conflicts.[7] On a map, one can still see the ghost of Hamburg's medieval walls encircling the city. After 1820, however, the encirclement comprised not barriers but bridges, houses, shops, and green spaces—especially on the west side, where a botanical garden encouraged burghers to stroll through their increasingly wealthy and confident city.

Having passed through the gates and gardens of the former walls, Franz and his father entered the increasingly narrow streets and canal passages of Hamburg's ancient urban core. In the young boy's imagination, the merchant houses there were themselves a type of fortress that was simultaneously intimidating and alluring. In his first journeys down the Steinstrasse toward his father's office building, Franz peered apprehensively through cavernous entryways into the merchant buildings' shadowy inner courtyards. He shied away from the "dark elements" who took refuge in the alleys, or who packed the areas around the canals as they loaded and unloaded goods.[8] Many of these men lived nearby, in an area called the *Gängeviertel*, or Alley Quarter. This thieves' den had grown narrower, dirtier, darker, smellier, more crowded, and more criminal as Hamburg's population swelled. Most men living there provided useful labor at the nearby docks, harbors, and warehouses, or in the booming construction industry. Working-class women became household servants or worked in textile factories. Eventually the growing number of laborers became a problem for the city fathers. Conditions had been deteriorating rapidly, turning the city's oldest and most central area into a crime-ridden slum rife with pickpockets, robbers, and general villainy perpetrated by and upon the recently arrived masses from the countryside.

Franz's father did not allow his son to enter these dangerous districts, wanting to shield the boy from the marginal inhabitants and their questionable lifestyles. Indeed, the pair never went as far as the city's western border of St. Pauli—a haven for sojourning sailors and hence a refuge for organized crime, rough language in many tongues, and far more adult entertainments than a respectable merchant would allow his young son to encounter. St. Pauli had always been somewhat of a borderland. Its most famous street, the Reeperbahn, acquired its name from the rope-makers who could practice their trade only outside the city limits. Outside the old walls but well within Hamburg's domain, St. Pauli became home to professionals of all stripes whose trades the city needed but also disdained for their din, their stench, or their disrepute.

With the arrival of steamships in the mid-19th century, the district quickly found an infamous new purpose. Although most cities and towns locked their gates at night, the iron barriers guarding St. Pauli remained closed during the day. At night the gates swung open and welcomed the Reeperbahn's famous nightlife. Taverns opened their doors. Dance halls and theaters raised their curtains. Sailors staggered drunkenly through alleys, fought locals and each other, passed out in piles, and were robbed of any coins they had not yet spent. On certain streets, lights from back-alley windows burst into red brilliance, illuminating the women who made themselves available to men—for a price. The scene degenerated further at Altona, where the Prussian takeover in 1864 had done little to reduce prostitution, and a street with the taunting name of Große Freiheit—great freedom—was home to a structure that Hamburg's solid Protestant leaders may have considered a second Babylon—the region's largest Catholic church. St. Pauli, Altona, and similar districts were at best necessary appendages to the central work life of a port city; at worst they were a constant source of disease, destabilization, and dismay. Respectable boys and girls had to be kept as far away as possible.

As Franz began to accompany his father into the far more tightly controlled world of the bourgeois merchants, his fascination with its solidity, its productivity, and its grand promises grew into adulation. His memoirs recall his growing interest in Hamburg's industrious bustle, which he later eulogized as a vanished "old-Hamburg world."[9] The green-tinged towers of the central churches rose above the clamor, their softly clinging bells uniting all below in marking the hours. Merchant houses clustered in the city center, growing ever taller and more grandiose, and buzzing with trade and commerce that refused to rest, even on Sunday. The masts and white sails of ships in the harbor shone through the morning mist, while the call of steamship whistles floated up from the docks. All these sights and sounds coalesced into a vast and varied commercial network that pulsed through the canals and inner streets of a *Welthandelstadt*—a world-class international trading city.

At the peak of their Sunday journey, father and son would arrive at August Christian's offices in the newly built Dovenhof, a massive and impressive building in the middle of Hamburg's central commercial district. Although young Franz would have always known the Dovenhof as a vital part of Hamburg's commercial scene, the new building actually represented a recent change in the city's architecture. Hanseatic merchant houses traditionally featured ground-floor shops and public spaces, warehouse rooms in the rear, and upper-story living spaces. The new style eliminated the residence, shop front, and warehouse elements in order to increase the amount of office space available for rent. These new "office buildings" had caught on like wildfire in London, New York, Baltimore, and Chicago, and their gradual takeover in Hamburg therefore showed how the city imported not only goods from overseas but also methods of doing business and ways of living. This connection to the larger Atlantic world of trade, with its openness to English and American business techniques, had long been one of Hamburg's strengths. In fact, the purpose of the Tügels' Sunday stroll was to enable August Christian to keep track of the outside world, which was reflected in the letters and other weekend mail that had piled up on his desk in the Dovenhof.

While Franz's father read his post at a leisurely Sunday pace, the boy would quietly amuse himself. Perhaps he would have carefully climbed on and off the fascinating paternoster elevator, a type of elevator cab recently imported from England. Franz's father might not have allowed him to do so unsupervised, however, as these constantly moving elevators had killed several people who mistakenly climbed onto the roof of the cab and were carried upward into the gears. Franz most likely would have sat at a desk next to his father's and watched the man review his business affairs. Or perhaps he sat at the window and looked out over the lower roofs of the old merchant houses. The office gave Franz a commanding view of the city, befitting the station of a rising merchant's son who expected to learn at his father's side and someday earn his own desk at the Dovenhof.

But this was not to be. Six years later, in 1904, while the family was living in Cologne for a time, August Christian Tügel suddenly died. Within a few short months, a man who had been perfectly healthy wasted away from a rapidly growing cancer. Franz was 16, and his world changed forever with his father's death.

"I cannot describe," he later wrote, "what went through my soul in that moment. Through my deepest sorrow grew an impassioned love for the heart that had ceased to beat, but whose unending care-taking had helped create for us such an easy and carefree childhood."

But now, he wrote, the "curtain had fallen; the world of childhood was forever closed to me."[10] Franz could never forget the sight of his father's coffin as it sat on the train that took the family back to their Hamburg home, on its way to be buried in the vast Ohlsdorf Cemetery. Ohlsdorf was one of the largest city cemeteries in the world, and it housed generations of Hanseatic patricians from Hamburg's historic past. August Christian now belonged to that past, yet his death was not just the end of one story. It was also, Franz wrote years later, a harbinger of the future.

"The death of my father," wrote Franz, "changed my life. Once again, I saw God's hand above me, as I had not seen since the striking pictures of biblical storybooks that I read during my earliest years in school. It gave me a powerful vision into the future of the land He wanted to show me."[11]

Ten years later, on the April day that would have been his father's birthday, Franz Tügel took the oath that made him a Lutheran minister. He did so in overt consciousness of upholding his father's worldviews—the "healthy opinions" of August Christian that Franz said had "entered my flesh and blood" at an early age and became "as self-explanatory as daily bread."[12] These views emphasized piety, tradition, self-restraint, and, above all, a strong connection between church and state as agents of God's order in the world. For the young "arch-conservative," as Franz proudly called himself, the "fatherly heritage" of his two fathers—literal and spiritual—demanded political conclusions. "Everything that looked like revolution or revolt," he wrote, "was high treason in my eyes."[13]

Franz Tügel seems not to have considered the possibility that his conception of his father's worldview was, at best, imperfect. Franz had only known his father as a relatively distant patriarch, a man who did not share nuanced or sophisticated aspects of his beliefs with children. Like most children, Franz knew only a highly idealized version of his father, and the man's early death prevented Franz from undergoing the periodic reevaluation of parental figures that most people experience throughout their lives. As Oscar Wilde wrote several years after Franz was born, "Children begin by loving their parents. After a time, they judge them. Rarely, if ever, do they forgive them."[14] Franz never reached the stage of judgment, critique, or forgiveness. Thus his childlike love for his father remained immature, unevaluated, and ignorant of the need to see which qualities of his father's generation had failed or done harm. Franz's political ideology therefore took on qualities similar to the emotional experiences that had birthed them—and in both realms, Franz masked immaturity with bombast.

Twenty years later, on March 5, 1934, an outwardly mature and confident Pastor Franz Tügel stood proudly before the members of Hamburg's Lutheran synod. They had just voted him bishop. Tügel, now a tall man with a pencil-thin mustache and slicked-back hair, did not wear the black robes of a minister on this day of triumph. He had chosen instead to don the brown shirt and swastika armband of a Nazi stormtrooper.

"It is a noteworthy coincidence," he said, "that the synod would meet today, the same day that one year ago saw for the first time the unfurling of the swastika-flag over the balcony of the *Rathaus* [city hall]. On that day, we National Socialists celebrated the fulfillment of our heart's old desire."[15]

It had been a time of long struggle, Tügel said, not only for the state and German society, but also for a church whose authority and influence had been attacked from all sides by sinister and destructive forces. But peace was at hand in both spiritual and secular life, "now that within the church the great meaning of the National Socialist movement for the German people has been recognized."[16]

In response to questions about the church's future plans, Tügel responded curtly, and to great applause, "I have no program. *I am the program.*"[17] He then finished his provocative address to the church he now led: "We have *one* solution only: In the spirit of Luther and Adolf Hitler, that church and *Volk* may become one heart and soul!"[18]

While his followers applauded the speech, Bishop Franz Tügel smoothed the contours of his uniform. Behind him, in the precise middle of the high table where the church's most notable members sat, a fellow clergyman wearing the black uniform of the *Schutzstaffel* oversaw the proceedings like a spider monitoring a well-spun web. Pastors and lay stormtroopers alike now joined in singing the first two verses of "A Mighty Fortress Is Our God," a powerful

Protestant hymn whose chorus now took on an especially aggressive tone. Before the ordination closed with the first verse of the stormtroopers' own anthem, the "Horst Wessel Lied," Franz Tügel raised his right hand in the Nazi salute.[19] Leading the group in three cries of "Heil Hitler!" he pledged his loyalty: to the Führer, to the state that his stormtroopers had helped create, and to the long-dead father Tügel thought he was serving by assisting in the Nazi takeover of the formerly Free and Hanseatic City.

Fathers, Sons, and Stormtroopers

Although Franz Tügel was just one man, his story is typical of the storm-troopers. Tügel described the pattern more clearly and directly than most of his comrades, but dead fathers loomed large in many stormtrooper writings across a variety of media. *Sturmabteilung* (SA) personnel records teemed with orphaned, abandoned, and estranged sons. When forced to defend themselves in legal proceedings, some SA men reliably raised the specter of a dead father as a defense for committing violent acts. Dead fathers also were a strong presence in the literature the stormtroopers later produced. In an array of books, poems, and newspaper articles, stormtroopers mourned their departed forebears and vowed to fight to recover a lost heritage. This theme played to a historic heroic archetype and to recent local history alike—Hanseatic merchant patriarchs seem to have made a habit of working themselves to death while their sons were still young, while working-class fathers also often died early, due to harsh labor conditions, poor sanitation, and substance abuse.[20]

But no matter how prevalent on an anecdotal and literary level, the SA's emphasis on dead fathers cannot be considered representative of all stormtroopers' experiences. Some of the Hamburg Nazi Party's brightest young stars, such as political leader Albert Krebs and SA general Alfred Conn, came to nationalist politics through the influence of their living fathers, and with the support of the socioeconomic circles that surrounded these patriarchs. However, their fathers did not always approve of the ultimate direction the stormtroopers chose. As Conn, Krebs, and other purportedly loyal sons would discover in the coming phases of the political conflict, living fathers at times condemned their sons' violent forms of political action, even if they sympathized with the youths' professed political goals. Living fathers also could pose overtly oppositional threats, as the working-class sons of socialist or Communist fathers discovered when they began to join the SA after 1929. Stormtrooper novelists portrayed this conflict in working-class families using caricatures of weak socialist fathers, who caused trouble for the protagonists' families through a conflicting combination of timid helplessness, overbearing paternalism, and backstabbing treachery.[21]

Indeed, father-son relationships in that era were often violent, as many fathers—whether liberal, monarchist, nationalist, or socialist—abused their sons. Even in families where physical mistreatment was not the rule, early psychoanalytic theories, such as the Frankfurt School's "authoritarian personality," gave great weight to the patriarchal family structure as a breeding ground for violent, authoritarian politics.[22] The popularity of this contested concept stemmed in part from the fact that imperial German fatherhood seemed especially heavy-handed across all social classes.[23] While elite and upper-middle-class fathers were mostly distant, cold, and demanding, lower-middle-class and working-class fathers tended to be directly abusive. A stereotypical father of this class worked 10–12 hours a day in a factory or shop, then proceeded to his local pub, and later returned to the family's small urban flat in a drunk and disagreeable mood. Once ensconced at home, he would subject his wife and children to verbal abuse that occasionally escalated to the point where he reached for his belt. Such fathers would not tolerate disagreement or discussion from those who lived under their roof.

According to the Frankfurt School, these encounters between powerful patriarchs and their dependent children had lasting consequences for both their individual and collective psychology.[24] This theory of the fascist father-son relationship, although intriguing and provocative when first presented, has not held up through decades of further research that has criticized its methodology, challenged its typologies, and revealed its sometimes circular logic.[25] The true importance of the abusive father as an explanation for the stormtroopers' violent political style therefore comes not from actual father-son relationships, but from the way stormtroopers conceptualized not only their own fathers but the men of the previous generation writ large. Whether they described these men as absent ghosts or as living disappointments, the stormtroopers' rhetorical reliance on the subject proved a key way to place themselves within a traditional and, they hoped, enduring context of legitimate social and political authority.

In politics, dead fathers are often more useful than live ones. Whether or not a stormtrooper had actually lost his father before, during, or after the Great War, most SA men fixated on a greater metaphorical sense of loss: the loss of the image of the exemplary gentleman capitalist, the merchant patriarch who had built Hamburg's glory and in whose footsteps the younger generation expected to follow. Even those whose fathers had come from outside Hamburg as part of the great throng of immigrants that swelled the city's population in the late 19th century had been raised to expect that the family would eventually establish itself in bourgeois circles. After 1918, however, stormtroopers came to believe that the prosperous Hanseatic city their fathers had bequeathed to them had fallen into decline and despair, and that their own potential to become—in the terms of historical scholarship—"gentlemen capitalists" or "hegemonic men" now proved impossible. Stormtroopers sometimes blamed their fathers for squandering their prosperity, mismanaging the empire, or turning to socialism. This confused mix of idealism and disdain persisted throughout the stormtroopers' public lives. Whether to honor their merchant fathers or to rebel against those who were socialists, SA men always claimed that they fought to resurrect a departed imperial past, to punish those responsible for destroying it, and to secure their own place as the latest generation of patriotic, prosperous leaders of a great northern city.

Hamburg's Political Heritage

To understand the psychology and motivation of the men who became Hamburg's stormtroopers, one must first understand their conception of the city itself. Its interests and its time-tested way of life, the stormtroopers claimed, were under attack and required a violent defense. Hamburg's streets and neighborhoods became the stormtroopers' trenches and battlefields. During the era of the Weimar Republic, the city's churches and taverns became fortresses and strongholds, the city hall and commercial centers became targets of political and economic conquest. But it was not the Hamburg of the late 1920s and early 1930s that dominated the stormtroopers' consciousness. These men had been born and raised into a very different Hamburg than the troubled postwar city they fought to defend. Their Hamburg was an idealized image from an earlier time—an imperial time, the prosperous and promising decades preceding the turn of the 20th century, when both Germany and Hamburg felt young, vital, and full of promise. It was a time when the Kaiser's race to establish German colonies and achieve naval parity with Britain seemed guaranteed to stimulate commerce as never before. The series of crises caused by Wilhelm II's policies and personal belligerence had not yet shaken Anglo-German relations, nor had the *Titanic*'s ignominious demise undermined the Atlantic bourgeoisie's sense of invulnerability. Before the war of 1914–1918, the hopes of Hamburg's merchant elite had not yet been battered on the rocks of the war, revolution, and general upheaval that ultimately sank the Free and Hanseatic City's long-sailing ship of state.

As children, the future stormtroopers had learned from teachers and schoolbooks to revere the German Empire and Hamburg's place within it. In some sense, however, that attitude fit poorly with Hamburg's traditional self-conception as a bastion of independence and democratic self-governance. Historians have called Hamburg a "special case."[26] It had been a Free Imperial City under the Holy Roman Empire since 1189, one of a few city-states allowed to run its own affairs with little interference from a distant monarch. Hamburg's advantageous position on the vital Elbe River allowed it to assist in, foster, and of course tax a vast portion of continental trade. Given the Elbe's cultural significance as a border between feudal eastern Europe and the booming merchant economies of western Europe, Hamburg became a key link in the chain connecting continental German lands to the wider world of the oceans.[27] Over the centuries, Hamburg helped protect the waterways, promote trade, and resist centralized imperial authority. Historians of the city's early years referred to antipiracy as "good work" in which Hamburg "honorably distinguished" itself.[28] In other words, the city was a responsible regional power that sought to protect trade, extend communication networks, and generally promote—although the term is anachronistic—liberal internationalism.

Hamburg used its advantageous geographic position to become one of the largest, richest, and most important towns of the medieval Hanseatic League. And while the rest of the League's cities declined in the mid-15th century, Hamburg remained a vital point of transit between the continent and the rapidly expanding English textile market.[29] By the 18th century it had grown increasingly prosperous, due in great part to the rise of the transatlantic trade. Unlike many other commercial cities, Hamburg accumulated its great wealth not through the export of local goods from its own agricultural territory, but by trading goods imported from the continent's interior in exchange for overseas products.[30] While the fellow Hanseatic town of Bremen enriched itself through the import of raw cotton and tobacco from America, Hamburg grew wealthier still as the key transporter of East Elbian grain and German machine parts to the wider world, while also coming to dominate European trade with South America.[31] Hamburg put a larger economic footprint on the region than any other German city, and its hinterland—a term that emerged in Anglo-German urban studies of the time—reached across all of Germany and into several other neighboring states.[32]

By the turn of the 20th century, the travel guides of multiple nations described Hamburg as one of the key elements of a world economic system that had brought great prosperity to Britain, Germany, the United States, and other great northern powers. As the 1900 edition of Baedeker's famous guide reported, "Hamburg, with 680,000 inhabitants, is the largest of the three free Hanseatic towns of the German Empire, and next to London, Liverpool, and New York must be counted among the most important commercial places in the world."[33]

These important commercial places shared not only economic interconnections but cultural ones as well. Hamburg's elite and bourgeois merchant classes, and those who hoped to climb into these ranks, clearly placed themselves within an Anglo-American or "northern" context. They were never English or American in their political loyalties, but they considered both of these peoples, together with the Scandinavians, the Dutch, and the "German Hanseatics," to be the torchbearers of progress and civilization. These free peoples of the north had protected the concepts of independence and free enterprise in the late feudal era, had defeated authoritarian religion during the Reformation, and had resisted the slave empires of Spain and France. In modern times, their development of industry and modern capitalism had brought the world out of darkness.

These sentiments contributed to a strong local identity that transcended even the bourgeois-liberal circles to which they most applied—indeed, even Hamburg's Nazis shared them. Hamburg: Chronicle of the Hanseatic City, coauthored by stormtrooper journalist Hermann Okrass, bore marked structural and thematic similarities with Anglo-American histories of Hamburg and the Hanseatic League.[34] The Chronicle began with a description of Hamburg's Saxon origins, which represented the Saxon (and Anglo-Saxon) people's "will for freedom," in contrast to the type of centralized authority found under authoritarian conquerors like Charlemagne. Both the Anglo-American and German histories emphasized early antipiracy campaigns, although the Nazi account predictably paid far more attention to such bloodthirsty elements as the famous beheading of an Elbe pirate-king and 70 of his associates in 1400.[35] Both types of histories also venerated a connection to England that developed in the following centuries, as English merchants immigrated in increasing numbers to Hamburg or established seasonal trading houses there.[36] As Okrass admitted in the *Chronicle*, immigrants to Hamburg at that time also included sizable numbers of Spanish, Italian, and Portuguese traders. The latter group even included a significant percentage of Jews. Here the Nazi coauthors surprisingly fail to insert the expected antisemitic commentary, even though Jews hardly counted as traditional elements of Hamburg's merchant elites. While the Protestant merchant patriarchs allowed a limited number of Jews to reside in the city, Hamburg's clan-based system of family firms usually kept them from gaining influence. This system worked to some extent against the Latin immigrants too; in Hamburg, both Catholics and Jews lacked the more perfect cultural union that Anglo-Americans enjoyed with Hamburg's elite Protestant burghers.

As the Hamburg Nazis' official history of their city reveals, even extreme nationalists felt pride in Hamburg's connection to English commerce, ways of life, political attitudes, and especially the long-shared sense of reserve, propriety, and what sociologist Max Weber had recently coined as a uniquely Protestant ethic of capitalism. By the early 19th century, according to the Nazi historian of Hamburg, "life in the city took on increasingly international forms" and "English ways of life became the fashion."[37] He did not mean this as an insult. The Hamburg Nazis' long fascination with and affection for England persisted far longer than most realize, mainly as wary appreciation for Britain's colonial and military success.[38] The connection was so close that later reading lists published by the Nazified Hamburg public library recommended that National Socialists seeking a proper Germanic consciousness should read works by British and American authors, as well as stories about these nations' most famous figures. Exemplary titles included Thomas Carlyle's *Heroes and Hero-Worship*, Heinrich Bauer's *Oliver Cromwell: Battle of Freedom and Dictatorship*, biographies of Queen Elizabeth I, *The Autobiography of Benjamin Franklin*, and, in a section on great seafarers and empire-builders, works by Francis Drake, James Cook, Henry Morton Stanley, and Rudyard Kipling.[39] Hamburg's Nazis gave these works of Anglo-American heroism equal prominence with German works of Hanseatic history, biographies of past German luminaries, and more predictable Nazi favorites such as the history of the swastika, the Nordic adventures of novelist Willi Vesper, and the racist theories of Adolf Hitler and Alfred Rosenberg. The Englishman Houston Stewart Chamberlain also made an appearance, as did the works of American eugenicist Madison Grant, which warned of the great civilizing Nordic races' supposed decline. Nazi hero worship in Hamburg transcended German nationality and embraced great men who lived in a variety of cities across the North Atlantic world.

All of these cities—and, to a lesser extent, imperial locales as far off as Bombay—had refashioned themselves over the course of the 19th century to become similar sites of global commerce that emphasized port construction, shipyards and naval expansion, financial services, and commodity transport.[40] A class of "gentlemanly capitalists" helmed these economies through their skillful use of finance, promotion of innovation, influence in government, and manipulation of public opinion through print media.[41] As scholars of the British gentleman capitalists have described, for these men "all the world was a stage, and as risk-taking merchant princes, investors, ship-owners, insurers, lenders, bankers, land speculators, projectors and adventurers they focused their profit-seeking attention on distant horizons."[42] They were "commercial sophisticates" who considered themselves "citizens of the world," or even, adding a global dimension to the traditional Germanic term for independent urban citizens, "burghers of the whole world."[43] To one historian who has studied Hanseatic families in Bremen, Baltimore, and New York, the transatlantic mercantile class formed a single though diffuse unit of "cosmopolitan conservatives"—a "Conservative International" whose business, social, and family networks mutually reinforced their conception of themselves as elites who were essential to the management of both local and world prosperity.[44]

The specific political forms generated by Atlantic merchant elites varied by nationality. Men later labeled "gentleman capitalists" dominated Britain's economic and politics from above; meanwhile, their American cousins had taken far more radical steps toward direct democracy and an unlimited male franchise. German Hanseatics called their system *Honoratiorenpolitik*, or the government of notables, which was a form of republican oligarchy in which the heads of prominent merchant families managed city affairs with an emphasis on independence, risk aversion, and collective prosperity. In 1712, when a new constitution empowered a bicameral legislature that included the Hamburg Senate and the *Bürgerschaft* (Citizens Council), this republican style of leadership became Hamburg's "perpetual, immutable, and irrevocable fundamental law."[45] This political form, according to its partisans, harkened back to ancient city-state models that combined a limited franchise with democratic modes of governance within elite circles. Practically speaking, city government functioned through committees composed of councilmen and prominent citizens. Senators guided the committees by taking expert testimony, drafting laws, and shepherding legislation through a full vote.[46] The dynamic brought economic growth, social stability, and political independence without courting the dangers of either monarchical tyranny or mob rule.[47] Hamburg's notables, like the citizens of an ancient Greek polis, assumed responsibility for the protection and promotion of their *Vaterstadt*. They earned the right to do so with their descent from established mercantile houses, their successful maintenance of that prosperity, and their conscious embrace of a corresponding set of civic virtues. These virtues—which above all included discipline, risk avoidance, and pragmatism—mandated utilitarian policies, maximal economic prosperity, and the promotion of the public good as a force to control social revolution from below. As such, the city-state conception of civic virtue was paternalistic and elitist, yet it also focused on public works and the idea that the rule of law brought security and common gain.[48] Civic values also lauded the educated middle classes. Not only merchants, but also lawyers, doctors, writers, pastors, and other intellectuals, made up Hamburg's civil society.[49]

Hamburg's connection to the great Anglo-American merchant cities therefore built not only commercial and political ties but also cultural, psychological, and familial bonds. Members of Hamburg's merchant elite, and those of the professional and middle classes that aspired to join its ranks, placed great stock in metaphors associating their Vaterstadt with its more literal merchant patriarchs. Carl Mönckeberg, author of one of the greatest works of late 19th-century Hamburg history, dedicated his magisterial *History of the Free and Hanseatic City of Hamburg* to—who else?—"my honorable father," the late senator Johann Georg Mönckeberg, as well as several other male relatives who wielded great political authority in Hamburg's halls of government.[50] "There is something special," Carl wrote, "about the love for a Vaterstadt, just as with the love of one's own father."[51] Although he admitted that some of this love came from nostalgia for one's own youth, he emphasized that admiration for fathers and father cities persisted not because of the riches or power these fathers wielded, but because virtue inspired loyalty that endured through the generations. After declaring Hamburg's kinship with "the small cities of ancient Greece," and even with "the Israelites' ability to maintain their self-consciousness as a people through centuries of condemnation in the eyes of the world," Mönckeberg declared that "Hamburg has from the beginning of its history belonged to the cities of which the Lord has said: Let this be a city on a hill, whose light will illuminate the world."[52]

Like America, the Free and Hanseatic City of Hamburg saw itself as a beacon of republican governance in the world. However, both polities were hardly favorable to the type of fully democratic politics a modern reader might expect. They instead combined concepts of independence and claims to political autonomy with limits on participation that today seem contradictory. Hamburg's political systems were both highly classist and heavily gendered, granting full political and economic rights only to those with enough property and financial independence to maintain both high socioeconomic status and practical control over aspects of city business. The voting system excluded working-class men and even many members of the middle class throughout much of the 19th century. As for women, no amount of property or wealth would bring political rights; even though elite Hanseatic women enjoyed a greater degree of financial independence than women in other European cities, that privilege did not extend to the vote.[53] Gender and class expressions of political hierarchy were of course intermixed, as was the case in many societies that mobilized gendered concepts of political authority and economic management. In a feat of circular logic, men of the era claimed to deserve economic and political authority because they were the heads of their households; conversely, they maintained authority over their families by citing their authority in the public sphere.

In Hamburg as elsewhere, men were firmly in charge. Not all men, however, could wield full political authority—political leaders had to conform not only to economic standards but to behavioral codes that marked them as bearers of the highest-ranking authority.[54] In addition to the staid Protestant virtues that had guided men for centuries, transatlantic mercantile society expected all men, and especially the gentlemanly elite, to partake in systems of consumption, acquisition, conquest, and production. Men's tastes and consumer choices confirmed their positions within a Victorian cultural sphere. They wore suits of dark English wool matched with colorful waistcoats of Oriental silk, smoked cigars from Central America, ate bananas and drank coffee imported from South America, and, by the turn of the century, walked on shoes soled with rubber from the Indies. In the 19th century, cultural connections based on global imperial commercial products brought England, America, and—through Hamburg—Germany ever closer.[55] Modes of dress and their equivalents in cuisine and home decoration solidified the Atlantic cultural sphere, provided guidelines for judging who could afford to partake in polite society, and therefore added to the cost of entry for political power.[56] Fashion thus served as part of a gatekeeping system, even as generally increased prosperity and the constant influx of new residents meant that by the late 19th century these gates were harder than ever to keep closed.

Paradigms of conquest and consumption as a means of establishing masculine authority extended into the realm of sexual relationships. Merchant elites could satisfy their desires not only with women, but also secretly with lower-ranking men. Although homosexuality and adultery were still illegal and sometimes subject to state interrogation, some high-ranking men could afford to conduct secret affairs—so long as they adhered to unwritten codes that cast their sexual dalliances in a masculine right. The master of a house frequently had affairs with his servant girls. Although his wife would run the household and manage relations with servants, the master held the moral right to oversee his female servants' social contacts and police their sexual morality. He could ask intrusive questions about the company in which a girl had spent her night off, or keep close eyes on the milkman lest he linger too long over deliveries. Sometimes the men of the household became aggressively controlling. In one famous case, the son of the master assumed his father's authority and ransacked a servant's room looking in vain for a suspected lover.[57] Such egregious cases could sometimes backfire to a man's detriment, but generally male heads of households—especially when they were business owners who conformed to social expectations for high-ranking men—found themselves able to practice and abuse a high degree of patriarchal authority. The pattern represented yet another similarity between Hamburg and the other transatlantic urban centers.

Merchants' privileges within their own homes also extended to sexual contact with male servants. This type of relationship was far more secretive and publicly suppressed than contacts with female servants, as it could endanger both partners if discovered; nevertheless, it had a well-established historical tradition as an essential component of male merchant privilege. Generally, these same-sex contacts involved an older wealthy man who made sexual overtures to a younger and socially inferior man, usually one of his servants or a soldier at a nearby garrison. Merchant masters secured trysts with inferiors through force, threat, or material inducements.[58] In aristocratic circles, same-sex relations formed a key part of patronage and client systems among nobles, as they had for Frederick the Great himself. However, in Hamburg's realm of the grand-bourgeoisie, same-sex contacts represented a system of economic rather than aristocratic domination. Unlike London, Amsterdam, and other important cities, Hamburg developed a same-sex subculture only very late.[59] By confining same-sex contacts to their homes, prominent merchants could keep allegedly destabilizing urges under control, in part by limiting their contacts to social unequals. An older, successful, and socially powerful merchant who took the "active" sexual role could often avoid sanction if he purchased sexual favors only from lower-ranking men. After all, such acts confirmed his status as the superior bearer of authority.[60]

Sexual commerce of this type was a secretive and dangerous way for merchant men to exercise their social and economic power. The man who carried his consumption too far risked losing his masculine authority through a decline into decadence. Modern Europeans borrowed the stigmatizing concept of effeminacy from the ancient Greeks, who had identified the trait through a man's overconsumption of alcohol and food, an obsession with women and sex, or a descent into the underworld of prostitution, sodomy, and foppishness.[61] As this last construction implies, hegemonic masculinity and the leadership of gentleman capitalists not only excluded women from political authority, it also banished from full republican citizenship a wide range of people who could not or did not conform to expected masculine traits. These people allegedly included the rough members of the working class, the dandies of the aristocracy, the shy and tentative, artists, foreigners, non-whites, Jews, and the French.

With these behaviors, Hamburg shared its conception of hegemonic masculinity with a constellation of northern European and American cities that were also led by male merchant elites. This group generally emphasized austerity, rejected ostentatious consumerism, and spurned the aspiration to gain titles, estates, and a place in the landed aristocracy. Hamburg's elite families in fact distrusted landed power for both social and economic reasons. Put simply, titled aristocracies bred indolence, entitlement, and corruption—all traits that were not good for business. In Hamburg, bourgeois notables expected that the members of each new generation would confirm their elite status through a display of individual responsibility, morality, and self-discipline.[62] By demonstrating these virtues, sons confirmed their worthiness to wield political power, rather than merely inheriting it.

Through the political upheavals of the late 18th century and the rising nationalism of the 19th century, Hamburg's notables steered an independent course. They sought merely to ensure that the city would run its own affairs, and they resisted being absorbed into larger states, whether French, Danish, or German. The most serious threat came from Napoleon, who like many French leaders before him resented Hamburg's close relationship with the English. According to Okrass' *Chronicle*, Hamburg "was only marginally interested in the new ideas" of the French Revolution; like the English, the people of Hamburg distrusted the revolution, as it was overly disruptive to practical affairs.[63] When Napoleon moved against England, he also struck Hamburg. In 1806, thousands of French troops marched into the city. They came bearing orders to arrest all English merchants, confiscate their property, and generally treat Hamburg as an outpost of the English enemy. In a sense, Napoleon was right to see Hamburg in this light. Unlike that of any other comparable city, Hamburg's Senate had long encouraged foreign merchants, particularly the English, to take up residence within its walls.[64] French troops now went on an extended hunt for these elements, going house to house in search of English merchants and bankers, whom they carted off as prisoners of war to the French fortress of Verdun.[65] Immediately following Napoleon's Berlin Decree, which banned all continental trade with England, his marshal in Hamburg forced the Senate to pass further punitive measures. Englishmen who did not surrender their property within 24 hours would be summarily executed. Hamburg's burghers had 48 hours to declare and surrender any property originating in England. All correspondence and contact with England or Englishmen were now banned.[66]

The French occupation, strongly resented across the German land, particularly vexed Hamburg's citizens, as it threatened to destroy the city's commercial and cultural exceptionalism. Even after the combined troops of Britain and Prussia thwarted Napoleon's plans to dominate the continental economy, the French occupation lingered in Hamburg's historical memory, ready to be used by Nazi historians like Okrass, who described 1815 as "one year of unbelievable suffering."[67] Okrass chronicled the confiscation of property and punitive taxes, daily arrests and executions, thousands of citizens being forced to labor on fortifications that strengthened foreign oppression, the systematic destruction of all homes outside the city walls, and the violent eviction—on Christmas Eve, no less—of 20,000 citizens who could no longer support themselves. One thousand of them died.[68] Okrass relished these details, not just due to a stormtrooper's sense of bloodthirstiness but because they provided a useful example of the consequences of national weakness. He continued:

> These inhuman sufferings made a deep impact on the spirits of Hamburg's population. If they had earlier stuck closely to ideas of world-citizenry, they now realized their common destiny with the other German lands, now began to feel German again, and now began to treasure their support from the greater German Volk. If they had earlier seen the world only through merchant eyes, and had only striven for their own advantage, now feelings of engagement with fellow citizens and a readiness to fight for the whole became part of their nature.[69]

Okrass' reading of these events in no way represented a unified Hanseatic consensus, but it did accurately reflect a mentality common among later nationalist generations. "A readiness to fight for the whole" was a key part of the stormtrooper mind-set, which they read backwards into historical memory as a justification for authoritarian militarism. In reality, Hamburg's merchant elite and general political affiliation throughout the 19th century continued to adhere to the city's traditional democratic strengths. Despite setbacks, Hamburg retained its self-governance for several more decades, during which it remained, according to Britain's most prominent modern scholar of Hamburg, "an island of republicanism in a monarchical sea."[70]

But monarchy's tide was rising. In the 1860s and 1870s, Prussia's wars of German unification ended Hamburg's official independence. To a great extent, memories of the Napoleonic occupation had indeed paved the way for this development—in Hamburg, as elsewhere in the German lands, Napoleon had taught many citizens of smaller states that the only way to preserve their independence would be to surrender it to a German monarch. In the past, Hamburg had always been one of the only cities in Europe able to remain a major economic power without the assistance of a larger nation-state.[71] This status quo, however, now seemed impossible to maintain. Prussian chancellor Otto von Bismarck thus found the Hamburg Senate more receptive than it otherwise might have been when, in 1864 and 1866, he pressured the city to participate in Prussia's wars against the Danes and Austrians. Some in the Senate and in society generally were enticed by Bismarck's skillful mobilization of long-standing resentment against the Danes, but most senators did not fully believe Bismarck's promises that a new German empire would respect Hamburg's political and economic independence. Even the doubters, however, feared that resisting Prussian plans would only bring outright annexation.[72] The Senate thus acquiesced and joined the war, and afterward the Prussian-sponsored North German Confederation. Hamburg was the last north German territory to compromise its sovereignty in this way. In 1871, all Confederation states were absorbed into the unified German Reich, and Hamburg's 700-year tradition of formal independence came to an end.

True to the fears of those who resisted unification, Hamburg's experience under the German Reich from 1871 to 1918 weakened the city's distinctive political forms. Although some continued to see imperial Hamburg as a "foreign body" in the monarchy, most scholars have noted that traditional republican values and practices declined after unification.[73] Elite resistance to titles and nobility weakened as the young empire became more integrated, and its imperial and Prussian character grew more entrenched. Before 1871, only one percent of Hamburg's wealthiest merchants held noble titles; over the next 40 years, however, ten times that number accepted titles from their new Prussian monarch.[74] The shift toward aristocracy took place only among the very elite merchant families, even though many of these families saw accepting titles as a radical change that could harm a family's good name.[75] This compromise of reputation was not merely symbolic, nor was it confined to elite mercantile circles. In fact, it formed one part of a generally increasing dissatisfaction with the notables' ability to govern.

A cholera epidemic in 1892 proved a crucial breaking point between political forms. The epidemic, one incident in a century-long pattern of diseases that terrorized Europe's crowded and poorly sanitized cities, was seen as proof that the city was growing out of control. Demographic turmoil came not only from the sheer number of residents—as of 1888, half a million—but also because these new masses increasingly clustered in dark, wet, and dirty slums. Yet the slum dwellers were not so physically distant from the city residents of longer pedigree and higher social standing. In August 1892, cholera struck Hamburg suddenly and brutally. Within a few weeks, ten thousand citizens of a city that valued propriety and dignity was suddenly hemorrhaging from all orifices, vomiting and defecating 25 percent of their bodily fluid in as little as five hours.[76] The disease—like its contemporary cousin, tuberculosis—disproportionately struck the poor and working classes, but it left none untouched psychologically.

The calamity crystallized growing doubts among Hamburg's elites and lower-class masses that the city's technocratic methods of liberal administration could manage rapid urban growth and destabilizing social change, as the notables had long guaranteed. The epidemic thus took as an additional casualty Hamburg's traditional political systems, which a wave of imperial, state-centered, and Prussian administration soon replaced.[77] The crisis also inaugurated the rise of mass politics. An expansion of citizenship and the franchise broke the elites' monopoly on political participation, birthed a politically aroused labor movement, and generated Germany's most powerful chapter of the Social Democratic Party, the SPD, which in some sense was Hamburg's first permanent political party. Before its rise, elite citizens considered parties less an expression of social class or identity than of immediate interests and specific issues.[78] The system worked because, in traditional Hamburg, all voters came from the same elite circles; they therefore found it easy to move between parties, shift alliances, and forge compromises.

The mobilization of the masses in the 1890s, however, changed both the style and the substance of political debate. Populist pressure groups arose to promote economic reform, leftist labor politics, and suffrage reform, while a new radical right conversely promoted antisemitism, militarism, and extreme nationalism. While the trend toward mass mobilization held true across the Reich, in Hamburg these new parties and pressure groups proved particularly destructive to traditional republican politics.[79] The police, which had traditionally taken its titles, uniforms, and practices from English models, refashioned itself in 1892 along Prussian lines. This new police force created a political division whose officers fanned out in disguise to spy on the labor movement.[80] As police reactions show, by the 1890s Hamburg's notables were losing power from two sides. From above they saw their independence diminished in favor of national policymakers in Berlin, while from below there arose a newly politicized lower-middle and working class intent on breaking the elites' political monopoly.

By the dawn of the 20th century, urban growth and economic progress had paradoxically strengthened the masses. More and more of the SPD's natural constituency of reform seekers now met the property requirements needed to vote.[81] In 1901, the SPD claimed its first seat in Hamburg's lower parliamentary house, the Citizens Council; almost a dozen more representatives followed in 1904.[82] The notables still held their grip through a three-tiered voting system that further imbalanced representation, even among the citizen class—essentially, half of the 160 Citizens Council seats were saved for elected "landowners" and "notables," with members of these top two tiers retaining the right to vote in lower elections as well.[83] The legitimacy of such a scheme was untenable so long as thousands of new workers continued to stream into the city and increase the potential power of the masses. Thus the notables faced a paradox: they could perhaps save themselves from the social unrest below, but only at the cost of imposing an authoritarian style of rule from above. While political elitism and assertions of social control were hardly in conflict with Hamburg's republican traditions, the Senate's 1906 plan to curtail democratic participation in Hamburg led to social unrest, economic disruption, mass demonstrations against the police, the first general strike in German history, and mass violence on the largest scale in living memory.[84] Police, overzealous in their desire to crush the revolt, caused Hamburg's vaunted republican government to appear more like Russian czarism than Anglophile democracy. The incident presaged a coming generation of increasingly brutal and violent political conflict, and few in the city still trusted paternalistic elites to manage local affairs with dispassionate concern for mutual benefit.

After the riots of January 1906 demonstrated that the city fathers had lost their hold on their father city, and as all sides grew ever more cynical, citizens' visions of the 20th-century city grew ever darker and more pessimistic. Hamburg was no longer the Hanseatic merchant town it had been for so long. Its continuing prosperity as an imperial city had come at great social cost and a high physical price: crowding, dirtiness, darkness, and disease. Hamburg was now, as socialist revolutionary Larissa Reissner described it, "as impermeable as a pilot's oilskins, steaming with moisture, reeking like a seaman's pipe, charred with the fires of the dockside bars yet standing firm under the torrential rain, with legs set wide apart as if on deck, planted on the right and left sides of the Elbe."[85] Industrial and human detritus choked its once-blue waterways, "disgusting black canal[s] into which factory waste flows from gaping pipes like inky vomit." In the center of it all, the bucolic Alster, a quiet tributary of the Elbe, still provided a refuge around which the nicest houses and richest families could focus on scenes of constructed beauty. Beside an artificial watershed, they ate ice cream and drank coffee in lakeside cafés, strolled carelessly under protective parasols, and sailed small boats in a defiant assertion of premodern ways in the face of new chaos.

Workers' quarters and electric trains now ringed the stately city center. The daily tide began to flow shortly after 6 AM. In the darkness of early morning, bourgeois merchants and unwashed laborers alike boarded squat streetcars and gleaming elevated trains, steamships ferried hundreds of thousands of workers to their places on the docks, and thousands more occupied the area in the hope of finding work. Across four bridges, the industrial underclass poured over the Elbe, a scene Reissner described as "a black oily Venice" illuminated by steamships' searchlights. Under the Elbe itself, workers had recently finished a massive tunnel, "a bright dry tube that pumps legions of workers across from shore to shore every morning." In a scene of the type later depicted in the dystopian film *Metropolis*, "at the end of this tunnel, elephantine lifts raise and lower this human torrent to and from the concrete exits. They move, these two lifts, screeching in their screw-like towers like two shovels unceasingly stoking living fuel into hundreds of furnace-like factories."[86] On the rails and in the tunnels, this brutally mechanized commute brought all citizens of Hamburg together in common participation, but they could not agree on its moral meaning. Hamburg's consensus had been fatally fractured—if it had ever existed in the first place. And if there was one thing on which the grand bourgeoisie, the squeezed middle class, and the laboring masses could agree, it was this: the shining city on a hill had become a dark metropolis, and a city of such contrasts posed a risk to all.

Hamburg's stormtroopers had experienced this grand imperial city as children or young men. They collectively saw the city from the perspective of both the established and the insurgent classes, for they came from both social spheres. Many leading members of the Hamburg SA came from the highest-ranking merchant families, and even more of the SA's most significant figures came from the middle-class professional backgrounds of shop-keeping, medicine, law, and government service. The SA's mass base, in contrast, originated on the lower rungs of the social ladder. Despite these differences, stormtroopers from all social backgrounds stood united in a common psychological reaction to their father city's recent history, a position of wounded pride that they expressed as resolve to restore a lost golden age. The question was how. As youths educated in the context of an expanding imperial German nation-state, they had learned that empire—both domestically in Europe and abroad in the world—had helped to create and secure Hamburg's pride of place in an intensely competitive world system. Empire must therefore be regained.

Many of these men's later writings demonstrate the resilience of their childlike conception of Hamburg's past. The Nazi history of Hamburg, *Chronicle of a World City*, tried to reconcile the paradoxical relationship between a "Free and Hanseatic city" and a unified German empire:

> Our city's historical development could well create the impression that Hamburg had placed its own interests ahead of Germany's. But it must not be overlooked that only through political independence could the Hamburgers develop the inner drive, courage for great undertakings, resilience through difficulties, and dexterity in conquering new markets that they unfurled within the German ranks. The successful deployment of these strengths for the city meant simultaneously service in German interests; for Hamburg's prestige in the world was Germany's worth in the world; Hamburg's economy was the German economy.[87]

There had been, the *Chronicle* warned, a danger that "foreign efforts" could threaten to undermine Hamburg's loyalty. The solid burghers, however, resisted "in their core" these foreign "customs and morals," and therefore "stayed essentially German" while using their connection to the wider world in the service of Germany's greater ambitions.[88]

Stormtrooper Hermann Okrass wrote these words, which reflect a contradictory assimilation of local tradition common to boys raised in Hamburg's late 19th century. Their history books and political culture recast Hamburg's long association with freedom and independence, and its relationship with England, as a service rendered to a mighty German empire.

Conversely, imperial strength guaranteed the city's future prosperity and world role. While not all children educated in this manner accepted such an imperialist framework, those who became stormtroopers largely embraced the narrative. As children, they had ingested ideologies that caused them to look upon war and empire as positive goods. They had also witnessed the great physical and social disruption that had resulted from, in their view, the city's departure from its traditional ways. These beliefs led the young men who became stormtroopers to volunteer for the Great War in great numbers, and later to react to the postwar republic's further changes with resentment and resistance.

Hamburg's young men had marched off to war in 1914 to protect their city's economic potential and aspirations for further growth. Many felt that they had returned four years later to a ruin, to a fallen Hamburg that had been taken over from within by a subversive mob. In reality, the halcyon world they recalled had already been swept away by a tide of rapid change—an ongoing and traumatic upheaval that, some historians have argued, itself generated the mad rush to a war intended to be a mechanism for re-forging social harmony. If that was in fact what the economic elites and populist masses alike hoped to gain through war, they failed. The war instead proved to be the most erosive tide that Hamburg had yet experienced. Afterward, the idealized golden-age Hamburg of stormtrooper memory, the city that had once stood solidly on the banks of the Elbe, had become a sort of Atlantis: a vanished world that inspired a lost generation to try to re-create its glory, never questioning whether that lost city had ever really existed as they now imagined it.

NOTES

1 Franz Tügel, *Mein Weg, 1888–1946. Erinnerungen eines Hamburger Bischofs* (Hamburg: Wittig, 1972), 8.

2 Note on sources: I have taken the route of this walking tour from Tügel's memoir, *Mein Weg*, which also includes detailed information on city scenes from this time. Physical descriptions of the city and its environs, in this chapter and future chapters, are based on maps, photographs, and descriptions appearing in the most popular travel guides of the time. They are, in chronological order of production: Robert Semple, *Observations Made on a Tour from Hamburg through Berlin, Gorlitz, and Breslau, to Silberberg; and Thence to Gottenburg* (London: Robert Baldwin, 1814); Albert Borchert, *Das lustige alte Hamburg. Scherze, Sitten, und Gebräuche unserer Väter* (Hamburg: F. Dörling, 1891); *Adler's Plan von Hamburg-Altona-Wandsbek und Umgebung* (Hamburg: C. Adler, 1891); Karl Baedeker, *Nordwest-Deutschland. Handbuch für Reisende* (Leipzig: Karl Baedeker, 1905); Edwin Clapp, *The Port of Hamburg* (New Haven, CT: Yale University Press, 1912); *Hamburg und Umgebung. Praktischer Rundführung* (Berlin: Albert Goldschmidt, 1912); Richters Guide-Books, *Hamburg and Its Environs: Practical Guide*, 7th ed. (Berlin and Hamburg: Verlaganstalt und Druckerei-Gesellschaft, 1913); Griebens Reiseführer Band 7, *Hamburg und Umgebung. Praktischer Reiseführer*, 24th ed. (Berlin: Albert Goldschmidt, 1913); Robert Medill McBride, *Towns and People of Modern Germany* (New York: Robert McBride & Company, 1927). Modern books of historic photography and Hamburg's urban history, which have also added to the account in this work, include: Carl Thinius, *Damals in St. Pauli. Lust und Freude in der Vorstadt* (Hamburg: Verlag Hans Christians, 1975); Jörg Duppler, *Hamburg zur See. Maritime und militärische Beiträge zur Geschichte Hamburgs* (Herford: Verlag E. S. Mittler & Sohn, 1989); Joachim Paschen, *Hamburg vor dem Krieg. Bilder von Alltag 1933–1940* (Bremen: Edition Temmen, 2003); Ortwin Pelc, *Hamburg: Die Stadt im 20. Jahrhundert* (Hamburg: Convent, 2002).

3 Tügel, *Mein Weg*, 8–9. For the importance of traditional "hometown communities" in Germany, see Mack Walker, *German Home Towns: Community, State, and General Estate, 1648–1817* (Ithaca, NY: Cornell University Press, 1971). These organic communities were, however, greatly disrupted throughout the 19th century. Franz Tügel's recollection has great similarities with how Walker described traditional towns. But the parallel is simultaneously apt and misleading: apt because the suburbs consciously functioned as re-creations of the former towns within a city context, and misleading because it insists on creating an unbroken continuity with the past that did not properly exist. For Walker, as will be seen in Hamburg's case, demographic pressures internally and the state's external pressure to cede control doomed town self-governance across Germany by the 1870s.

4 Adler, *Adler's Plan*, 23–25.

5 On August Christian Tügel's background, see Tügel, *Mein Weg*, 4–6. On the large-scale movement to Hamburg during the imperial period, see Richard Evans, "'Red Wednesday' in Hamburg: Social Democrats, Police, and Lumpenproletariat in the Suffrage Disturbances of 17 January 1906," *Social History* 4, no. 1 (1979): 19–22.

6 Tügel, *Mein Weg*, 9.

7 Griebens Reiseführer, *Hamburg und Umgebung*, 60.

8   Tügel, Mein Weg, 10.

9   Tügel, Mein Weg, 10.

10   Tügel, Mein Weg, 35.

11   Tügel, Mein Weg, 35.

12   Tügel, Mein Weg, 40, 218.

13   Tügel, Mein Weg, 218.

14   Oscar Wilde, An Ideal Husband (Boston and New York: C. T. Brainard, 1909/1895), 95.

15   Tügel, Mein Weg, 430.

16   Tügel, Mein Weg, 431.

17   Tügel, Mein Weg, 434.

18   Tügel, Mein Weg, 435.

19   Tügel, Mein Weg, 436.

20   On the universal elements of this theme, see Joseph Campbell, Hero with a Thousand Faces (New York: Pantheon Books, 1949). Locally, Lars Maischak demonstrated the early death of Hanseatic merchant men in "A Cosmopolitan Community: Hanseatic Merchants in the German-American Atlantic of the Nineteenth Century" (dissertation in history, Johns Hopkins University, 2005), 101.

21   As in Bernhard Voss, Willi Dickkopp. Aus dem Tagebuch eines unbekannten SA Mannes (Rostock: Bernhard Voss, n.d.).

22   Wilhelm Reich, The Mass Psychology of Fascism (New York: Farrar, Straus, and Giroux, 1970/1933); Max Horkheimer, ed., Authorität und Familie (Paris: Alcan, 1936).

23   For more about domestic violence by imperial German men, see Volker Berghahn, Imperial Germany, 1871–1918: Economy, Society, Culture, and Politics (New York: Berghahn Books, 2005), 72–73.

24   T. W. Adorno, Else Frenkel-Brunswik, Daniel J. Levinson, and R. Nevitt Sanford, The Authoritarian Personality (New York: Harper & Brothers, 1950), 6.

25   John Levi Martin, "'The Authoritarian Personality,' 50 Years Later: What Lessons Are There for Political Psychology?" Political Psychology 22, no. 1 (March 2001): 1–26.

26   P. E. Schramm, Hamburg. Ein Sonderfall in der Geschichte Deutschlands (Hamburg: Christians, 1964). Schramm's term has become a rallying point for historians of Hamburg, who have taken the term as a point of pride for the city even as they critique the accuracy of a "special case." For one such critique, see Mary Lindemann, "Fundamental Values: Political Culture in Eighteenth-Century Hamburg," in Peter Uwe Hohendahl, ed., Patriotism, Cosmopolitanism, and National Culture in Hamburg: Public Culture in Hamburg 1700–1933 (Amsterdam and New York: Rodopi, 2003), 17–32.

27   Erik Lindberg, "The Rise of Hamburg as a Global Marketplace in the Seventeenth Century: A Comparative Political Economy Perspective," Comparative Studies in Society and History 5, no. 3 (2008): 648.

28   Karl Baedeker, Northern Germany as Far as the Bavarian and Austrian Frontiers (Leipzig: Karl Baedeker, 1900), 163.

29   William E. Lingelbach, "The Merchant Adventurers at Hamburg," American Historical Review 9, no. 2 (1904): 267. See also Philippe Dollinger, The German Hansa (Stanford: Stanford University Press, 1970), 281–311.

30   Lindberg, "The Rise of Hamburg," 648.

31 Maischak, "A Cosmopolitan Community," 46–47. See also Victor Böhmert, "Die Stellung der Hansestädte zu Deutschland in den letzten 3 Jahrzehnten," *Vierteljahrsschrift für Volkswirtschaft und Kultur* 1 (1863): 73–115.

32 The term *hinterland* itself reflects a high degree of intercommunication among English- and German-speaking scholars of urban spaces—the word was originally German but quickly caught on in English, French, and Italian. On theories of Hamburg's hinterland in the context of larger British "hinterland studies" of the mid-20th century, see F. W. Morgan, "The Pre-War Hinterlands of German North Sea Ports," *Transactions and Papers (Institute of British Geographers)* 14 (1956): 45–55; Guido G. Weigend, "The Problem of Hinterland and Foreland as Illustrated by the Port of Hamburg," *Economic Geography* 32, no. 1 (1956): 1–16; and the founding text of the discipline, A. J. Sargent, *Seaports and Hinterlands* (London: A. and C. Black, 1938).

33 Baedeker, *Northern Germany*, 162.

34 Johannes Sass and Hermann Okrass, *Hamburg: Chronik einer Hansestadt* (Hamburg: Hamburger Tageblatt, 1941), 8. Sass claims first billing on the title, but Okrass exercised significant control in his capacity as editor of the Nazis' Hamburg newspaper, which published the volume.

35 Sass and Okrass, *Hamburg*, 20–21.

36 Sass and Okrass, *Hamburg*, 26–27.

37 Sass and Okrass, *Hamburg*, 45.

38 To some extent, the Nazis tried to foster Anglophilic elements within the party at large, but this fight was a losing battle, even in Hamburg, once it became clear that Britain would stand in the way of Nazi war plans. See Gerwin Strobl, *The Germanic Isle: Nazi Perceptions of Britain* (Cambridge, England: Cambridge University Press, 2000).

39 Emma Schiller and Willi Wendling, *Nordischer Gedanke und nordische Leistung* (Hamburg: Hans Christian, 1938).

40 Sandip Hazareesingh, "Interconnected Synchronicities: The Production of Bombay and Glasgow as Modern Global Ports ca. 1850–1880," *Journal of Global History* 4 (2009): 7.

41 See P. J. Cain and A. G. Hopkins, *British Imperialism: Innovation and Expansion, 1688–1914* (Harlow, England: Longman, 1993). Cain and Hopkins' work kicked off a larger debate about the concept of gentlemanly capitalism and its relevance for the rise of the British empire. See Raymond E. Dumett, *Gentlemanly Capitalism and British Imperialism: The New Debate on Empire* (London and New York: Routledge, 1999); Anthony Webster, *The Debate on the Rise of the British Empire* (Manchester, England: Manchester University Press, 2006). For comparative perspectives on these debates, which places "gentlemanly capitalism" in a larger global context, see John Darwin, "Globalism and Imperialism: The Global Context of British Power, 1830–1960," in Akita Shigeru, ed., *Gentlemanly Capitalism, Imperialism, and Global History* (New York: Palgrave, 2002), 43–64.

42 H. V. Bowen, "Gentlemanly Capitalism and the Making of a Global British Empire: Some Connections and Contrasts, 1688–1815," in Shigeru, *Gentlemanly Capitalism*, 20–21.

43 Bowen, "Gentlemanly Capitalism." See also M. Daunton, "'Gentlemanly Capitalism' and British Industry 1820–1914," *Past and Present* 122 (1989): 119–158.

44 Maischak, "A Cosmopolitan Community," 7, 16.

45 Lindemann, "Fundamental Values," 18. Ironically, this constitution came about through the intercession of Holy Roman Emperor Joseph I, whose imperial commission resolved a dispute between Hamburg's political and religious factions that had been a source of conflict since the 1680s. See Gerd Augner, *Die kaiserliche Kommission der Jahre 1708–1712. Hamburgs Beziehung zur Kaiser und Reich zu Anfang des 18. Jahrhunderts* (Hamburg: Verein für Hamburgische Geschichte, 1983).

46 Richard Comfort, *Revolutionary Hamburg: Labor Politics in the Early Weimar Republic* (Stanford, CA: Stanford University Press, 1966), 16.

47 Lindemann, "Fundamental Values," 19.

48 Katherine Aaslestad, *Place and Politics: Local Identity, Civic Culture, and German Nationalism in North Germany during the Revolutionary Era* (Leiden and Boston: Brill, 2005), 33–45.

49 Aaslestad, *Place and Politics*, 56–68.

50 Carl Mönckeberg, *Geschichte der Freien und Hansestadt Hamburg* (Hamburg: H. D. Verstehl, 1885). Carl's son, whom he named for the boy's grandfather, himself went on to become First *Bürgermeister* during the 1890s. It is his name that Hamburg's famous shopping street bears.

51 Mönckeberg, *Geschichte der Freien*, 1.

52 Mönckeberg, *Geschichte der Freien*, 2.

53 Maischak, "A Cosmopolitan Community," 101–109.

54 While the exact behaviors and traits expected of male leaders vary over time, most societies come to laud one type of adult male identity over all others. It then becomes what scholars call "hegemonic masculinity"—the type of male identity that grants men who conform to its traits political, economic, and personal power over women, children, and nonconforming men. See R. W. Connell, *Masculinities*, 2nd ed. (Berkeley and Los Angeles: University of California Press, 2005), 76–84. The "patriarchal dividend" gained thereby includes authority, honor, the ability to command obedience, as well as a number of legal and material benefits (Connell, p. 82). Hegemonic men—in Hamburg's case, the merchant elites and those lower-ranking men who could best imitate elite forms of family life—also claim the exclusive right, based on their moral standing as the proper kind of man, to use violence to defend their privileges, to turn back systemic challenges, and to bolster their own position vis-à-vis other men (Connell, p. 83). The specific qualities of an era's hegemonic masculinity vary with economic and social conditions, and they are constantly under challenge. (For modern examples, see Lynne Segal, "Changing Men: Masculinities in Context," *Theory and Society* 22, no. 5, Special Issue: Masculinities [1993]: 625–641.) However, hegemony implies the ability of the reigning group to convince others in society that the hierarchy is natural, normal, universal, and irresistible. Mike Donaldson, "What Is Hegemonic Masculinity?" *Theory and Society* 22, no. 5, Special Issue: Masculinities (1993): 645.

55 Richard Evans, "Family and Class in the Hamburg Grand Bourgeoisie 1815–1914," in David Blackbourne and Richard Evans, eds., *The German Bourgeoisie: Essays on the Social History of the German Middle Class from the Late Eighteenth to the Early Twentieth Century* (London and New York: Routledge, 1991), 115–139.

56 Maischak, "A Cosmopolitan Community," 23. See also Eric Hobsbawn, *Age of Capital: 1848–1875* (New York: Vintage, 1996/1975), 230–248, 277–302.

57 Katharina Schlegel, "Mistress and Servant in Nineteenth Century Hamburg: Employer/ Employee Relationships in Domestic Service, 1880–1914," History Workshop 15 (1983): 71.

58 Jakob Michelsen, "Von Kaufleuten, Waisenknaben, und Frauen in Männerkleidern. Sodomie im Hamburg des 18. Jahrhunderts," Zeitschrift vor Sexualforschung 9, no. 3 (1996): 205–237.

59 Jakob Michelsen, "Die 'Blame' des Senatsekretärs Schlüter. Ein Sodomiefall aus dem Hamburg des 18. Jahrhunderts," Frühneuzeit-Info 16, nos. 1 & 2 (1996): 59.

60 Michelsen, "Die 'Blame,'" 58–60.

61 Kathleen Wilson in Philippa Levine, ed., Gender and Empire (Oxford, England: Oxford University Press, 2007), 18–19. On Greek conceptions, see George Mosse, The Image of Man: The Creation of Modern Masculinity (Oxford, England: Oxford University Press, 1998), and David Halperin, One Hundred Years of Homosexuality: And Other Essays on Greek Love (London and New York: Routledge, 1989).

62 Richard Evans, Death in Hamburg (Oxford and New York: Oxford University Press, 1987), 560–563.

63 Sass and Okrass, Hamburg, 45.

64 Lindberg, "The Rise of Hamburg," 656.

65 Lingelbach, "The Merchant Adventurers," 283.

66 Lingelbach, "The Merchant Adventurers," 283.

67 Sass and Okrass, Hamburg, 48.

68 Sass and Okrass, Hamburg, 48.

69 Sass and Okrass, Hamburg, 48–49.

70 Evans, Death in Hamburg, 2.

71 Lindberg, "The Rise of Hamburg," 654.

72 On Hamburg's relationship with Prussia in the last years of the Vormärz, see Detlef Rogosch, Hamburg im Deutschen Bund 1859–1866. Beiträge zur Deutschen und Europäischen Geschichte Band 2 (Hamburg: Krämer, 1990).

73 Ekkehard Böhm, "Wirtschaft und Politik in Hamburg zur Zeit der Reichsgründung," Zeitschrift des Vereins für Hamburgische Geschichte 64 (1978): 52.

74 Dolores L. Augustine, "Business Elites of Hamburg and Bremen," Central European History 24 (1991): 2, 134. Augustine notes that the elite merchants of Hamburg and Berlin were therefore, by the period 1907–1911 at least, more similar to each other in this and some other respects than previously believed.

75 Evans, Death in Hamburg, 561.

76 Evans, Death in Hamburg, vii, 227.

77 Evans, Death in Hamburg, viii.

78 Comfort, Revolutionary Hamburg, 16.

79 Jan Palmowski's analysis of Frankfurt reveals similarities with Hamburg at this time. See Urban Liberalism in Imperial Germany: Frankfurt am Main, 1866–1914 (Oxford and New York: Oxford University Press, 1999). For the national picture, see Brett Fairbairn, "Political Mobilization," in Roger Chickering, ed., Imperial Germany: A Historiographical Companion (Westport, CT: Greenwood Press, 1996), 303–342, and Chickering, We Men Who Feel Most German: A Cultural Study of the Pan-German League, 1886–1914 (London: George Allen & Unwin, 1984).

80 Richard Evans, *Kneipengespräche im Kaiserreich. Die Stimmungsberichte der Hamburger Politischen Polizei* 1892–1914 (Hamburg: Rohwolt, 1989), 10–14.

81 The SPD had already come to dominate Hamburg's delegation to the national *Reichstag,* since these votes were based on universal male suffrage. Locally, between two rounds of suffrage controversies in 1896 and 1906, the SPD's growing power seemed poised to increase its influence and allow it to join forces with liberal elements that had previously turned against the labor movement. But possibilities for a new left-liberal cooperation quickly faded as the SPD became increasingly self-confident and unwilling to accept traditional terms of political debate. See Jennifer Jenkins, "Social Patriotism and Left Liberalism: The Hamburg People's Home, 1901–1914," *German History* 21, no. 1 (2003): 33–35. Jenkins argues that both elite and working classes tried in this brief window to use cultural forms—in this case, an educational project borrowed from England—to unite the classes.

82 Richard Evans, "'Red Wednesday' in Hamburg: Social Democrats, Police, and Lumpen-proletariat in the Suffrage Disturbances of 17 January 1906," *Social History* 4, no 1 (1979): 3–5.

83 For a useful review of the tiered system, see Comfort, *Revolutionary Hamburg,* 15–18.

84 Evans, "'Red Wednesday,'" 4. Hamburg had already seen massive strikes over labor issues, the largest in 1892, but this strike transcended specific workplace grievances and extended into a massive social protest.

85 Larissa Reissner, *Hamburg at the Barricades and Other Writings on Weimar Germany* (London: Pluto Press, 1977).

86 Sass and Okrass, *Hamburg,* 62.

87 Sass and Okrass, *Hamburg,* 62.

88 Sass and Okrass, *Hamburg,* 63.

SHATTERED SONS

2

Near the center of Hamburg's old city, the narrow ancient streets suddenly open up into a market square. A canal along one side connects the shops and warehouses of the mercantile quarter to the smaller of Hamburg's two central pleasure lakes, the Binnenalster. The buildings bordering the square, then as now, hosted the main offices of banks, newspapers, and other city institutions, all clustered around the area's major feature, the Rathaus. Across the Hanseatic cities, generations of merchant elites met in town halls to negotiate tariffs, set taxes, plan public works, and plot an independent political path for their free city.

Most Hanseatic city halls tended to be quite old, and therefore small, cramped, and heavy with stone and timber. Hamburg's, however, had burned down in a great fire in the 1840s. The new Rathaus had been rebuilt in the 1880s and 1890s as a neo-Renaissance giant that boasted several stories surrounding a looming central tower, a graceful yet imposing monument to the wealth and confidence of the age. Its hundreds of rooms—more than in Buckingham Palace—included the mayor's office, the Senate council chambers, apartments of state, countless offices, and a basement wine cellar and restaurant. Befitting its status as a secular cathedral, its walls featured statues of prominent leaders, including a mosaic of Hammonia, Hamburg's patron goddess. This mosaic, which today still stands vigil over the mayor's balcony that overlooks the central square, depicts her in traditional garb, wearing a crown shaped like the city walls and holding the wheel of a ship in one hand. Above her the city motto proclaims, "Let posterity preserve the freedom our elders have won." Hammonia represented the city's values of freedom, harmony, prosperity, and free trade. The building testified to both Hamburg's successful legacy and its hopeful future.

Four years after the beginning of the First World War, as the new year of 1919 turned, this once-hopeful future seemed sour. The marketplace in front of the Rathaus—and, indeed, the entire city—now pulsed with the beat of revolution. For months, massive demonstrations and rallies held by the prewar underclass had combined with postwar economic woes to undermine and overthrow traditional authorities on both the local and national level. The previous November, armed revolutionary sailors had taken up watch outside the front doors of the Rathaus, thus asserting a new regime's authority over the old symbol. On the balcony above them, looming over the Hammonia mosaic, a red flag now flew.[1]

Close by this tumult, Deputy Mayor Carl August Schröder sat in his office. In Hamburg, the deputy or second mayor came from within the ranks of the senators, who chose one of their own as the mayor's designated successor to ensure an orderly transfer of power at the end of the term (or life) of the current mayor. Schröder had in fact been both deputy and mayor before, but he must have wondered if his second stint as deputy would again evolve into the mayorship. Although he still held his title, he had surrendered most of his authority over the city to Social Democratic revolutionaries. He therefore had time to ponder his answer to a young man who had written him for advice. Alfred Conn, a young war veteran and the son of an old schoolmate of Schröder's, had recently returned from the front. He now wrote his father's famous friend with a cry of distress. He had gone to war to defend his city and had returned to find it in tatters. He saw the revolution as a betrayal of his sacrifices, a crime against his city, and he now declared himself prepared to fulfill his oath of loyalty. Together with like-minded comrades, he would take up arms to reconquer the city from its usurpers, if only the senators would ask. The elders, however, rejected this course of action. "His Magnificence impressed upon me to stay away from such things," Conn wrote in his memoirs. "And surely he was correct. The Bürgertum [citizenry] from which I descended had grown afraid of confrontation, and had allowed itself to be trampled by a handful of rebellious sailors. Was it worth it then to defend them in the future?"[2]

Schröder could only answer no. Within months of his exchange with Conn, the deputy mayor found himself out of a job, deposed in the first elections of a new form of government. He apparently had assessed the situation correctly, as the city's traditional leaders had indeed surrendered control. As for young Conn, he did not entirely follow his honored elder's advice. Instead of removing himself from politics and concentrating instead on following in his father's merchant footsteps, he joined a local nationalist club and took up the self-appointed task of protecting his neighborhood from disreputable elements. From there, he and his comrades fell in with the Nazi stormtroopers, who were then but one of many paramilitaries seeking to turn the clock back on the revolution, impose a nationalist dictatorship, and wage a war of vengeance against everyone they blamed for the chaos of 1918–1919.

Conn eventually came to lead the Hamburg SA, and his experiences in 1918–1919 provide an important window into the mind-set of the type of young man who became a stormtrooper. These young men demonstrated a toxic combination of resentment, alienation, and testosterone that fueled SA recruitment. Disillusion, depression, and a sense of anxiety about the future dominated their thoughts. Their political, economic, moral, and generational panic shaped the Nazi movement by creating a desire for community so strong that it became one of the Party's most important principles. But the Nazis—and especially the stormtroopers—built their community in divisive ways, and they used both rhetorical and literal violence against those they saw as being outside their family. However, the attempt to form a united nationalist family often foundered because of an inherent conflict between competing social networks. At this early stage, the conflict was as much generational as anything else. Conn and his comrades sought to extend their hypermasculine "community of the trenches" into postwar political life, rejecting their fathers' methods of politicking in favor of more direct and violent measures. These actions appealed to their sense of youthful certainty and vigor, and provided them with a community of comrades that disguised their otherwise stunted political and personal maturation.

Political and Psychological Legacies of the German Defeat

By 1918, despite the claims made on the Rathaus balcony, many of Hamburg's citizens feared that prosperity and security now existed only in the past. The brutal stalemate of war not only had killed millions on the battlefield, it had prompted a British naval blockade that brought millions more to near starvation in the "turnip winter" of 1916–1917. Even turnips, themselves a poor substitute for the scarce potatoes, had to be rationed.[3] Despite the general lockdown on social activism during the war, and despite the Hamburg Senate's establishment of "war kitchens" to mitigate the hardship, hunger riots and labor unrest increased.[4] The war and the blockade had crippled Hamburg's economy by siphoning off workers and material, diverting production to wartime needs, and cutting off the city's vital connection with the outside world. Hamburg's population fell by over one hundred thousand, and those who remained worked more and consumed less than ever before.[5] Yet none of these sacrifices had brought victory. The defeat of Russia in 1917 had seemed a welcome development, but by 1918 it was clear that the revolutionary movement in Russia in the aftermath of the war posed a new and powerful danger. Meanwhile, the German resources that had been freed from fighting Russia in the east had failed to win the war in the west, where the newly arrived and energetic Americans had upset the balance of forces. In September 1918, Germany's military leaders suddenly and surprisingly told the Kaiser that they were about to lose the war, and they began secretly exploring the possibility of an armistice. By October 1918, as Germany's last offensive had turned into an increasingly disorganized retreat, the public was becoming aware of the numerous setbacks the army had formerly concealed.

When open revolt broke out against the miseries of war, it started in the Hanseatic towns that had always considered themselves bastions of independence and freedom. On October 28, sailors at the naval base in Wilhelmshaven learned that the fleet admirals planned to sally forth in a final, apocalyptic confrontation with the superior British fleet. The action would not change the course of the war, but it would salvage the naval elite's sense of honor, which had long resented the fleet's inability to engage the enemy. Ordinary sailors, however, felt differently about such a suicidal plan, and they declared open mutiny. The revolts spread to other north German coastal towns and then rapidly throughout the empire.[6] What had begun as a mass mutiny, itself previously unthinkable in the German military, had now joined with a rebellious working class that for decades had threatened to rise up against distrusted political leaders.[7] This revolution spread easily to the Free and Hanseatic City of Hamburg, with its numerous connections to naval logistics, production, and basing, as well as its large and politically active working class.

In less than a week, the naval mutiny had turned into an uprising of the underclass that supplanted traditional authorities in most of Germany's northern coastal cities. By November 9, workers' councils had appeared across the empire, in cities as distant and diverse as Bremen, Munich, and Berlin. The Kaiser and his advisors surrendered power. Wilhelm II fled the country, took refuge in the Netherlands, ended the military dictatorship that the war had imposed, and left the shattered country in the hands of a civilian government led by Social Democratic forces. They soon declared a democracy, the Weimar Republic.

The Political Legacy of the Great War

Because it originated during the collapse of the war effort and the resulting tragic consequences, the new republican system was inherently unstable from the beginning.[8] On the right, the youths who became stormtroopers nurtured deep resentment against all who took part in or even merely tolerated the revolution, seeing socialists, Communists, republicans, liberals, and even members of more moderate conservative and nationalist parties as traitorous domestic enemies. "Who had betrayed us?" a stormtrooper asked rhetorically in a later autobiographical essay. "Our fathers, our brothers? No! A thousand times no! . . . The enemy must be behind the front as well as across from us."[9]

This idea that people on the home front had given the war effort a Dolchstoss—a stab in the back—quickly became popular on the political right, promoted by its leading figures and universally accepted among its rank and file. The phrase itself had appeared even before Germany's defeat, when the highest military leaders began campaigning to shift the blame from their own shoulders. In the fall of 1918, General Erich von Ludendorff, the quartermaster who had risen to army chief of staff and virtual dictator of Germany, had already begun spreading the word that civilian political leaders had hamstrung his war management and that they should take the blame for defeat. He and his boss, Field Marshall Paul von Hindenburg, had studiously kept the public and even the Kaiser in the dark about the true state of the war. When Ludendorff finally came clean, he recommended that the Kaiser turn the government over to civilians so they could take the blame for the humiliation to come.[10] Ludendorff's strategy may have been dishonorable, but even politically moderate officers thought it wise. Lieutenant-General Wilhelm Groener, Ludendorff's successor and later an important official in several Weimar governments, admitted in his memoirs that, "strictly legally seen," the army's refusal to assume responsibility was "without justification." But he excused it based on the army's need to defend its reputation—in his words, to "keep the armor shining."[11] Groener wanted the army to retain enough authority to help stabilize whatever German state emerged from the defeat, and he could forgive a few lies in the service of a clean image. He failed, however, to see how damaging the Dolchstoss myth would be.

Ludendorff had himself proposed the armistice, but once the proposal became a reality he turned against the idea and resigned his commission. He then devoted his newly free time to slandering civilian political groups, whom the nationalists dishonestly accused of disloyalty. A few days before the armistice was signed and revealed to the world, one of Ludendorff's subordinates compared him to the Germanic hero Siegfried, who in the final act of Wagner's epic Ring Cycle is stabbed in the back by a racially impure schemer, thus initiating the "Twilight of the Gods" that destroys the existing order.[12] Ludendorff approved of the image, and he approved of his subordinates and ideological fellows enthusiastically spreading his preferred version of events. Ludendorff even propagated the myth in British circles, when he met after the armistice with the head of the British military mission in Berlin for a fateful dinner, which many later claimed was where the "stab-in-the-back" phrase originated. The British officer supposedly reacted to Ludendorff's description of the war effort by saying, "It sounds as if you were stabbed in the back!" Only then, in Ludendorff's telling, did the scales fall from his eyes. He now realized the betrayal.[13]

In reality, of course, Ludendorff himself created and tirelessly promoted this myth. His efforts soon expanded from private dinners to public propaganda. When the Weimar government commission investigated the war defeat in 1919, Ludendorff conspired to cement the Dolchstoss in the public's consciousness. The commission had subpoenaed Hindenburg, one of the few men who knew that the armistice idea had in fact come from Ludendorff. Ludendorff informed Hindenburg that, unless he testified in support of Ludendorff's version of events, Ludendorff would slander him in his upcoming memoirs. In collaboration with nationalist politicians, Ludendorff prepared a statement for Hindenburg to read before the commission. It turned out to be Hindenburg's only testimony on the subject of whom to blame for the defeat:

> The parties shook the homeland's will to resist . . . [They also] planned the secret decomposition of the fleet and army, and the attrition of the front through revolution. And so our operations had to fail, it had to come to a collapse. The Revolution was only the capstone. An English general said rightly to me, "The German Army was stabbed in the back."[14]

That Hindenburg cited the British general in his testimony shows that the myth had come to maturity in its life cycle as a political lie. The Brit's original exclamation, itself possibly a figment of Ludendorff's imagination, had turned into a declarative statement, the neutral and reliable observation of a disinterested outsider. The revered Hindenburg's use of the already popular myth cemented it forever in the German nationalist consciousness. In Hamburg, the bourgeois-conservative press *Hanseatische Verlagsanstalt* pushed this line of argument in many of its books, including one that called the 1918 revolution "the most disgraceful treason known in the history of mankind," a product of "malicious agitators" who "kindled it" for their own selfish gain.[15]

Once established, the myth motivated nationalist war veterans to join radical political movements. Even many years later, these men spoke in Ludendorff's terms. Stormtroopers' autobiographical sketches often contained the "backstab" legend, especially in essays by men old enough to have ingested it firsthand. As one stormtrooper veteran wrote of his tumultuous homecoming:

> People who never saw a battlefield, who had never heard the whine of a bullet, openly insulted men who through four and a half years had defied the world in arms, who had risked their lives in innumerable battles, with the sole desire to guard the country against this horror.
>
> For the first time I began to feel a burning hatred for this human scum that trod everything pure and clean underfoot. Young as I was, I determined that I should never have anything to do with these people.[16]

Another asked:

> Was it for this that the fresh youth of Germany was mowed down in hundreds of battles? It almost seemed as if that might be the answer—treason to the Fatherland, and the celebration of veritable orgies . . . My soul rebelled against this shame and baselessness.[17]

Such accounts ignored the fact that the revolution had in fact begun within military ranks. Ironically, young nationalists who had been at the front should have been in the best position to see this. The wartime sections of Franz Tügel's memoirs, for instance, describe what he saw as a dangerous degradation of faith within Hamburg's Infantry Regiment 76, where he served as chaplain (Figure 2.1). While his first wartime sermons were orderly and even peaceful, he had to shout his final sermons over the sounds of "fanatically wild" fighting and exploding artillery shells close by.[18] During the breakdown of military order, Tügel tried frantically to preserve political

FIGURE 2.1

Franz Tügel and wife

Franz Tügel, in uniform, sits for a photograph
with his wife, taken just before his departure
to join what he called "the male church of
war." Serving "beside the field-gray men of the
front" in the Great War hardened his views on
Germany's political and gender order.
Source: StAHH 662-1 Familie Tügel.

and spiritual order, but to no avail. As he described it, he dedicated his service in "the manly church of war" to bolstering the soldiers' sense of obedience and trust in their leaders.[19] But his efforts often came to naught, given the "bottomless depravity" of rumors spreading from the home front, stories of revolution and defeat that offended "the German sense of male honor" and weakened military order.[20] Tügel's account inadvertently shows, however, that German soldiers participated just as much as sailors, workers, and other revolutionaries in rejecting the increasingly false promises of their authoritarian military government. During the retreat across the Rhine, soldiers criticized their leaders and openly advocated for the Kaiser's removal from power. Even Tügel's fellow chaplains, he claimed, abandoned their responsibility as supporters of order and instead "began to howl with the wolves."[21] The experience shattered his confidence that society still supported the type of social and spiritual order he believed in, yet he refused to believe that the soldiers themselves could have played a role in undermining it. Meanwhile, even his own memoirs showed that they did.

As Tügel's memoirs illustrate, stormtroopers' writings tended to embrace a fundamental error concerning the causes of revolution. They clung to an inappropriate division between revolutionaries and loyalists that aligned perfectly with their preexisting political positions. Authoritarian nationalists had always distrusted the loyalty of socialists, Jews, women, working-class men, most liberals, and all civilians generally, and now a newer and even more terrifying embodiment of disorder had emerged in the form of homosexuals, atheists, and Communists. In this oversimplified categorization, the hard men of the front represented masculine loyalty, self-sacrifice, political and spiritual reliability, and opposition to revolution. The truth was far more complicated, as the mutinous sailors and even Tügel's army memoirs demonstrated, but stormtroopers tended to be less interested in facts than in the psychological comfort that convenient myth could provide.

Many men who became stormtroopers never abandoned their rejection of reality on this subject. One expressly denied in his autobiography the idea that "the soldiers themselves had brought on the revolution, and were therefore responsible for the frightful things that followed."[22] Such strong denial of incontrovertible fact should remind us that we must consider the stormtroopers' own writings as illustrations of their psychological state and unconscious bias, rather than as accurate descriptions of events. This stormtrooper's statement clarifies a second fundamental error that SA men made in judging the relationship between the lost war and the revolution. Rather than accepting that defeat caused revolution, they insisted that revolution caused defeat. Believing these two errors, despite evidence to the contrary, the youths who became stormtroopers nursed resentment against the new German government. These grudges drove them almost immediately to form counterrevolutionary militias. In Hamburg, Einwohnerwehr (citizens' militias) sprang up as partnerships between generations of nationalist men. The younger ones became the troops and field leaders, while the older men offered their authority and logistical support. General Paul von Lettow-Vorbeck put out one typical call for recruits by telling nationalist youths that their lives would forever be on hold unless they acted now to secure order. He said, "What's the use of studies, and what's the good of business or a profession? Enemies within and beyond are burning down our house. Help us, in the spirit of German comradeship and loyalty, to restore our power of national defense!"[23] In St. Georg, Conn took charge of a militia funded by his father's circle. This militia played a key role in putting down the riots and protests in 1919.[24]

The first elections of the Weimar Republic took place on January 19, 1919, in an atmosphere of open Communist revolt and rightist militia violence. The vote did generate a solid 76.2 percent for the three parties representing the republican form of government: the SPD, the Catholic Center Party, and the DDP.[25] But it was a devil's bargain for the young Republic, which had survived only because of actions taken by the rightist militias, who put down Communist uprisings and murdered their leaders. On the left, cooperation between republican and rightist forces poisoned relations between the moderate and radical left for the entire Weimar era, leaving the Communists alienated from a state and system that supported workers' needs better than any realistic alternative. On the right, the pact reinforced a belief popular among nationalist militiamen that their violence was legitimate, necessary, and protective of Germany.

Many historians have observed that the Weimar Republic was "a republic without republicans"—a system in which a majority of the citizens did not believe in its basic right to exist. Moreover, none of the major factions had gotten what they wanted out of the postwar settlement. While the SPD had finally achieved a fully democratic state and a leading role for itself, its performance was continually handicapped by total resistance from other factions, treachery by its political allies, and numerous external crises. Many of these crises were an inevitable result of the lost war and Germany's subordinate international position, a situation the SPD did not cause but for which the parties of the right eagerly blamed it at every opportunity. On the center right, the nationalist, national-liberal, and other traditionalist parties only reluctantly accepted the loss of the former system. While they had surrendered to and now tolerated the Republic, they proved indifferent to its fate and unwilling to defend it at key stages. The extreme right, born in opposition to the revolution itself, subscribed to the stab-in-the-back legend and viewed the republicans as traitors. For them, only a fascist coup, whether paramilitary or electoral, would restore Germany's strength. Meanwhile, the fascists' mirror image, the Communists, felt that the center-left had betrayed the revolution through its cooperation with the center-right. They too sought the destruction of the democratic system, which they wanted to replace with a Communist one.

All these groups, aside from the Social Democrats, had in common was their refusal to come to terms with the establishment of a postwar democratic system. The great historian Hans Mommsen labeled these reactions "the inner rejection of the peace," a phrase that describes the political conflicts of the Weimar years as an expression of the nation's social and psychological fissures over the lost war.[26] The revolution of 1918–1919 was not merely a normal political event whose consequences the elites could manage; it was a systemic destruction, a time of political and economic transformation combined with social and generational upheaval. The resulting Republic spent its early years frantically attempting to deal with repeated political crises, periodic economic calamities, sustained demographic disruption, and perpetual outbreaks of violence, as increasingly numerous and ever more radical political factions tried to conquer their domestic enemies.

The Socio-Sexual and Familial Legacy of the Great War

Fittingly for the era's new psychoanalytical way of thinking, the challenges many Germans faced in the postwar era bred a variety of politicized psychosexual obsessions. The good citizens of Germany became obsessed with the idea that the lost war and revolution had led to a vast increase in social malevolence, including divorce, unwed motherhood, venereal disease, homosexuality, rape, and even cannibalism. To some extent, their fear was justified. The immediate postwar years did see a rise in demographic markers of instability, such as divorce and disease. These trends also became more acute during two periods of great economic instability that followed: the 1923 hyperinflation crisis, and the global depression that began in 1929. But even during Weimar's "golden years" of relative stability in the mid- to late 1920s, a broad spectrum of civic, political, and artistic leaders became obsessed with stories of decadence, urban decay, and a general dissolution of society. The power and endurance of these fears reflected the very real tensions that the war had exacerbated, and which continued to gain strength as the new form of government failed to overcome the numerous crises it faced.

In their later writings about how they came to their Nazi beliefs, many stormtroopers described how they resented the new system for causing the decay of morality and family life. The decline, however, had actually begun during the war. As one stormtrooper later wrote of his wartime childhood, "All family life was at an end."[27] Because the fathers and older brothers had gone to the front and women had to take the men's place in the workforce, children saw neither father nor mother. "So we grew up," he wrote, "amid hunger and privation, with no semblance of a decent family life."[28] Such a description of course reflects a great degree of class bias, since its sense of what constituted "a decent family life" had not existed even before the war for many working-class children. This class bias perhaps reveals why so many of the early stormtroopers insisted that the revolution had caused social upheaval rather than realizing the truth—that wartime privation had caused revolution.

Most of Hamburg's early stormtroopers came from middle- and upper-middle-class circles. They joined right-wing militias because of a desire to defend a class and political system that had worked well for their families before the war. Conversely, youths from working-class families who had not been as prosperous under the imperial system initially had little sympathy for National Socialism. However, this dynamic changed after 1929, when the global depression radicalized broad masses of German society and brought the Nazi and Communist parties into direct competition for recruits from the working class. But in the early years, most young men who joined militias—whether of the right, left, or center—did so in professed allegiance to their families' values. As one of the earliest men to join the Hamburg SA, a stormtrooper named Schipper described the origins of his nationalist politics:

Having been raised from my youth as a nationalist, I recognized quite early that the political fragmentation and the Marxist course would lead to the powerlessness and death of our *Vaterland*. In accordance with my upbringing, I joined the so-called nationalist camp.[29]

Schipper had learned nationalism as a self-evident value that suffused daily family life. SA man Werner B., who after the war had moved to Hamburg from its Prussian outskirts in search of economic opportunity, agreed, writing that "Communist ideas were foreign to me, having grown up in an East-Prussian family of teachers with strong *vaterländisch* [patriotic] orientation."[30] One proud father of a young stormtrooper expressed similar sentiments when he credited his son's SA membership to "a strict breeding and sense of order learned in his parents' home."[31] Many stormtroopers saw their political ideology as a natural inheritance, as part of a middle-class family life that for decades had stood for patriotism, patriarchy, nationalism, and antisocialism.

The ideal of middle-class family life, which included a particular form of masculinity that supported and ennobled it, was always partially fantasy, and it was never as stable as its devotees insisted. Even so, it had been a pillar of the state, and now both state and ideal had toppled. Statistical and demographic evidence attest to this fact, but contemporary psychological evidence also loomed large. Artists and social scientists began exploring and publicizing more than ever the types of people who did not fully conform to the social ideal—however, they did so not to keep them marginalized but to help integrate them into society.

Magnus Hirschfeld, the pioneering "sexologist" who had made headlines discussing homosexuality before the war, spearheaded a groundbreaking study after the war that called attention to a hidden history of the conflict. He called it *The Sexual History of the Great War*. Together with a dozen other contributors, many from his Scientific-Humanitarian Committee in Berlin, Hirschfeld collected and parsed the growing body of work that psychiatrists and social scientists had generated about the sexual experiences of wartime. The resulting project, eventually published in full in 1930, contained chapters on venereal disease, army brothels, prostitution, "war wives and immorality," the eroticism of nurses, and other timeless but rarely discussed aspects of warfare. Stormtroopers likely took little issue with topics like these, since they merely reinforced masculine stereotypes of warfare as a realm in which men behaved as men, conquering enemies on the battlefield and in the bedroom. Even chapters that depicted sexualized war crimes, rape, and "the bestialization of man" fell into that ironically comfortable category.[32]

Other topics, however, posed a greater psychological threat. The Great War had been a period of potential female empowerment, and Hirschfeld and his contributors consequently highlighted the impact of women soldiers, women spies, and women working on the home front. Hirschfeld argued that women's increased prominence after 1914 grew out of three prewar trends: a general embrace of eroticism by both men and women, growing political equality between the sexes, and women's increasing participation in economic life.[33] These developments had gained strength during wartime, a time of emergency that "swept away prejudices which had already been tottering." An array of "dammed-up instincts" now "rushed out in a veritable moral chaos which reached its peak, curiously enough, not during the war but in the first post-war years."[34]

Demographic evidence certainly seemed to confirm a dissolution of the idealized social norm, and this dissolution was one of the disturbing features of postwar life that radicalized young men who were caught up in the transition. Stormtroopers therefore may have applauded a work that decried "moral chaos" in postwar sexuality. Hirschfeld, however, was unconcerned with delivering a condemnation. He instead presented his work as empirical and documentary, and in the service of these goals he analyzed additional phenomena that made the Nazi war veterans shudder indeed. *The Sexual History of the Great War* contained chapters on the "sensuality of the trenches," "homosexuality and transvestism" among the soldiers, genital injuries and psychosexual conditions caused by war, "war eunuchs," and the sex life of prisoners of war.[35] It depicted a failed abstinence campaign that German political and scientific authorities had promoted on the theory that sublimation and self-denial would "treasure up the best powers of the body" to serve the war effort.[36] Authorities told soldiers to concentrate on self-control, which supposedly would mold them into superior fighting men and bring victory. Hirschfeld described the idea as a "bastard hybrid of psychoanalysis and patriotism" that was utterly inappropriate to a long and all-consuming war, and which was in fact refuted by that experience.[37] Sexologists, psychiatrists, and other social scientists like Hirschfeld found that soldiers continued their erotic lives in the trenches through dreams, fantasies, masturbation, and same-sex attraction that included sexual acts.

While homosexuality in military circles had come to public light in the years immediately preceding the war, wartime conditions further magnified the association. This awareness in part reflected a natural drift toward what psychologists today refer to as "situational homosexuality" among men in same-sex environments. As Hirschfeld wrote at the time, "It will not escape even the most superficial observation that in a war where tremendous masses of men were deprived of every contact with the other sex, homosexuality would be bound to play an important role."[38] Although the concept is familiar now, Hirschfeld's depiction scandalized his contemporaries because it showed how even ostensibly heterosexual soldiers indulged in the occasional homosexual experience.

Alongside this dynamic, the number of military men who openly identified as homosexual—at least to themselves and their trusted friends—increased as well. Hirschfeld claimed that of the scientists and staff of the Scientific-Humanitarian Committee who identified as homosexuals, at least 50 percent had enlisted in the German military at the outbreak of war.[39] The Committee knew of thousands more who went to great lengths to join the mobilization, including men whom the state had persecuted for their homosexuality. Some who had exiled themselves after receiving convictions under Paragraph 175 now returned, and officers whom the services had dismissed for homosexuality now sought permission to rejoin. Once in the trenches, according to Hirschfeld's researchers, homosexual soldiers often made the most capable servicemen. They tended to care more for the general social welfare than men who headed their own families, proved more dedicated to their comrades because of their emotional attachment to them, and fought more fiercely due to a psychological need to prove themselves to a society that often challenged their patriotism.

In some respects, this image resembled the long tradition of military camaraderie that had developed throughout the 19th century, which had increasingly linked militant masculinity to citizenship, state formation, and governing. Service in the army thus confirmed a man's leading social status while simultaneously marking as inferior those men not allowed to serve. Ironically, however, this formulation also physically and emotionally isolated soldiers from the society they protected. Literary works of the time represented soldiers as psychologically estranged from the nation-states they served. Rejected by women and bourgeois society, they longed for new wars that would allow them to participate again in a "fantasy of manhood."[40] Any hardships endured due to this fantasy were made easier by a compensatory sense of camaraderie, which filled the emotional void that wartime conditions created, encouraged group loyalty, and motivated men to conduct feats of heroism. Camaraderie thus sustained social and political structures across Europe, but especially in the German lands, where the ideal gained central importance in the dominant definition of normative masculinity.[41]

By World War I, the homoeroticism of the imperial military, as well as in schools, associational life, and public service, had become a much-remarked trait of German life. In March 1914, the homosexual American artist Marsden Hartley traveled to Berlin, where he painted works in praise of the "essentially masculine" country and wrote letters to friends describing the close bonds between German men.[42] During the war, Hans Blüher, a prominent articulator of German same-sex affections, claimed that erotic bonds between men offered a force for social and political cohesion superior to that of the heterosexual family.[43] In his 1917 work, *The Role of the Erotic in Male Society*, Blüher wrote that a system that segregated itself into a male public sphere and a female private sphere, and which based its legitimacy on this demarcation, would prompt an outpouring of social, patriotic, political, and military advances.[44] Blüher's concept of the *Männerbund*, or men's society, became an important concept to many stormtroopers. It already existed in state institutions including the army, military academies, all-male boarding schools, sporting clubs, and youth groups—institutions that formed the basis of the imperial state and gave members a path to social power, economic self-sufficiency, and political authority.[45]

The system reached its peak during the Great War, which many combatants viewed as a transcendent male experience. Nationalist literary responses to the war from authors such as Ernst von Salomon, who later became a high-ranking SA officer, and Ernst Jünger claimed that combat had forged war veterans into an elite fraternity whose allegiance to outside groups paled in comparison to their obligations to one another. This elite group, however, grew estranged from the rest of society, as evidenced by the letters, diaries, and memoirs of right-wing war veterans who joined the postwar militias, which they called the *Freikorps* (Free Corps). As psychoanalyst Klaus Theweleit demonstrated in his strange yet pioneering study of these men, they wrote only rarely about the women in their lives. When they did, they usually lamented the lack of connection and incomprehension between the sexes, which war had exacerbated. "How can women understand us," asked one, "when they gave nothing, when they shared nothing of our experiences during those years of torment?"[46] This writer's insistence that women "gave nothing" surely ignores the sacrifices and hardships that those on the home front bore during the war—but that is precisely the point. Although membership in the Freikorps and SA never perfectly overlapped, the most zealous adherents of both groups shared the same mentality: loyalty to comrades balanced by alienation from others. The more entrenched their narrow view of militarized masculine hegemony became, the more they disdained any group they interpreted as an opposing stereotype. The most important of these stormtrooper counter-types, besides women, were the SA's most resented opponents: civilians, pacifists, liberals, effeminate homosexuals, and Jews. Stormtroopers adhered to a bifurcated image of political citizenship in which men who had served in the military constituted legitimate political actors, with a lesser degree of influence allowed the civilians who gave such men their full and unqualified support. Right-wing militants thus considered themselves the postwar heirs of powerful male bonds forged during wartime, and they rejected as full citizens to those who did not (or could not) take part in that experience.

The close association between masculinity, warfare, and the health of the state proved powerful, but it also created great risk. If such a system met defeat in war, it would mean defeat not just for individual men but for masculine ideals generally and any political system based on them. This is exactly what happened after the Great War. The depersonalized and industrial nature of the war mocked assertions of traditional valor, showed the physical frailty of the male body, and proved the helplessness of masculine political and military organizations.[47]

Scholars now recognize that this sense of embattled masculinity was less monolithic among the men of the Weimar Republic than is often believed.[48] Nevertheless, none dispute that the German nationalists—and especially the stormtroopers—believed in an aggressive masculine paradigm. In fact, traditions of camaraderie were a powerful draw for young nationalists who respected the imperial period and longed for its unabashed celebration of militant masculinity, which they hoped to re-create in their own lives. They saw the postwar Republic as feminized and weak, and they hoped to redeem Germany's martial honor by elevating militarized masculine values and ties of male affection.

Masculinity thus formed the foundation of the SA's political practices, but this foundation contained several dangerous fissures. Publicity generated by the social scientists, sexologists, psychoanalysts, and novelists who called increased attention to the sexual or erotic side of male affection jeopardized movements that relied upon that male energy. As Hirschfeld wrote in his great work, comradely ties could be broken down into three categories: open eroticism, sublimated or unacknowledged eroticism, and the absence of eroticism. A more modern set of terms would label these categories as homosexuality, homoeroticism, and homosocialism. The differences among these three concepts became of paramount importance to the SA as it developed into a self-consciously masculine political movement that played to all three sides of same-sex male attraction. On the one hand, the SA emphasized its homosocial nature, since this quality reinforced its appeal as a vigorous defender of an uprooted patriarchal order. It drew on homoerotic bonds as a way to integrate its members and strengthen itself as a fighting community. It loudly and publicly denied that this emotional stance made it attractive to homosexuals, even while it simultaneously incorporated talented homosexuals whose devotion to a group of comrades might prove extremely useful. The SA thus had to exert extraordinary effort to weld these three concepts into a coherent whole that would ensure that masculinity and same-sex attraction could offer a secure base on which to build a movement.

Masculinity, Camaraderie, and the Founding of the SA

Nationalist politics in both the imperial and Weimar eras mainly took place in same-sex spaces. Political parties met in men's clubs, taverns, public houses, and other drinking establishments to hear speeches and engage in vigorous, alcohol-soaked debates about Germany's future. Other political movements also followed this trend, creating a constellation of competing taverns that openly advertised their affiliation with a particular political party. While these gatherings rarely formally banned women, in practice the only women likely to be present were waitresses or barmaids. Social democratic politics proved an exception, encouraging women to play active roles and even electing them to office in extraordinarily high numbers, at least as compared to women's relative absence among other factions. This gender equality was among social democracy's most distinctive features, as attractive to adherents as it was repellent to rivals. Rightist parties therefore kept their meeting spaces exclusively masculine to express and reinforce their insistence that politics remain, as it had been in the past, a decidedly male realm.

But this tradition now met with change. As the old form of masculine political life evolved during the turbulent Weimar period, young men who frequented political taverns exhibited increasingly combative and violent tendencies. When this new affinity for violence pushed parties to establish protection squads to guard their meetings, the squads themselves increased the overall level of violence by conducting both offensive and defensive operations. This masculine political environment eventually spawned the SA as a particularly paranoid and aggressive participant in the tavern-brawl political style.

During the imperial period, taverns had dominated Hamburg's political life to such an extent that the city's unusually active political police regularly sent undercover agents to monitor the guests and record their views on imperial politics.[49] In contrast to the beer halls and outdoor beer gardens of southern Germany, which were often massive spaces filled with long tables, large speaking platforms, and orchestra stands, Hamburg's taverns were mainly unpretentious one- or two-room establishments with rough wooden tables and chairs. The typical tavern offered space for 15–20 customers, who bought beer, schnapps, and simple food to soak up the alcohol. Taverns with two rooms marked the second one as a "club room" that allowed space for more formal meetings, lectures, and political discussions. The owner and his family, who helped run the establishment, lived above or next to the tavern, while the customers were the men who lived or worked nearby.

Guests usually visited the pub on their way home from work, drank a few pints, and read aloud articles from newspapers that the tavern keeper made available. The choice of newspaper signaled the pub's political affiliation, an important factor in drawing or repelling customers. Tavern owners tended to agree with—or at least cater to—the mood of the neighborhood. Pubs in working-class areas near the docks featured the socialist *Hamburger Echo*, while taverns in wealthier areas around the Alster (such as the St. Georg district where Alfred Conn and several other early stormtroopers lived) or Hoheluft (where the university had just been founded) carried liberal papers like the venerable *Hamburger Nachrichten* and *Hamburger Fremdenblatt*. They also sometimes offered radically nationalist and antisemitic magazines. These publications formed the basis of discussions that, as the political police reported, often gained their energy from alcohol.

Formal meetings and lectures took place at the pubs several times a week. Meetings often began with music or patriotic entertainment—German songs, German dances, or readings from the German classics. Formal speeches by local party activists followed the cultural program. The evening's central element would be a political speech by a local expert or invited guest, who addressed attention-grabbing issues in an organized and forceful manner that often connected with the audience's concern for their city.[50] For instance, a speaker might excoriate the Treaty of Versailles by illustrating its negative impact on Hamburg's shipping industry, or criticize the postwar French occupation of German soil by comparing it to the Napoleonic army's predatory behavior in historic Hamburg. The best speakers fully engaged the audience, whose members spontaneously interjected rebuttals and catcalls when provoked or offended. Both bonds and divisions between speaker and audience, and among the audience members, grew stronger as they consumed large amounts of alcohol before, during, and after the event.[51]

Hamburg's taverns had long been politicized spaces where people stridently disagreed with one another, but they were traditionally not violent spaces. If a tavern keeper's politics did not match his neighborhood's political tenor, the worst he could expect would be a boycott and customers' defection to other taverns. Customers complained with their pocketbooks, and a tavern keeper who misjudged his neighborhood's political orientation soon had to close shop or sell the business to someone better attuned to local sensibilities. Violence and tavern brawls—at least those that originated from political disputes—were unusual.[52] This changed after 1918. The taverns' political role remained the same while the membership numbers of old-style political clubs reached new highs.[53] However, from 1918 to 1924, the destabilized political situation changed the old form of conduct. There were now more parties competing for voters' loyalty. Moreover, and most important in terms of understanding the SA, a generational shift had taken place. By the early 1920s, many young men considered their fathers' mode of political life too soft, too weak, too non-confrontational, and ultimately too ineffective at turning back the tide of democratic and socialist revolution.

A stormtrooper who later wrote a proud essay about his turn to Nazism expressed the generation gap quite eloquently. He had been a sailor in Kiel during the revolution, but he had not supported it and in fact deeply resented the military governor's order that troops should not fire on the rebels. To a young future stormtrooper, this inaction encapsulated the weakness and vacillation of the prior generation's approach to political threats. After 1918, such youths resented their elders for failing to defend the prewar ways of life they had promised to pass on to their sons:

> Completely disconcerted, a bourgeois generation faced the new world of 1918. It had managed during the war, adapting itself to all the unaccustomed limitations, suffering bitter need in the belief that some time, after peace was made, it would be able to continue down the broad, comfortable avenue it had traveled before. Now it found itself confused and frightened . . . There was a gaping abyss between fathers and sons. We soldiers of the front had never known the fabulous comfortable road; nor did we feel any longing for it. Fighting had become our life purpose and goal; any battle, any sacrifice for the might and glory of our country.[54]

This describes a common mind-set among the stormtroopers: resentment at being denied the life of steady bourgeois progress that their forefathers had enjoyed, then denial that they wanted it in the first place, then a resolution to favor conflict over comfort. This is a familiar psychological defense mechanism common in many eras. After failing to achieve an aspiration, people can convince themselves that they in fact never hoped for the outcome they failed to achieve. For the stormtroopers, the vehemence of their denial betrayed their despair at the situation. Such duality marked stormtrooper politics throughout the life of the SA, as the SA men openly portrayed combat and conflict as their true joy, yet simultaneously claimed to fight only as a means to regain the comfortable life they had originally wanted. The paradox closely parallels another psychological rift in the movement: the conflict between comrade and family as the emotional basis of SA politics.

Another insight provided by this autobiographical passage is its elaboration of the generation gap that defeat and revolution had opened up between fathers and sons. As in Conn's experience in the Rathaus, many young nationalists wanted to resist the revolution, but the older, cooler heads of the prior generation had ordered them not to. Ironically, the only time counterrevolutionaries were able to smash the socialists was when the SPD enlisted them against the Communists to protect the hated Republic. A sense of being abandoned by their patriarchs thus drove young nationalists toward paramilitary politics. "One must bear these things in mind to understand the course of our lives," the stormtrooper sailor wrote, "to comprehend how two generations became estranged in a few days. In those days, our trust in the old leaders, in the old generation, was destroyed, struck dead. We had to take our fate in our own hands."[55]

The generation gap showed clearly in the early stormtroopers' political and economic careers. Many of the future stormtroopers at first joined their fathers' political parties, as Alfred Conn did with the German National People's Party (DNVP), one of the new entities that had emerged as a successor to the old-line conservative, nationalist, and national-liberal parties.[56] Conn's father and his friend Dr. Holzmann led DNVP local politics in St. Georg, and his father's house became the party's election center in the Republic's early months. Conn also joined his father's merchant firm, which had been in his family for generations. Many of Hamburg's early stormtroopers who came from merchant families followed this pattern, either working directly for their fathers or using their fathers' contacts to start businesses of their own.[57] Many future SA doctors began their careers by following their fathers into medicine, and even stormtroopers who pursued careers different from their fathers' often allowed their fathers to have significant influence over their choices.[58] Stormtrooper Hans M. described in his party autobiography how he had come to a career as an upholsterer "in compliance with my father's wishes."[59] Future stormtroopers also found work by mobilizing traditional forms of male associational life, such as fraternities. Albert Krebs, a young war veteran who became an important local journalist and Nazi political leader, got a job in this way with a conservative nationalist trade union called the German Nationalist Workers Association (DHV).[60]

However, even young Nazis who had begun their political and economic lives by conforming with their fathers' ideologies later came into conflict with those sensibilities. In fact, most considered the contrast with an older political style to be the very reason they joined the *Nationalsozialistische Deutsche Arbeiterpartei* (National Socialist German Workers Party, or NSDAP)—commonly referred to as the Nazi Party. This new party proclaimed the same goals as the old-line conservative parties, but it embraced new means that radicalized youth found more appealing. Conn described the younger generation's frustration with its elders in the context of a DNVP national meeting in Berlin that he attended with his father. It seemed very well organized, he said, but it was also dry and boring, an expression of "the old bourgeois

style" that accomplished nothing.[61] He returned to Hamburg disappointed, and complained to Dr. Holzmann that such a desiccated party would
not be able to win wider support. The conservatives had to seek newer and
broader alliances. Holzmann professed superficial agreement but showed no
interest in the project; he told Conn to attempt it himself. Conn's reaction
to this conversation is illustrative. Rather than work within the DNVP, he
drifted away. He soon joined the *Deutschvölkischer Schutz- und Trustbund* (German
Nationalist Protection and Defiance Federation), a new antisemitic association with close ties to the DHV and the venerable Pan-German League, but
which sought a more radical approach. Conn also founded a group of his
own: the German People's Fraternity Sigfried [sic], a student society that required its members to show their ancestry and swear to their blood purity.[62]
Here, too, this small but growing group came into conflict with more traditional student fraternities, which often professed the same goals and beliefs
but considered these young upstarts too dogmatic and aggressive.

As Conn found, national socialist or *völkisch* youths often had to defend their political beliefs against accusations that they were merely young
and naïve. Krebs' patrons in the DHV chuckled when he told them of his
Nazi sympathies. One of the elders there called the Nazi Party an "enfant
terrible," a well-intentioned but overly wild outburst of "confused youth"
that would have to mature before others would take it seriously.[63] The older
generation failed to realize, however, that a raw, aggressive, and youthfully
belligerent tone proved attractive rather than repulsive. Committing acts of
violence offered a way for new groups to gain attention among Weimar's
myriad parties, and it provided opportunities to draw members away from
apparently weaker groups.

In Munich, the Nazi Party also refashioned itself in just this way: as
an innovative and increasingly successful competitor in the ecosystem of
southern German nationalist politics. The Party began in 1920, when Adolf
Hitler took over and rebranded the German Workers Party, bringing a new
approach to old-style beerhall politics. His new style directly opposed the
previous generation's more dignified speeches and lectures, emphasizing
instead a tone of confrontation, anger, and aggression as a way to bring
notice to itself and frustration to its enemies. Hitler's new visual style appropriated old nationalist symbols like the swastika, while also borrowing
imagery formerly common to the left, such as the color red, which it combined with the black and white of the old Prussian flag. The combination

was purposefully explosive, and his meetings grew ever larger as people flocked to see a guaranteed confrontation between Hitler's ferocious rhetoric and the outbursts it would draw from a drunken and ideologically mixed audience.[64] The first SA units in Munich, and therefore the first stormtroopers, grew out of this environment, as the Party needed a troop that could eject protestors without relying on the police. Moreover, by positioning themselves as defenders of a political speaker's right to debate, the members of this extralegal gang could also pose as defenders of bourgeois order against an increasingly aggressive and violent generation of socialists.[65] But the stormtroopers embodied better than anyone the new, violent generation of politics. Hamburg's stormtroopers existed within this paradox as well; they claimed that their warlike tendencies and pursuit of violent political struggle merely defended a traditional way of life. Their actions, however, contradicted the very values that way of life had promoted: bourgeois standards of moderation, compromise, civility, and restraint, which the stormtroopers decried as decadent weakness in the postwar era.

The Birth of the Hamburg SA

The Hamburg chapter of the Nazi Party was founded on January 24, 1922, by Joseph Klant, the elderly proprietor of a cigar store in the upscale neighborhood of Rotherbaum.[66] He and the other four founding members began to campaign by word of mouth, enlisting friends, relatives, and acquaintances to join the Party.[67] The group thus began as the very type of "bourgeois debating society" that Hitler and the stormtroopers habitually mocked.[68] But it, too, like the Munich Party chapter, formed a protection squad quite early on, thereby demonstrating that it engaged in the new generation's preferred form of politics. Unlike Hitler's Munich SA, the Hamburg group declined the euphemism of a "sport division" and called itself a "hall protection division," or simply "storm troop."[69] The independent inventions and difference in names shows that, during the movement's early phase, Nazi Party cells outside Munich could remain relatively independent of the national Party.[70] The Hamburg Nazis formed their SA not on Munich's orders but because they faced the same problem as their comrades in the south: disruption of and attacks on their taverns by socialist and Communist groups.

The Hamburg SA's first conflicts became local legend, much as the Munich SA's first battle in the Hofbräuhaus became part of the national

Party's founding myth. Police reports and the SA's own accounts testify that confrontations with political opponents began in the local Party's earliest days, the inevitable result of Klant's decision to hold the first Party meetings in a famed socialist tavern decorated with portraits of Marx, Engels, and other leading personalities of the left.[71] After only a few meetings, however, the regular pub-goers began to threaten the interlopers, and Klant soon moved his meetings elsewhere. The Nazis later claimed that the socialists followed them wherever they went, provoking and persecuting them until the Nazis had no choice but to strike back. According to one later tribute to the Hamburg SA's early accomplishments, the group faced its first "test of fire" on September 25, 1922, when a group of "socialists and Communists" sneaked into a Nazi meeting and attempted to "blow it up," a preferred term on both sides for disrupting enemy meetings:

> The attempted disturbance soon developed into a brawl during which the red bully-brothers were shown the door. The noise drew the curious, and the fight broke out again, shots fell, and finally the police appeared, restoring the peace through the application of their nightsticks. That was the first meeting-hall battle faced by the Hamburg group.[72]

As with other Nazi sources, the accuracy of details mattered less than the creation of a myth. In this case, the story of the first battle argued that the Nazi Party had first attempted honest debate, only to suffer constant violence by hordes of Marxist thugs who feared Nazi ideas:

> The opponents of the NSDAP would not fight the new movement through spiritual weapons, but rather used violence and terror; this brought the party to organize its own storm troop to defend against the brutal attacks and to keep order within its meetings.[73]

The Nazis also believed that the socialists had the support of state and police agencies that overtly opposed the nationalists:

> The experience showed that the police either came too late to the opponents' attempts to disturb our meetings, or intervened only when forced to, and then not against the Marxist disturbers of the

peace but against the hated National Socialists, who were worked over with nightsticks just for seeking to exercise their rights. In principle, the ruling system wanted the meetings of the NSDAP to end in brawls and tumult, with broken chairs and busted skulls. The guardians of order could then prove the conduct of the party to be disturbing to the peace and dangerous to the state, and they could then justify their bans to the public.[74]

In interviews conducted after the war, some antifascists who had fought the SA during the *Kampfzeit* (time of struggle) admitted their role in provoking tavern violence. Like the stormtroopers, they too saw tavern battles, which mainly took place in the border neighborhoods between bourgeois and working-class quarters, as defensive actions. Paul M. described his group's efforts in Eimsbüttel to keep out "National Socialist strength, German-national, whatever you want to call them," as an especially aggressive effort to attack a particular tavern, which his friends assaulted using hit-and-run tactics to damage the building's windows and exterior.[75] Heinz Preiss, a Communist youth group member in the late 1920s, bristled when an interviewer asked how his group had "provoked" the Nazis in St. Georg, in the taverns, and on the streets. Preiss claimed it "would probably give a false impression to say" that his deeds were provocations. He preferred instead to characterize them as "specific counter-actions" by groups "created for the protection of the [Communist] Party." Preiss admitted that "the way things are talked about today, it would come close to terrorism. But it wasn't . . . That's different."[76] The language of the two sides is striking in its similarity. Both claimed that their paramilitary efforts were entirely defensive, while also admitting—and at times bragging—that their sense of what constituted defensive measures drifted far into the offensive realm. For the SA and other paramilitaries of the time, violence and fighting were not just defensive tactics to protect existing party members; violence also offered a chance to spread a party's fame and attract new members.

The SA made a striking visual impression while standing guard, even before they swung into action. Once they did, the violence itself held positive appeal. Conn described the first time he attended a Nazi meeting as just such an experience. He had traveled to Wedel, a neighboring town where he sometimes went to represent his father's business interests. This Nazi meeting had come under siege by its enemies, but it enjoyed the protection of a local SA-Freikorps alliance:

The mood was tumultuous. In the square before the tavern was a gesticulating mob, quite openly Communist-led, which demonstrated against our event. But here was no young *Bürgerverein* [bourgeois club]. Here we didn't go for passive resistance like the German nationals; we were active instead. In all entrances of the hall stood martial men, mostly from the Freikorps Raven, in closed formation, ready to beat back the expected attack on the tavern.[77]

Conn's use of an inclusive "we" in this passage is retroactive, in that he had not yet joined the Party. However, he found easy and immediate identification with the group, given his service in a Freikorps unit and a citizens' militia. The alliance between SA and Freikorps men in Wedel showed him that the Nazi Party sought to represent nationalist causes in the most militant manner possible, and this demonstration began his path to the Party. Many other stormtroopers had similar experiences.[78] They had joined various *Wehrverbände* (combat leagues) as an early expression of their patriotism and to defend national and local stability, and they now grew ever more attracted to the Nazi Party because of the prominence of the SA.[79] *Sturmführer* (company leader) Schipper had first joined the *Jungstahlhelm*, the youth division of the predominant veterans group, the *Stahlhelm*. Despite the Stahlhelm's nationalist and rightist orientation, it considered itself a force of moral authority that transcended the parochial interests of specific political parties. Schipper and men like him, however, sought out militias that embraced party affiliation, and they hoped that building a strong party militia could unite all nationalist factions under one banner. Schipper himself converted to National Socialism after hearing a Hitler speech that made promises along these lines. As Schipper put it, "Unity brings strength."[80]

Unity demanded the total commitment of those who advocated it, and Schipper believed that only the Nazi Party and its SA offered such a style. "I am an SA man," he wrote in a later essay contest, "because here I have the best chance to actively struggle with my entire being, to fight . . . in the front ranks of the struggle."[81] Another Sturmführer echoed Schipper's feelings using much the same words: "Why am I an SA man? Because my very being demands that I stand as a fighter, and enter at the point of struggle with my entire being."[82] These statements reflect the dominance of a particular kind of militant and valorized masculinity that lay at the center of the SA's political practices. Heroic, self-sacrificing violence gave the SA an integrative force that helped it claim that it transcended the boundaries of class, religion, and other non-ethnic social categories. As long as a man held true to the masculine ideal and had the proper ethnic background, he could belong. Conn claimed that, in the SA, "all the German classes were united in brotherhood."[83] SA general Manfred von Killinger later explained this sentiment in his book, *Men and Might: The SA in Words and Pictures*:

> The SA won't ask you where you come from; what's your name; what kind of schooling do you have; what is your father, is he a worker of a government minister—but rather what kind of guy are you; what can you do; what can you achieve? You will now be thrown into the water. Swim. If you can't, then save yourself on the shore and another guy will take your place.[84]

Military masculinity was therefore a factor that could unite a fractured society. The SA chose as its leaders men who embodied the principle. The three men who led the Hamburg SA during the drive to power—Arthur Böckenhauer, Paul Ellerhusen, and Alfred Conn—were all war veterans and members of close-knit militias who retained their men's loyalties throughout the vagaries of political disagreement and infighting. They also proved adept at attracting and retaining men of varied social classes and education levels, even though all three were themselves from the ranks of Hamburg's traditional notables.

Nationally, SA leadership also embodied the principles of military masculinity. Ernst Röhm, the founding figure and eventual SA chief of staff, enjoyed unimpeachable credentials as a fighter in the Great War. His face bore the scars of combat, and he loudly advocated the personal benefits of military experience and the moral superiority of men who fought on their country's behalf. His background, personality, and physical presence offered the ultimate example of the fighting men the SA hoped to attract as their "political soldiers." Röhm did not just practice military masculinity— he also theorized and wrote about its meaning. He argued that men alone should hold political authority. He claimed that the Weimar Republic and democracy had destroyed masculine values in favor of feminine ones, thus accelerating the country's decline. The solution, he said, would come only by uniting around the concept of military masculinity. He called his autobiography *The Story of a Traitor*, a title that conveyed his view that Germany had so far departed from its traditional values that even a loyal son such as himself became suspect. The work went through several editions during the Weimar era.[85] Although Röhm constantly tinkered with its contents, editing and revising to suit momentary political needs, one theme remained constant: his connection of patriarchal warrior masculinity to German national might. Röhm believed that Germany's changing gender order, in which women gained increasing equality and men found options other than a monolithic martial identity, was both a cause and an effect of the nation's decline. As he wrote, "Times of state power and greatness, eras of struggle, have never tolerated a leading position for the female sex." Alexander the Great and Frederick the Great, he said, would never have "bowed to feminine influences."[86] Most stormtroopers shared these views. The SA's newspaper, *Der SA Mann*, later explained the embodiment of the "SA spirit":

> The organized will, the power, and the masculine, German, mentality of our brown army [are] the undefeatable source of strength from which leader and man continually reap new motivation, new confidence, and new will to victory.[87]

The connection of militarized masculinity to concepts of disciplined, organized power stemmed from an ideal of male *Soldatentum* (soldierhood) that had dominated the imperial period, and which the stormtroopers hoped to enshrine anew in a fascist state. As the stormtrooper newspaper explained:

> He who holds as the highest ideal the avoidance of every disturbance in his comfortable lifestyle, who avoids every difficulty, who runs from every obstacle in his way, who puts himself before everything else, is no soldier—and in the end, not even a real man. As every real man is by nature a soldier.[88]

In the SA, this ideal even competed with racist antisemitism for status as the Nazis' great unifying solution. But basing a political movement on a hegemonic conception of masculinity also carried risks, because it forced the stormtroopers to constantly fend off challenges to their self-conceptions.

Ernst Röhm embodied the dilemma best, since he had more than one reason to laud military heroes such as Alexander and Frederick. Like these men, he too was a homosexual. In the early 1920s he had not yet come to grips with his own orientation, but in the future it became known to everyone—first among his comrades, then among his political allies, and finally to the nation and the world, when a socialist newspaper published evidence of his orientation. By the mid- to late 1920s, as future chapters of this book will describe in detail, homosexuality in SA ranks became a prominent feature that both attracted and repelled adherents of the Nazi movement. However, the presence of homosexuals in the SA even in the early years should remind observers that many stormtroopers never had all the traits their pure version of the masculine stereotype demanded. That vision simultaneously enshrined military service, economic independence, and familial authority as the necessary identities that together justified po-litical authority. But the SA—both in its early years as a sporting club and protection troop and later in its maturity as a mass paramilitary army—at-tracted primarily the young. Many of the earliest SA men were 20 years old or even younger; some were as young as 15.[89] But even those who had reached their mid-20s felt that wartime service had stunted their personal and professional growth, interrupted their normal life path, put their career and marriage on hold, and consequently denied them many markers of full manhood. The youngest stormtroopers had watched their fathers and older brothers march to war but had been too young to participate in this important experience before the nation suffered its ignominious defeat. The SA therefore represented a collection of men psychologically riven by a wholehearted embrace of male roles that they only imperfectly embodied: would-be soldiers denied an army in which to serve; men who wanted to start a family but who could not afford to marry; and homosexuals who be-lieved their military service should trump their sexual nonconformity. These men exerted great effort to construct themselves as traditionally heroic male warriors, and they believed that they could transcend their differences and individual failures through these efforts. In short, through the SA they could become the type of man they wanted to be.

A political movement based on masculinity and male camaraderie can-not merely assert these qualities, nor are such traits a simple inheritance of lineage, class, profession, or education. Men instead have to create, demon-strate, and constantly perform their masculine identity. This is true even among men who appear to conform most easily to its stereotypes. Among men who do not, performance and assertion become even higher priorities. Unfortunately for the stormtroopers, their opportunities to perform heroic violence soon became limited indeed.

Trials of the Early SA in Hamburg, 1922–1928

The young Hamburg Nazi Party and its SA fell victim to broader national developments before its first year had even passed. On November 20, 1922, following the lead of the Prussian state government, Hamburg's political police banned the Nazi Party and SA under the provisions of the Law for the Protection of the Republic. The police accused the Nazis of conducting "antisemitic, anti-republican hatred" in coordination with other rightist groups, and of exchanging suspicious regular correspondence with the Nazi headquarters in Munich in the aftermath of the murder of foreign minister Walter Rathenau by right-wing assassins.[90] The killing was just one incident in a wave of terrorist violence and "revenge killings" perpetrated by self-appointed execution squads that murdered over four hundred government officials. Although the killings took place mostly in southern and central Germany, they drew a police spotlight onto rightist paramilitaries in all regions. The Hamburg police thus singled out the SA in their rationale for banning the Nazi Party, saying:

> The reasons for the dissolution of the NSDAP in Prussia are valid for Hamburg as well. In particular, it has built a *Sturmtrupp*, which possesses a flag and demands from its members a loyalty oath upon this flag, that they will keep loyalty and obedience to their leaders until death, and to the flag loyalty and allegiance until victory in the final battle is celebrated.[91]

Both the party and SA responded by re-forming under an ever-shifting array of cover names. The underground period magnified the existing division between the two different sides of the movement. The Party represented the more traditional and intellectual body, posing as an array of political clubs that had titles not affiliated with any particular party, such as the German Building and Economic League, the Ruhr-Aid Society (dedicated to helping Germans in the territory occupied by France), the Club for Classical Music, the Club for Modern Culture and Seafaring Education, and the Club for Biology and Racial Science.[92] These new clubs met in members' homes, where the men would talk politics while the wife served tea and snacks. When they met in taverns, Klant found a variety of cover stories to camouflage Nazi meetings from police. These schemes grew increasingly elaborate, and they often emphasized the family nature of the dormant Nazi movement. In one case, Klant booked Hamburg's largest meeting hall, Sagebiel, which would allow a larger audience than the living room gatherings. However, the meeting needed a disguise to deflect police attention, so Klant masked the event as an engagement party. A young woman volunteered to play the bride, and Klant ordered a Party member to play the groom. The event played out as a celebration for the promising young couple, who stood in metaphorically for the future of Germany. Klant's toast to their fortunes became a lecture on the fortunes of Germany, which lasted for several hours and promoted Nazi solutions for the problems young people, and a young nation, faced in building their future.[93]

Official Party accounts claimed that the group continued to thrive during this time, but other sources disagreed. Conn recalled that a small network of 20–30 members attended the household meetings in various combinations, with the overall number rising only slightly over time.[94] The secrecy and deception involved in the gatherings made it difficult for the Party to attract new members in public ways, and allowed it to recruit only through word of mouth and existing personal relationships. Even these men sometimes proved difficult to mobilize, as Conn recalled in a story about trying to get a friend to join him at an evening hosted by the Club for the Preservation of German Song. His friend expressed reluctance at going to such an esoteric and backward-looking event, and sat unhappily in confusion until Klant took the stage and began speaking on the need to preserve German songs. "But it was necessary first to know," Klant said in Conn's recollection, "what is German in the first place. And then Klant opened fire with all registers of his speaking ability. Only then did my acquaintance realize that the evening concerned forbidden topics."[95]

The Party therefore retained its powerful personal appeal and continued to work through direct social contact. It suffered, however, under a paradoxical situation: The more effectively it hid its political identity from the police, the harder it was to recruit more friends. Conversely, the more the Nazis articulated their true principles, the greater their risk of discovery. In the end, political action under these limitations proved self-defeating. If the Nazis' guests, like Conn's friend, could figure out the hidden message, so could the police. By the middle of 1923, they did. On July 8, policemen raided the Party's secret headquarters in Klant's cigar store near the university. There they found a poorly hidden stash of illegal propaganda materials, as well as a cigar box full of membership cards that they gave to the courts for further investigation. Klant was immediately arrested; he was later sentenced to four months in jail and fined 500 Marks.[96]

This ignominious episode cemented the lack of respect that many Party members—and especially the young men of the SA—had for Klant and his circle. Conn had never approved of him, calling him "the old man."[97] Conn claimed that Klant's "somewhat raw, blood-raising antisemitic tone" was an anachronism, and that Klant had failed to grasp that the younger generation preferred more sophisticated constructions of nationalist and racial ideology.[98] Joseph Goebbels called him "Father Klant," which he did not mean as a compliment, and Hamburg's younger Nazis criticized their elder's lack of interest in recruiting younger members.[99] Klant's failure to hide incriminating materials, especially the damning membership cards whose capture put all Party members in legal jeopardy, seemed like the failure of a doddering old man. Young stormtroopers saw it as typical of his disorganized leadership, which in the end destroyed even the underground Nazi Party. Attempts to preserve the movement by re-forming under a variety of cover names further alienated many young stormtroopers, who saw the development as a retreat into the fragmented "club mentality" from which they had hoped the SA could rescue nationalist politics.

The SA itself remained true to its origins and refashioned itself as a sporting club that drew its members from existing male networks of militias and paramilitaries. They called themselves the Blücher Gymnastic, Sport, and Hiking Club, which was founded on February 12, 1923, by Arthur Böckenhauer, a 24-year-old former police officer who had lost his job due to his participation in anti-republican politics.[100] Of the five founding members, only Böckenhauer developed into an important player in local Nazi politics. His importance is vast: He held the SA together during its time in the wilderness and even increased its numbers. He maintained contact with the myriad other paramilitaries that young Nazis founded in the period, including Conn's "Kameradschaft Conn," which kept together a group of comrades who had traveled in tandem through the ever-changing landscape of right-wing militias.

The hidden SA of this period was small and poor. It boasted only 16–18 members in the summer of 1923, and it could not afford uniforms.[101] The men tried at least to wear the same color of military surplus jackets.[102] Despite the lack of materials, the group achieved some measure of success

FIGURE 2.2

SA march

Stormtroopers march back into Hamburg
on February 22, 1925, after a hike in the
countryside to celebrate the anniversary of
the Nazi Party's founding. Events like these
served to maintain the SA's identity as part
of the general popularity of youth groups,
sporting clubs, and friendship groups.
Source: Arthur Böckenhauer, 10 Jahre SA in
Bildern mit verbindendem Text (Hamburg, 1932).
Collection of Archiv FZH

FIGURE 2.3

SA gymnastics training (interior, sport hall)

Stormtroopers train in gymnastics shortly after the movement's
return to legality, circa 1926–1927. Throughout the SA's life as an
organization, sports were an important way for members to see
the movement as a vehicle to better themselves. *Source:* Arthur
Böckenhauer, *10 Jahre SA in Bildern mit verbindendem Text* (Hamburg,
1932). Collection of Archiv FZH

FIGURE 2.4

SA gymnastics training (exterior, partner exercises)

Partner exercises demonstrate stormtrooper beliefs that they were training each other in physical and mental discipline. They also reveal the physical and emotional intimacy shared by the group.

Source: Der SA Mann, date unknown. Photo taken by author from copy of newspaper in Library of Congress.

for its few members. Böckenhauer sought to make the undercover SA into a training ground where youths who no longer had an army to join, and who expected to face urban combat against political enemies, could learn pseudo-military skills. He used sports to inculcate discipline, self-reliance, duty, loyalty, persistence, and camaraderie—a theme that continued through all phases of the SA's organizational life (Figure 2.2). The Blücher Club met weekly at the gymnastics hall of a boys' school near the Berliner Tor for gymnastics and free exercises (Figures 2.3 and 2.4). They sang nationalist and military songs before taking leave with a hearty "Heil!"—a greeting originally common to 19th-century sporting and gymnastics societies. The club also held marches and gathered for other sporting activities, to which members brought friends in the hope that the comradely atmosphere would seduce them into regular participation and gradual politicization. However, it still faced problems stemming from its ad hoc nature, as shown by one embarrassing episode in which a new recruit arrived at the starting point for a proposed march and found just one member in attendance.[103]

An SA so weak and disorganized could serve no useful role in the underground Nazi Party, nor could the banned party help build the SA. Both elements could only watch and wait while further coup attempts from both radical extremes took place throughout 1923. Hyperinflation had been wreaking havoc on the German economy since the beginning of the year, erasing decades of personal savings, driving food prices almost out of reach, imperiling anyone relying on pensions and other fixed incomes, and playing into the hands of speculators. The crisis atmosphere further radicalized both left and right, and across the Republic a new series of uprisings began. In October, passive resistance against the French occupation in the Ruhr district erupted into open combat. That same month in Hamburg, the local Communists, eager to lead a national revolution and possibly acting on misinterpreted orders from Moscow, called for an uprising. They attacked police stations, seized weapons, built barricades, and tried to rally the populace to support them. Parallel risings broke out in a constellation of towns that traditionally looked to Hamburg for their politics, including the suburb of Altona, where street violence led by Communists festered throughout the Weimar period.

Most of these local uprisings quickly collapsed, except for those in Barmbek, a working-class district east of the Alster that was one of the Communist Party's main strongholds. There the revolutionaries drew on local support for provisions and protection, and thereby held out through protracted exchanges of fire with police. By October 26, however, they realized that they had not achieved the broader rally they had hoped for. They abandoned their positions in the middle of the night—just in time to avoid a massive police assault the next morning, which demolished their barricades and ended the revolt. The death toll included 17 police officers, 24 Communists, and 61 civilians. Police arrested more than 1,400 people in the aftermath.

In this atmosphere of crisis, Hitler stepped forward to seize the moment. On November 9, 1923, in an atmosphere of confusion and conflicting agendas among Munich's nationalist factions, he stormed a meeting led by Gustav Ritter von Kahr, the nationalist militia leader who had just been appointed a near dictator in Bavaria's state of emergency. Surrounding the room with his SA men and firing a pistol into the ceiling to gain the crowd's attention, Hitler declared that he would lead the nationalist factions in a Bavarian revolution, after which they would march to Berlin to seize power nationwide. But Hitler's behavior toward the other nationalist leaders was schizophrenic. He placed them under arrest and threatened them with his pistol while simultaneously giving them high positions in his self-declared new government.

Meanwhile, several blocks away, Röhm took over the local army headquarters and rallied the SA and its allies. Throughout the evening, small bands of militiamen marched through the streets, celebrating, threatening, and posturing as the mood stuck them. The putsch, however, came to grief from disunity, lack of organization, and ill-conceived execution. As the leaders rushed around the city, their troops at the beer hall grew restless and uneasy as they waited without orders. They had eaten and drunk their way through an astonishing amount of bread and beer, which the Nazi party later had to pay for. Cigarettes began to run low as well. Most of the rival nationalist leaders whom Hitler had forcibly recruited to the cause took their first opportunity to abandon it, and by morning Hitler had to send stormtroopers in search of money to buy the men's loyalty. They wound up looting a nearby printing press of a pallet of 50 billion Mark notes.[104] As the stormtroopers often did, they decided by noon that the only solution to their frustration lay in violent action. They gathered some two thousand men and marched toward the war ministry, but they soon encountered a strong police barricade. Nobody knows who shot first, but the ensuing firefight killed several people, nearly including Hitler himself. He, Röhm, and the other leaders of the putsch were eventually captured, thrown in jail, and tried for treason.

In Hamburg, Böckenhauer and many of his stormtroopers heard of the uprising the night it took place. They gathered together and stayed up until morning in a state of readiness, hoping to receive word from a victorious nationalist regime in the south. They would then begin their own revolution, although none could have said how they would accomplish it with so few members. Like Hitler, they seem to have thought that the population supported them, and that the masses would rise up at the first sign of nationalist strength. In any case, the call from Munich never came, and the Nazis had to face the fact that they lacked widespread support. Conn later wrote that "unripe fruit can't be picked."[105] Left with no party to support, the Blücher men tried to maintain their group coherence through social events. In December they held a Christmas party at their local pub, Zur Post, at which a Christmas tree gleamed, small gifts were exchanged, the wives of married men attended, and "good, German Christmas feelings reigned."[106]

Thus far, both the political and paramilitary wings of the Nazi movement had failed miserably. The political police proclaimed the Party all but dead, riven by factionalism among its most important members on the political side.[107] But this period of covert operation and endemic infighting saw the key development that drove the Nazi Party to the front of the pack among Hamburg's nationalist parties after 1929: the rise of an activist SA. When a new national socialist coalition, the National Socialist Freedom Bund, held its first meeting in April 1924, the small number of assembled Nazis, in Conn's description, "vanished completely within the teeming mass of enemy visitors."[108] The meeting degenerated into a predictable brawl between socialists and members of the underground SA, who fought until police arrived to clear the hall. The meeting ended prematurely, but Conn proclaimed the stormtroopers "quite pleased with the results." To the SA, a violent meeting proved its success.

By mid-1924, Böckenhauer and Conn between them boasted some 30–40 men for hall protection.[109] The groups became more aggressive in leafleting and pasting posters, especially in socialist areas of the city. Such actions caused the ideological conflict to materialize in public spaces. Each night in the weeks leading up to the several elections held in 1924, groups of three to five men fanned out through the darkened city with posters,

FIGURE 2.5

SA poster column

Stormtroopers hang posters during an election campaign. They often ran afoul of police, property owners, and rival paramilitaries while postering buildings, making these activities a source of increasingly violent political confrontations.
Source: Arthur Böckenhauer, *10 Jahre SA in Bildern mit verbindendem Text* (Hamburg, 1932). Collection of Archiv FZH

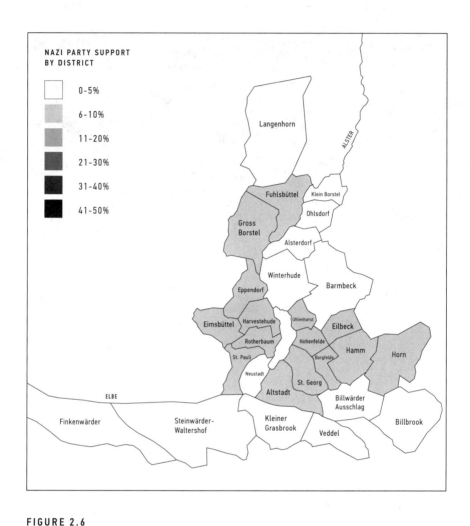

FIGURE 2.6

Nazi Party support by electoral district, May 4, 1924

Source: Created by author. Data from Richard Hamilton,
Who Voted for Hitler? (Princeton, NJ: Princeton University Press, 1982).

wheat paste, and other propaganda materials, often clashing with the poster teams of opposing parties.[110]

The SA's overt political activities in these realms often started small. One representative photograph from the elections of late 1924 shows a group of six stormtroopers standing proudly in front of one lonely poster (Figure 2.5). In the coming years, however, the SA poster columns grew in strength, and in time they could cover an entire street with swastikas, slogans, and Hitler's grim visage in a single night. Yet even the early efforts represented an important shift toward the public display of powerful visual symbols, especially in neighborhoods that turned out to vote for the Nazis in the Reichstag elections of May 4, 1924 (Figure 2.6). In addition to its intensifying poster campaigns, the SA promoted itself as a symbol in its own right with its emphasis on uniforms, flags, and music squads (Figure 2.7). Even before the Party had become the National Socialists, the SA was branding itself as a premier force within the larger national socialist movement. As the Party prepared to re-form itself, the SA leaders, especially the aggressive and ma-nipulative Böckenhauer, began to play a decisive role in the power struggle over who would control the movement.

In January 1925, Hamburg's political police considered the National Socialists divided and leaderless. Their report said that "a mad confusion" ruled within the movement, which had splintered "to the point where the actual existence of the group can no longer be spoken of."[111] The police be-lieved that the chaos stemmed from the fact that Hitler, newly released from prison, hesitated to immediately proclaim a new, unified party. Nobody doubted that Hitler intended to do so, however, so potential leaders of a new party conducted an array of schemes. SA leaders played key roles in the competition. Heinrich Lohse, the SA leader in Schleswig-Holstein, who controlled the stormtroopers of Hamburg's suburbs, ordered his men to join the Nazi Party in late January, before it had even formally declared its resurrection, hoping to mark himself as the area's leading stormtrooper.[112]

On February 13, Klant held a meeting in Sagebiel's largest hall, where he declared that only Hitler could lead the völkisch movement for Germany's resurrection. The police report on the rally recorded it as the death of the placeholder group, the National Socialist Freedom Movement (NSFB), and the point of inevitability that the Nazi Party proper would return.[113] Klant made it official on March 5, announcing his own position as Gauleiter (dis-trict leader, the party's top level of regional political leadership).[114] Not all

FIGURE 2.7

Three of the earliest stormtroopers pose with the group's
first flag. Small variations in their uniforms show that they
had not yet developed the standardized iconography that
became such a powerful draw for recruits.

members greeted the news with joy, especially those who had worked the hardest for the NSFB. Conn, for one, considered the previous year and a half of work wasted, and he, like many stormtroopers, had no faith in Klant's older leadership style.[115] Conn and men like him, the sometime-stormtroopers of the front generation who had bounced between various völkisch paramilitaries, declined at first to join the new party. The police interpreted these tensions as evidence of the movement's decline, declaring in an April report that "the völkisch-national socialist movement here is currently without meaning."[116] At the end of 1925, the police estimated the combined membership of the Hamburg Nazi Party and the lame-duck NSFB at no more than five hundred.[117]

Dissatisfaction with the leaders of the Nazi Party's political wing continued for over a year, and it degenerated to a crisis level by the end of 1926. Police reports in the autumn of that year continued to document complaints against Klant from younger Nazis dissatisfied with his leadership style, his lethargic collection of membership dues, and his continued appeals to Munich to quash dissent.[118] In July, Klant had countered an attempt to remove him from office by having Munich eject his opponents from the Party.[119] Throughout the struggle over his leadership, Klant hoped that Hitler would come to Hamburg to demonstrate his support. This of course was an impossibility, given that, as a (technically stateless) foreigner found guilty of treason, Hitler had been banned from the city.[120] Given Hitler's inability to dominate the northern Party cells, and considering the political wing's miserable performance to date in Hamburg, local SA leaders emerged as the movement's kingmakers. Böckenhauer had declared even before the official re-founding of the Party that he would place his Blücher Club at its disposal.[121] On March 31, the latent SA shed its mask and declared its return to Hamburg with a torchlight parade that led to the giant Bismarck monument overlooking the Alster.[122] The new SA counted around 60 men in its ranks at the time of the re-founding, and they wore their old, makeshift uniforms from the underground period.[123] These stormtroopers were overwhelmingly young men who had stuck with Böckenhauer and considered him their personal leader.[124]

The concept of personal, comradely connections at the heart of the SA received a boost at the time when the national SA reorganized itself. In the disappointing aftermath of the 1923 putsch, Röhm had left Germany for a position advising the Bolivian army. His replacement, Franz Pfeffer von

Salomon, a stormtrooper leader in the Ruhr and an experienced fighter against the French occupation, solidified the inner organization of the SA and its subordinate relationship to the Party. He did so in a way that reinforced the independence and vitality of the SA's smallest organizational unit, then called the group and later the *Schar*. Pfeffer said that a squad should be composed of six to twelve men, ideally men who were already friends, neighbors, schoolmates, or sporting teammates. As the official catechism of the SA described:

> The squad builds the basis and foundation for the entire operation and expansion of the SA. The entire organization of *Truppen, Stürme,* etc. builds itself outwards from the squad. The squad should be made up of comrades who have the same sensibilities and a common connection, founded on youth friendship, school camaraderie, or similar work experience. Geographical proximity is also desired, so that closeness proliferates and immediate collective action is possible.[125]

Stormtrooper leaders saw emotional connections between their men as a paramount quality in combat. Camaraderie, loyalty, preparedness, and fighting ability developed in concert, especially among stormtroopers with long-standing emotional ties who could be counted on, "when attacked, to work together best for defense."[126] In fact, Nazi leaders encouraged the stormtroopers to concentrate their energy on solidifying and extending their personal bonds, rather than on spreading an ideological message. That was the Party's job. Pfeffer declared a strict separation of tasks between the Party and the SA. The Party controlled the content of political propaganda, while the SA carried out propaganda actions using its network of comrades.[127] This choice signaled that Hitler and Pfeffer did not intend to rebuild the SA as a paramilitary group seeking violent revolution, as it had formerly been in Bavaria and had wished to be in Hamburg. The SA was now a subunit of a party pursuing a faux-legal strategy of winning elections in order to destroy democracy. The Party would therefore allow the SA to develop semi-independently with its own organizational culture, in contrast to the Party's "civilian" members.[128] In theory, the SA would not seek to shape the Party itself. In Hamburg, however, the SA's symbolic power and its popularity among the young Party activists gave it a great deal of influence in the context of the local group's ongoing leadership crisis. In fact, during the complicated struggles that played out over the next several years, storm-troopers and their tight-knit factionalism proved key to both provoking and resolving controversies over who would lead the local Nazis.

Klant's worst failing as a leader lay not merely in his general lassitude but in his resistance to the SA's buildup. According to the police, Klant had "fallen into disfavor among many members of his party for not being radical enough, and especially for resisting every expansion of the storm-troopers. He has recently expelled a great number of members from the Party."[129] Klant declined alliances with other nationalist militias, an act that sowed doubt about whether he really supported the paramilitary style of politics preferred by the younger men.[130] Böckenhauer soon openly defied Klant by courting comrade networks that opposed the elder leader. In April 1926, Böckenhauer declared on his own authority that 50 former party members whom Klant had expelled would be welcomed back as Hamburg's first SS unit. According to police reports on the ensuing conflict, the new SS planned a coup against Klant to punish him for his lack of radicalism.[131] Klant survived the challenge, due largely to his backing by the national Party and its control over district-level appointments, and he expelled the would-be SS men from the Party.[132] Many of them talked their way back in, however, by getting comrades to vouch that "their morals and character were unquestioned."[133] Others found refuge in suburban Party cells that lay under the authority of the Prussian Party leadership.

Böckenhauer himself escaped unscathed from his defeat, and by autumn he felt strong enough to again flex his influence. He suddenly announced that the SA would no longer take orders from Klant or carry out its hall-pro-tection duties.[134] This indictment of Klant's leadership by the young activist core proved too much for Klant to overcome. On November 4, 1926, Klant resigned as leader of the Hamburg Nazi Party. Although he continued to hold his elected office in the Hamburg Citizens Council, he agreed to abstain from trying to influence the Party internally.[135] Lohse, the SA leader from Altona, was named provisional commander until a new Hamburg leader arose. While Böckenhauer's 60 SA men controlled a majority at a key membership meet-ing held to decide the leadership question, Böckenhauer himself declined the role. He claimed only to be interested in leading his stormtroopers.[136]

The Hamburg party, downgraded from a *Gau* (administrative district) to an *Ortsgruppe* (local group), chose Albert Krebs as its new leader. Now in his fighting prime at 28 years old, Krebs had been a member of nationalist youth movements, a dueling fraternity, and the Freikorps von Epp. Krebs' background indicated that the party sought a leader who would engage with rather than marginalize the SA. At first it seemed that Böckenhauer and Krebs had common goals and methods, and that both men benefited from the partnership. Krebs used the SA to its fullest, a fact the police noticed as early as January 1927, when a uniformed SA troop guarded a high-profile speech Krebs gave on the subject of "people without space."[137] Krebs believed, and many Party members agreed, that his new speaking style contributed to a doubling of the Party membership, from three hundred in 1927 to six hundred the following year.[138]

Part of the movement's success in 1927 came from poaching members of other rightist paramilitaries. These groups had previously worked together on specific protest issues. During religious holidays like Pentecost and secular events that honored service in the Great War, the rivals' common nationalism and militarism could overcome their factional differences. On Bismarck's birthday, for example, some thirty thousand marched together.[139] But the SA and the other paramilitaries were still natural competitors, as they all sought allegiance from the same young nationalist demographic. While Nazi political leaders at first allowed joint demonstrations, they soon discovered the power of monopoly. They declared that all stormtroopers could belong to only one militia, the SA, and they threatened to expel anyone who did not quit their membership in a competing militia. This canny strategy recognized that the SA and the Nazi Party were proving better at combining the immediate attractions of a paramilitary lifestyle with the long-term potential of a political party.

The focus on attracting preexisting groups of comrades began to pay off in 1927, when the *Verband* (Association) Hindenburg, led by Paul Ellerhusen with Conn as his deputy, split over disagreements concerning an officer who had married a Jewish woman. When the group fractured, Ellerhusen and Conn led their loyalists into the SA. Their choice highlighted the wisdom of Pfeffer's restructuring. The SA eagerly kept existing groups together, and in this case it simply created a new unit to be led by Ellerhusen, with places for however many men were willing to follow his defection.[140] Conn summarized the spirit of unquestioning comradely loyalty in his immediate reaction to the split itself. He said that he had not changed his allegiance because of the issue under debate, but rather out of loyalty to his comrades. As he later wrote, "I stood at once on our boys' side."[141] He also stated more generally that he "lost more and more feeling" for Party political groups as entities and retained loyalty only to his comrades in the militia.[142] Ellerhusen's men thus renounced their memberships in other militias so they could stay together under his banner.

This group represented the largest single defection, but many other new recruits had behaved the same way, moving in packs between one paramilitary group and another. Every time a group of comrades felt organizationally marginalized or ideologically offended—which happened constantly within the dozens of competing völkisch factions—Pfeffer's new administrative structure allowed them to transfer as a team to the SA. The SA at this time also reincorporated members who had previously broken off because of their dissatisfaction with "Father Klant." By the middle of 1927, the police estimated that the SA had siphoned off enough of these comrade groups to double its strength to 350 members; more than 200 had come from Ellerhusen and Conn's group alone.[143]

Besides the SA's soft appeal to emotional ties, it also employed a harder edge. Stormtroopers not only wooed competing groups, they openly fought against them. In fact, physical contests seemed part of the wooing process. The SA therefore disrupted meetings of rightist groups whose ideology and style were closest to their own, attacking other nationalists to ensure that only their party would represent national socialism. The SA also enforced iron discipline against its own inevitable defectors—a necessary caution, since the tactic it used to induct existing groups made it vulnerable to organized internal opposition. In two consecutive summers, 1926 and 1927, groups of SA men attempted coups against Böckenhauer's leadership. The first insurrection involved a group of war veterans who sought to take command based on their age and common experience at the front, but their claim failed to resonate outside the mutineers' own clique.[144] The second attempt involved a different unit, but it too failed because of the group's isolation within the larger SA; in fact, about 20 would-be putschists were driven out.[145] In the end, however, the SA gained more men than it lost through these maneuvers. Police estimated that it boasted around five hundred stormtroopers by the end of 1927.[146]

The stormtroopers' growing numbers and internal cohesion prompted further schemes by Böckenhauer, who now resented and resisted Krebs as much as he had his predecessor, Klant. None of the men who later described the conflict between Böckenhauer and Krebs could ever discern what had set the former against the latter. Böckenhauer seems simply to have been the type of leader who solidified his authority by undermining anyone who could rival him for his subordinates' affection and loyalty. Conn reported that Böckenhauer spied on Krebs, sought to secretly review his decisions, and spread libelous rumors alleging that Krebs was guilty of corruption and financial mismanagement.[147] Böckenhauer charged Krebs with running a "boss system" that dealt favors to his cronies while undercutting the SA and young activists.[148] When Böckenhauer eventually ordered the SA to stop protecting meetings, the conflict came to the national Party's attention. Hitler sent Gregor Strasser, an old Party ideologue who often represented the socially revolutionary and stormtrooper wings of the Nazi movement, to resolve the issue. Strasser declared Böckenhauer's accusations unfounded, but he could not bridge the personal grudges that truly drove the conflict.[149]

Soon Pfeffer himself arrived to broker a solution. He called a membership meeting for April 21, 1928, in the Wilhelm *Gymnasium* (secondary school), a symbolically meaningful school that the Nazis liked to use for important gatherings. Hamburg had just been raised again to Gau status, and Krebs' promotion to Gauleiter had to be confirmed by a membership vote. Under other circumstances, this confirmation would have been almost automatic. As the meeting opened, however, Böckenhauer appeared with his band of followers. Neither Pfeffer nor Ellerhusen's local SA intervened to stop him from again dominating a discussion of political leadership. Krebs, despite enjoying the national Party's backing, could not control the situation. Unable to diffuse the challenge to his leadership by Böckenhauer's tight-knit loyalists, Krebs resigned on May 1. Lohse again controlled the Hamburg Nazi Party from Altona until a permanent resolution emerged.[150] It would take over a year.

Conn described the crisis, a needless sowing of division by the volatile and insular Böckenhauer, as a "hard blow" that shook the Party's spirit mere weeks before an important election.[151] Yet this proved the final leadership struggle of the Hamburg Nazi Party, as well as Böckenhauer's final act of interference in such matters. His unreliable, aggressive, and self-aggrandizing style, combined with a recent conviction for assault that embarrassed the Party, finally convinced the political leadership to expel him on May 8. Although Böckenhauer eventually wormed his way back into the ranks of SA leaders, the party was spared his divisive influence for the near future.

After Böckenhauer's ejection, the older and more restrained Ellerhusen took charge of the Hamburg SA. This proved a salutary development for the SA's relationships, not only with the Party but also with the other nationalist paramilitaries. Böckenhauer had taken a combative approach toward leadership, recruiting, and retention—in fact, his assault charge resulted from an attack he had led against members of an SA splinter group.[152] Ellerhusen had come from a rival group, and he therefore tended to reject open violence against fellow nationalists. His reserve was a personal trait, but it was also a political choice that stemmed from the SA's continued identity as a young upstart group trying to win respect in the right-wing political ecosystem.

On June 3, 1928, the Stahlhelm held a major rally in Hamburg that was attended by 138,000 people.[153] Nationalists would see any violence against the solid, respected members of the Stahlhelm by the young toughs of the SA as patricide, which thus would have challenged the SA's image as good sons of German fathers. So Ellerhusen withdrew his SA from the city altogether. He sent 240 stormtroopers, almost half the total number, on an all-day cruise down the Elbe River, along with their wives and girlfriends.[154] Instead of engaging with their older counterparts in battle, the SA addressed them through a series of articles in the *Hamburger Volksblatt*, the Nazis' weekly newspaper. There Ellerhusen stressed the values the two groups shared, especially the superiority of the "front-soldier spirit."[155] Ellerhusen, however, accused the Stahlhelm of falling short in its pursuit of these values, and he claimed that its political leadership had degenerated into "parliamentarism" and become the slave of the "stateless forces of Jews, Jesuits, and Freemasons." Ellerhusen feared that the Stahlhelm declined to resist these forces with proper vigor. Those truly interested in defending the nation from its international enemies should therefore join the SA, currently strong in spirit but weak in numbers. "If we, like the Stahlhelm," Ellerhusen wrote, "had all the front soldiers in our ranks and could command the 140,000 Stahlhelmers who marched in Hamburg, we would have power over the state and the entire people behind us."

In the summer of 1928, the outlook for the Hamburg SA seemed precarious but optimistic. It had survived a difficult period where it numbered no more than a small collection of friends and family members, meeting in living rooms and disguising themselves as members of wedding parties. The SA had become a major force within the Party and an independent source of power that attracted new members, but it had also posed a problem that the political leadership had to face. While the Nazi Party still fell short of its goal to lead the völkisch paramilitaries, it had firmly established the principles and philosophy that would eventually allow it to do so.

The SA's strength, it was discovering, came from mobilizing and enhancing existing loyalties and emotional ties among the most militant young nationalist men, who could be secured through a combination of catering to their insularity and promising them free reign to lash out against their enemies. These men's loyalties would transfer to the militia that promised most convincingly to use them as a cohesive fighting unit in the service of nationalist and counterrevolutionary politics. Establishing this strategy, however, also created a series of paradoxes and difficulties that grew stronger over time. The SA had arisen as a movement based on male warrior camaraderie, and it therefore risked seeming cliquish, exclusive, and even morally suspect. Stormtroopers therefore had to find ways to transform their continual acts of violence into well-intentioned acts of local and national renewal. In the coming years, stormtroopers sought to portray their violence as productive rather than destructive, patriotic rather than criminal. They also had to show that they were not a small private circle of comrades, and were instead connected to deep and enduring structures of family, religious, and civic life. These associations, which along with the SA's increasingly successful staging of public violence as civic virtue, were then advertised as evidence of the stormtroopers' ultimate morality and thereby resolved the tension between family and camaraderie that so plagued SA politics.

NOTES

1   Joachim Paschen, *Freiden, Freiheit, Brod! Die Revolution 1918/19 im Hamburg* (Hamburg: DOBU Verlag, 2008), 39–40.

2   Archiv der Forschungsstelle für Zeitgeschichte in Hamburg (hereafter, Archiv FZH), 11C1 Alfred Conn, memoirs, 10.

3   Uwe Shulte-Vanderhoff, *Die Hungerunruhe in Hamburg im Juni 1919 – eine zweite Revolution?* Beiträge zur Geschichte Hamburgs, Band 65 (Hamburg: Hamburg University Press, 2010), 23.

4   Pierre Broué, *The German Revolution 1917–1923* (Leiden and Boston: Brill, 2005), 60.

5   Richard Bessel, *Germany After the First World War* (Oxford, England: Clarendon Press, 1993),18.

6   Broué, *The German Revolution,* 140–151; Robert Rosentreter, *Blaujacken im Novemberrevolution. Rote Matrosen, 1918–1919* (Berlin: Dietz Verlag, 1988).

7   Friedrich Meinecke, "Unfortunate Collapse—A Liberal View," *The Creation of the Weimar Republic: Stillborn Democracy?* in Richard Hunt, ed., *The Creation of the Weimar Republic: Stillborn Democracy?* (Lexington, MA: D. C. Heath and Company, 1969), 11.

8   Richard Hunt, ed., *The Creation of the Weimar Republic: Stillborn Democracy?* (Lexington, MA: D. C. Heath and Company, 1969); Samuel Halperin, *Germany Tried Democracy: A Political History of the Reich from 1918 to 1933* (New York: Thomas Y. Crowell, 1946).

9   Theodor Abel, *Why Hitler Came into Power* (Cambridge: Harvard University Press, 1986/1938), 27.

10 Albrecht von Thaer, *Generalstabdienst an der Front in der O.H.L. Aus Briefen und Tagebuchaufzeichnungen 1915–1919,* Siegfried A. Kaehler, ed. (Göttingen: Vandenhoek & Ruprecht, 1958).

11 Quoted in Francis Ludwig Carsten, *The Reichswehr and Politics, 1918–1933* (Berkeley: University of California Press, 1973), 5–6.

12 MacGregor Knox, *To the Threshold of Power: 1922/33,* Volume 1, *Origins and Dynamics of the Fascist and National Socialist Dictatorships* (Cambridge, England: Cambridge University Press, 2007), 199.

13 John W. Wheeler-Bennett, "Ludendorff: The Soldier and the Politician," *The Virginia Quarterly Review* 14, no. 2 (Spring 1938): 187–202.

14 Quoted in Lars-Broder Keil and Sven Felix Kellerhoff, *Deutsche Legennden. Vom "Dolchstoss" und anderen Mythen der Geschichte* (Berlin: Christoph Links Verlag, 2002), 33.

15 Gottfried Zarnow (Ewald Moritz), *Der 9. November 1918* (Hamburg: Hanseatische Verlaganstalt, 1933). Reprinted as "Stab in the Back—A Nationalist View," in Hunt, *The Creation of the Weimar Republic,* 16–24.

16 Abel, *Why Hitler Came into Power,* 24.

17 Abel, *Why Hitler Came into Power,* 26.

18 Franz Tügel, *Mein Weg, 1888–1946. Erinnerungen eines Hamburger Bischofs* (Hamburg: Wittig, 1972), 144.

19 Tügel, *Mein Weg,* 116.

20 Tügel, *Mein Weg,* 134.

21 Tügel, *Mein Weg,* 144.

22 Abel, *Why Hitler Came into Power,* 28.

23 Abel, *Why Hitler Came into Power,* 39–40.

24 Archiv FZH, 11C1 Alfred Conn, 15.

25 Volker Berghahn, Modern Germany: Society, Economy, and Politics in the Twentieth Century (Cambridge, England: Cambridge University Press, 1987), 66.

26 Hans Mommsen, The Rise and Fall of Weimar Democracy (Frankfurt am Main: Propylaen Verlag, 1989). English translation by Elborg Forster and Larry Eugene Jones (Chapel Hill: University of North Carolina, 1996), 89–128.

27 Quoted in Abel, Why Hitler Came into Power, 15.

28 Quoted in Abel, Why Hitler Came into Power, 15.

29 StAHH, 614-2/5 Nationalsozialistische Arbeiterpartei (NSDAP) und ihre Gliederung B228.

30 NARA A3341 SA Kartei: 039 Werner B.

31 NARA A3341 SA Kartei: 206 Günther H.

32 Magnus Hirschfeld, The Sexual History of the World War (New York: Cadillac Publishing Co., 1946 edition/1930), ix.

33 Hirschfeld, The Sexual History, 13.

34 Hirschfeld, The Sexual History, 20.

35 Hirschfeld, The Sexual History, ix.

36 Hirschfeld, The Sexual History, 64–66.

37 Hirschfeld, The Sexual History, 64–66.

38 Hirschfeld, The Sexual History, 110.

39 Hirschfeld, The Sexual History, 112.

40 Patricia Anne Simpson, The Erotics of War in German Romanticism (Lewisburg, PA: Bucknell University Press, 2006), 15–19, 76.

41 Thomas Kühne, Kameradschaft. Die Soldaten des nationalsozialistichen Krieges und das 20. Jahrhundert (Göttingen: Vandenhoek & Ruprecht, 2006).

42 Patricia McDonnell, "'Essentially Masculine': Marsden Hartley, Gay Identity, and the Wilhelmine German Military," Art Journal 56, no. 2 (1997): 62–68.

43 Andre Gisselbrecht, "Hans Blüher et l'Utopie du 'Männerstadt,'" Revue d'Allemagne 22, no. 3 (1990): 391–399; Harry Oosterhuis, "Medicine, Male Bonding, and Homosexuality in Nazi Germany," Journal of Contemporary History 32, no. 2 (1997): 196–198.

44 Hans Blüher, Die Rolle der Erotik in der männlichen Gesellschaft, vol. 1. (Jena: E. Diedrichs, 1921), 6–7.

45 Thomas Kuhne, "Comradeship: Gender Confusion and Gender Order in the German Military, 1918–1945," in Karen Hagemann and Stefanie Schuler-Springorum, eds. Home/Front: The Military, War, and Gender in Twentieth-century Germany (Oxford, England: Berg, 2002), 233–254; George Mosse, "Friendship and Nationhood: About the Promise and Failure of German Nationalism," Journal of Contemporary History 17, no. 2 (1982): 351–367.

46 Klaus Theweleit, Male Fantasies: Volume 1: Women, Floods, Bodies, History (Minneapolis: University of Minnesota Press, 1987), 61.

47 Karen Hagemann, "The Military, Violence, and Gender Relations in the Age of the World War," in Hagemann and Schüler-Springorum, Home/Front, 4–41.

48 Birthe Kundrus, "The First World War and the Construction of Gender Relations in the Weimar Republic," in Hagemann and Schüler-Springorum, Home/Front, 159–180.

49 Richard Evans, *Kneipengespräche im Kaiserreich. Die Stimmungsberichte der Hamburger Politischen Polizei, 1892–1914* (Hamburg: Rowolt, 1989), 21–30.

50 Roger Chickering, "Political Mobilization and Associational Life: Some Thoughts on the National Socialist German Workers Club (e.V.)," in Larry Eugene Jones and James Retallack, eds., *Elections, Mass Politics, and Social Change in Modern Germany* (Cambridge, England: Cambridge University Press, 1992), 307–328.

51 A vast historical literature exists on the utility of alcohol in forming social bonds among unrelated men in northern Europe, including: James S. Roberts, *Drink, Temperance, and the Working Class in 19th Century Germany* (Boston: George Allen & Unwin, 1984); Hasso Spode, *Der Macht der Trunkenheit: Kultur- und Sozialgeschichte des Alkohols in Deutschland* (Opladen: Leske & Budrich, 1983).

52 Evans, "Kneipengespräche," 28.

53 Herbert Freudenthal, *Vereine in Hamburg. Ein Beitrag zur Geschichte und Volkskunde der Geselligkeit* (Hamburg: Museum für Hamburgische Geschichte, 1968), 329.

54 Abel, *Why Hitler Came into Power*, 44–45.

55 Abel, *Why Hitler Came into Power*, 46.

56 Lewis Hertzman, *DNVP: Right-Wing Opposition in the Weimar Republic, 1918–1924* (Lincoln: University of Nebraska Press, 1963), 32–55.

57 NARA A3341 SA Kartei: 006 Otto A., 030 Herbert B., 071 Franz H., 096 August K., 123 Paul B., 141a Adolf L., 205 Kurt H.

58 NARA A3341 SA Kartei: 060 Freidrich F., 105 Friedrich O., 092 Karl K.

59 NARA A3341 SA Kartei: 048b Hans M.

60 Albert Krebs, *The Infancy of Nazism: The Memoirs of Ex-Gauleiter Albert Krebs* (New York: New Viewpoints, 1976), 4–5.

61 Archiv FZH, 11C1 Alfred Conn, 11.

62 Archiv FZH, 11C1 Alfred Conn, 12. No reference exists to this supposed group in M. Doeberl's *Das akademische Deutschland* (Berlin: C. A. Weller, 1930), a 2,400-page reference book claiming to list all student fraternities of the Weimar era.

63 Krebs, *The Infancy of Nazism*, 5.

64 Ian Kershaw, *Hitler: Hubris* (New York: W. W. Norton & Company, 1999), 144–147.

65 Peter Longerich, *Geschichte der SA* (Munich: Verlag C.H. Beck, 2003), 23.

66 Arthur Böckenhauer, *10 Jahre SA in Bildern mit verbindendem Text* (Hamburg, 1932), 32.

67 Alfred Bordihn, *10 Jahre Kreis Rotherbaum der NSDAP* (Hamburg: Paul Meyer, 1935), 5.

68 Adolf Hitler, *Mein Kampf* (Boston and New York: Houghton Mifflin Co., 1999/1925), 504. See also Chickering, "Political Mobilization and Associational Life," 309–313.

69 Böckenhauer, *10 Jahre SA in Bildern*, 4.

70 Andreas Werner, *SA und NSDAP. "Wehrverband," "Parteitruppe" oder "Revolutionsarmee"?* (doctoral dissertation, University of Erlangen, 1964), 50.

71 Wilhelm Recken and Julius W. Krafft, *Hamburg unterm Hackenkreuz. Eine Chronik der nationalen Erhebung in der Nordmark 1919–1933* (Hamburg: Paul Hartung Verlag, 1933), 55.

72 Recken and Krafft, *Hamburg unterm Hackenkreuz*, 55.

73 Recken and Krafft, *Hamburg unterm Hackenkreuz*, 55.

74 Recken and Krafft, *Hamburg unterm Hackenkreuz*, 60.

75   Werkstatt der Erinnerung (in the Forschungsstelle für Zeitgeschichte), 123T.

76   Archiv FZH/WdE, 247T Heinz Preiss.

77   Archiv FZH, 11C1 Alfred Conn, 32.

78   Hermann Okrass, *Hamburg bleibt Rot. Das Ende einer Parole* (Hamburg: Hanseatische Verlaganstalt, 1934), 60; Ulf Böttcher, *Die SA in Hamburg, 1922–1934. Politische Rolle und innere Struktur* (Examensarbeit at University of Hamburg, 1982), 7.

79   StAHH, 614-2/5 *Nationalsozialistische Arbeiterpartei (NSDAP) und ihre Gliederung,* B170.

80   StAHH, 614-2/5 *Nationalsozialistische Arbeiterpartei,* B228.

81   StAHH, 614-2/5 *Nationalsozialistische Arbeiterpartei,* B228.

82   StAHH, 614-2/5 *Nationalsozialistische Arbeiterpartei,* B228.

83   Archiv FZH, 11C1 Alfred Conn, 72.

84   Manfred von Killinger, *Männer und Mächte: Die SA in Wort und Bild* (Leipzig: R. Kittler, 1934), 11.

85   Heinrich Bennecke, "Die Memoiren Ernst Röhm. Ein Vergleich der Verschiedenen Ausgaben und Auflagen," *Politische Studien* 14, no. 148 (1963): 179–188.

86   Ernst Röhm, *Die Geschichte eines Hochverräters* (Munich: Franz Eher Verlag, 1928), 258. See also Eleanor Hancock's discussion of this passage in "Ernst Röhm and the Experience of World War I," *Journal of Military History* 60, no. 1 (1996): 57.

87   "SA-Geist," *Der SA-Mann,* March 1, 1932, 2.

88   "Das Wesen der SA," *Der SA-Mann,* January 19, 1932, 2.

89   Thomas Krause, *Hamburg wird braun. Der Aufstieg der NSDAP von 1921–1933* (Hamburg: Ergebnisse Verlag, 1987), 51.

90   Bordihn, *10 Jahre Kreis Rotherbaum,* 10.

91   Bordihn, *10 Jahre Kreis Rotherbaum,* 10.

92   Böckenhauer, *10 Jahre SA in Bildern,* 4; Freudenthal, *Vereine in Hamburg,* 421–423.

93   Recken and Krafft, *Hamburg unterm Hackenkreuz,* 58.

94   Archiv FZH, 11C1 Alfred Conn, 35.

95   Archiv FZH, 11C1 Alfred Conn, 33.

96   Bordihn, *10 Jahre Kreis Rotherbaum,* 6.

97   Archiv FZH, 11C1 Alfred Conn, 38.

98   Archiv FZH, 11C1 Alfred Conn, 32.

99   Krause, *Hamburg wird braun,* 76.

100 Krause, *Hamburg wird braun,* 50.

101 Krebs, *The Infancy of Nazism,* 42; Böckenhauer, *10 Jahre SA in Bildern,* 4.

102 Recken and Krafft, *Hamburg unterm Hackenkreuz,* 62.

103 Recken and Krafft, *Hamburg unterm Hackenkreuz,* 62.

104 Kershaw, *Hitler: Hubris,* 205–209.

105 Archiv FZH, 11C1 Alfred Conn, 33.

106 Recken and Krafft, *Hamburg unterm Hackenkreuz,* 64.

107 StAHH, 331-3 *Politische Polizei,* Band 1 1097, reports of April, May, and September 1924.

108 Archiv FZH, 11C1 Alfred Conn, 35.

109 Archiv FZH, 11C1 Alfred Conn, 35; Recken and Krafft, *Hamburg unterm Hackenkreuz,* 70.

110 Böckenhauer, *10 Jahre SA in Bildern,* 7; Recken and Krafft, *Hamburg unterm Hackenkreuz,* 70.

111 StAHH, 331-3 *Politische Polizei,* Band 1 1097, report of January 3, 1925.

112 Recken and Krafft, *Hamburg unterm Hackenkreuz*, 74.

113 StAHH, 331-3 *Politische Polizei*, Band 1 1097, report of February 28, 1925.

114 Werner, *SA und NSDAP*, 319.

115 Archiv FZH, 11C1 Alfred Conn, 43.

116 StAHH, 331-3 *Politische Polizei*, Band 1 1097, report of April 1, 1925.

117 StAHH, 331-3 *Politische Polizei*, Band 1 1097, report of November 19, 1925.

118 StAHH, 331-3 *Politische Polizei*, Band 1 1097, reports of September 4, October 12, October 19, and November 18, 1926.

119 StAHH, 331-3 *Politische Polizei*, Band 1 1097, report of September 4, 1926.

120 Hitler had renounced his Austrian citizenship in 1925, but he did not gain German citizenship until 1932, when he needed to do so in order to run for president. StAHH, 331-3 *Politische Polizei*, Band 1 1097, report of October 19, 1926.

121 Archiv FZH, 922 SA, document of February 2, 1925.

122 Recken and Krafft, *Hamburg unterm Hackenkreuz*, 74.

123 Böckenhauer, *10 Jahre SA in Bildern*, 12.

124 Krebs, *The Infancy of Nazism*, 42.

125 Draft document reprinted in SA education files of StAHH, 614-2/5 *Nationalsozialistische Arbeiterpartei (NSDAP) und ihre Gliederung*, B223. See also Peter Longerich, 58–59.

126 Pfeffer quoted in Longerich, *Geschichte der SA*, 58.

127 Werner, *SA und NSDAP*, 378.

128 Werner, *SA und NSDAP*, 217, 270.

129 StAHH, 331-3 *Politische Polizei*, Band 1 1097, report of December 17, 1926.

130 StAHH, 331-3 *Politische Polizei*, Band 1 1097, reports of August 18, 1925, September 15, 1925, October 19, 1926, and November 18, 1926.

131 StAHH, 331-3 *Politische Polizei*, Band 1 1097, report of April 16, 1926.

132 StAHH, 331-3 *Politische Polizei*, Band 1 1097, report of June 15, 1926.

133 StAHH, 331-3 *Politische Polizei*, Band 1 1097, report of September 4, 1926.

134 Ursula Büttner and Werner Jochmann, *Hamburg auf dem Weg ins Dritten Reich. Entwicklungsjahre 1931–1933*. Document 80 (Hamburg: Landeszentrale für politische Bildung, 1985), 243.

135 StAHH, 331-3 *Politische Polizei*, Band 1 1097, report of November 18, 1926.

136 StAHH, 331-3 *Politische Polizei*, Band 1 1097, reports of November 18 and December 20, 1926.

137 StAHH, 331-3 *Politische Polizei*, Band 1 1097, report of January 20, 1927.

138 Krebs, *The Infancy of Nazism*, 61.

139 StAHH, 331-3 *Politische Polizei*, Band 1 1097, report of April 16, 1926.

140 Böckenhauer, *10 Jahre SA in Bildern*, 13.

141 Archiv FZH, 11C1 Alfred Conn, 50.

142 Archiv FZH, 11C1 Alfred Conn, 52.

143 StAHH, 331-3 *Politische Polizei*, Band 1 1097, report of June 17, 1927.

144 StAHH, 331-3 *Politische Polizei*, Band 1 1097, reports of May 16 and June 15, 1926.

145 StAHH, 331-3 *Politische Polizei*, Band 1 1097, reports of June 14 and October 24, 1927.

146 StAHH, 331-3 *Politische Polizei*, Band 1 1097, report of December 21, 1927.

147 Archiv FZH, 11C1 Alfred Conn, 60.

148 StAHH, 331-3 *Politische Polizei*, Band 1 1097, report of June 30, 1928; Albert Krebs, 65.

149 Archiv FZH, 11C1 Alfred Conn, 60.

150 Krebs, *The Infancy of Nazism*, 67.

151 Archiv FZH, 11C1 Alfred Conn, 61.

152 Archiv FZH, 922 SA.

153 Berghahn, *Modern Germany*, 112.

154 Archiv FZH, 11C1 Alfred Conn, memoirs, 62–63. Total membership figures for this time come from StAHH, 331-3 *Politische Polizei*, Band 1 1097.

155 No issues of the *Hamburger Volksblatt* for this year survive, but a summary of the articles and quotations of several passages can be found in StAHH, 331-3 *Politische Polizei*, Band 1 1097, report of September 2, 1928.

STORMTROOPERS CONFRONT *THE CRIMINAL*

3

The SA advertised itself as a masculine society, a group whose combat in the trenches and battles in the streets had forged an emotional bond of camaraderie that offered solace in troubled times. Although its size in 1925 paled in comparison to what it would become, it had already collected a respectable number of adherents by assimilating entire networks of friends, militiamen, and neighbors. These men spent an extraordinary amount of time together. They attended and protected meetings, spent their free time in their chosen tavern, and socialized mainly with one another. The SA's homosocial spaces grew stronger over the years, eventually expanding into barracks and kitchens where stormtroopers never needed to live apart from their comrades.

But not all German men found attractive the idea of living in an all-male society, devoted to urban warfare and distant from emotional connections with women. In contrast to nationalist homosociality, socialist organizations mixed the sexes far more regularly and therefore worked according to an entirely different model. According to Heinz Preiss, a Communist youth group member who fought the Nazis in St. Georg, the SA's Männerbund repelled youth who preferred mixed company.[1] Such young men tended in general to have a more modern outlook. They therefore saw the stormtroopers' glorification of militant male camaraderie as an artifact of the 19th century, a way of life connected to the militant and aristocratic cliques whose imperialist machinations had caused the Great War. Homosociality therefore offended antifascists who feared or loathed homosexuality. However, it also turned off those who supported homosexual emancipation because it revealed the Nazis' goal of rolling back modernity and re-imposing imperial modes of political sexuality.

Nationalist homosociality took on new meaning in a time when homosexuals first began to identify themselves openly and to seek public tolerance, if not yet acceptance, for their new subculture. While this phenomenon also had its roots in the 19th century, it took on new life in the Weimar Republic, when it reached a level that many gays and lesbians today look back on as the first emergence of a mature homosexual subculture. In the Weimar era, German homosexual rights groups were the largest and strongest in the world, and the homosexual scene in Berlin became a prominent feature of German culture. Homosexual bars and taverns opened in most major German cities, including Hamburg, although none was as world famous as Berlin's Eldorado, where cross-dressing wait staff and performers catered to a worldly and urbane crowd.

In this new era, stormtroopers faced a problem that their 19th-century forebears did not: the chance that outsiders would interpret their open praise of fellow men as evidence of homosexuality. A reputation for being a band of homosexuals would seriously weaken the stormtroopers' attempts to portray themselves as the authoritative men they claimed to be. After all, the standard vision of masculinity claimed that homosexuals were weak, effeminate, and unreliable. Homosexual rights activists, Hirschfeld foremost among them, had done themselves no favors in strongly supporting a feminized view of homosexuality, thus solidifying the stereotype anew. For the stormtroopers, as with theorist Adolf Brand, homoeroticism and homosociality had nothing to do with femininity, representing instead the peak of masculinity.

Even though Röhm was no longer in charge, the SA still adhered to a mentality he had expressed: "Nothing is more false than the so-called morality of society."[2] This Nietzschean sentiment reinforced the SA's tendency to hold its members only to internal codes of behavior—and these always boiled down to whether or not a transgression helped or harmed the movement. The SA was rarely inclined to discipline its own members for moral or criminal misbehavior against outsiders, especially sexual acts that counted as misdeeds only to a stodgy society. Stormtrooper leaders boasted of creating a fighting community, meaning that they would welcome anyone who could effectively protect friends and battle enemies. As Röhm put it in his autobiography, "Prudery certainly does not seem revolutionary to me."[3] Homosexual stormtroopers—whether they identified as such or not—therefore felt that they could exist in the SA with the protection of its highest leaders, as long as they conformed to the other markers of masculinity that stormtroopers of all sexualities embraced. The SA therefore welcomed some transgressors of traditional gender orders to a movement that claimed it fought to uphold those orders. It was a paradox similar to the one seen in the SA's views of the bourgeois political style: simultaneously envious and dismissive.

Such a balancing act could work only so long as the actual presence of homosexuals within the SA remained secret, and the organization could thus retain the public denial that its homosociality hid homosexuality. Stormtroopers who did have same-sex desires therefore tended not to flaunt their homosexuality. They often remained guarded around their comrades, many of whom felt threatened by any personal association with homosexuality. Other stormtroopers, and many members of the political side of the Nazi movement, expressed their open enmity toward homosexual stormtroopers, a problem Röhm had encountered during his time in charge.[4] Above all, homosexual stormtroopers had to take care that their orientation never came under public scrutiny, since revelation of one stormtrooper's homosexuality could undermine the entire group's masculine self-image.

Hamburg's SA therefore tried at several points to prevent men known for having a same-sex attraction from joining its ranks. In 1926, members of the Schlageter Bund (society), a militia that sympathized with the national socialists, attempted to join SA ranks. They had named themselves after Albert Leo Schlageter, a nationalist hero of the Ruhr campaign against French occupation, and therefore seemed well attuned to the SA's preferred image of self-sacrificing national heroes. The Schlageter Bund also shared common origins with Böckenhauer's original group, in that both had been founded by former police officers. The Schlageter Bund founder, however, had the reputation of being an open homosexual. The SA therefore not only refused to accept his group, whose 36 members would have significantly enhanced the SA ranks at that time, but also managed to pressure it into disbanding altogether.[5] The SA thus pushed away a potential supporter of some influence, rejecting the type of comradely group it claimed to prize because it deemed associating with a known homosexual too dangerous to its reputation.

This action, however, was an exception to the SA's general desire, both in Hamburg and nationally, to simply ignore the paradox with which it lived. The number of stormtroopers with a same-sex attraction continued to grow, and it was only a matter of time before one slipped up and came to public attention. This happened in Hamburg in 1928, in the context of a murder case whose combination of politics, violence, sex, and scandal brought unwelcome attention to this side of the SA's politics.

The Outing of SA Man Gerhold

In September 1928, during the run-up to the latest round of elections, four young men of the Reichsbanner militia were heading out for a night of drinking along a popular bar street near the Schlump train station, when they spotted another group of youths hanging election posters. Thinking they were their social-democratic comrades, they approached before realizing that the poster party was in fact a troop of SA men. An argument began over the posters, with the Reichsbanner men citing election laws that prohibited hanging posters on private property without the owner's permission. When one of the Reichsbanner men grabbed the posters from a stormtrooper's hands, another stormtrooper punched him in the back of the head. A brawl began. Most of the SA men took flight, claiming later that they had been unarmed while facing an enemy wielding nightsticks and other clubs. Their flight left a stormtrooper named Gerhold in the clutches of four opponents. Surrounded, he drew a pistol and shot a Reichsbanner man named Wulf. The shots drew reinforcements on both sides while the remaining original combatants fled the scene. Newly arriving Reichsbanner men placed Wulf in the back of a taxi and took him to a nearby hospital, where he died. Gerhold was arrested and put on trial for murder.

This incident confirmed the stormtroopers' preferred understanding of themselves and their battles. They often claimed to have been attacked while attempting innocent electioneering, which forced them to use violence in defense of their political rights and personal safety. When the trial began later that month, Dr. Korn, who frequently served as a lawyer to indicted stormtroopers, charged the Reichsbanner men with initiating the fight by inappropriately assuming police powers to enforce election laws. The judge found sympathy in this argument and bemoaned both sides' new style of politics.[6] Gerhold told the court that Communists had attacked him in a similar situation just weeks earlier, which was why he had acquired a firearm for self-defense. The prosecutor countered that Gerhold had "crossed far beyond the line of self-defense," but the judge found Gerhold's claim sympathetic.[7] He agreed with Korn's argument that the Reichsbanner had begun the fight by claiming the powers of the police, and agreed as well that the republican militia had chased down its fleeing opponents, surrounded Gerhold, and made him fear for his safety. Gerhold, the judge continued,

> had already had terrible experiences with the Communists and believed himself to be in danger. His exercise of self-defense should not be denied, even if he overstepped its bounds. And if he did overstep, he did it in the context of his past terrible experiences. This must stand to his favor.[8]

The judge therefore acquitted Gerhold of murder, although he did sentence him to a year in jail for not having a firearms license.

The sentence was on the high end for the weapons charge, but still far more lenient than the murder conviction the Reichsbanner had hoped would result. The social-democratic *Hamburger Echo* called the verdict a "miscarriage of justice that all right-thinking people must deeply bemoan," and predicted that "this monstrous judgment, which has given the criminal nationalists a free pass to continue their murderous deeds, will make it difficult to keep the peace."[9] The *Echo* also complained about the paternal attitude the judge displayed toward the defendant. The paper described the judge's tone as unusually soft, with requests to "Please take your seat" and "Would you please come up here for a bit?" rather than his usual "Accused, sit down!" and "Accused, approach the bench!"[10] The judge also gave the defendant a bit of fatherly advice at the trial's close. "One would think," he said, "that you, young man, would have had enough. A child who burns himself should fear fire. This isn't a criticism though—you haven't done anything more than all the other parties do." In closing, the judge admonished Gerhold to work on his own personal development rather than busy himself with party politics.

Given the judge's paternal attitude, it seems as if the SA could have come through this incident unscathed. The verdict validated SA propaganda that the stormtroopers only defended themselves against violent Marxist thugs. The warmth and concern with which the judge treated the killer symbolically reinforced the SA's self-image as the decent sons of good German fathers. The trial, however, also revealed another aspect of Gerhold's past, one that caused far more embarrassment to the SA than a murder conviction would have carried.

During the judge's questioning of the defendant, he asked, "A gun isn't a children's toy. Haven't you made mischief with one before?"[11] Gerhold had: he had previously been investigated but not charged with extortion and attempted murder for shooting in the head (but not killing) a Jewish merchant. The two men had been having sex. Gerhold then repeatedly pressured the man, known only as M. in accounts of the trial, for money. He played on M.'s affections and made him feel guilty until M., short of money himself, finally offered to make a loan. Gerhold, frustrated at his failure and likely paranoid that the affair could come out, took a gun to their next meeting. Standing behind M. in the close quarters of a darkroom while M. developed photographs, Gerhold shot his lover in the head. He claimed later that the gun had gone off accidentally. M. naively believed the claim and declined to press charges. During Gerhold's murder trial in 1928, however, M. took the stand to recount the incident and to say that he no longer believed the shooting was accidental.

The prosecutor then elaborated on the alleged connections between

Gerhold's sexual history and his criminal political behavior. He told the court, "The personality of the defendant has been seen here to be dangerous and risky, and it would be praiseworthy if he was eliminated from the public. His love relationship also makes clear the accused's lack of scruples."[12] The judge ignored this part of prosecution's argument, but the media did not. The presence of a former lover in court made the SA man's same-sex past a highlight of the case. The intimate setting of a darkroom recalled the dim and mysterious images associated with homosexual men, whom the public believed to be sneaky, furtive, manipulative, and conspiratorial. The very word "darkroom" had associations of male-male sex, for that was the term used for the poorly lit sections of bars in which men could meet for anonymous encounters.[13] The twice-murderous intentions of the homosexual SA man thus signaled a depth of melodrama and depravity to which such a character was supposedly prone. Gerhold's story in the end carried an array of negative homosexual associations, the very ones the SA sought to avoid at all costs.

The resulting publicity of a stormtrooper's homosexuality created difficulties for the SA at the same time it was trying its best to woo members of the other hypermasculine paramilitaries. To overcome its public embarrassment, the SA conducted a high-profile action designed to deflect accusations of homosexuality by demonstrating its homophobic bona fides. Public protestations of disgust at homosexuality could also offer a cover story to those stormtroopers who battled their own same-sex attractions. Modern psychological studies have identified this dynamic as a process of reaction formation, in which people with intense resistance to their own same-sex desire proclaim vehement opposition to homosexuality, hoping thereby to convince both others and themselves of their heterosexuality. The concept has long-standing support in psychological theory, as well as in historical experiences throughout the modern era.[14]

Individual stormtroopers and the SA as an organization both acted in this sense. Beginning in the immediate aftermath of Gerhold's embarrassing outing, stormtroopers found that the solution to their psychological dilemma lay not in trying to avoid the issue of homosexuality but in publicly engaging with it in the most negative way imaginable. Homophobic activism would immunize them from accusations of homosexuality, bolster their self-image as hypermasculine warriors, and in the end preserve their standing among traditional conservatives, prudish bourgeois elites, and militant militiamen—with all of whom the SA desperately wanted to associate itself, despite its equally desperate feelings of resentment against them.

Protesting *The Criminal*

In December 1928, only a few months after the Gerhold trial, the SA put its new strategy into action by protesting a play that had just premiered in Hamburg. Ferdinand Brückner's *Der Verbrecher* (*The Criminal*) portrayed the troubles of young homosexual men in a big-city boarding house. To some extent, it adhered to tropes of homosexuality common to the German stage at the time, when young men who were same-sex oriented appeared only as doomed outsiders leading lives destined to end in tragedy.[15] Yet *Der Verbrecher* modified the formula, in that its main character's doom did not come from the mere fact of his homosexuality, which in traditional plays earned a homosexual death as the inevitable wage of his sins. Here the main character's downfall began in the first act, when a blackmailer discovered his homosexuality and threatened to inform the police if he was not paid. In the second act, when the case went to court, the youth faced the dilemma of either admitting the truth and facing criminal penalties, or of perjuring himself— thus becoming the eponymous criminal in either outcome. The character thus became a double victim: of the blackmailer and of the law.

Given this plot, *Der Verbrecher* departed from traditional plays that showcased homosexuality in order to reinforce the stigma against it. Plays featuring homosexuality had actually become increasingly common in German theater throughout the 1920s—a high point not reached again until the 1970s.[16] Brückner himself had even premiered another play dealing with homosexuality just two years earlier: *Krankheit der Jugend* (*Sickness of Youth*), in which two lesbians killed themselves rather than succumb to social pressure to deny their love. This play did not provoke the kind of rage within the SA that *Der Verbrecher* later did, perhaps because depictions of lesbianism are less threatening to men than portrayals of male homosexuality. Moreover, the characters' fates did adhere to the image of homosexuals as victims of their orientation: the two lesbians' suicides reinforced negative stereotypes of homosexuals as weak, immoral, and self-destructive, even if the play ultimately sympathized with them as victims of society. *Der Verbrecher*, however, took sympathy to a new level, openly proclaiming that Paragraph 175 placed an unfair burden on private life, encouraged crimes such as blackmail, and made otherwise law-abiding citizens into criminals. The true criminal, the play argued, was not the homosexual but the law itself. This revolutionary statement earned Brückner praise from more progressive quarters. The *Hamburger Echo* called the play "a valuable and meaningful document of the times."[17]

The Nazis felt differently. Many stormtroopers seemed especially threatened by the play's exposure of homosocial male environments as locations that facilitated homosexual contact. The Sports Club depicted in the play, ostensibly a place where men met to discuss common masculine interests, also provided a site at which homosexual men met others, learned the scene and its culture, and pursued sexual encounters. The play hinted at the dangers of male friendships, as one of the main character's closest friends eventually turned on him and became an untrustworthy blackmailer. To the SA, this seemed like an accusation—a scenario disturbingly close to the one that Gerhold's trial had just revealed.

Both homo- and heterosexual stormtroopers therefore had reason to resent and fear this play. Alfred Conn, who had emerged as one of the local SA's most ardent homophobes, wrote in his memoirs that the play represented everything the Nazi Party opposed "as part of our fight against shame and filth." He and his men hoped that protesting it would show that "the Party was prepared to fight with all the means at its disposal against all tendencies that threatened to bury morality and family."[18] The SA had not mobilized against previous plays, but the combination in this case of substance and circumstance now led it to organize massive and violent protests, fighting Brückner's play as a way to overcome its own public embarrassment at being associated with homosexuality.

Conn took the lead in organizing the protests. His SA units began by assembling groups of students and members of *völkisch* youth groups to sneak into the theater and disrupt the performances. They yelled "fire!" blew whistles, or set off sirens during the play. The police, Conn recalled, "did everything to stop our disruptions, and things soon developed into a question of prestige between the Party and the police."[19] Conn and Wilhelm Hüttmann, the Nazi member of the Citizens Council, soon planned a more elaborate disruption of the play's performance on November 31. Conn took obvious pride in this attack against the unsuspecting theatergoers, who, according to his account, consisted entirely of effeminate Jews and homosexual esthetes—an unthreatening audience that in retrospect seems a dishonorable target for the SA's self-proclaimed warrior band. The lack of equality between forces does not seem to have bothered him, and that night remained so clear and proud in his memory that he could, decades later, recount its planning and execution in great detail.

As the audience took its seats, the youngest SA men smuggled in simple noisemakers and stationed themselves in the upper balcony. Conn and two comrades sat in the front row of the first balcony, bringing with them smoke bombs as well as homemade capsules of itching and sneezing powder. Conn's deputy Trzebiatowsky took charge of the arsenal and sat between his comrades to shield the stash from discovery. They would arrive separately and begin the disruption once their young comrades above created a diversion with their noisemakers. Conn himself went undercover for this mission, dressing in a smoking jacket and carrying a copy of the *Berliner Tageblatt*, a newspaper he thought would disguise him as a Jewish intellectual. The trick seemed to work when "a Jew"—typically for a Nazi, Conn does not say how he knew him to be one—sat down to Conn's right and, based on seeing the "Jewish reading material," felt safe enough to speak with him.[20] They speculated on the possibility that there would be a disruption, which Conn pretended to dismiss as unlikely, given the large police presence.

The first act passed with no signal from the SA students in the upper balcony. Conn assured his Jewish neighbor that this meant the play was in the clear, but the latter shook his head and meekly replied, "You never know." The second act began. As the main character endured his trial onstage, debating whether to confess to perjury or to reveal his homosexuality and attract a charge under Paragraph 175, Conn saw Trzebiatowsky nervously juggling the capsules in his hand. He seemed unable to make up his mind to let loose, and Conn quietly prompted him with increasing urgency as the homemade capsules began to disintegrate. Finally, Trzebiatowsky threw the stink bombs from the balcony into the main seating areas below. The result was "an immediate and violent tumult."[21] The lights went up and a police company stormed the theater. Conn pretended ignorance while his Jewish neighbor, he claimed, began to exclaim wild and inaccurate theories as to where the disturbance had come from. In Conn's depiction, it was as if this Jewish homosexual was so unacquainted with military matters that he could not recognize the basics of an operation that had been carried out under his nose. In the meantime, the SA youths up top had begun their disturbance, drawing the attention of the police, who apprehended them and escorted them from the theater. The guests below "sprayed many bottles of cologne to cover the bestial stench," and the play eventually resumed.[22]

Meanwhile, Hüttmann had assembled a mob outside the theater, which he besieged with an army of paramilitary men from a variety of cooperating factions. They harassed the exiting theatergoers and antagonized the police, who eventually arrested 19 people, including Hüttmann himself.[23] At a second protest on December 9, Hüttmann's mob was so large and impassioned that it trapped the theatergoers inside, which obliged the police to bring in reinforcements to clear a path to the train station.[24]

The *Hamburger Echo* claimed that the Nazi protests "expose[d] the spiritual nature of these people more clearly than any pamphlet."[25] Though it meant the statement as an accusation, the Nazis themselves agreed—as did others on the right, where the SA's homophobic protest won it newfound sympathy and allegiance. One Council member from the nationalist German National People's Party applauded his colleague Hüttmann's assertion that the National Socialists fought "against the Jews' dirty fantasies."[26] He added, "The author of this play insults the German court system. That is a scandal. Our German people is a race in chains so long as such a play is allowed to continue. If the German youth disrupts such proceedings with stink bombs, then I can only agree."[27] When new sessions of the lower house opened in January, the Nazi representative Brinkmann asked if the body had any plans to punish the theater.[28] Of course it did not. This negative answer confirmed the stormtroopers' disgust with parliamentary democracy's unwillingness to defend conservative definitions of the German family. It also disappointed them because they hoped to keep the issue alive through the coming weeks, as it had been so successful in supporting the Party's political arguments.

Police observers of the protests saw the event's importance immediately: "The different rightist groups whose members made up the protests were completely united, even though they usually fought each other at every opportunity."[29] Before the *Verbrecher* protests, SA propaganda had claimed that it shared values with the other nationalist militias and that it would be the most effective agent of counterrevolution. The people targeted by the militiamen's propaganda, however, often doubted the claims, especially when events like the Gerhold trial portrayed SA men as members of subordinate and lesser male subgroups rather than the dominant types they claimed to be. The *Verbrecher* protests solved this problem. By targeting a homosexual subculture that was newly visible but still widely hated—even among the normally staid middle class and otherwise liberal socialists—they created a chance for cooperation between political rivals, and they furthered their argument for the legitimacy of violence as a political tactic.[30] The protests therefore increased the SA's standing on the right as a defender of conservative values while simultaneously countering accusations—and evidence—of homosexuality in its own ranks. The theme of homosexuality that rivals could have used against the SA now counted in its favor.

The Political Function of Homophobia

Mere weeks after the protests against Der Verbrecher, Ernst Röhm arrived in Hamburg in the company of an attractive 19-year-old art student, a protégé who called him "Uncle Röhm." The two apparently platonic companions checked into the posh Hotel Atlantik on the shores of the Alster, where they spent an afternoon enjoying fine food and drink while waiting to board a ship to South America. Röhm had been offered a position as a military advisor in Bolivia, where a large number of Germans served as technical and organizational advisors to the relatively new nation. Although Hitler had just recently pressed him again to accept the position as SA leader, Röhm's financial difficulties and political frustrations had pushed him to accept a new kind of adventure, in a land where he could free himself from the obstacles he believed existed in a struggling Germany.[31] While in Bolivia, he continued to pay close attention to German politics, and indeed he would not remain in Bolivia for long. But while he was gone, any homosexual stormtroopers who had joined the movement must have marked his absence with wariness. Although Röhm's departure had nothing to do with the protests against Der Verbrecher, and although he had not been in charge of the SA for years, the two events combined to create an impression that the era of toleration for sexual dissidence might end. With Röhm gone, and with National Socialism shoring up its rightist credentials through homophobic violence, any remaining homosexual stormtroopers existed within a threatened space.

A high-ranking Hamburg SA officer named Bisschopinck was one such figure. Bisschopinck was a war veteran, an "old fighter" in the SA ranks, and, in the testimony of his fellow old fighter Franz Koeberle, an "unsurpassed treasurer" who was among the Hamburg SA's leading lights.[32] His unit, Sturm 6, had come intact to the SA from its previous associations in the postwar years, and thus represented the type of comradely circle the

SA honored above all others. Many of these men, however, were either homosexuals or tolerant of homosexuality, being ultimately loyal to their leader, Bisschopinck, who had joined the SA in 1927. He had at some point lost his leadership position for unspecified reasons, but Ellerhusen reinstated him soon after he took command of the Hamburg SA, an act of loyalty that stormtroopers normally favored. Homosexuality, however, complicated the picture.

Alfred Conn had always clashed with Bisschopinck for explicitly personal reasons: Conn described his rival as having a "known deviant tendency."[33] Ellerhusen, like Hitler in Röhm's case, already knew about Bisschopinck's orientation when he appointed him the leader of Sturm 6, a decision he made despite his old comrade Conn's reservations. During a train trip to Hannover, Ellerhusen and Conn argued about the situation. Conn insisted that he "would not work with such people" whom he suspected of being "counter to 175."[34] In January 1930, when Conn learned that Ellerhusen had promoted Bisschopinck, Conn called the act "a completely unbelievable decision."[35] He had to express this shock in a letter, since at this point Ellerhusen was avoiding contact with him, despite their long and comradely association.

Ellerhusen's choice enraged Conn, who now conspired against Bisschopinck with vigor. Conn's reasons did not originate in any professional or political shortcomings his enemy had displayed. Instead, his ire focused on the relationships among the three men involved. Above all, he bristled at the growing closeness of his old comrade Ellerhusen to the emotional interloper Bisschopinck. Conn wrote to Ellerhusen that "with such actions, you snub your best friends and allow yourself to be led astray."[36] Here, Conn employed coded language. His writings betrayed his jealousy that Bisschopinck had come between him and Ellerhusen, who by January 1930 had begun ignoring his old friend in favor of his new relationship. Conn's letters to Ellerhusen took on increasingly maudlin tones. "Since you've gone out of your way to avoid speaking to me," Conn wrote in January, "I will not be attending the [SA leadership] meeting tomorrow."[37] After not hearing from Ellerhusen for another month, he asked, "What is the real reason you're so intentionally avoiding me?"

Bisschopinck was the reason. Conn claimed that, after Ellerhusen became the Hamburg SA leader, he "gave himself over to the company of bloodsucking cronies"—that is, Bisschopinck and his allegedly homosexual circle.[38] The group supposedly overindulged in alcohol and lived a generally debauched lifestyle, which "began to cost [Ellerhusen] more and more of his old energy; he lost his drive and became anchorless."[39] As this description shows, although Conn's campaign against Bisschopinck was rooted in his own insecurities about his relationship with Ellerhusen, his attacks expressed themselves through old tropes about homosexuals. These men, Conn insinuated, were dissolute, libertine, seductive, and cliquish, and enervated any who encountered them. He warned that they would ultimately fall into self-destructive habits and abandon their former sources of strength and stability. Before Bisschopinck's entrance on the scene, Ellerhusen and Conn had enjoyed "untarnished camaraderie."[40] Now they fought passive-aggressive emotional battles over competing friendships. Conn took allegations against Bisschopinck to Hamburg's leading Party members, thereby spreading word of things the SA generally sought to keep secret.[41] He threatened his own resignation in a letter, whose histrionics pleaded for a response: "From your conduct," he wrote to Ellerhusen, "I have to understand that you value your cooperation with B. more clearly than [your relationship] with me . . . and I regret that for your part you have decided to ignore me until the end."[42]

Conn won his war against Bisschopinck. The complete records of and reasons for Bisschopinck's removal no longer exist, but at some point in April 1930, Ellerhusen transferred him and other members of the suspect group to the small Silesian town of Golar, where they could continue to serve the movement in a lower-profile setting.[43] "We are finally rid of Bisschopinck," crowed Conn. "Everyone is breathing a sigh of relief."[44]

But not everyone breathed easily after this affair. Although the SA leadership had solved the immediate problem of the disruptive relationship triangle, the emotional turbulence on display troubled stormtroopers who were aware of the situation. Some felt that good men were being driven out of a group that still sorely needed their skills. Koeberle, the old fighter who had written to defend Bisschopinck, feared that the SA was drifting into "puritanism" more suited to the staid parties the Nazi Party was trying to supplant. On the other hand, Koeberle also admitted that the SA had to "give walking papers" to those flaunting an act "forbidden" to soldiers.[45] This side of his conflicted view aligned more closely with that of the homophobes and anti-homosexual crusaders, who felt that to retain homosexuals in the organization, even privately, would be disruptive and scare off potential recruits. In any case, neither side with strong feelings on the matter fully won its argument. For now, the paradox persisted.

Certainly, the presence of known homosexuals in the movement complicated stormtroopers' efforts to display the type of masculinity that would generate social and political power. Homosexuality was thus not a private fact but a public one. Seen in this light, the personal motivations of the anti-homosexuals in the SA do not matter. Although it might be tempting to identify Conn as a latent homosexual or a man trying to deny to himself that he was attracted to his comrades, we can never know his true thoughts or feelings. We can also rarely determine whether the Nazis' ardent anti-homosexuals pursued their vendettas based on moral, political, or personal feelings. But we do not need to do so. Homosexual stormtroopers, homophobic stormtroopers, or—the most problematic category—stormtroopers whom modern psychiatrists would possibly label as latent or self-loathing homosexuals all had to grapple with homosexuality's political meaning in the same way.

What were the terrible offenses of the homosexual stormtroopers? The fact of homosexuality in and of itself, to be sure, inevitably angered some. But the SA had proved that it cared little about offending others, and in fact it continually sought to offend middle-class sensibilities when it saw a political advantage in doing so. The group could thus treat homosexuality as a private matter, in specific cases. What it could not countenance, however, was associating itself with the array of negative stereotypes connected to homosexuality, including excessive affection, self-interest, and conspiracy.

Despite homosexuals' increasing visibility in the recent decades, many stormtroopers seem in fact to have been quite ignorant of its reality—a fact attested to by Koeberle's description that Bisschopinck and comrades engaged in "lesbian love."[46] A man more attuned to actual male homosexual experiences would hardly describe them in those words. What all stormtroopers certainly knew, however, was the vision of authoritative and powerful masculinity to which they aspired. This was a time when proper men possessed characteristics of rationality, restraint, and discipline—all of which made them the only legitimate holders of political power, which they would wield for the good of the community rather than for their own self-interest. In contrast, this view held, homosexuals were emotional, decadent, and inclined toward conspiracies to advantage their circle at the expense of their public duty.

Even many antifascists often saw politics in this way. One of the best examples comes from British journalist William Shirer, whose famous book, *The Rise and Fall of the Third Reich*, for a time appeared ubiquitously in train stations and airports across the English-speaking world. His sensationalist book described SA leaders as "notorious homosexual perverts" who "quarreled and feuded as only men of unnatural sexual inclinations, with their particular jealousies, can."[47] This description reflected the common and unexamined prejudices of many who lived through the Nazi era. The prevalence of homophobic myths therefore created in the SA an incentive for homophobic discourse and action no matter what individual stormtroopers may have thought about their comrades' sexuality, or their own.

Homophobic incentives were the greatest for organizations that, like the SA, based their legitimacy around standard conceptions of masculinity and close bonds between men. The great historian of gender, Eve Sedgwick, who established the term homosocial in her groundbreaking study of "homosocial desire" among 19th-century men, showed that public homophobia was not just persecutory, it was also productive in the ways it manipulated relationships among ostensibly heterosexual men.[48] Seen this way, Nazi actions against their homosexual stormtroopers, and especially public actions against homosexuals in general, served a creative purpose: they helped the remaining stormtroopers reinforce their self-definition as men who did not share the traits they displaced onto their homosexual comrades. As the homoerotic love triangle between Bisschopinck, Conn, and Ellerhusen showed, homosexuals hardly had a monopoly on the types of intrigues with which Shirer so casually slandered them. Heterosexual men could prove just as emotional as women and homosexuals, and they could allow these feelings—forbidden in and of themselves, regardless of their object—to complicate and contaminate political dealings.

The need to cover up their own flawed nature was therefore a critical element of the Nazis' homophobia throughout the movement's life cycle. At this point, the SA's need to balance homosocial appeal with professed allegiance to traditional gender roles was paramount, and the SA used the Verbrecher protests to solidify both internal and external support. Although it would be some time before the SA and Nazi Party again targeted homosexuals for public violence, the principle of their homophobia in fact retained its power by revealing their broader techniques of integrative violence. Soon after Bisschopinck's expulsion, in fact, the Hamburg SA became embroiled in its most public and spectacular confrontation yet—an event that helped unite the SA internally while permanently establishing the Nazi Party as the Weimar era's premier vehicle of nationalist politics.

NOTES

1   Archiv der Forschungsstelle für Zeitgeschichte/WdE (hereafter, Archiv FZH), 247T Heinz Preiss.

2   Quoted in Eleanor Hancock, "Only the Real, the True, the Masculine Held Its Value: Ernst Röhm, Masculinity, and Male Homosexuality," in *Journal of the History of Sexuality* 8, no. 4 (1998): 623.

3   Quoted in Hancock, "Only the Real," 623.

4   Eleanor Hancock, *Ernst Röhm: Hitler's SA Chief of Staff* (New York: Palgrave Macmillan, 2008), 88.

5   StAHH, 331-3 *Politische Polizei*, Band 1 1097, report of February 18, 1926.

6   *Hamburger Echo*, September 27, 1928.

7   *Hamburger Echo*, September 27, 1928.

8   *Hamburger Echo*, September 27, 1928.

9   *Hamburger Echo*, September 27, 1928.

10 *Hamburger Echo*, September 27, 1928.

11 *Hamburger Echo*, September 27, 1928.

12 *Hamburger Echo*, September 27, 1928.

13 It is difficult to determine when the word became the common currency it now carries, but some sources suggest a quite early start. On the scene in general, see Clayton Whisnant, "Hamburg's Gay Scene in the Era of Family Politics" (doctoral dissertation, University of Texas–Austin, 2001), 12–16.

14 See David F. Greenberg's description of Freud's formulation in *The Construction of Homosexuality* (Chicago: University of Chicago Press, 1988), 13–14, as well as the study by Henry Adams, Lester Wright, and Bethany Lohr, "Is Homophobia Associated with Homosexual Arousal?" *Journal of Abnormal Psychology* 105, no. 3 (1996): 440–445.

15 Laurence Senelick, "The Homosexual as Villain and Victim in Fin-de-Siècle Drama," *Journal of the History of Homosexuality* 4, no. 2, Special Issue, Part 1: Lesbian and Gay Histories (1993): 201–229.

16 Richard Allen Korb, *Victimization and Self-Persecution: Homosexuality on the German Stage: 1920s and 1970s* (doctoral dissertation, University of Pittsburgh, 1998).

17 *Hamburger Echo*, December 1, 1928.

18 Archiv FZH, 11C1 Alfred Conn, memoirs, 64.

19 Archiv FZH, 11C1 Alfred Conn, 64.

20 Archiv FZH, 11C1 Alfred Conn, 65.

21 Archiv FZH, 11C1 Alfred Conn, 65.

22 Archiv FZH, 11C1 Alfred Conn, 65.

23 *Hamburger Echo*, December 1, 1928.

24 *Hamburger Echo*, December 10, 1928.

25 *Hamburger Echo*, December 1, 1928.

26 *Hamburger Echo*, December 8, 1928.

27 *Hamburger Echo*, December 8, 1928.

28 "Aus der Bürgerschaft," *Hamburger Echo*, January 17, 1929.

29 StAHH, 331-3 *Politische Polizei*, Band 1 1097, report of December 12, 1928.

30 George Mosse, *Nationalism and Sexuality: Respectability and Abnormal Sexuality in Modern Europe* (New York: H. Fertig, 1985); Isabel Hull, "The Bourgeoisie and Its Discontents: Reflections on 'Nationalism and Respectability,'" *Journal of Contemporary History* 17, no. 2 (1982): 247–268.

31 Hancock, *Ernst Röhm*, 96–100.

32 Archiv FZH, 991 OSAF , Franz Koeberle letter of March 2, 1931.

33 Archiv FZH, 11C1 Alfred Conn, 69.

34 Archiv FZH, 922 SA, Conn to Ellerhusen letter of January 28, 1930.

35 Archiv FZH, 922 SA, Conn to Ellerhusen letter.

36 Archiv FZH, 922 SA, Conn to Ellerhusen letter.

37 Archiv FZH, 922 SA, Conn to Ellerhusen letter.

38 Archiv FZH, 11C1 Alfred Conn, 69.

39 Archiv FZH, 11C1 Alfred Conn, 69.

40 Archiv FZH, 11C1 Alfred Conn, 69.

41 Archiv FZH, 922 SA, Conn to Korsemann letter of January 28, 1930.

42 Archiv FZH, 922 SA, Conn to Ellerhusen letter.

43 NARA A3341 SA Kartei B104: Gunther P. P. was a member of the clique.

44 Archiv FZH, 991 OSAF, Conn to Korsemann letter of May 15, 1930.

45 Archiv FZH, 991 OSAF, Franz Koeberle letter of March 2, 1931.

46 Archiv FZH, 991 OSAF, Franz Koeberle letter.

47 William Shirer, *Rise and Fall of the Third Reich* (New York: Simon & Schuster, 1990/1960), 120.

48 Eve Sedgwick, *Between Men: English Literature and Male Homosocial Desire* (New York: Columbia University Press, 1985), 1, 16, 83–96.

THE BATTLE OF STERNSCHANZE

4

On October 29, 1929, a series of massive losses in the American stock market caused the U.S. economy to crash. The Great Depression had begun—not just in the United States but across the world. Although the speculation and stock market chicanery originated on Wall Street, the contagion spread quickly from America to Europe, due to the tangled financial web that had been woven in the aftermath of the Great War. Britain and France owed the United States large sums, which they had sought to recoup from Germany in the form of war reparations. The Weimar Republic, stricken by the reparations and resentful of the attached blame for the war, had already tried to inflate its way out of its debt in 1923, with disastrous consequences. After 1929, the Republic had few tools with which to counteract the worldwide economic catastrophe. With international support nonexistent, its war debts pressing, and its industries failing through a lack of national and international demand, Germany joined most other major economies in a time of prolonged misery.

Although the Depression radicalized politics in many countries, the effect in Germany proved especially severe. The crisis reminded Germans of the miserable conditions under which the Republic had begun, which allowed the extremist parties to seem more persuasive in their claims that democracy did not work. Many histories of the Nazis' rapid rise in 1930 thus begin within the crucial context of the Depression's effect on wealth, welfare, and especially unemployment, which some historians claim permanently alienated a generation of young men from the republican system.[1] Historians of the SA in other cities have emphasized how unemployment bred frustration and scorn for traditional politics, fueled the strategies of the Nazi and Communist fighting organizations, and allowed the Nazis to seduce adherents by concentrating on social welfare. In Nuremberg, the SA increased its membership sevenfold in just two years.[2] In Hamburg's suburb of Altona, the Depression eroded middle-class trust in government and in traditional bourgeois parties. After the crash, the middle class turned away from the bourgeois parties supporting the Republic and toward the Nazis.[3] The same process took place in Hamburg itself. The Depression hit the Hansestadt particularly hard, since it relied so much on international trade and shipping. Since 1918, the Hamburg Senate had steadily ceded its ability to set economic policy to the national government, leaving it unable to play its traditional role as guardian of local economic prosperity.[4] Studies of Hamburg's working-class families have concluded that simply putting food on the table became people's primary concern and a cause of great uncertainty.[5] Younger members of Hamburg's middle classes fell into this state of uncertainty as well, especially those whose families could not step in to compensate for their economic struggles. The crisis thus brought a new generation of stormtroopers into the Nazi fold. The Hamburg SA grew almost fourfold during the 18 months of the Depression—from around 400 members in the summer of 1929 to 1,500 in April 1931.[6]

However, young men alienated by democracy's perceived failures did not automatically flock to the Nazi banner. Many chose to join the Communists and their fighting organization, while others turned to the myriad non-Nazi hypernationalist factions. The SA had already discovered one way to attract young rebels in the large-scale demonstrations it had perfected during the *Verbrecher* protest, but the tactic of creating public chaos carried risks as long as the Nazis claimed to be a party of order. This dilemma stands in for the general problem of stormtrooper politics at this phase of the movement. The SA used violence to bolster its internal coherence and cater to its members' emotional needs, but this use of violence could also threaten its broader appeal. The group thus had to transform its desire for violence into something that was attractive rather than repulsive.

It did so in two ways, both of them essential to the success of politics in the era. First, the Party created newspapers that could solidify a Nazi sense of community. Second, it crafted situations that would lead the public to view its violence sympathetically. These two ways of shaping public debate combined to encourage ever-greater numbers of Hamburg citizens to accept the stormtroopers' own understanding of their movement, thus helping the Nazis convert their strong internal cohesion into wider public appeal. In this way, the year 1930 became among the most crucial of any in the Hamburg SA's rise to power. That year it developed its key tactics of fighting a double battle: the first in the streets against its Communist enemies, and the second in the pages of the city's newspapers as part of a struggle to define the meaning of public political violence.

"Storm Column": Hamburg's Nazi Media, 1928–1930

During the Weimar Republic, any party that hoped to gain notice in a chaotic political environment had to publish a newspaper. Of course, the media environment was as frenzied and unmoored as the nation's political life.

Along with the proliferation of parties, the Republic generated a torrent of new newspapers—over 700 in the period 1923–1929 alone.[7] Almost half of these papers officially claimed links to political parties, such as Hamburg's *Echo* (Social Democrats) and *Volkszeitung* (Communists), while others pursued consistent political philosophies without being bound to a single party. Newspapers voiced explicitly political positions that attracted even readers of other parties, who were often interested in what their rivals had to say. The *Hamburger Fremdenblatt*, which promoted "Hanseatic-mercantile interests" independent of any party, was particularly popular in German-speaking Europe and even America as a paper of record for the merchant class—a kind of *Wall Street Journal* for business-minded German speakers.[8] Nazi newspapers, however, had been slow to emerge because of financial constraints and organizational rivalries. A series of agreements at the 1928 Party congress established clear rules for the first time, instituting a system under which the national Party would give its stamp of approval to locally financed papers that met the central leadership's standards of conduct.[9] Nazi papers proliferated following this agreement, led by titles produced in traditional German publishing centers like Hamburg.

In 1928, Party member Hans Hesse founded the Hamburg Nazi Party's first newspaper, the *Hamburger Volksblatt*. In naming the paper, Party leaders had rejected Hesse's more belligerent suggestions, including the *Storm Signal*, in favor of the recognizable title of a defunct Social Democratic paper. The *Volksblatt* operated by subscribing to Gregor Strasser's Combat Press in Berlin, which sold content to other National Socialist papers and thus functioned as a kind of Nazi wire service.[10] Hamburg's party leaders liked the *Volksblatt* at first, and they pledged to make up any debts it assumed to Strasser. Hüttmann, however, rescinded this guarantee during his brief tenure as local Party leader. Hesse then filled the *Volksblatt*'s pages with increasingly sensational content that Krebs described as "something halfway between *Der Stürmer* and the *Nachtpost*."[11] He did not mean it as a compliment: *Der Stürmer* was Julius Streicher's infamous Nuremberg Nazi tabloid that distributed lurid images of hypersexualized violence against blonde women, and which appealed to the rawest and most offensive racial paranoia. The *Nachtpost* was a local Hamburg tabloid that was not as racist as *Der Stürmer* but still reveled in lowbrow tales of crime, sex, and scandal. Party leaders judged this content inappropriate on several levels: it was too disreputable to appeal to Hamburg's respectable classes, and it had no power to engage the newspapers of other parties in political debate. By the end of the *Volksblatt's* run it barely even discussed politics at all. The Party tried to remedy this situation with a new paper, the *Hanseatische Warte*, which premiered on January 1, 1929. It almost immediately gained a reputation as the Party's official paper, and Hesse's *Volksblatt* went into financial freefall. Krebs and his ally Brinkmann, who ran a publishing house of his own, bought out Hesse and continued to publish his paper until April, when the two papers merged under the *Warte's* banner.[12]

The *Hanseatische Warte* proved more successful than the irregular and unreliable *Volksblatt*. On the most basic level, it appeared regularly—an obvious but essential element to its mission to foster the sense of community and identity that the stormtroopers sought. The paper also presented itself in a more reputable style. While Krebs at times criticized its lack of "a cutting edge" and was at times frustrated with his relationship to the political leadership, he agreed that the paper had to tread carefully between political extremes.[13] The *Warte* consciously sought to present what Krebs called a measured, "specifically Hanseatic contribution to German politics," while at the same time speaking directly to the Party's younger and rougher rank and file.[14] This he accomplished by featuring stormtrooper reporters such as Hermann Okrass, who wrote the "Storm Column" page. Krebs also gave a regular column to a butcher who wrote in the local Plattdeutsch dialect under the pseudonym "Fietje." The column, called "Shut Your Trap and Listen to Fietje," mirrored a similar Berliner character in Goebbels' *Der Angriff*, which dealt with politics from an uncultured but relatable and affectionate local perspective.

Sales of the *Warte* struggled through 1929, but they picked up in 1930 during that summer's national political crises. By that time, citizens of democracies worldwide were realizing that the previous year's financial crash had inflicted unprecedented economic damage on almost every industrial economy. Foreign and domestic conflict dominated the *Warte's* headlines, which included stories about the dissolution of the *Reichstag*, a ban of the SA, and heated protests against the Young Plan—the latest attempt to get Germany to pay its war reparations by lowering the amount owed. Even a reduced amount, however, outraged many Germans because of the inherent moral guilt that payment implied, not to mention the immediate material impact on the German economy. These events of 1930 helped to increase interest in the Party's perspective while also adding to its ranks.

Sales, subscriptions, and advertising revenues at the *Warte* also increased, and the paper moved to a bigger office. All these developments meant that the growing stormtrooper movement had a way to build and sustain its internal sense of community, which proved particularly important as the movement entered a new offensive phase. As the offensive began, more people read to learn the Party's perspective not only on political events but on the nature of the movement itself. Even if new readers were not yet ready to join the Party, they began to pay increased attention to its perspective.

Journalists of the other parties' papers also read the new Nazi publication with increased interest. The Social Democratic *Echo* and Communist *Volkszeitung* naturally disputed almost everything they found in the *Warte's* pages. Other papers, most notably the venerable liberal organs the *Hamburger Fremdenblatt* and *Hamburger Nachrichten*, began subtly to reflect elements of the *Warte's* coverage. Ernst Baasch, a historian of Hamburg's newspaper industry, noted in 1930 how papers that based their appeal on "tradition"—especially those that held unbroken political or managerial continuity—enjoyed far more influence than upstart papers linked to new parties.[15] Paradoxically, however, the venerable papers often survived by adjusting their coverage to prevailing political forces.[16] The Hugenberg Press papers that were aligned with the German National People's Party (DNVP) displayed this tendency in the extreme. According to one historian critical of their coverage, the Hugenberg papers led their readers astray beginning in 1930, inducing their formerly liberal-nationalist audience to abandon the liberal side of that position in favor of imperial and militarist ideas that sped those readers' paths to Nazism.[17] In the theaters, Hugenberg's newsreels played a similar role.[18] The Nazi movement came to rely on these other media to repeat National Socialist claims to an audience that might have resisted the same message from Nazi sources. This cooperation, sometimes unwitting and sometimes overt, became one of the most important ways for the SA to recast stormtrooper violence as patriotic rather than treasonous, and communal rather than chaotic.

The "Neighborhood Offensive": SA Violence and Public Presence

During the SA's push into Hamburg's neighborhoods, the group employed violence of three main varieties. First, they initiated or were victims of unplanned attacks that originated in the rhythms of everyday life. Most of the many fights, beatings, ambushes, stone-throwing, property damage, and other violent incidents involving stormtroopers took place spontaneously. They emerged out of random but predictable encounters between stormtroopers and their political opponents, encounters that turned violent when an individual lost control and attacked, or when one side found itself with such numerical or tactical superiority that it could not resist letting loose.

Second, stormtroopers planned organized marches, mostly on Sundays, which generated fights between small bands traveling to or from the marches. Public marches formed the face of the National Socialist movement. Historian Sven Reichardt has identified these marches as the core element of the SA's public activities, especially as they showcased the movement's claims to discipline, order, and unity.[19] Marches were part of a "neighborhood offensive" designed to prove to residents of dangerous and depressed areas of the city that the Nazis could restore order and bring prosperity.[20] Stormtrooper marches most often began in relatively safe neighborhoods, such as Conn's home territory of Hoheluft, but then proceeded to neighboring areas in order to win converts in contested regions and extend Nazi strongholds into new areas. Nazi newspapers and pamphlets included the first-person testimonies of these converts, who had been inspired to join by the imagery and emotional impact of a march. One such report came from a resident of a "bright red district" west of the Alster, who had "always held himself at a distance" from National Socialism. However, this convert wrote, "the disciplined behavior of the SA during the march, its stalwart bearing, and above all the lightning in the eyes of these youths ripened in me the decision to join as a Party member. And I've since found out that many more residents of our house joined the Party on the same day."[21]

As this passage shows, for a march to fulfill its purpose, it had to proceed with discipline, police tolerance, and great emphasis on decorum. In this spirit, SA leaders repeatedly banned provocative or overtly antisemitic songs, such as one that included the infamous lyric, "when Jewish blood sprays from our knives," or another that exhorted the stormtroopers to "grab hold of the hand grenades."[22] These bans show the importance SA leadership placed on mitigating violence during marches—although, of course, the fact that they repeatedly had to prohibit these songs also shows that their pugnacious troops eventually returned to singing what they liked, not caring if they provoked violent responses or even eager to do so.

The marches, by their very existence, antagonized non-Nazi residents of the neighborhoods in which a stormtrooper column marched. Stormtroopers, however, brashly asserted a philosophical right to march, claiming the streets as a public forum available for the use of any citizen. In Conn's words, "The streets belong to everyone, not just the ones who live on them."[23] Stormtroopers therefore claimed a right to march where they pleased, regardless of whether or not the residents approved of their presence. Even if we grant that the stormtroopers truly did believe this, the concept was myopic, disingenuous, and self-interested. Conn may have told himself that he and his friends were merely strolling through their city, but they purposefully did so in a confrontational way that they knew would raise the temperature of political conflict. In fact, that was the whole point: marches reliably sparked scuffles between marchers and bystanders, which made further public violence more likely, and at times even spawned large-scale riots.

The third and most noteworthy form of violence was not a difference in type but of degree. Both large- and small-scale incidents eventually, and inevitability, led to deadly encounters in which one faction finally killed an enemy. When such an event took place, the political murder gripped the public consciousness and defined the SA's reputation—for good or ill. Fatalities created spectacular press accounts in the weeks following a death, during which a contest over the public representation of victims and aggressors played a key role in the development of Nazi politics.

SA street politics therefore rotated through three forms of violence. Stormtroopers marched on Sundays, navigated a series of everyday encounters during the week, and nursed violent thoughts over months of low-level combat. Every six months or so, tensions erupted into spontaneous or organized acts of deadly conflict. This dynamic crystallized in the election campaign of September 1930, a breakthrough for the Nazis' political fortunes, when months of low-level violence and public campaigning culminated in the Battle of Sternschanze. The event became legend in the Hamburg SA, a successful contest over the public interpretation of violence that created the template for later stormtrooper strategies.

The Battle of Sternschanze: September 7, 1930

The confrontation at the Sternschanze train station came not by design but by accident. It began with an SA march through the city—a normal event, if ambitious in its scale—that was meant to be the greatest display Hamburg's SA had shown to date. This would-be triumph, however, in fact ended in ambush, defeat, and the fatal stabbing of one of the group's most powerful personalities, *Truppführer* Heinrich Dreckmann. Many Nazis initially considered Dreckmann's death a devastating personal loss, a practical setback for the Nazi Party's plans, and a humiliating indictment of the Hamburg SA's directionless leadership. Yet the public reception of the battle transformed tactical defeat into strategic victory. Hamburg's newspapers—not only the *Hanseatische Warte* but also the most prominent papers of the center-right—rewrote the incident as a moral victory that demonstrated Communist criminality and stormtrooper heroism. The story of Sternschanze was therefore the tale not only of a street fight but of a battle to define the incident. It is the story of the SA discovering its most powerful political narrative: the heroic male martyr's public blood sacrifice that renews the political community.

Hamburg's SA had been especially busy during the first week of September. It had marched in friendly Rotherbaum and in far-off Langenhorn. It had protected daily Party meetings at locations throughout the city. And it had spent weeks preparing for a major propaganda march on September 7, during which the brigade would march for the first time with more than one thousand men, complete with standardized uniforms, flags, a musician troop, and flatbed trucks. The Hamburg police, however, had to approve the routes of political marches that were conducted in closed formation or accompanied by vehicles. Although the police had granted approval for smaller marches as recently as the previous week, the SA's request to hold its largest march yet posed too great a threat to public order. As Hamburg police captain Lothar Danner noted in his memoirs, the Prussian police, who had just banned the brown shirt, had recently warned other agencies against the National Socialists' "illegal political methods." A police circular issued on August 12 declared that SA politics had returned to "the type that led to the Hitler putsch in 1923."[24] The Hamburg police therefore declined the SA's request to march.

There was, however, a loophole. Only marches in closed formation or with vehicles came under police jurisdiction, thus the SA could forego its vehicles and march either without its uniforms or in open ranks. If it did so, it could proceed without prior approval. Ellerhusen decided that a march without uniforms would admit weakness and accomplish nothing, so he chose to march in open formation confined to the sidewalks. The stormtroopers could thereby continue to rely on the strained interpretation that they were merely private citizens exercising their right to walk through their hometown. Conn, however, did not approve of this decision. He doubted that the thousand men of the brigade could maintain contact while arrayed in such an extended formation, and he feared the consequences of surrendering the SA's traditional march discipline.[25]

Around noon on September 7, the SA began to assemble at the Wandsbeker Chaussee rail station near Hamburg's northeastern border. The march would take the form of a "walk" with around five hundred men in uniform, with an equal number of non-uniformed SA and Party members.[26] They set out at 2 PM and proceeded via Lübeckerstrasse to the city center (Figure 4.1). The stormtroopers proceeded without incident through the center of Hamburg's wealthy government-commercial corridor at Mönckebergstrasse, the Rathausmarkt, and Jungfernstieg. As the loose columns of brown shirts proceeded in lively and exuberant fashion, they became increasingly spread out and disconnected. Rather than one brigade that marched together in step through the center of the street, the group broke down into its constituent parts of smaller troops and squads pushing their way along the sidewalks, singing battle songs, and enjoying feeling emboldened by the presence of a thousand comrades.

Conn, an officer of the SA's motorcycle unit, motored through the streets to monitor the march's progress. He returned to meet Ellerhusen at the head of the column around the time it reached Gänsemarkt. Here Conn made an unpleasant discovery: Ellerhusen had planned the march route only up through Mönckebergstrasse. "He had proceeded," wrote Conn, "in the conviction that the police would in any case move against us by that point. They hadn't done so. And now no one knew where we should go next."[27]

Ellerhusen spontaneously decided that the march should proceed to the Wagner pub on Gabelsbergerstrasse, home to Sturm 2. Conn could not understand this reasoning, as the SA men at the column's front hailed from Barmbek, on the other side of the Alster. Therefore they did not know the neighborhood well, nor did Ellerhusen. Sturm 2 itself was marching near the rear of the column and could not help guide the group, but even if the brigade arrived intact at Wagner's, one pub could not contain a thousand men. Ellerhusen told Conn, who lived nearby, to lead the column west toward the Schanzenviertel, a working-class neighborhood heavily contested by the Nazis and Communists. Neither SA leader knew that the Communists had already assembled there, at the Neuer Pferdemarkt, for a propaganda rally of their own.

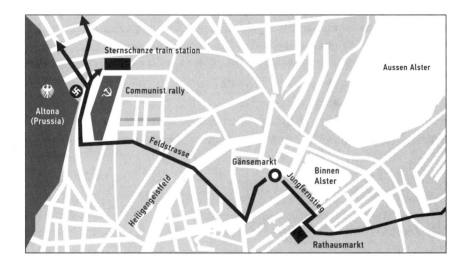

FIGURE 4.1

**Map of the march route and battle zone,
September 7, 1930**

Source: Created by author, based on a map in Karl
Baedeker's *Northern Germany as Far as the Bavarian and
Austrian Frontiers: Handbook for Travelers* (New York:
Charles Scribner's Sons, 1910).

The leading Sturm discovered the danger with little warning. Crossing the Feldstrasse bridge, it encountered a police cordon, behind which seemingly innumerable masses of Communists were loading up over 60 wagons, singing fighting songs, and waving red flags.[28] The way through the Neuer Pferdemarkt was closed to the Nazis. The SA column again stalled, but this time it had few options of where to proceed. Its right flank was constrained by the Communist demonstration and the police, who had closed off most of the small streets around the marketplace and placed officers on balconies throughout the neighborhood to monitor the situation from above. On the SA's left, the Hamburg-Altona border at Schulterblatt formed an invisible yet impenetrable barrier. Since Altona was Prussian territory, where authorities had banned the brown shirt, crossing the street would expose any stormtrooper to immediate arrest. The Hamburg SA therefore had but one option: to march straight down Schanzenstrasse, then use the SA tavern at the Hotel Adler as a protective strongpoint that would allow a breakout to the park surrounding the rail station and the open streets to its north. Once there, they could leave behind the contested wards of the inner city for the browner pastures of Eppendorf and Eimsbüttel. Until they could reach the hotel, however, the march route was a narrow canyon perfect for an ambush, and the SA would have to traverse this space without the benefit of closed ranks, which would have protected them from the Communists but would also have drawn the ire of the police.

Ellerhusen's lack of planning had left the SA no choice but to run a gantlet of quick-tempered Communists and edgy policemen, without any tactical options to lessen the danger. Conn sped up and down the column on his motorbike, warning SA officers at every point of the situation and ordering them to keep their men as close together as they legally could. He also emphasized the need for the men not to respond to inevitable Communist provocations—a prescient warning, since the SA's self-image of restraint in the face of provocation was usually more fiction than fact.

By the time Conn had returned to the column's lead elements, they had passed through the gauntlet and were now marching through to the open north. But Conn and his motorcycle troop were not the only mounted units that day. The Communists had motorcycles of their own, and eventually one broke through the police cordon separating the antagonists. It buzzed the edges of the SA column, its rider waving a red flag just out of reach of the angry stormtroopers. Conn wondered how the police, "who had all the tools they needed to prevent it," had allowed "such an obvious provocation."[29] When SA men caught the cyclist, tore his flag from him, and knocked him off his vehicle, the potential violence that had been building throughout the encounter finally erupted. Policemen drew their clubs and began to arrest the stormtroopers who had attacked the motorcyclist. SA men from the rear rushed forward to protect their comrades from the police. Policemen linked arms in a vain attempt to keep Kampstrasse closed, but the Communists broke through and attacked. Conn and the motorized SA men sped to both ends of the extended column to summon reinforcements. The SA's limited range of movement made its progress slow, but there were no restrictions on where the Communists' flatbed trucks could go. They circled around into Altona to attack the SA's exposed western flank, and within minutes the entire district had become a war zone. SA men battled Communists and police, civilian sympathizers and Party members added to the ranks of combatants, women and children were caught in the middle of the brawl or sought refuge in the houses and shops on Schanzenstrasse, and the police eventually gave up on making arrests and sought only to defend themselves.

In the absence of central leadership from any faction, the riot degenerated into hundreds of small-scale conflicts among the police, Communists, and stormtroopers. Even the combatants found it difficult to distinguish the factions. As Conn later noted:

> Everything had fallen apart. No leader had his people, no people their leader, and in the middle of it all were party members, women, and passersby. Nobody listened to orders anymore. The troop was fully divorced from its leadership, as much as it can even be called that.[30]

Ellerhusen and other leading SA officers had already reached as far as Christuskirche, where they directed fleeing SA men into the rail station and away from danger. Conn, still in the thick of the melee, steered surrounded stormtroopers to escape via the Sternschanze station or to safety in the Hotel Adler. *Sturmführer* Stäublin and several other SA men fled to another pub and barricaded themselves inside.

By the time most of the combatants had dispersed and the police had restored order, the scale of the SA's defeat had become clear. At least 34 stormtroopers had been arrested, dozens had been wounded, and on the corner of Susannenstrasse and Schanzenstrasse lay the cooling corpse of

Heinrich Dreckmann, one of its most beloved leaders.[31] The next day, the police banned the brown shirt. They declined to put equal restrictions on the Communists. In the face of this disaster, local party leaders and SA rivals denigrated Ellerhusen as an incompetent drunk, deposed him as *Brigadeführer*, and set him on the margins of the movement. It was a humiliating battle-field defeat for National Socialism's "political soldiers."

But the SA soon recovered its pride. It did so by constructing a heroic narrative of the day's events, in which the stormtroopers were innocent, outnumbered, persecuted, and ultimately martyred to the forces of corruption and disorder that had assailed the peace of the Hansestadt. With their physical presence on the streets reduced, the stormtroopers labored instead to influence public perceptions of the battle: who had caused it, why the police had been unable or unwilling to prevent it, and what meaning the stormtroopers' struggle held for the movement's moral authority.[32]

As the stormtroopers disingenuously claimed to believe, their march had been peaceful in purpose—an innocent Sunday stroll that had provoked unreasoned violence. The true villains of the story were the Communists, whose rage against the SA had been more powerful than the police's ability to hinder it. Police failures and biases, the Nazis argued, demanded that the would-be forces of republican order also bear equal responsibility for the violence. The *Warte* wrote that the Communists would not have dared to attack if the police had allowed the SA to march in formation, or if they at least had kept Communist provocateurs from harassing the innocent stormtroopers. To the *Warte*, this had amounted to the police taking the Communists' side against the SA, thus forcing the stormtroopers to fight on two fronts, with reduced numbers, and against an emboldened foe.[33] In short, the police had colluded with Communism. "Instead of controlling the situation," Conn wrote, the police "went against the SA, arrested a whole mass of storm-troopers who were only defending themselves against the Communists, and drove them off in paddy wagons."[34]

According to the *Warte*, in the aftermath of the fighting the police did nothing to prohibit 58 Communist vehicles from taking triumphal drives through the streets, even while holding back SA medics from helping wounded comrades. The police also arrested 34 stormtroopers, including a stormtrooper medic who tried to examine Dreckmann's body, which police then refused to release to his widow for several days. The *Warte* complained that all of the arrested men had languished in jail, "even though they are completely innocent," which meant that they would likely lose their jobs. The total ramifications of the unequal arrests, wrote the *Warte*, comprised "a terror, a chicanery that one can't even put into words."[35]

The SA remained steadfast in its conviction that it had faced a double assault that day: physical violence by the Communists and legal persecution by the police. This view was unfair to the police, who had guarded the registered Communist rally in the same way they had guarded official Nazi meetings on other occasions. Police officers on that day faced a tense situation made suddenly worse by the entry of a thousand Nazis insistent on passing directly through the area of a Communist rally, with no warning given to help them prepare to diffuse a confrontation. It is therefore entirely likely that the police did consider the SA to be at fault, but even so, this hardly made them biased. What choice did they have but to do their duty—to keep the two sides separate, break up any fights that began, and arrest any lawbreakers? The 34 stormtroopers arrested likely deserved their fates. The fact that no Communists were arrested—if this Nazi claim was even true—would likely have stemmed from the fact that the police had long ago banned Red Front uniforms.[36] Any of their fighters would therefore have been harder to identify and arrest. Ironically, police measures against the Communists in a prior phase of conflict now created the situation that the Nazis claimed showed anti-stormtrooper bias.

However, as much as the *Warte* emphasized victimhood, it could not portray SA men as weaklings lest it undermine the image of masculine virtue that the group continually worked to display. Nazi accounts of the battle therefore had to make the outnumbered stormtroopers into heroes who had stood alone or in small groups against powerful larger forces. The enemy, according to this narrative, sought the stormtroopers' destruction not only as men but as symbols of a political movement that worked for German renewal against the efforts of corrupt policemen and criminal Communists. The *Warte* thus emphasized individual stories of heroic resistance against what it claimed were overwhelming odds in the form of two to three thousand Communists.[37] Its reportage of "how it happened" gathered the stories of many different stormtroopers, using a testimonial motif—"I saw"—to strengthen group cohesion and to tie individually repeated themes into a unified whole. The anonymous stormtroopers testified:

> I saw how a group of Communists, containing about ten men armed with long iron staves, struck into the SA and police. One Communist had a pistol. I saw how a Communist beat an SA man with a heavy iron cudgel. I saw how a Communist hit an SA man in the face with a large glass bottle. I believe that this was Truppführer Dreckmann.
>
> I saw many knives among the Communists. Above all they had iron rods. One Communist sought to throw a homemade bomb in the face of an SA man. During the throw he fell over, the bottle slipped, and he burned his own hand almost completely.[38]

The tone of this testimony emphasized the fine line between oral and written accounts of stormtrooper adventures. In this case and others, the first action reports were always carried by word of mouth, passed around the *Sturmlokale* (SA taverns), and carried into wider circulation throughout the Nazi movement. After important battles, Nazi journalists merged multiple accounts into an official narrative in the Party paper. The effort laid bare the work required to fashion the stormtroopers' heroic self-images: they needed to fight, but they also needed to shape the resulting battle's story into one that cast them as protagonists rather than villains.

The masculine warrior archetype most favored by stormtroopers was hardly unique to their movement. It was in fact among the most common Western heroic myths, one that reached back to the Greek legends of Thermopylae and the 300, saw service in WWI through the youthful sacrifice at Langemarck, and came to the SA via the fantasies of the Freikorps men.[39] All the stories were the same: a small group of iron men stands against a teeming mass of enemies who seek to breach civilization's walls and wash away a people's civic independence. The SA shaped the Battle of Sternschanze into this favored narrative: a small group of heroic stormtroopers had come under attack by a superior number of enemies, whom they resisted long enough to save their comrades. They could not always save themselves, however, and sometimes fell in defense of comrades, *Volk*, and nation. These fallen became the martyrs of National Socialism.

In its basic structure, the myth of fallen stormtroopers belonged to a thematic family that contained some of Germany's most powerful founding narratives. Its general outlines placed it into a category that historian Hayden White described as a romance—a drama of good's victory over evil through the power of transcendent self-sacrifice.[40] Such stories describe a hero's journey through a series of trials and adversities, which transform innocence into maturity, strength, and eventual triumph. A narrative similar to the myth of the Spartan 300 appeared in numerous legends of the Holy Grail, including the Wagnerian interpretation of Parsifal that was so popular among modern German nationalists, and the mythic histories of the Teutonic knights' blood sacrifice that claimed areas of central and eastern Europe for Germanic civilization. The narrative also tracked closely with more secular works of modern political history, including the predominant strain of 19th-century German historicism, the "Prussian School," in which a scattered and weakened German people is redeemed by the rise of the Hohenzollern monarchs and a brotherhood of warrior masculinity that unites a new German empire through victory on the battlefield.[41] Stories of stormtrooper martyrs thus recalled much deeper historic and mythic masculine traditions, presenting the SA struggle as merely the latest chapter of an eternal spiritual-historical crusade fought by the heroic men of the German past: Parsifal, the Teutonic Knights, and even, perversely, Christ himself.[42]

Just as the nascent Christian community circulated letters written during their martyrs' final days, Nazi newspapers wrote about Dreckmann's death to bolster their political community.[43] Goebbels had drawn on Christian myths of "resurrection and return" in his lionization of the "martyred" Horst Wessel earlier that year.[44] Now the Hamburg Nazis had their own fallen stormtrooper to cast as a sacrificial savior. In the *Warte*'s account of his fatal battle, Dreckmann led his five-man unit back into the thick of fighting to stave off a flood of Communist reinforcements that came down Susannenstrasse from the west. He and Sturmführer Paschke fought to keep the men around them in a tight formation, but a few became separated from the SA phalanx and came under attack. The *Warte* described how Dreckmann leapt to their defense in a heroic climax to his valiant life:

> With senseless fury [his] empty hands grappled through swinging iron clubs and naked knives. The Commune broke into wild flight. The comrades were free. But in this moment some 500 Communists came from the flank and from behind . . . Eyewitnesses report that he held out long. But he was struck with a knife through his throat, while almost simultaneously a sledgehammer smashed in his head. As his body fell, it was further struck with numerous stabs. He was trampled almost to unrecognizability.[45]

The Nazi warrior had protected his comrades among a sea of enemies and could only be struck down by superior numbers and multiple blows from all quarters. Both immediate and later Nazi accounts embellished the melodrama of Dreckmann's story. His initial obituary described how, during ceremonies that surrounded Hitler's speech the previous week, Dreckmann had "looked his Führer Adolf Hitler in the eyes and allowed himself to be honored by him, and then a day later had to seal his oath of loyalty with death."[46] The story noted a happy home life with his wife and 16-year-old daughter, as well as his doomed farewell to them on the eve of the march. When the wife complained that he would not stay home despite the risk, Dreckmann supposedly responded like a model of masculine stoicism: "It can't be changed. Service is service. Maybe in the coming years Germany will be better. But until then you must master yourself. We don't live for ourselves alone."[47]

Later stormtrooper histories and books that lauded the Hamburg SA gave even more elaborately maudlin details. In Okrass' official history of the Hamburg stormtroopers, Dreckmann's wife asked when her husband would spend more time with the family. "When the Third Reich is established," he supposedly replied. "It's not about us. It's about Germany."[48] Both versions of the story emphasized the subordination of the individual family to the political family the Nazis sought to build. Although the differences in the tales imply that Nazi propagandists simply invented both versions, the common messages of martyrdom, persecution, and sacrifice resonated strongly within the movement.

The Nazis, however, still lacked the publishing capacity to propagandize Dreckmann's death outside their own circles. The *Warte* appeared just once a week, thus the Party was able to publish only one round of stories before the crucial election the following week. The true test of the efficacy of their narrative was its ability to be reproduced in non-Nazi newspapers, which would spread their framing of Dreckmann's death to new audiences. The most important "transmitter" in this respect was the *Hamburger Fremdenblatt*, the venerable national-liberal organ of Hamburg's business and bourgeois communities. The paper's anti-Communism led it to swallow many Nazi tropes, which it inflicted on its readers with little apparent thought as to how that could undermine its other efforts to strengthen a "bourgeois middle" based on liberal principles.[49]

Before Sternschanze, the *Fremdenblatt* had previously ignored news of stormtrooper deaths. In March 1930, it reported that 12 Nazis suffered injuries in an attack, and in the evening edition relayed police assurances that "although deadly weapons must have been used, the injuries were not of a serious nature."[50] The paper did not report that one of the stormtroopers, Paul Kessler, later died of his wounds.

The *Fremdenblatt* showed no such reticence with Dreckmann's high-profile demise (Figure 4.2). "Bloody election battles in Hamburg's streets!" blared the *Fremdenblatt* on September 8. "Communist attack on Hitler demonstrators—1 dead and 10 seriously wounded."[51] The story did not absolve the Nazis of blame for the incident, noting their failure to register the march with the police, but it also placed the riot in the context of the "radicalism" of both extremes. The liberal paper described "brutal acts of barbarism by the Communists," during which "one Communist repeatedly screamed 'Kill them all!'"[52] Meanwhile, its portrayal of the Nazis echoed the type of victimhood seen in National Socialist papers, where the stormtroopers were depicted as hopelessly outnumbered and driven to flight. Finally, the paper emphasized how even the police could barely defend themselves against the Communist mob, thereby linking the Nazis with the police as common enemies of the extremist left. In this context, the *Fremdenblatt's* warnings against political violence sounded similar to Nazi rhetoric:

> State authorities must use all their means to prevent in all cases the repetition of yesterday's proceedings. Sentimental hindsight does not suit a place where life and health are at risk even more than is the authority of the state.
>
> Only then can yesterday's events have a positive outcome: if the voters of Hamburg use it as proof that no land and no Volk, no Bürger, no worker, no public official, no merchant, neither woman nor man can found the future of their Volk or the well-being of their family on a party that only preaches hate and self-slaughter, and with raw brutality of the fist seeks to trample spiritual and moral principles.[53]

The *Fremdenblatt* addressed these words to both Communists and Nazis, but the language of bourgeois respectability was also Nazi language. The desire to protect "spiritual and moral principles" against a Communist party that preached "hate" and "self-slaughter" was the stormtrooper's professed goal—even if he at times rejected the constraints of bourgeois morality in the service of its defense.

FIGURE 4.2

A Nazi portrait of stormtrooper leader
Heinrich Dreckmann, one of the Hamburg
SA's leading lights before his 1930 death in a
streetfight. Source: Collection of Archiv FZH

Public disturbances of the scale and deadliness of the Battle of Sternschanze increased a bourgeois sense of besiegement and led to calls for stricter action by the state. These calls played into Nazi hands, as did the *Fremdenblatt*'s willingness later that month to cover the Berlin trial of Horst Wessel's murderers. In the aftermath of Dreckmann's death, which had solidified in Hamburg the trope of the murdered Nazi luminary, such stories sold. But they also had consequences. The *Hamburgischer Correspondent*, a less influential liberal paper that held Nazism at a distance, noted the implicit danger of this dynamic in its story about the Reichstag's new composition. "National Socialism," it declared, "draws its best strength from the pessimism of the Bürger."[54]

Bourgeois pessimism featured prominently in the pages of the *Fremdenblatt*, *Correspondent*, *Hamburger Anzeiger*, and other leading liberal papers. They only haltingly supported the period's governing coalitions, which they saw as an ideologically incoherent and politically untrustworthy defensive alliance. The *Fremdenblatt* in particular had rapidly lost hope that a "bourgeois alliance" could regain political power, govern with traditional restraint, and defend liberal business interests.[55] Another bourgeois paper—the prestigious, national-liberal and DNVP-sympathetic *Hamburger Nachrichten*—reported positively on Hitler's election speeches and debunked reports of Nazi treason issued by the interior minister shortly before the election. A few days before the vote, the *Nachrichten* grouped the Nazi Party with the DNVP, German People's Party (DVP), and other rightist parties as reasonable options that shared broad agreement on national questions. "All six of these parties are trustworthy and nationalist," it wrote. "[They] struggle against the internationalist Marxist parties, the Social Democrats and Communists, who would destroy people and nation, family and German spirit."[56]

Many traditional newspapers thus had some sympathy for the Nazi self-image. They did so for reasons of their own and with some consciousness of the dangers involved, and they did not dismiss SA violence that offended their bourgeois sensibilities. When such incidents took place, these papers generally followed police accounts for the details, and criticized or (worse) mocked the stormtroopers when appropriate.[57] Despite all that, however, these papers played a key role in legitimizing the stormtroopers' self-image of heroic victimization during a time in which the Nazis did not yet have a daily paper of their own. The would-be centrists' complicity had begun in the summer of 1930 by lending approval to the

Nazi Party's activism against the Young Plan to readjust Germany's postwar reparations debt.[58] After Sternschanze, the papers' support moved beyond targeted sympathy for Nazi foreign policy goals and toward a broader use of Nazi rhetoric to describe the political scene. As the Social Democratic *Echo* complained in October, the "Nazi-friendly *Fremdenblatt*" and other organs of "the bourgeois press" increasingly wrote reports "based on Nazi sources."[59] These papers' coverage proved crucial as the election campaign continued in the week after the Battle of Sternschanze.

During the time between the battle and the election, the SA—with many of its members in jail and its symbols banned from public display—issued no new provocations. Its most visible presence was at Dreckmann's grave, where the Hamburg Nazi Party for the first time engineered a funerary spectacle in which it transformed the martyr's death into an act of communal renewal. The effort to depict Dreckmann's death as heroic martyrdom proceeded in both word and deed. The funeral itself attracted hundreds to the Ohlsdorf Cemetery, in whose chapel only a small number of intimates could gather. Outside, the Hamburg SA and other Party members stood under gray skies. The *Hanseatische Warte* described a strong wind that blew "brown leaves" to the ground—an image meant to naturalize the fallen brown shirt as part of a holy German landscape.[60] The Nazi defense attorney, Korn, had freed five of the arrested stormtroopers in time for them to attend the funeral, and their presence bolstered the morale of the movement's warrior core.[61] A pastor named Koopmann gave the funeral oration, in which he highlighted Dreckmann's war service, his 21-year marriage to a loving wife, and his self-sacrifice for Volk and *Vaterland*. Koopmann claimed that Dreckmann had died to "give us this day our daily bread," and he encouraged the assembled SA to consider similar acts of breadwinning self-sacrifice in the future.[62] *Gauleiter* Kaufmann brought forth the grieving widow and daughter, and he promised the fallen Dreckmann, "We will take over the protection of your family!"[63]

At the end of the funeral the SA changed the words of the "Horst Wessel Lied" to highlight the "burning rage in our hearts" and to promise Dreckmann, "*Kamerad*, your red blood was not spilled in vain!"[64] In short, Dreckmann's funeral was choreographed by the SA, narrated by the *Hanseatische Warte* and bourgeois-liberal papers, and interpreted by the public in general as a political gathering. It was an act of necromancy that used Dreckmann's corpse to bind together the disparate elements of the movement while fracturing bourgeois rivals and leftist enemies. The band of SA warriors, the political leaders, the nuclear families, and the religious leaders who participated in the funeral thus emerged from their defeat with strengthened resolve.

If the bourgeois papers declined to cover Dreckmann's funeral with excessively sympathetic rhetoric, they nevertheless endorsed the other side of the Nazi narrative: Communist criminality during the "Bloody Sunday" of Sternschanze. The *Fremdenblatt* reprinted the "bloodthirsty" words of the Communist *Volkszeitung*, which had crowed, "Yesterday's Sunday was a day of triumph for Hamburg, a sign of the will that shall help the KPD to victory. The next Sunday will be more arduous yet, but the red election helpers will go to work to fulfill their revolutionary duty."[65] Bourgeois papers often played up the Communist statements most likely to scare the Hansestadt's staid citizens. These papers intended to repudiate all radicalism—hence the *Fremdenblatt*'s election-day exhortation to "vote the liberal middle!"—yet their effect weakened the parties of the center by heightening an atmosphere of emergency and threat.[66]

On September 13, Hamburg went to the polls. The *Fremdenblatt* reported the results as a "victory of the extremists."[67] Moderate conservative parties, like the DNVP and DVP, lost much of their strength to the rising National Socialists (Table 4.1). The Hamburg Nazi Party had only 1,659 members at this time, but it won an astonishing 145,000 votes.[68] Hamburg historian Ursula Büttner has called the result "a monstrous increase" in the Nazi vote, the moment the Party finally won significant notice outside its own circles.[69] The election also cemented the Nazis' neighborhood ties in the upscale areas that bordered mixed middle- and working-class neighborhoods near the Elbe (Figure 4.3). These new Nazi strongholds forced the Senate to fight a strong anti-republican party not only from the left but from the right.[70]

In the months after the Sternschanze defeat and the election victory, the Nazi media portrayed the SA as quiet but resolved, protective of its home territories but not seeking battle unless attacked. In the *Warte*'s final September issue, stormtrooper journalist Hermann Okrass described the stormtroopers' proud return to the streets as they set out to protect a meeting at Sagebiel. Their march to Hamburg's premier meeting hall was not stopped, he wrote, by police, Marxists, cold, or rain.

The election had proved that the SA would only benefit from public display, despite the physical dangers involved. Any other choice, Okrass wrote,

	ELECTION			
	May 4 1924	December 7 1924	May 20 1928	September 14 1930
SPD	27.5%	32.1%	36.8%	31.8%
USPD	.5%	.2%		
KPD	18.8%	14.7%	17.3%	18.7%
ZENTRUM	1.6%	1.8%	1.6%	1.5%
DDP	13.1%	12.7%	11.8%	8.7%
DVP	11.7%	12.7%	13.2%	9.0%
DNVP	19.4%	21.4%	12.6%	4.0%
NSDAP	6.1%	2.3%	2.6%	19.0%
OTHERS	1.3%	2.0%	4.1%	7.4%
PARTICIPATION	**79.0%**	**76.5%**	**80.1%**	**84.6%**

TABLE 4.1

Reichstag election results in Hamburg, 1924–1930

Source: Created by author, data from Richard Hamilton,

WhoVoted for Hitler? (Princeton, NJ: Princeton University Press, 1982).

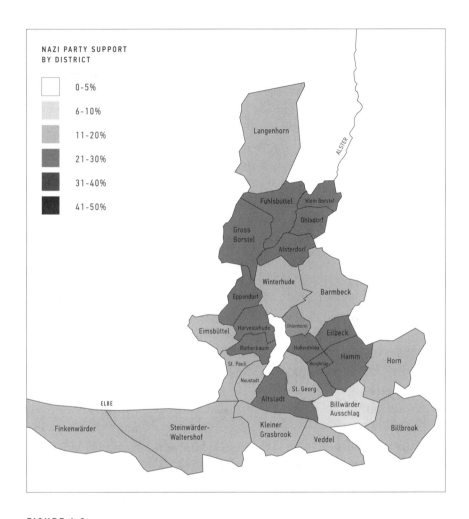

NAZI PARTY SUPPORT BY DISTRICT

- 0-5%
- 6-10%
- 11-20%
- 21-30%
- 31-40%
- 41-50%

Langenhorn

ALSTER

Fuhlsbüttel   Klein Borstel

Ohlsdorf

Gross Borstel

Alsterdorf

Winterhude

Barmbeck

Eppendorf

Eimsbüttel   Harvestehude

Uhlenhorst

Eilbeck

Rotherbaum

Hohenfelde

St. Pauli

Burgfelde

Hamm

Horn

Neustadt

St. Georg

ELBE

Altstadt

Billwärder Ausschlag

Finkenwärder

Steinwärder-Waltershof

Kleiner Grasbrook

Veddel

Billbrook

FIGURE 4.3

Nazi Party support by electoral district, September 14, 1930

Source: Created by author, data from Richard Hamilton,
Who Voted for Hitler? (Princeton, NJ: Princeton University Press, 1982).

would be "moral suicide."[71] The SA had to stay active in order to keep its members' interest and energy intact, but it could not appear too aggressive lest it bring down more sanctions from the police. Therefore, when the *Warte* proclaimed in October that "the quiet pause after the election has ended," the SA focused its energies outside Hamburg.[72] It still protected meetings in the city, but its public projections of strength thrust outward into neighboring towns such as Altengamme, Bergdorf, Elbstadt, Geesthacht, Halstenbek, and Reinbek. All these places saw large-scale SA marches in October's early weeks, and some of these marches led to confrontations with Communists. The distance from the far-flung country towns to the city center meant that skirmishes in the towns often went unreported or underreported in Hamburg's media. The *Echo* alone continued to draw attention to SA violence, but the only local cases it described were small-scale incidents that arose from personal disagreements, not political strife.[73]

As the year ended, it seemed as if the Hamburg Nazi Party and SA had discovered a powerful formula that the Party afterward sought to perfect. In December, Krebs—who had retained his editorial role at the paper despite his removal from political leadership—replaced the *Hanseatische Warte* with a new daily paper, the *Hamburger Tageblatt*. For the expansion, Krebs used 5,000 Marks that the *Warte* had in reserve. He could now hire more staff, rent larger offices, and, after a rocky start, deliver a more technically sophisticated product.[74] The rewards were clear: the Nazis could now more effectively and immediately influence political debates over SA violence, and the initial five thousand subscriber list increased steadily.[75]

But to Krebs' personal dismay, he now had to surrender his independence and allow the *Gau* far more control over editorial content than he had previously done. The new *Tageblatt* functioned as one star in the larger constellation of Nazi press operations, one of 36 dailies whose total circulation reached half a million per day.[76] Its reporters and editors now relied on wire copy and Party press releases for its most important stories, which they then adapted for local relevance. A page or two of Hamburg news covered strictly local events. Other page-long features addressed core Nazi constituencies, such as students, sailors, and the stormtroopers themselves, whom the *Tageblatt* reliably depicted in the images of heroic martyrdom developed in the context of Sternschanze. As an episode in the Nazi Party's intellectual and regional history, the limits and control imposed on the *Tageblatt* signaled the movement's increasing centralization and ability to impose

authoritarian discipline outside the Munich inner circle. These trends eventually led Krebs, Strasser, and a number of other independent-minded
national socialists to become alienated from the movement. Nevertheless,
the founding of a more disciplined daily paper was an unqualified boon to
the movement as a whole, which could now quickly mobilize its rhetoric
of respectability in response to incidents of political violence. It also heavily
promoted the SA's ties to family, church, and the city in order to make the
SA men seem still more respectable.

In 1932, the Party also established a national newspaper for the stormtroopers, *Der SA Mann.* This weekly paper had an important national function
as a forum through which the SA leadership could promote a coherent
group identity in the face of larger ideological rifts within the Nazi movement.[77] It was written by the stormtroopers themselves, based on their own
experiences, in their own voices, and encouraged by SA leadership.[78] The
two new papers gave the stormtroopers much greater power to shape their
own images, to influence coverage from neutral or sympathetic papers, and
to translate these two results into increased numbers for the movement.
From 1930 to 1933, the SA combined its two labors of representation—
the public events themselves, and the effort needed to cast these events in
sympathetic light—to convince many of Hamburg's citizens that National
Socialism could rescue the state and society from factional violence.

NOTES

1   Peter Merkel, *Making of a Stormtrooper* (Princeton, NJ: Princeton University Press, 1980), 3–20.

2   Eric Reiche, *The Development of the SA in Nürmberg, 1922–1934* (Cambridge, England: Cambridge
    University Press, 1986), 89.

3   Anthony McElligott, *Contested City: Municipal Politics and the Rise of Nazism in Altona, 1917–1937,*
    Social History, Popular Culture, and Politics in Germany (Ann Arbor: University of
    Michigan Press, 1998), 154–159.

4   Ursula Büttner, "Das Ende der Weimarer Republik und der Aufstieg des Nationalsozialismus
    in Hamburg," in Ursula Büttner and Werner Jochmann, eds., *Hamburg auf dem Weg ins Dritte
    Reich* (Hamburg: Landeszentrale für politische Bildung, 1983), 16.

5   Karen Hagemann, "Wir hatten mehr Notjahre als reichliche Jahre . . . Lebenshaltung und
    Hausarbeit Hamburger Arbeiterfamilien in der Weimarer Repbulik," *Journal Geschichte* 2–3
    (1991): 33.

6   Thomas Krause, *Hamburg wird braun. Der Aufstieg der NSDAP von 1921–1933* (Hamburg:
    Ergebnisse Verlag, 1987), 143.

7   Heinz-Dietrich Fischer, *Handbuch der politischen Presse in Deutschland, 1480–1980* (Düsseldorf:

Droste Verlag, 1981), 282.

8 Jürgen Fromme, *Zwischen Anpassung und Bewahrung. Das "Hamburger Fremdenblatt" im Übergang von der Weimarer Republik zum Dritten Reich. Eine politische-historische Analyse.* Beiträge zur Geschichte Hamburgs, Band 17 (Hamburg: Christmas Verlag, 1981), 15.

9 Oren Hale, *The Captive Press in the Third Reich* (Princeton, NJ: Princeton University Press, 1964), 40.

10 The Nazis did not set up an official wire service, however, until after they took power. Albert Krebs, *The Infancy of Nazism: The Memoirs of Ex-Gauleiter Albert Krebs* (New York: New Viewpoints, 1976), 102.

11 Krebs, *The Infancy of Nazis*, 89.

12 Krebs, *The Infancy of Nazis*, 92–94.

13 Krebs, *The Infancy of Nazis*, 95.

14 Krebs, *The Infancy of Nazis*, 96.

15 Ernst Baasch, *Geschichte des hamburgischen Zeitungswesens* (Hamburg: Friederichsen de Gruyter & Co., 1930), 150.

16 Baasch, *Geschichte des hamburgischen Zeitungswesens*, 128.

17 Emil Dovifat, "Die Publizistik der Weimarer Zeit," in Leonhard Reinisch, ed., *Die Zeit ohne Eigenschaften. Eine Bilanz der zwanziger Jahre* (Stuttgart: W. Kohlhammer Verlag, 1961), 124, quoted in Heinz-Dietrich Fischer, *Handbuch der politischen Presse in Deutschland, 1480–1980* (Düsseldorf: Droste Verlag, 1981), 282.

18 Conan Fischer, *The Rise of the Nazis* (Manchester, England: Manchester University Press, 2002), 69–70.

19 Sven Reichardt, *Faschistische Kampfbünde. Gewalt und Gemeinschaft im italienischen Squadrismus und in der deutschen SA* (Cologne: Böhlau Verlag, 2002), 114–119. See also Dirk Schumann, *Politische Gewalt im der Weimarer Republik. Kampf um die Strasse und Furcht vor dem Bürgerkrieg, 1918–1933* (Essen: Klartext Verlagsgesellschaft, 2001), 245–269.

20 McElligott, *Contested City*, 191–194; Pamela Swett, *Neighbors and Enemies: The Culture of Radicalism in Berlin, 1929–1933* (Cambridge, England: Cambridge University Press, 2004).

21 "Was man fürchtet," in *Hanseatische Warte*, 1st September Aufgabe, 1930.

22 StAHH, 614-2/5 *Nationalsozialistische Arbeiterpartei* (NSDAP) und ihre Gliederung B28, Böckenhauer letter to H. J. Gau Hamburg of January 6, 1933; see also StAHH, 614-2/5 *Nationalsozialistische Arbeiterpartei* (NSDAP) und ihre Gliederung B105 Band 2 and B197.

23 Archiv FZH, 11C1 Alfred Conn, 67.

24 Lothar Danner, *Ordnungspolizei Hamburg. Betrachtungen zu ihrer Geschichte 1918–1933* (Hamburg: Verlag Deutsche Polizei, 1958), 209.

25 Archiv FZH, 11C1 Alfred Conn, 93.

26 "Wie es geschah," *Hanseatische Warte*, 2nd September Aufgabe, 1930.

27 Archiv FZH, 11C1 Alfred Conn, 94.

28 "Zu den Wahlkampf-Schlägereien am Sonntag," *Hamburger Fremdenblatt*, September 9, 1930.

29 Archiv FZH, 11C1 Alfred Conn, 95.

30 Archiv FZH, 11C1 Alfred Conn, 95.

31 "Wie es geschah," *Hanseatische Warte*.

32 This work's discussion of how stormtroopers represented their public violence owes much to Pierre Bourdieu's concept of "labor of representation," which describes the

efforts groups make to construct their public identities through a combination of action and discourse. See Pierre Bourdieu, *Language and Symbolic Power* (Cambridge, England: Cambridge University Press, 1994). Other scholars have used his approach to analyze similar patterns in street demonstrations, parade violence, and political conflict. See Dominic Bryan, *Orange Parades: The Politics of Ritual, Tradition, and Control* (London: Pluto Press, 2000).

33 "Und die Polizei?" *Hanseatische Warte*, 2nd September Aufgabe, 1930.

34 Archiv FZH, 11C1 Alfred Conn, 95.

35 "Wie es geschah," *Hanseatische Warte*.

36 "Zu den Wahlkampf-Schlägereien am Sonntag," *Hamburger Fremdenblatt*.

37 "Wie es geschah," *Hanseatische Warte*.

38 "Wie es geschah," *Hanseatische Warte*.

39 Jost Hermand, *Old Dreams of a New Reich: Volkish Utopias and National Socialism* (Bloomington: University of Indiana Press, 1992).

40 Hayden White, *Metahistory: The Historical Imagination in Nineteenth Century Europe* (Baltimore: Johns Hopkins University Press, 1973), 8–9.

41 Georg Iggers, *The German Conception of History: The National Tradition of Historical Thought from Herder to the Present* (Middletown, CT: Wesleyan University Press, 1968), 6–13, 90–123.

42 Andrew Wackerfuss, "The Myth of the Unknown Stormtrooper: Selling SA Stories in the Third Reich," *Central European History* 46, no. 3 (2013): 305–306.

43 Elizabeth Castelli, *Martyrs and Memory: Early Christian Culture Making* (New York: Columbia University Press, 2004), 69–104.

44 Jay Baird, "Goebbels, Horst Wessel, and the Myth of Resurrection and Return," *Journal of Contemporary History* 17, no. 4 (1982): 633–650. See also Daniel Siemens, *The Making of a Nazi Hero: The Murder and Myth of Horst Wessel* (London and New York: I. B. Taurus, 2013).

45 "Wie unser Kamerad fiel," *Hanseatische Warte*, 2nd September Aufgabe, 1930.

46 "Heinrich Dreckmann, Truppführer Sturm 50," *Hanseatische Warte*, 2nd September Aufgabe, 1930.

47 "Heinrich Dreckmann, Truppführer Sturm 50," *Hanseatische Warte*.

48 As in Hermann Okrass, *Hamburg bleibt Rot. Das Ende eine Parole* (Hamburg: Hanseatische Verlaganstalt, 1934), 209.

49 Fromme, *Zwischen Anpassung und Bewahrung*, 81. The concept of "transmitters" comes from David Neiwert, a journalist who has studied neo-Nazi paramilitaries and rightist movements in the United States. His use of the term describes individuals, groups, or institutions that "straddle both the mainstream and extremist sectors of the right" and lend the extremist positions "a veneer of legitimacy that they would otherwise utterly lack." David Neiwert, "Rush, Newspeak, and Fascism: An Exegesis," part VIII, Official Transmitters. Available at http://www.cursor.org/stories/fascismviii.php.

50 "Communisten überfallen Nationalsozialisten," *Hamburger Fremdenblatt*, March 25, 1930.

51 "Blutige Wahlkämpfe in Hamburgs Strassen," *Hamburger Fremdenblatt*, September 8, 1930.

52 "Blutige Wahlkämpfe in Hamburgs Strassen," *Hamburger Fremdenblatt*.

53 "Blutige Wahlkämpfe in Hamburgs Strassen," *Hamburger Fremdenblatt*.

54 "Der Deutsche Reichstag radikalisiert!" *Hamburgischer Correspondent*, September 15, 1930.

55 Fromme, *Zwischen Anpassung und Bewahrung*, 100.

56 Richard Hamilton, *Who Voted for Hitler?* (Princeton, NJ: Princeton University Press, 1982), 123–128.

57 *Hanseatische Warte*, 4th September Aufgabe, 1930.

58 StAHH, 331-3 *Politische Polizei*, Band 1 10977 report of November 29, 1930.

59 "Das nazifreundliche *Fremdenblatt*," *Hamburger Echo*, October 7, 1930.

60 "Über Grabern vorwärts . . ." *Hanseatische Warte*, 3rd September Aufgabe, 1930.

61 Archiv FZH, 991 SA Opposition Gau Hamburg, Korn to Uschla, February 4, 1931.

62 "Über Grabern vorwärts . . ." *Hanseatische Warte*.

63 "Über Grabern vorwärts . . ." *Hanseatische Warte*.

64 "Über Grabern vorwärts . . ." *Hanseatische Warte*.

65 "Zu dem Wahlkampf-Schlägereien am Sonntag," *Hamburger Fremdenblatt*.

66 "Geht zur Wahl—der Stadt seid Ihr!" *Hamburger Fremdenblatt*, September 13, 1930.

67 "Die Reichstagwahlen in Gross-Hamburg. Der Sieg der Extremisten," *Hamburger Fremdenblatt*, September 14, 1930.

68 Ulf Böttcher, "Die SA in Hamburg, 1922–1934. Politische Rolle und innere Struktur" (Examenarbeit at the University of Hamburg, 1982),17.

69 Ursula Büttner and Werner Jochmann, *Hamburg auf dem Weg ins Dritte Reich. Entwicklungsjahre 1931–1933* (Hamburg: Landeszentrale für politische Bildung, 1985), 16, 24–25.

70 Ursula Büttner, "Der Aufsteig der NSDAP," in Josef Schmid, ed., *Hamburg im "Dritten Reich"* (Göttingen: Wallstein, 2005), 46.

71 "Unter dem roten Sturmfahne des Nationalsozialisten," *Hanseatische Warte*, 4th September Aufgabe, 1930.

72 "Nach dem Sieg der Kampf," *Hanseatische Warte*, 1st October Aufgabe, 1930.

73 As in the *Echo*'s October 3 report, "Nationalsozialistische Rache," in which a group of SA men marching to a Wandsbek campsite was hit by a truck, stormed the vehicle, and beat the occupants.

74 Krebs, *The Infancy of Nazis*, 68.

75 Krebs, *The Infancy of Nazis*, 101.

76 Hale, *The Captive Press*, 59.

77 Richard Bessel, *Political Violence and the Rise of Nazism: The Storm Troopers in Eastern Germany, 1925–1934* (New Haven, CT: Yale University Press, 1984), 57-74; Fischer, *Stormtroopers*, 159–169.

78 StAHH, 614-2/5 *Nationalsozialistische Arbeiterpartei (NSDAP) und ihre Gliederung* B220 Lutze to Untergruppe Hamburg letter of November 9, 1931.

COMMUNITY AND VIOLENCE

By 1930, the SA had cohered into the form that entered historical memory. The growing number of stormtroopers, seeing themselves as besieged outsiders, relied on one another for physical, economic, and psychological protection from the Great Depression. They had used public violence to elevate themselves to a leadership position on the nationalist right, and they had also positioned themselves to expand the ranks of the right by drawing in middle- and even working-class voters who had been radicalized by the economic disaster. The SA supported Nazi goals by emphasizing community, which they presented as a cure for the country's allegedly shattered identity. Nazi recruiting strategy thus functioned through social networking as much as ideological indoctrination.

Seeing Nazi mobilization in this way shows how its various subgroups overlapped, but it also reveals how imperfectly these groups coexisted. Despite its members' significant shared ideological and social backgrounds, the SA could never fully unite the economically marginalized neighborhoods with the elite merchant districts, the majority Protestants with the dissident pagans, or the laddish brawlers with the would-be family men. During the *Kampfzeit*, political and literal warfare kept these groups cohesive, and the SA proved relatively adept at using its institutions as the thread that stitched together its various social fabrics. In its peak pre-power years, the SA concentrated its efforts on three sources of social unity: family, church, and comrades. It combined these into a self-contradictory but effective politics of domesticity, in which association with women, children, and religion sanitized the violent stormtroopers of the barracks hall. This combination of community and violence attracted and integrated more recruits into the SA as reliable members of the Nazi movement.

Family Instability and the Growth of the SA

Many of the short autobiographies the SA asked its stormtroopers to write contained a common story.[1] It told the tale of a young single man trying his best to establish himself professionally while lacking support from an absent or degraded family, and therefore being continually thwarted by the Depression until he found economic and spiritual succor in the stormtrooper movement. This new "family" would sustain him until the day it achieved political victory, which would renew the nation and allow him to find his feet as the respectable family man he had always wanted to be.

The life of *Scharführer* Paul B. provides a typical example. In his SA auto-biography, Paul B. related a personal history that had "led me over hard streets."[2] He was born in 1904, the son of a merchant whose Hamburg firm traded glassware and porcelain "in all corners of the world." This classic Hamburg father died in 1919, however, and the family's inheritance vanished in the inflation of 1923. Paul's older brother, a naval officer in WWI, had been held for 2½ years in an English POW camp, where his health was broken.

Upon his release, the brother spent two years of "unspeakable suffering" in a Hamburg hospital before dying in 1921. When Paul's next eldest brother died from a botched operation in 1924, only Paul remained to head the household. He was 21 years old. Fortunately, he had apprenticed in his father's profession, so his father's contacts in Hamburg's merchant community were able to place him at a successful import firm. This hopeful future came to an abrupt end, however, when the American stock market crash cut off the flow of goods from the United States. Paul was let go, and he found no work for the next four years. His remaining family being unable to help him, he found a surrogate home in nationalist politics, with which he had flirted since the age of 17. His militia group joined the SA en masse once the SA agreed to keep the comrades together. In the SA, Paul later wrote, he saw the best chance to further a set of political principles that he explicitly connected with his departed father, whom Paul seemed to believe had been unable to serve in the imperial military because he was an orphan. The orphan story was unlikely but emotionally powerful, a fatherly legacy of denial that came full circle once the son came into the SA's embrace. While the father had been unable to serve the state as he wished, the *Vaterland*'s weakness and its inability to defend Hamburg's commercial interests had foiled the man's peaceful efforts to provide for his children. Paul, a second-generation orphan, was now determined to redeem the family legacy by joining the most militant nationalist faction, which he believed would secure economic independence for his family and absolve the past generation's defeat.

Paul B. was a stormtrooper typical of those too young to have fought in World War I, who had lost fathers and older brothers to the conflict but, because of a lack of firsthand experience in the trenches, retained a belief in the power of will and warfare to secure personal and national goals.

Even older stormtroopers had often taken a similar path to the SA, having experienced a certain stunting of their lifelines due to the political and economic pressures of the times. Karl B., born in 1895, also claimed in his

SA autobiography to have "worked without interruption for the national renewal."[3] He, like Arthur Böckenhauer and other prominent SA officers, was a policeman whose enmity for socialism stemmed from the revolutionary behavior of the KPD. After 1923, Karl B. became increasingly radical himself, until a 1924 confrontation with Communists led to his dismissal from police ranks. He described the incident to the SA as "having gone too far in self-defense in my capacity as a police officer"—in other words, for abusing his authority by assaulting a suspect.[4] His firing began his long slide down the socioeconomic ladder, which led him to commit further criminal acts. During a dispute with his landlord—an argument that he blamed on her Jewishness but in fact stemmed from his inability to pay the rent—he broke a window, threw its fragments at her, and was eventually convicted of destruction of property. Upon his release from jail the next year, he was immediately sent back for having unsuccessfully suborned perjury in his previous trial. Karl B.'s story shows the reality of the connection many stormtroopers made between their economic and moral fates: financial difficulties led stormtroopers into personal and social disputes that brought them into conflict with their community and with the law.

The files of the Hamburg Justice Department are filled with crimes that SA men committed in the 1920s and 1930s. Some of these crimes had overtly political motives and could not be blamed on economic troubles. Even in such cases, however, economics influenced patterns of criminality—unemployment could turn a mild fine into significant jail time. Hans Friedrich L. had let an underage friend handle his unlicensed pistol. He was convicted of an illegal weapons violation in June 1930 and sentenced to a 100 RM fine, which long unemployment left him unable to pay. He thus faced ten days in jail. Hans Friedrich's SA-sponsored lawyer wrote the court to petition for more time to pay the fine, in light of the lasting harm a jail sentence could do to the young man's future. The lawyer said Hans Friedrich hoped to find work at his former firm, which would not be possible if the court send him to jail:

> The convicted has already been told that the possibility to work at his old place of employment would end if he had to serve his punishment. Without this position, the convicted would be sentenced to further unemployment of indeterminable duration, which would further endanger his character and make even more difficult his resumption of an orderly life.[5]

Stormtroopers thus feared the Depression's effects not just on their pocket-book but on their character and family stability.

These fears were justified. Economic woes drove stormtroopers, like many down-on-their-luck men of any era, to commit a wide variety of financial crimes. The Hamburg justice files, as well as SA records from a 1934–1935 review of personnel, record hundreds of cases of embezzle-ment, fraud, extortion, and counterfeiting, as well as thefts both petty and grand.[6] But as was the case with sexual irregularities within SA ranks, the Kampfzeit SA met these criminals with understanding—provided the re-cruits arrived with the requisite attitude of pugnacious nationalist solidarity. As Böckenhauer said of Karl B.'s case in 1935, in the context of clearing Karl's criminal record so the SA could secure him a job, "He was merely, even if in an illegal way, protecting his own skin."[7] The phrase well encapsulates the SA's attitude toward its own political and personal misdeeds: a claim of self-defense, however thin, sufficed to forgive any crime. The SA had been born of a need to physically defend Nazi speakers, but stormtroopers who found themselves in personal, financial, or legal jeopardy extended their concept of self-defense to include family members and the community at large. This expansive definition conveniently excused a wide range of crim-inal behavior.

Karl B. received sympathy from his comrades because he was not only looking out for "his own skin" but for the welfare of his dependents—his wife, in this case. To the stormtroopers, the worst aspect of the economic depression, besides its obvious physical miseries such as hunger and home-lessness, was its degenerative effect on the German family. This theme played a powerful role in the works the SA published about itself, which showed stormtroopers plunged into broken family situations that only their political victory could resolve.

A 1934 work of stormtrooper history, *Ehrenbuch der SA* (*The SA Book of Honor*), presented two Hamburg stormtroopers as archetypes of young men shaped by the impact the Depression had on their families. The first had lost his father as a boy, after which he could only look on helplessly as his mother experienced a moral decline. She began hanging around bars and eventually took a much younger boyfriend, a Communist who would disappear for days at a time to conduct "terror actions" against National Socialists.[8] Both the boy and the mother were damaged by the spell of this violent, oversexed Communist: "The boy saw how his mother was used as a sex object by her boyfriend, which fully ruined him even if his youth and inexperience could not understand all the complications, the spiritual and physical effects that such a relationship entailed."[9] The mother soon stopped caring for her son, and the story hinted that she became a prostitute. Mother and son now lived in a tavern in a state of degeneracy. The boy had no chance at a real education or a stable family life, but he found salvation in the baker's son down the street, who had lied about his age to get into the SA and had given the fallen woman's son his first glimpse of the SA uniform. The boy's "longing for purity," the story related, then led him naturally into the SA.[10] The following years featured a chronicle of violence, combat, and electioneering typical of stormtrooper lives, especially those in contested Communist neighborhoods. The young man's new political orientation alienated him from his mother and her Communist friends, and he eventually left home to live with the stormtroopers. On the day of the Nazi takeover, the story concluded, he returned to the tavern in triumph. He entered in uniform, gave a loud "Heil Hitler," and none dared attack him as they had in the past. This boy's story, which had begun with his father's death and his mother's descent into sexual and political depravity, ended with the boy using the Hitler uniform to impose his "natural sense of purity" over the degraded dens of his youth.

Given the prominence of lost fathers in stormtroopers' biographies and mentalities, it is not surprising that the stormtrooper heroes of novels and films took over the role of family provider.[11] Another case from the *Ehrenbuch* tells the story of a young bank teller who had just begun his career when the inflation of 1923 wiped out his earnings and eventually his job. The elder bank employees—who represented a discredited older generation and its failure to deal with new realities—had little to offer their younger colleagues but mockery: "The youths of the bank came to the older employees, who stood clueless concerning the worthlessness of money, laughed at their difficulties, and recommended they put away paper marks or speculate on the market."[12] The poor young banker, who lost his place as a promising aspirant to Hamburg's commercial society, degenerated into renting a room in "a miserable alley" with a Communist family that had "criminal inclinations."[13] The family at first seemed to treat him as one of their own, but he soon discovered that the daughters were wanton and lewd and that the parents saw him as a meal ticket. When his savings eventually vanished, "the family's love ceased, and turned to dim hate."[14] After this false Communist family failed him, his true family intervened. His brother, a house painter, gave him a job that offered salvation not only economically but also politically and even spiritually—for here he met his first SA man. This stormtrooper "had something like a holy fire in him," and he set the fallen banker on the path to "a fully new spiritual world."[15] The hardships of poverty and unemployment had introduced the youth to the dark family life of the Communist underclass. It had also caused him to recognize the causal chain that had so plagued him: the political situation had destroyed the German economy, and the devastated economy in turn undermined the German family. Through the fortunate intervention of his brother and the stormtrooper, the former banker discovered in Nazism a way to recover from his personal troubles, rebuild his city's economy, and found his own family:

> He had raced through the years, and sometimes the great shadows of his life suddenly became all too clear, and gripped him by the throat, and he could no longer help it and drank the whole night through. But that became much more seldom—yes, it stopped altogether as he met a girl, had a child, and saw the small creature fidget and laugh. He sees in him the youth of the Third Reich, and . . . he knows this child will never know danger, just as he knows that his superiors will step up and make sure that his convictions vanish from the record, as the broken and overthrown system had vanished.[16]

Stories the SA told about stormtroopers before and after the Nazi takeover presented the men as having struggled to find work, to marry their girlfriends, and to raise a family. The Weimar Republic's notorious economic instability had made these goals difficult to pursue. The stormtroopers therefore blamed the republican system, "parliamentarism," and socialism for Germany's inability to defend its borders, pursue an independent trade policy, and build the German economy to provide for German families. They continued to blame "the system" for pushing them into a life of crime, and then embraced National Socialism as a way to build a new foundation for their own individual lives.

Biographical data from the SA personnel files support these idealized self-images to some extent. The vast majority of the stormtroopers were single during the Kampfzeit—71.8 percent of the Hamburg stormtroopers whose marital status can be identified in a sample of the personnel files did not marry before 1933.[17] About a third of these men remained single even into the late 1930s. The nearly 30 percent of stormtroopers who were married before 1933 tended to have been born earlier than the majority and to have started their families during the marriage boom that occurred in the first years after the Great War. These married men also tended to join the SA later than their bachelor comrades. Stormtrooper marriage rates fluctuated through the rest of the 1920s due to economic instability, before rebounding in a wave of stormtrooper marriages after the Nazi's takeover of power in 1933–1935. Stormtrooper childbirth rates fell along a similar curve, with an especially sharp drop in 1930, when the Depression began. In short, these data show how economic problems, marriage rates, and stormtrooper membership combined to promote a young bachelor cohort of stormtroopers whose numbers were more than double those of the smaller group of older married members. In other words, economic woes and the barracks-hall SA lifestyle discouraged stormtroopers from starting families and discouraged family men from being stormtroopers.

The SA as an organization also believed that political struggle and political identity developed out of individual family situations. While it kept no systematic data on whether stormtroopers were married, had children, or were fatherless, the personnel records it did keep consistently contain accounts of family troubles as they inevitably arose. The prevalence of family woes in the SA's administrative files testifies to the group's concern with the state of the stormtrooper family. The files also provide several concrete cases of the classic myths stormtroopers held dear about themselves, their comrades, and their families.

Hans Friedrich L., the stormtrooper who faced jail time for nonpayment of a firearms fine, would have been able to avoid jail if his family had not been so destitute. His father, the SA's letter informed the state, earned only 140 RM a month, with which he had to support his sick wife, unemployed son, and underage daughter.[18] That sum represented only slightly more than half of what a working-class family needed to support itself at that time.[19] As in this case, young stormtroopers often could not count on their families to bail them out of financial, political, or personal trouble, and therefore any problem in one of these realms quickly bled over into the other two. In 1928, SA man Karl V. met a girl shortly before his 21st birthday. Six months later he learned she was pregnant—a "fait accompli," he called it, implying entrapment and victimhood for himself.[20] "Despite my parents' insistent warnings," he later wrote, "I decided, as an upstanding and perhaps naïve young man, to accept the consequences and marry her."[21] He joined the SA shortly afterward, feeling the call to protect his young family. However, his National Socialist activity got him fired from his job, and he had to move his family to his in-laws' apartment. Here the difficulties continued, as the young stormtrooper refused to give up his SA duties even while remaining unemployed, which the father-in-law, "a card-carrying member of the SPD," opposed on both economic and ideological grounds. The situation eventually destroyed the young stormtrooper's family, when he and his father-in-law came to blows during an argument: "I saw myself obligated to present my wife a choice between myself and her parents. When her decision fell against me, I saw myself obligated to leave the house."[22] Karl's wife convinced him to take responsibility for the ensuing divorce, a suggestion he says he did not resist because of his "spiritual collapse."[23] Taking the blame left him open to her retroactive financial demands when he found work after 1933, using the SA's connections. Karl V.'s file concerns his failure to pay child support for the years between the divorce and her demands, of which he claimed to be unaware. He claimed that she had waited until the moment he was back on his feet to destroy him and the new family he was trying to found.[24] As Karl V. reminded the now-Nazified court,

> My monstrous debt-load came, in addition to other disadvantage, not only through unemployment but also from my many years of active service for the Nazi Party. I must also say that [while living in Hamburg] as a citizen of Danzig I received no social assistance for months at a time, so that I had to rely on donations and loans from comrades to keep my head above water.[25]

Karl V.'s case combined many elements of a fallen manhood narrative that reinforced mutual dependency between the SA and its stormtroopers. He had come to Hamburg in the first place as part of a German exodus from the Danzig corridor, which Germany had to surrender to Poland after the Great War. Germany's failure to defend its borders had therefore disrupted Karl V.'s life and created a sense of victimization that he carried over to his later personal and financial problems. He described himself, as did most stormtroopers in similar situations, as an upstanding but perhaps naïve young man who was merely trying to live up to his obligations. When his political duties conflicted with his family responsibilities, he justified his choice of Party over family using the SA's preferred terms of service and duty, as seen in his repeated use of the phrase, "I saw myself obligated." In the end, the SA helped him "keep his head above water" until the Nazi takeover of the state granted the stormtroopers the power and influence to defend their own interests.

Karl V. claimed in his letter to the court that, if not for the need to tend to his new wife's poor constitution, "there would be nothing else for me but to end my terrible distress with a bullet."[26] This was not an idle threat: suicide was an intellectual fascination among writers of the Weimar period, but for the Kampfzeit SA it was also an ever-present danger.[27] Some storm-troopers who faced both family and financial distress took their own lives. Stormtrooper Heinz Grosser shot himself on June 19, 1931. A report by his commander explained:

> The reasons lay partially in family burdens and partially in econom-ic misery. The father is a drinker who had left his family in the lurch, while the mother is in a sanatorium. Otherwise, he was also unem-ployed and received not the slightest support; his love life, the press has reported, drove him to his final end.[28]

Grosser was "always a good and true comrade," and the SA regretted his death.

The SA's reluctant support of stormtrooper Pawlowski a few months later can be seen in the context of financial threats to the family. The police had arrested Pawlowski in late 1931 for embezzlement and theft. He had already been convicted in the past of fraud and forgery; this history, plus his attempt to flee the arresting officer, caused his bail to be set at 200 RM. Dr. Walter Raeke, the SA's main lawyer in Hamburg, investigated the matter to determine if the SA could assist. His clerk visited Pawlowski's home, and while Pawlowski himself "didn't make a bad impression, . . . the impres-sion made by his family (wife, mother) is entirely bad."[29] The SA leaders in charge of the case, "in light of the poor impression made by the family," which had made "no real effort to raise the bond themselves," considered denying the petition. Yet Raeke had already taken it upon himself to supply the bond out of sympathy for the man's wife, who had been hospitalized after a troubled childbirth.[30] Pawlowski in return praised Raeke for providing a Christmas miracle. "I would like to convey my personal thanks to you," he wrote Raeke, "as well as wishes for a merry Christmas from myself and my family. I am already so indebted to you in thanks; I will in the future conduct myself as a true German man."[31] The SA assisted Pawlowski reluctantly: his crimes were not political and therefore seemed self-interested, while his family seemed lethargic and lacking motivation to better itself. Such families did not fit the SA's self-image. But Pawlowski had been a stormtrooper since 1927, and in the end the SA intervened to protect his family when economic hardship threatened to destroy it.[32] In return, the SA received Pawlowski's pledge of loyalty and his promise to behave according to the standards of a "true German man"—the definition of which, of course, Pawlowski had learned from the SA itself. In short, the economic and moral troubles of the German family may have posed a crisis for individual stormtroopers, but they presented an opportunity for the organization.

SA *Heime* and Kitchens: Social Assistance and Ideological Conditioning

As the SA grew in strength, it increasingly provided extensive social services that ultimately included legal aid, health insurance, food, and lodging. By doing so, the SA made good on its promise to deliver "socialism of the deed" and to rescue the movement's men from character- and family-endangering poverty. Stormtrooper leaders knew that such programs could also create dependency, which in turn bred loyalty. In the SA Heime (hostels) and kitchens, where many stormtroopers came to live, eat, and otherwise organize their daily lives, the SA offered a homogeneous social space in which stormtroopers could train one another in ideological and behavioral codes that matched the group's conception of German manhood. This self-organized training came organically, through the mentorship of respected comrades who provided models of behavior. It was therefore more immersive and experiential than it was formally educational, although formal lectures could still be effective if delivered by those inside the stormtroopers' trusted world.

Personal contact and an immersive environment attracted many working- and middle-class men into the movement. The radicalizing effect the Great Depression had on the economically threatened could have drawn them to any number of extremist parties. As Richard Hamilton noted in his study of the Nazi rise in neighboring Kiel, the parties relied instead on "mediating forces" to attract potential recruits.[33] In Hamburg, these forces included an array of local institutions, like Lutheran churches, neighborhood associations, newspapers, family networks, and organizational cells within the city's most prominent seaborne industries. The SA, because of its extensive social services, thus became one of the Nazis' most powerful attracting forces. As the legal efforts of Dr. Korn and Dr. Raeke on behalf of accused SA criminals clearly demonstrated, aiding a stormtrooper earned his enduring loyalty. In 1930, the SA expanded its social assistance into a comprehensive network of institutions that provided unemployed young men with food, shelter, and a surrogate family that would protect them from economic upheaval.

The Hamburg SA had tried since 1925 to provide for comrades injured in battle. Soon after the SA's re-founding that year, a group of nationalist paramilitaries had come together to create a group insurance plan through which members could pay 1 RM quarterly to ensure that they had healthcare benefits if they were injured during official political activities. The SA, however, soon decided to create its own plan, as other nationalist groups were notoriously unstable and always covetous of one another's members, and associating too closely with rivals would therefore pose risks. This strategy had the advantage of not mixing SA finances with those of other groups. Going it alone also allowed the SA to develop a more comprehensive plan than the scheme offered by the other paramilitaries. The SA's plan not only insured members for injuries incurred during party events, it also paid out for injuries of any kind suffered while traveling to and from political events. This was an important element of the plan, since a high percentage of political attacks happened at those times, when comrades traveled in smaller groups. By offering this broader frame of support, the SA showed itself both more aware of and more concerned with threats to its members' well-being.

Once SA leaders arranged the details and secured the financing, they took the plan to Hitler himself, who backed the arrangement and allowed the SA to promote the program under his name. In March 1929, stormtroopers received letters titled, "What Many Still Don't Know," which informed them of the plan's benefits, as well as the horrific consequences risked by anyone who failed to take advantage of the SA's assistance. Many local stormtroopers had already signed up for the plan, which in Hamburg was managed by *Sturmführer* Bisschopink, until Conn drove him from the city because of his homosexuality. That unseemly side of the story was of course not mentioned in the letter, which instead described the great care the plan gave to its early adopters. Most of these men lived in contested or Communist-dominated areas, but many SA men who lived in less-disputed areas had not yet signed up. That, the letter said, was a mistake:

> Many members have not yet taken up this offer because they assume that the SA Insurance pays out only for attacks by Marxists, and that in their neighborhood things have not yet reached that depth. This is an error! SA Insurance pays out not only for injuries from attacks, but also for all accidents taking place while traveling to or from a Party event.[34]

The letter cited cases of two women Party members. One had been hit by a car while returning home from a meeting; she was bedridden and unable to work for two weeks. Thanks to her SA Insurance, however, for the affordable price of 20 Pfennig a month she received 42 RM in benefits. The other woman had been attending a meeting at which "a tumult suddenly erupted"; she was caught in the melee and bedridden for eight days.[35] The use of women to convey the need for insurance told the SA men that politically related injuries posed a constant threat no matter how geographically or socially insulated one might be. If even women fell victim to Marxist attacks and car accidents, a stormtrooper who lived in Hamburg's most heated neighborhoods could only imagine what he risked. The letter urged all SA men to join in order to protect themselves and their families. The appeal seems to have borne fruit: by April 1929, 408 Hamburg stormtroopers had signed up—almost every stormtrooper in the city.[36]

Stormtroopers needed financial support not only when they were victims of catastrophic injuries but also in their daily efforts to feed and clothe themselves. These daily struggles had in fact occurred before 1929, as many young stormtroopers had never been in a stable financial position. Hamburg attracted many youths from the countryside and from other German cities who hoped to find work in Hamburg's shipping industry. Those with existing Nazi ties often contacted the SA about housing upon their arrival, as Ernst Blücher did when he moved from Kiauschen in East Prussia. Before leaving Kiauschen, he wrote to then SA general Böckenhauer to inquire about lodging for himself and his sister; he seems to have believed that he could live at the SA's main office. But the SA of that time was in no position to help, and Böckenhauer regretfully replied that the SA had no lodgings. The SA could only offer to try to find a member to take Blücher in until he found his own room.[37]

When the Depression began, the Party and the SA hoped to move beyond the ad hoc measures seen in Blücher's case. They came to the stormtroopers' aid not only because they genuinely wanted to help, but also because they relished the propaganda value. For these same reasons, the SA established a series of soup kitchens and group homes called SA Heime. Although any translation of "Heime" would be imprecise, "hostels" best conveys the idea that these places catered to young, poor, unemployed, and potentially transient young men who sought a place to eat and sleep safely among trusted comrades.[38] Conn established Hamburg's first SA Heim in October 1930.[39] He gathered needed materials largely from individual donors, which he solicited through classified ads in the Nazi paper:

> For the erection of an SA Heim for unemployed SA men we require: wool blankets, bed sheets, electric lights, tables, chairs, cabinets, curtains, and draperies. Party members or ideological friends who can make such materials available are asked to contact the SA office at [Grosse] Bleichen 30 either by letter or telephone.[40]

The idea quickly gained popularity within the movement. A Party member named Tesch wrote to SA headquarters in November offering to rent his three-story house to the SA for use as a second Heim. The SA, while thanking him for his offer, declined. The group could not afford the rent, wrote the responding adjutant, since "the already great financial strains on the SA at present cannot bear more expenses."[41] Furthermore, he wrote, "the rooms in their present condition are not suited to SA purposes, and the costs of reconstruction would be considerable." The latter reason showed a substantive rather than a merely financial objection to this offer: the house was a traditional single-family row house with separate rooms for sleeping and studying, not a group home for young men who wanted to live in the manner of a military barracks. The SA wanted to give its comrades a place to sleep, but it needed one that held true to its vision of an appropriate living environment. It did not want to run a hotel in which each stormtrooper received a private room; it wanted to offer a communal living situation that would encourage social bonding and mutual reliance among its men. The men wanted this as well, being attracted to a life spent among comrades. Tesch's home was therefore "out of the question," but the SA encouraged him to approach the group again the next year, in case its finances improved and they could afford to remodel along communal lines.[42]

Unable to extend the promising Heime system due to a lack of money, the SA instead established soup kitchens in early 1931. These provided comrades with hot meals for the affordable price of 10 to 20 cents.[43] Of a kitchen in Bramfeld that had opened on March 6, the Hamburger Tageblatt wrote, "In a time when some men don't know where their next warm meal should come from, this kitchen is a vision of the future for the many who are down on their luck."[44] The opening of these kitchens helped those they fed, but they also helped the Party propagandize its generosity, which it called "socialism of the deed." The phrase embodied the Nazis' effort to cast themselves as practical, involved problem-solvers who worked with local communities, in contrast to the other titular socialist parties, whom the Nazis accused of using socialism as an over-intellectualized cover for their indifference and failure to solve public problems.[45] While it is true that the SPD was older, more intellectual, and more inclined toward technocratic and systemic socialism rather than direct local action, both it and the KPD did try to offer practical assistance in ways similar to the Nazis. The KPD, for instance, set up "Red Help" soup kitchens, as well as a small number of "canteens" that met with little success.[46] Nazi newspapers, if they ever mentioned such efforts, discussed only their failure, which the Nazis took as confirmation that the KPD was less interested in actually helping the impoverished masses than in politicizing the unemployed for its own purposes.

The Tageblatt highlighted Nazi social assistance as the heroic efforts of socially conscious citizens, who stepped in to correct the alleged failures of socialist governance. Stories of SA social work often used gripping narratives to win the audience's emotions. One such example, a Tageblatt story that appeared on April 16, 1931, with the typical stormtrooper title, "Fight Hunger in Our Ranks," began in medias res, during a triumphant Hitler rally that had taken place in Hamburg four months earlier. "A thick and hot air lay over the meeting," the reporter wrote, "of the type that only emerges when thousands stand pressed together indoors."[47] Stormtroopers lined the front of the stage, "German men holding in hard fists motionless staves of oak." However, the classic stormtrooper image hid something that was amiss beneath the hard bodies of these party fighters:

Along this front a single red flag made itself seen. First a slight waver, then it began to sink. An attendant sprung in and swiftly grabbed the banner, so that it would not fall into the dust of the hall. The flag-carrier sank to the ground unconscious.

The haggard face had grown pale. The lips almost white. We know these outer signs. When one suffers from hunger, when the mouth has nothing to bite all day long, this color comes.

The *Führer* clenched his teeth. He himself, a soldier and worker, knows what hunger is: he knows the embarrassing pain and knows too how quickly hunger, the adversity of the belly, weakens everything else.[48]

Among the stormtroopers' many enemies, hunger was perhaps their greatest fear—not for its physical unpleasantness, which they claimed to embrace as ennobling, but for its effects on their masculine self-image. It indicated an embarrassing inability to establish oneself as self-sufficient, self-reliant, and worthy of authority over self and others. Worse, it left obvious physical markers on the masculine body that displayed these failures to the public. As in the *Tageblatt* account, hunger could transform a strong, upright warrior into a pallid, weakened husk. Even if he remained steadfast in inner conviction, the "outer signs" of hunger would weaken his body and leave him in "embarrassing pain," ending in his utter helplessness. Fortunately, the *Tageblatt* proclaimed, Hitler and his fellow Nazi leaders not only understood the plight of their men, they also had a plan to combat it:

One day came the order: The local groups have established SA Kitchens. These kitchens are now everywhere. Every day thousands of our brown shirts and their families go to these kitchens, where selfless women have prepared a hearty, nutritious soup.

Farmers send free potatoes, meat, and vegetables. Members of the NS Automobile Corps transport the goods. NS grocers provide the spices. NS women cook. None seek reward. Nor thanks. A striking proof of our will. And the hungry SA man needs not offer great words of thanks. This is how we seek to help the hungry workers of the fist. It's not much, but we do what we can.[49]

The article's note of humility rings false when compared to the great role the SA kitchens and Heime played in Nazi propaganda. This article, and others like it, exaggerated the programs' ubiquity, at least in the years before the 1933 Nazi takeover of power, after which the Nazis could amplify their efforts using state resources. The "workers of the fist" formulation was yet another SA subversion of socialist rhetoric, which often lauded "workers of the hand and head"—the lower- and middle-class voters that most parties competed to represent. The Nazis now added the stormtroopers as a third socially productive constituency that had been ill served by republican governance. Despite the misrepresentations of this framework, the article did accurately refer to the coordinated efforts needed to open and run the kitchens. The "socialism of the deed" on display was not just about feeding the stormtroopers but about demonstrating unity and common purpose among farmers, drivers, grocers, housewives, and other sectors of a population that felt increasingly fragmented and isolated in the turbulent times. This idea of unity and purpose attracted citizens who feared the social effects of the chaotic postwar and Depression years just as much as it directly assisted those who needed services.

The SA kitchens grew steadily throughout 1931–1932. They also expanded early on to include the Nazis' preferred "workers of the head," students belonging to the National Socialist Student Union (NSDStB). This group had had difficulty attracting and retaining members, especially in Hamburg, and the Party now hoped to adopt the SA's successful recruiting techniques.[50] Previous attempts to recruit students, such as the group's short-lived rebranding as the SA University Group in 1929, had met with strong resistance from students who felt that anti-intellectual thugs had no place at a German institution of higher learning. Eventually, however, the emergence of the SA's strong networks of social support began to lead students, always a financially marginal group, to see the SA in a more palatable light. Although the name change did not stick, dual membership grew, and by 1932 about half the members of the NSDStB also claimed membership in the SA.[51] For a short time, the Party tried to make SA membership mandatory for all Nazi-affiliated students. This merger, however, was also short-lived, since the all-encompassing demands of SA service meshed poorly with the competing commitments of student life. After all, as shown by the SA's emphasis on communal living and eating, Party leaders and prominent stormtroopers all agreed that the SA offered members an immersive way of life.

The ideal image of the SA as lifestyle became more concrete in June 1931, when leaders finally found enough money to open a second Heim, which they financed through donations and by charging a small amount of rent. The Heim combined the advantages of a meeting tavern, a residence, and a soup kitchen, and it therefore streamlined the SA's social services in one location.[52] The model proved successful and spread throughout the city. How many ultimately existed, in Hamburg or elsewhere, can no longer be determined. The Communist paper *Hamburger Volkszeitung* counted 28 local SA Heime in 1932, mostly in working-class areas hit hard by the Depression.[53] Given that 58 percent of stormtroopers were unemployed that year, the demand was greater than the SA could meet.[54] Only after the takeover of power could the Hamburg SA establish enough Heime to accommodate all would-be residents. During the Kampfzeit it often had to send its men to the Altona SA, which resented having to feed and clothe the "wandering SA men" it continually found at its doorstep.[55]

The total benefit to the regional movement, however, more than repaid the local costs to Altona. SA Heime drew potential recruits into the movement for its practical benefits, then once the recruits were on the inside made them feel welcome with full stomachs, a warm bed, and emotional support from a tightknit masculine community. Nazi social support through charitable institutions, when contrasted with the failure of SPD and KPD efforts, became a central point of contrast between the SA and its main political rivals. The difference showed, the stormtroopers argued, that Nazi aid to the poor would help not only their material condition but their social and moral state as well.

SA Heime became legendary in the stormtroopers' understanding of themselves and of the Nazi movement. Living together, sharing experiences, and sharing the necessities of life taught SA men true camaraderie, as the *Ehrenbuch* described:

> If an SA man has only one cigarette, he breaks it in two and gives his fellow a half. Or they smoke it together. That's thriftier, because only one stump remains. A third comrade then gets the stump for his pipe. And so three men get their enjoyment, and three are content.[56]

Stormtroopers who lived together would repeat the cigarette sharing ritual many times throughout the day. Its essential elements also held true for food, drink, and sleeping arrangements—all the aspects of daily life that the stormtroopers experienced together. Sharing meant more than just providing for each man during a time when goods were scarce. It also showed the stormtrooper's true personality and revealed whether he had the sense of true camaraderie so valued by the organization and its men:

> Above all one notices immediately who is a real comrade. If some-one gives ungenerously, if someone provides perhaps only because he thinks he is going to need something for himself later that after-noon, he thereby makes himself unloved and soon must move out.[57]

Descriptions of SA life after the takeover like this one from the *Ehrenbuch* assured readers that selfishness "happened only seldom."[58] In reality, how-ever, SA communal spaces had an extensive record of petty thefts. Most potential members chose to ignore this reality, remain idealistic, and accept the Party's positive propaganda. Moreover, the SA's zealous prosecution and expulsion of anyone caught stealing from a comrade reassured the storm-troopers that the group remained true to the ideal. As the literature said, anyone failing to live up to the ideal had never really been a stormtrooper in the first place.

The SA's social-welfare institutions trained the stormtroopers to asso-ciate being well provided for with having fought hard for the movement. Food, clothing, and housing were not charity but payment for their tireless activity and physical struggle. This association was a key part of a storm-trooper mentality that decried reliance on the socialist state's benefits, which stormtroopers alleged to be destructive of a self-reliant work ethic. Yet the stormtroopers themselves relied on charity. They therefore described their own acceptance of benefits as a fair bargain in which they earned their keep by working hard for a small reward.

Stormtrooper poet Heinrich Anacker, who set his verses in the Kampfzeit milieu, often illustrated the links between work, militarism, and humble re-ward. In "Peas with Bacon," stormtroopers returned to their Heim after a hard day's march to be rewarded with the titular favorite, if humble, meal (see next page).

The poem was in some ways a typical soldiers' song, complaining about the officer's demands yet ending with a satisfying reward. Here, howev-er, the poet linked military patterns with daily life in ways that traditional soldier songs, set during wartime, did not. This story took place during a civil war for German streets. The "goulash cannon," a type of wheeled soup

LOOSE TRANSLATION	ORIGINAL
Today our leader wore us out,	Heut hat der Staf uns recht geschlaucht,
'Til all our bones were shaking,	Das alle Knochen klirrten,
He really ran us all about—	Und hat uns auch mal angehaucht—
But something good is making;	Nun lassen wir uns bewirten;
First dirt and fleas	Nach Drill und Dreck
Then bacon and peas,	Gibt's Erbsen mit Speck,
Boom! From the goulash cannon!	Bumm! Aus der Gulaschkanone![59]

cauldron used to feed troops in wartime, reinforced the cross-connection, but it now carried extra meaning as a concrete image of how the warring parties weaponized food and sustenance (Figure 5.1). As the poem proceeds, its later stanzas reveal a disturbing narrative pattern. While earlier stanzas were situated in the daily struggles of the local neighborhood, later stanzas move to an actual battlefield, where stormtroopers-turned-soldiers again enjoy their favorite soup. In the final stanza they eat peas and bacon in "soldiers' heaven" as an eternal reward for a lifetime of struggle in service to the Party. As the poem makes clear in verse, men living together in the SA not only received peas, bacon, and other physically nourishing foodstuff; they also ingested a militant ideology that preached combative struggle against neighborhood political rivals, naturalized the idea that local conflict would eventually expand into future wars between nations, and promised transcendent reward and ascension into a Valhalla-like afterlife. In this afterlife, the stormtrooper's heavenly father would provide eternal reward, just as his SA leaders in life had kept him fed in exchange for service.

The combination of physical and ideological support offered through the SA's communal living arrangements more than justified the effort and expense they required. The institutions greatly aided Party recruitment among both the stormtroopers directly assisted and the civilians attracted by this demonstration of social values. But the program also created tension between the movement's paramilitary and political wings, within the SA itself, and between the stormtroopers' lived experiences and their public self-positioning as members of traditional German families.

FIGURE 5.1

A goulash cannon

Stormtroopers serve soup out of a "goulash
cannon" to hungry comrades. This provisioning
method, which recalled the stormtroopers'
psychological roots in the Great War, was usually
used on marches and expeditions, or to supplement distribution at SA kitchens that could not
handle the high demand for their services.
Source: Heinrich Hoffman, *Das braune Heer. 100
Bilddokumente. Leben, Kampf, und Sieg der SA und SS*
(Berlin: Zeitgeschichte, 1932).

Nazi political leadership had long feared a strong and internally coherent SA just as much as it had needed such a group. During the Kampfzeit, local and national Party leaders often clashed with their SA counterparts, and some of these conflicts intensified as the SA grew. The Berlin SA even broke into open revolt on two occasions, the first in August 1930, when its leader, Walter Stennes, led the SA in a strike. Stennes had pressured SA chief Pfeffer to ask that Hitler order more stormtroopers onto the Party's list of electoral candidates. During the Weimar Republic, the process for electing members of the Reichstag compared a party's percentage of the vote to its list of candidates. The more votes, the more members of that list would take a seat. Stennes' demand for more stormtroopers in higher places on the list thus formed part of the stormtroopers' continual requests for deeper social support, as Reichstag membership carried a variety of financial and other privileges. When Hitler refused this request, Stennes resigned and his SA units refused to carry out their duties. Hitler himself traveled to Berlin to broker a solution, which involved him personally assuming the role of the top SA leader.[60]

Hitler's leveraging of personal authority and loyalty succeeded in reuniting divergent Nazi factions, as it almost always did when he personally intervened in intra-Party disputes. It worked in this case because it deployed the emotional bonds stormtroopers felt for their Führer, who they believed personally cared for them and would guard their interests. Hitler himself therefore convinced the Berlin comrades—for a time, at least—to be patient in their expectations for support. Party leaders knew, however, that they would soon have to make a concrete commitment to meet the stormtroopers' social demands.

In Hamburg, most formal conflicts between the Party and the SA had already been resolved through Karl Kaufmann's elevation to Party leader. Kaufmann kept a wary eye on the SA, however, given the context of Stennes' rebelliousness and Hamburg's past experiences with the volatile Böckenhauer. When Conn built the SA's first Heim on his own initiative, without Kaufmann's permission, Kaufmann at first called the action "ominous." Even if he did not fear the rivalry between Stennes and Goebbels, Kaufmann wondered if SA Heime threatened to inappropriately bolster the SA's already strong sense of itself as a separate subculture within the larger National Socialist movement.[61] As Kaufmann complained to the national Party office in January 1931, "I believe that there is no Gau in the Reich that has, considering all the bounds of possibility, provided as much for the welfare of the SA as this one."[62] However, he described these welfare efforts with the tone of a father frustrated with the ingratitude of children who fail to appreciate the work that goes into their care, which included "entire wagonloads" of goods trucked in from the agricultural hinterlands.[63] Despite these initial frustrations, however, Kaufmann and other local political leaders in the end seem to have realized that providing for the SA was the best way to ensure its loyalty.

Having committed to support the stormtroopers in their preferred way, the Party and SA now faced an array of problems in delivering on their promises. The greatest difficulty came in countering the headaches well known to anyone responsible for housing masses of young men: cleanliness and upkeep. A series of SA Heime that looked run down and smelled like cesspools would only harm the movement's image. Yet the stormtroopers were often—by nature and by acculturation—difficult to tame. The Marine SA proved particularly troublesome. This special division, headquartered in Hamburg, involved men who came from the merchant marine and therefore had no permanent German address. Marine stormtroopers often stayed at SA Heime during the weeks between voyages, an arrangement that embodied perfectly the SA's claim to support honest workers in Hamburg's traditional ways of life. However, these stormtrooper sailors were often drunk and destructive. Their boorishness eventually prompted a stern warning from Marine *Sturmbann* I, which issued a series of orders in August 1932 that official accommodations had to be better cared for. The orders cited several egregious lapses in respect for property, such as broken windows, tables, and chairs.

But the main problem seemed to be the stormtroopers' general slovenliness. In contrast to the idealized propaganda images of cleanliness, order, and wholesomeness, stormtroopers served by the Heime often displayed behaviors more typically matching their reputation as rough young men (Figure 5.2). They loitered in front of buildings and stairwells, causing resentment among the janitors who had to clear away their trash and cigarette butts.[64] They often left their bicycles in places that obstructed entrances and stairs. They took little care with interior spaces as well; window frames warped from having been left open in the rain, bathrooms festered without cleaning, and toilets stopped up because of "evidently large objects" thrown into them.[65] The SA reminded its slovenly stormtroopers that the

FIGURE 5.2

Life in the Heime

Stormtroopers outside an SA Heim wash up
in the morning. Although this image, taken
by Hitler's official photographer, conveys
cleanliness and respectability, it also shows
the conflicted intimacy of life in the SA
Heime. Neighbors often complained of the
stormtroopers' impropriety, rowdiness, and
occasional lack of clothing.

Source: Heinrich Hoffman, *Das braune Heer. 100
Bilddokumente. Leben, Kampf, und Sieg der SA und SS*
(Berlin: Zeitgeschichte, 1932).

cost of repairs and upkeep ultimately came out of their own pockets, and it appealed to the men's sense of camaraderie to contain the damage: "He who wantonly harms our property thereby directly injures his comrades, since it is with his comrades' money that the injuries have to be made good."[66] In some cases, the SA expelled stormtroopers for transgressions against the ideals of the SA Heim, failing to pay the rent, or stealing from comrades or from the Heim itself. Most of the expelled stormtroopers had racked up several different violations, such as SA man Hoffman, who was ejected in late 1931 for failing to pay rent, keeping for himself 21 RM he had collected for the SA, and making off with a pair of boots.[67] Unfortunately for the group's image, the shaky finances of individual stormtroopers that had created the need for the Heime made these crimes more common than the SA wanted to admit.

The tension between safety and suspicion further strengthened the cliquishness already present in SA politics. Stormtroopers warned one another not to trust outsiders, even "wandering" SA men from other units who turned up seeking assistance. Leaders said it was simply too difficult to separate the honest applicants from those who sought their own gain. This attitude held true even for those already in the Party, if local stormtroopers did not recognize them. As Böckenhauer instructed *Standarte* 15:

> So-called "wandering" national socialists should not be allowed to receive support, since 99% of these people are thieves, or are not worthy of aid for other reasons. It cannot be helped that if 1% are respectable people, they must suffer along with the vast majority of un-respectable people.[68]

SA Heime and kitchens functioned best when they catered to the needs of the neighborhood stormtroopers, who often knew one another from childhood or other earlier associations. These were the "respectable people" described in Böckenhauer's letter. Yet other members of the movement began to suspect that the SA's living arrangements were anything but respectable. The more the SA support networks grew, the more its political supporters—and worse, its enemies—began to see a sexual threat in the SA's nontraditional ersatz family.

Women in SA Spaces

Stormtroopers were attracted to the youthful, masculine environment of SA spaces, which they considered a safe haven that had rescued them from the hazards of life during the Depression. These safe spaces, however, sometimes created their own moral threat by removing stormtroopers from the families they claimed to protect and cherish. The moral danger came partially from the fact that stormtroopers now lived outside of traditional social settings that supervised and regulated young male sexuality. A lack of adult or familial supervision threatened to allow uncontrolled stormtroopers to make SA Heime into dens of immorality rather than bulwarks against it.

Some party members feared that unsupervised SA men would prove too active in their heterosexual conquests. The sexuality of stormtroopers and Nazi youths has in fact received increased scholarly attention in recent decades, which contrasts with the long-standing tendency to see the Nazis only as prudes. The Nazi movement did in fact seek to limit or eliminate types of sexual activity that it did not approve of—but it also encouraged expressions of sexuality that fit with its ideological focus on promoting ethnic German reproduction. For the young especially, this element of sexual permissiveness was part of what made Nazism a movement of its times, one that made concessions to the relative sexual liberalization of the Weimar era just as much as it decried other types of sexual modernism.[69] In fact, socialist and Communist groups faced similar difficulties in negotiating the era's more liberated spirit. Older leaders rarely wanted to discuss matters of sexual liberation, while the younger members saw sexual freedom as a defining element of modern politics. As Wilhelm Reich wrote in an essay titled "Politicizing the Sexual Problems of Youth," parties seeking to mobilize young people had to tread carefully. On the one hand, Reich agreed with Lenin's decree that "there were more important things to be done" in political life than to pursue sexual freedom.[70] On the other hand, Reich and other prominent Communists believed that the left should stand for "joy of life, power of life, and a satisfied love life" as part of a greater liberation from the constraints of bourgeois oppression. After all, the bourgeoisie based its political control partly on its ability to instill a mentality of obedience within the unsuspecting masses, making sexual authoritarianism "one of the bourgeoisie's strongest ideological props."[71] According to these interpretations of political sexuality, youthful sexual liberation fit well with leftist politics.

In practice, Social Democrats and Communists did indeed prove to be stronger proponents of rights for women, homosexuals, heterosexuals who used contraceptives, and anyone who pursued a lifestyle contrary to a rigid bourgeois morality that allowed sexual activity only within a legally sponsored, heteronormative framework. The Social Democrats had long since proven their modernity on questions regarding women and homosexuals, although they retreated from this stance as their political position became threatened.

The Communists initially supported sexual modernity, but they eventually abandoned most of their sexually liberal positions as their movement increasingly rejected its emancipatory origins in favor of its authoritarian impulses.[72] The parties of the left therefore had a mixed record on sexual matters. Even so, they proved far more enlightened than conservative and fascist political movements, which consistently, openly, and strongly favored monolithic and authoritarian forms of family life. The Nazis, recognizing the powerful allure of sexual liberation among the rising generation, sought to synthesize their traditionalism with youthfulness by creating a concept of Germanic sexuality that would leverage young sexual energy toward the goal of a utopian racial state. This concept offered the movement a chance to embrace approved categories of sexual behavior while still encouraging the persecution of any sexual life outside a fascist political framework.

Discussion of these subjects caused deep tension within political movements. Among National Socialists, disagreement and wariness over the sexuality of young Nazis often aligned with the movement's other organizational and generational splits, as the older members of the political wing looked askance at younger members' failure to adhere to bourgeois morality. The complaint of a Hamburg Party member to the SA in September 1932 exemplifies this dynamic. The letter writer claimed that a failure to enforce gender segregation and sexual restraint in SA spaces would weaken the Party's claim to distinction from the Communists, whose alleged sexual immorality the conservative and middle-class parties often criticized. This Party member claimed to have observed similar transgressions in SA Heime:

> I feel it is my duty to inform you that in the SA Heim on Heimhuderstrasse 14, an SA man lives together with his girl. We work for a pure Germany. Such wild marriages should not be allowed. It excites scandal, and could then cause more SA men to want their girls to live with them, and then our communal enterprise would be finished.[73]

The SA dismissed the complaint when its investigation revealed that the couple had since married. It did not investigate whether or not the woman had actually lived with her stormtrooper husband in the Heim before their marriage, despite the breach of policy this arrangement would represent.

The SA's lax attitude toward this case contrasts with its general stance that allowing women to move into SA Heime would dilute the purpose of the enterprise. The letter writer himself seems to have followed this line of argument, making his appeal based on emotional camaraderie rather than on middle-class morality. As the SA knew, the Heime's masculine environment drew young men to the group's ranks, encouraged the recruits' mutual emotional bonds, and intensified their commitment to more combative interpretations of masculine behavior. This living situation also made them available as a quick-response force against local Communist attacks. These politically useful traits countered the risks the Party took in gathering volatile young men together. The distracting presence of women could dilute these effects, but trying to erect a wall between stormtroopers and women would pose several dangers. The Nazi Party needed women supporters, voters, and members in order to win any real place in a now-egalitarian electoral system. It also needed to appeal to all classes and genders as a way to emphasize its claim that ethnicity, not class or any other category of identity, formed the only legitimate basis of social organization. If the Party claimed to offer a totalizing solution to a fragmented and squabbling society, it needed to show it could integrate women as well as men.

Women thus played a large but overlooked role in the SA. Although they could not themselves be stormtroopers, and although extreme proponents of the SA's masculine ideology often discounted their contributions, women filled a variety of support roles in the movement's official activities and in the stormtroopers' daily lives. The SA, never a rich organization, needed help to keep its members in uniforms and boots, which the stormtroopers had to buy from Nazi suppliers. To reduce the cost of these items in the impoverished early years, the SA sometimes assembled stockpiles from donated materials that Nazi women would patch up and repair.[74] Local chapters of the Nazi women's section offered occasional resoling of boots at reduced prices to unemployed stormtroopers, a service the SA closely monitored for abuse.[75] When stormtroopers were hospitalized with injuries from political actions, the SA contacted the women's section to arrange for wounded comrades to receive visitors and emotional support.[76] Some women also went outside normal channels, supplementing their official Party work with personal offers of shelter in their own homes. Some offered a place at their Sunday supper tables for stormtroopers in neighborhoods far from SA kitchens.[77] The SA coordinated such matches, further anchoring individual stormtroopers to neighborhood families. The SA and the women's section also cooperated in providing temporary housing for out-of-town stormtroopers who could find no room in the official homes, or for whom a different location was more convenient.[78] In these ways, women leveraged their traditional roles as mothers, wives, and providers in the home. Using these traditional social roles, women found a place that would not challenge the traditional conceptions of family that the Nazis claimed to defend.

Behind every stormtrooper unit stood several women who helped keep the men dressed and fed, and who comforted them when sick. Women therefore earned a vital but limited place in the movement as mothers, sisters, or desexualized political associates.[79] In contrast, Communist and socialist groups did at times allow women to take more prominent roles, including in leadership and even in fighting organizations. Still, women's roles within the socialist parties were not as straightforwardly positive as is often assumed, and although many socialist theorists placed high value on women's liberation and equality, practitioners of leftist politics often did not.[80] The Nazis aligned their gender ideology and practice more closely. Stormtrooper women functioned comfortably as provisioners of private life and standard bearers of cultural values in public life, but they could never participate in the SA's central function and defining experience: the milieu of male bonding and physical combat against political enemies. Since women could not literally be fighters, SA rhetoric emphasized their role as moral examples and as a source of spiritual strength for male warriors. By psychologically empowering women who remained in traditional roles, SA rhetoric bridged the disconnect between stormtroopers' view of women as objects to be protected and the reality in that era of women as political actors in their own right. The SA and the Nazi Party therefore lauded a conservative definition of femininity as a source of strength for individual women and for the movement, and, ultimately, for the nation.

Stories in the *Tageblatt* about women's subtle heroism echoed tales with stormtrooper protagonists. Both relied on the anonymous hero. One example described an encounter the narrator, a stormtrooper, had with a comrade's mother. The family was poor, with both son and father unemployed and the sister earning a meager salary at the Karstadt department store. The narrator never knew where his comrade, affectionately nicknamed Heini, managed to get the sandwiches he brought to SA marches and gladly shared with hungry comrades. A visit to Heini's home and an encounter with his mother revealed the answer. At first the narrator had resisted Heini's invitation to afternoon coffee, as he did not want to strain the family's resources, but he could not long refuse without offending. When he finally made the visit he was impressed with the level of hospitality the poor family could offer:

> What can I say about how Heini's mother laid the table? A fat-bellied coffee pot on a pretty and colorful tablecloth, cute little cups from grandmother's time, and as the pride of the day an actual, fragrant cake. "Baked it myself," commented the mother offhandedly. And it tasted wonderful. [81]

The narrator kept his astonishment to himself until late in the evening. As Heini escorted him home, the narrator finally asked, "Tell me, how do you guys do it at home?" Heini, "as if it were self-evident," replied in charming Hamburg dialect, *"Je, Mudder kann allens!"* ("Hey, Mom can do anything!"). The tale revealed the woman as the source of the family's strength and cast the stormtrooper son's positive attitude as the product of generations of female domestic integrity. The story ended with an explicit statement of the importance such women played in National Socialism: "If in later years someone should write a history of today's difficult times, then the mothers must take a place of honor in that book." [82]

Nazis who discussed women's role in this way often referred to them as "culture bearers." Party member Maria Adelheid Konorath spoke on this subject during a special Nazi Party lecture series in 1932. According to the *Hamburger Tageblatt*, she struck a special chord with women attendees, who sympathized with her call for a return to a gender order supposedly present among ancient Germans. Women and men alike, Konorath argued, must be "links in the chain" connecting past and future generations. Women bore the special role of creating those generations—not just in the physical act of childbirth but in the spiritual sense of transmitting unchanging values across generations. "Our forefathers' worldview held that women should be considered man's highest ideal," Konorath explained, meaning that women inspired men's heroism, their victory in combat, and their defense of a threatened homeland. By the 20th century, however, both women and men had become estranged from their essential natures, a lapse from a supposedly natural state of affairs that brought about defeat in the Great War. In her argument, Konorath mobilized a gendered version of the stab-in-the-back legend, explaining that women's increasing complaints about wartime food shortages and other difficulties on the home front disheartened the men at the front and sped the army's collapse.[83] Women's failure to uphold supposedly tireless notions of inspirational femininity had therefore caused Germany's defeat—but the restoration of proper gender roles could bring Germany's resurgence. "The German renewal can only come through the woman," Konorath told her Nazi audience. "The man can surely achieve the other manifestations, but still the inner spiritual freedom will be won only by the woman."[84]

In the Nazis' feminine equivalent of male heroism, women provided material and psychological support for the men, encouraged militant attitudes in men, and bore with pride their own sorrow when men fell in battle. This combination of emotional investment and emotional detachment bridged the gap between the stormtroopers' conflicting roles as warriors seeking martyrdom and men seeking fatherhood. As the *Ehrenbuch der SA* explained:

> One might think that the SA man who is also a family man would become soft and slack off. Certainly, it is hard for an SA man to see his family suffer because he fights for the Führer; his dependents have to sacrifice much, or his marriage comes into difficulty. It is a silent and great heroism, what the women of many SA men bear, when they go through years of unemployment, when every time their husband leaves the house they must ask: "Is he coming home? Is he going to land in the hospital or dead in the morgue? Where and how will I see him again? Will I ever see him again, or will he lie beaten to death in a river or canal?"[85]

These were very real concerns for stormtroopers' wives and mothers, whose fears could easily come to pass every time a stormtrooper engaged in political combat. SA writings therefore encouraged Nazi women to embrace the potential tragic heroism inherent in their roles by giving them behavioral models for how loyalty after death could win the affection and allegiance of a far larger circle of men than the single one they had lost.

In the SA novel *Gotthard Kraft*, the titular hero's death leads to stronger emotional bonds between his mother and his comrades. This theme became even more fully elaborated in the only known example of a stormtrooper novel written from a woman's perspective: Gudrun Streiter's *Dem Tod so nah . . . Tagebuchblätter einer SA-Mannes Braut* (*With Death So Near . . . Diary Pages of an SA Man's Bride*). The name Streiter was most likely a pseudonym, given its adherence to the mythic naming conventions of SA literature. Streiter claimed to have been given these diary pages by an old school friend who wanted her to understand the women's side of the stormtrooper struggle. The resulting book, published with a foreword supposedly written by the anonymous SA wife's pastor, described the marriage as drawing its passion from the couple's joint work for the Party. This is how they had met, grown close, and come to see the potential of their partnership. When it came time for a marriage proposal, they spoke more of the Party than of themselves. After asking her to marry him, the stormtrooper urged consideration of their political life and the dangers it carried:

> "Before you give me your affirmation . . . think that to be an SA man's wife demands sacrifice and going without certain things. Can you promise me that you'll never put limits on my duties for the Hitler movement, that you're ready at any time to give your last and dearest for your fatherland?" Never was God so near to me as at this hour. I felt fate's hand burning in my soul. I knew that hard tests lay before me. Love for the Fatherland burned within my heart. But I never felt so strong as in the moment I gave my affirmation to this man, whom I loved with my entire soul, and swore to him to sacrifice everything for the Fatherland.[86]

The writer's words prove prophetic when her betrothed is shot and killed just before they can marry. The pastor who was to marry them helps her maintain her strength by reminding her that she is an SA man's fiancée, after which she conducts the funeral as a gesture of support to the movement they both had loved:

> Not in the black garments of mourning was I clad. No, I walked as the fiancée of an SA man, as a Hitler girl behind the hearse, in Hitler's brown garment. I will not dress in clothes of mourning.

Only my brown Hitler dress, my fighting dress will I wear. I will not disappear in my pain. I need my strength for the fight. Nothing will separate me from Wolfgang. Our souls are forever united.[87]

Such stories taught a woman to use a stormtrooper's death to renew her commitment to the Nazi movement, channeling her pain into an intensified social bond between her and the fallen one's comrades. In doing so, she would fulfill what National Socialists believed to be the ancient role of Germanic women—to provide a model of virtue that would inspire intensified struggle in defense of the Vaterland.

Models of the stormtrooper family did not exist only in the movement's didactic myths and propagandistic "honor books." As with its acts of violence, the SA proved quite adept at staging events to concretize its self-image. To create the reality of the family bonds they publicly claimed, the SA hosted well-publicized gatherings that united the masculine warriors with their female partners and child dependents. Events like feasts for area children would prove that, as one local SA leader declared at a "Feeding of Five Thousand" in September 1931, "The smallest of the small, the future of our *Volk*, should feel at home with us, should be the guests of the SA."[88] The children themselves paid no attention to the speeches during the event: "They had to make sure first that the mountain of cookies, the dear donations that had been arranged for them, disappeared. And at the same time they had to apply themselves to drinking up the cocoa served to them by brown-clad girls." When the evening grew late, the adults put the children to bed, held a singing contest and a German dance, and talked of the National Socialists' plan to protect the future for the children they had just entertained.

The group held similar celebrations during the Christmas season of 1932, which included a massive party hosted by the women's section and the Marine SA in a hall near the zoo.[89] These occasions gave both men and women opportunities to perform the gender roles the movement expected of them. Women provided food, decorations, and a festive atmosphere in an interior space made safe by the presence of militant men who guarded its borders. These events also encouraged courtship between National Socialist men and women, so that the movement's young people could find appropriate spouses. One stormtrooper wife described decades later that she had met her husband in this way:

My cousin and her parents, they were avid Nazis. And I always went along to their dances . . . they were really upstanding young people there, not like the criminals who run around today. And if people say today that they too weren't good for much, [I would reply that] yes, I came to support Adolf Hitler, but only because there was order in the land. You can really believe that. The whole thing that people complain about, I didn't know anything about that. But that's where I met my husband.[90]

This woman's whitewashing of stormtrooper crimes both before and during the Third Reich was not (or not merely) an artifact of the interview's later date; it was also a statement of how she always had seen the movement. The SA members, she believed, were upstanding people. Their crimes vanished from her consciousness, because to focus on them would undercut her belief in people she had been raised to see as respectable. Her family supported her courtship and marriage to the stormtrooper, even if, as happened, she became pregnant before they were married. Rather than causing her rejection, the pregnancy and resulting marriage confirmed her membership in a respectable community: "My mother was happy, because I became an upstanding person [ein ordentlicher Mensch]."[91]

Events promoting SA families thus literally created those families, which the Nazi press and word of mouth then advertised as examples of the socially cohesive, integrated community that National Socialism promised to deliver. The Tageblatt's description of a June 1931 "Wedding in Brown Shirts" described how the ceremony united not only the bridal pair but also the attendees of varying social classes and backgrounds, "the dock worker next to the student, the SA Führer next to the SA Mann." The pastor's wedding sermon echoed the National Socialist emphasis on community and collectivity, contrasting it to a spirit of selfishness and decadence the Party alleged was promoted by socialists, democrats, and Jews. According to the pastor:

There was a time in Germany when people sought to make their lives as "comfortable" as possible. The interest of the Ego had become the priority, and that of fellow man and the nation had become secondary. It is, thank God, different today. A movement has arisen whose motto is: common good before private gain [Gemeinnutz vor Eigennutz]. This slogan embodies true Christianity. As the Nazarene said: "Whatsoever you do to the least of my brothers, you do to me."[92]

A "brown shirt wedding" embodied the Nazi Party's promise to heal a society broken by war, depression, and the struggles of modern urban life. The idea appealed both to potential stormtroopers, who themselves had experienced trouble forming the healthy families they felt to be their birthright, and to the larger voting public, whose dissatisfaction with the moral state of Weimar Germany had only intensified with the coming of the economic depression. Indeed, the connection between economic misery and family instability had long plagued young men of Weimar Germany.

Stormtroopers therefore found themselves rooted in two competing conceptions of family. First they were, or tried to remain, loyal to an idealized version of the biological families in which they had been raised. They sought healthy relationships with their mothers and fathers, and they had the goal of eventually finding a partner with whom they could begin a family of their own. Yet they also found themselves drawn to their family of comrades, the homosocial environment of intense male bonding found in SA Heime and in constant rounds of Party activities. These two families existed in natural conflict, which the SA tried to dispel through rituals of family and community that united competing members of the stormtroopers' tribes. The two, however, inevitably clashed, as the stormtroopers spent their nights in the barracks and their days as paramilitary fighters in an urban civil war.

The conflict proved especially severe during the Christmas season, when daytime public violence clashed with the evening's promise of peace amid the family. During the Christmas seasons of 1931 and 1932, the police imposed a ban on paramilitaries, marches, rallies, and other disruptive forms of political contest. Stormtroopers thus had a quieter time in which to consider their familial loyalties in light of the Christmas celebration, as one anonymous SA man did in an article for the *Tageblatt* in 1931:

> "And now go home to your houses, be joyful under the lighted trees, be joyful in the circle of your family. Christ is risen, peace on Earth, Christmas is here!"
>
> So will the Pastor speak in the church tonight. He'll speak of the gospel, of the son of God, of belief.
>
> And we men will go home and be joyful and will forget all else. We'll remember that it's Christmas, the celebration of love, the celebration of family.

And we? We of the SA?

We will try to be joyful, we'll say to mother that we're happy to be by her again, we'll tell the wife that we're at peace and try to wipe the troubles from her brow. We'll tell the children happy stories—and nevertheless, always return in our thoughts to those whom we call comrades.[93]

This same unknown stormtrooper recalled these comrades with sympathy for the disconnect between the promise of the Christmas season and the reality of their lives during the Depression:

One of them sits on a cold floor. He stares out into the night, sees candles burning and people laughing. Sees his dear mother somewhere in his thoughts, and hears her thoughts. That it is Christmas today.

Cold shivers in his marrow, hunger gnaws at his body.

He goes restlessly here and there. Thinks about the hours with his comrades, through burning sun and winter storms, in woods and fields with his comrades singing consoling songs and following with laughter Hitler's red banner.[94]

Another stormtrooper, locked in prison for political crimes, drew strength from the fact that his comrades had not forgotten him. Another "had to leave his mother and father so that he may go toward Hitler's banner." A third lost dear friends and gave up his girlfriend "because he followed Hitler's drumbeat." Others lost jobs, lost their savings, or were "beaten and violated" for their loyalty to the Party. Yet they all had one consolation:

We have lost everything, we have gained everything. We gave up father and mother and fiancée and friend, gave up money and goods and our blood. Some of these things we gave easily, some with more difficulty, but we have all gained one things that no man or God can rob from us—we have gained our comrades.[95]

Stormtroopers who so valued male camaraderie could only exist uneasily in a movement that ideologically promoted heterosexual marriage and nuclear family life. Most of them claimed that camaraderie could coexist with heterosexuality, as indeed it can and did. But the stormtroopers' constant and effusive professions of emotional attachment to their fellow men, combined with their same-sex living arrangements and increasing emotional attachments, made them particularly prone to accusations of homosexuality—especially once the fact of some stormtroopers' homosexuality became a matter of national conversation.

Röhm's Return: Homosexuality in SA Spaces

Although most of the stormtroopers who joined the SA during the Depression were heterosexuals, rapid expansion naturally drew a number of new recruits who were attracted to their fellow men. Quick growth also prompted the reappearance of one whose homosexuality was known, and known well: Ernst Röhm, who in November 1930 returned to Germany from Bolivia, where he had worked as a consultant to the Bolivian army. Within weeks of Röhm's return, Hitler called SA leaders to Munich to discuss appointing him chief of staff. North German SA leaders raised the strongest objections to Röhm, fearing the cliquishness and favoritism they had seen in the past with the old Bavarian guard.[96] While opponents seem not to have related their concerns to Röhm's sexuality, knowledge of it would have reinforced north Germans' fear of emotional and incestuous southern leadership. Hitler, however, had his way. On January 5, 1931, he named Röhm SA chief of staff. Although Hitler himself kept the highest position of ceremonial leadership and was as willing as ever to intervene when the mood moved him, many people now considered Ernst Röhm to be the Nazi movement's second most important man.

From the start, the choice angered Röhm's internal enemies, including many SA leaders who feared that his elevation marked a consolidation of Hitler's personal power over the SA and the SA's ultimate subordination to the Party's political wing.[97] Stormtrooper and Nazi adherence to the National Socialist "leadership principle," in which Hitler's personal will provided policy guidance that no Nazi could question, made opposing the Führer's choice a difficult and dangerous path for anyone who sought to stay within the movement. SA leaders who resisted the recent structural decisions therefore relied on personal attacks against Röhm, which allowed them to oppose the organizational changes without seeming to contradict Hitler's judgment. Hitler, however, quashed these sentiments as well. He announced that the SA "was not a school to educate the daughters of the upper classes, but rather a formation of rough fighters," a statement picked up by the SPD's newspaper *Vorwärts*, which was eager to fan the flames of the Nazis' intra-party bickering.[98]

Röhm's elevation came at the same time the Hamburg SA established its first systems of social support. Across Germany, other local SA units began doing the same, thus furthering the group's rapid expansion. Central Party and SA leadership reacted to this success by increasing the number and power of its top leaders, in order to keep greater control and to administer stormtrooper services more effectively. In his staffing of SA leaders, Röhm's initial actions in some ways played to his enemies' fears. He appointed an array of friends and old comrades as his subordinates, and he advanced the careers of other favorites connected to this circle. Contrary to popular belief both then and now, however, he did not surround himself only with fellow homosexuals. Some of his associates did fit the label, but the true common thread in Röhm's choices lay in values of long-standing camaraderie, trust, and personal loyalty to Röhm and to Hitler that had nothing to do with sexuality. Röhm prioritized consolidating the SA under Hitler's personal directive, forcing it to adhere to the path of legality that Hitler had proclaimed while maintaining the SA's rough energy as a point of attraction for young recruits.[99]

In many ways, Röhm's war record, past achievements, and personality as a rough brawler who cared little for conventional middle-class morality endeared him to the stormtrooper rank and file. This fact made rivals hate him all the more. Hitler's choice of Röhm seems to have been one factor in alienating anew the rebellious Stennes, who in April 1931 again led his Berlin SA into revolt. This time the clash centered on whether to obey a recent state order to notify the government in advance of political rallies, which the combative Stennes refused to do. Hitler expelled Stennes from the Party and demanded that all remaining SA leaders take an oath of personal loyalty to Hitler. Rather than blaming Hitler in the aftermath of this humiliation, Stennes focused his ire on Röhm. Later that summer, Stennes tried to have him killed.[100]

Röhm's problems extended from internal difficulties with Party rivals into the public realm, where his troubles risked embarrassing the entire SA. Throughout the month of June 1931, the Munich Post published a series of attacks that climaxed in a scandalous article, "Homosexuality in the Brown House. Sexual Life in the Third Reich." In an echo of the Social Democratic

FIGURE 5.3

Stormtrooper camaraderie

Stormtroopers in an SA Heim display their camaraderie
for Hoffman's camera. This official propaganda image
meant to appeal to the stormtrooper recruits' desire
for close male relationships and emotional connections
to other men. But the homosocial lifestyle that the SA
fostered in the Heime strengthened the antifascists'
accusations of stormtrooper homosexuality.
Source: Heinrich Hoffman, *Das braune Heer. 100
Bilddokumente. Leben, Kampf, und Sieg der SA und SS*
(Berlin: Zeitgeschichte, 1932).

outing campaigns of the late imperial period, the paper accused Röhm of committing offenses against Paragraph 175, of furthering the interests of a militaristic homosexual clique, and of corrupting German youth. It was an old attack from the standard playbook. However, this time the story included copies of private letters Röhm had sent to a friend, letters that not only connected him to known homosexuals but included passages in which Röhm openly admitted his attraction to men.

Röhm's friend Dr. Karl-Günther Heimsoth, the recipient of these letters, had achieved some measure of notoriety as a theorist of the homosexual emancipation movement. Along with author and publisher Adolf Brand, Heimsoth belonged to the faction that rejected Magnus Hirschfeld's scientific and liberal approach that at the time saw homosexuality as an effeminate "third sex." Brand, Heimsoth, and their intellectual kin held instead to the romantic-militaristic view of male homosexuality that Röhm shared, one in which ultra-masculine warrior love furthered the goals of civilization. Heimsoth did much to enshrine racism and ethnocentrism in this model, claiming that heroic homoerotic love could truly occur only among Aryan men (Figure 5.3).[101]

Heimsoth and Röhm began corresponding in 1928, when Heimsoth interpreted passages in Röhm's autobiography as a confession of homosexuality. Heimsoth then approached Röhm by letter in the hopes of enlisting an ally on the right for the battle to repeal Paragraph 175. Röhm responded to the approach positively but guardedly, as in one of the letters the newspapers now revealed: "Of course I fight against moral laws, above all P175. Is that not clear? In my first draft I had written a more detailed account of the subject, but on the advice of friends, who find this [evasive] kind of writing to be more effective, I have changed it to this formulation."[102] The letter expressed affection for an array of obviously homosexual persons and figures, including Hans Blüher, whose Role of the Erotic in Society had greatly influenced the early pro-homosexual movement, and whom Röhm now told Heimsoth he "would like to meet."[103] Röhm also thanked Heimsoth for having sent him a copy of Heimsoth's own recent work, Constellations and Character: With Special Concern for Same-Sex Matters, a work of astrology that sought to connect homosexuality to astral alignments. Röhm affectionately joked that the book was too difficult for him to understand, but he said too that he had "extraordinary interest" in the subject.

Thus far, Röhm's words had admitted nothing illegal, and they could have been explained away as typical of a politician's vague words of support for a petitioner's pet project. The next letter, however, written from Bolivia, contained clear and direct statements of Röhm's own sexuality. By this time Röhm had read through Heimsoth's work of astrology, and he now claimed that it affected him deeply: "I imagine myself to be same-sex oriented, though I only really 'discovered' this in 1924. I can remember earlier an array of same-sex feelings and acts during my childhood, though I have gone with many women. Without particular pleasure."[104] Röhm described himself as distant from his father and brother, yet totally devoted to his sister and mother—ironically, a psychological alignment that did not match Heimsoth's and Brand's mode of militant homoeroticism so much as it resembled their mutual enemy Hirschfeld's construction of effeminate male homosexuality. Röhm's affection for his female relatives was well known among all of his associates, but it did not lessen his credentials as a masculine warrior, who after all was capable enough to have been recruited to Bolivia for a military purpose. Röhm claimed satisfaction with the new position in Bolivia, which offered stimulating work, an Alpine climate, and even good German food. One thing, however, was missing:

> I would be in the best order, if I was not missing an object of love. I even took a companion with me, a 19-year-old Munich artist. I'm very close to him, and him with me; when, for example, he leaves on a student trip, it's very hard for him to take leave of me. Sexual acts between us, however, are out of the question: he has no desire for it, thinking that such pleasure has to be taken with girls. Also I have no real desire for it, although he is quite the cute little thing (or I would not have brought him along).[105]

Although Röhm claimed not to pursue his interest in the artist, other passages in the letter detailed his attraction to young men. He expressed frustration that the local youths in the streets of La Paz did not shy away from physical affection with each other, "to the point where you would think everyone on the street is Schwul."[106] Röhm's use of the colloquial "Schwul," which had not yet gained wide usage, revealed him as an insider to homosexual circles. Yet these circles did not exist in La Paz, and he could not find the time to go to Buenos Aires. This left him no choice but to conduct a life of celibacy—at least, he said, until the time when he could "continue my attempts to spread" same-sex ways of life.[107] Such candid prose played into the era's worst stereotypes concerning homosexuals' alleged attempts to seduce heterosexual youths. A third letter commented on the attractions of "hot-blooded, fresh young lieutenants" under his command, again awakening allegations that homoerotic feelings inappropriately warped command relationships in military and political organizations.[108]

The Munich Post's story was local at first, but it quickly inspired similar articles in a variety of Social Democratic and other anti-Nazi newspapers, which used the item as evidence of a broader claim that Röhm and his party did not "possess the moral qualities" needed for political leadership.[109] The SPD's Hamburger Echo particularly enjoyed raising the subject of "des schwulen Hauptmann Röhms" (the gay captain Röhm), as it did in September 1931 in response to a Nazi campaign flier on "a clean Germany, a true family life."[110] The article also noted an array of other Nazi sex crimes, including those against underage girls. However, Röhm continued to be the prime subject of salacious political reporting, the symbol who stood in for the trend allegedly suffusing National Socialism. Writing about a Hitler Youth leader sentenced to four years in prison for molestation, the Echo described the man as "following in Röhm's footsteps."[111]

Although Röhm at this point began to restrain his private sexual life, the public issue refused to die. In April 1932, his letters again appeared in print, this time not only in newspapers but as a 16-page pamphlet. The publisher, Dr. Helmut Klotz, had been a Nazi who was committed enough to know many Party secrets, but by 1932 he had defected to the SPD in order to wage a propaganda war against his former associates. His book, The Röhm Case, reproduced copies of the original handwritten letters and included a timeline of "Facts!" that tracked Röhm's many failed attempts in court to bar the book's publication. As Klotz explained, Röhm's first lawsuit failed when a Munich court ruled, "The petitioner Röhm does not deny having written the letters. If someone publishes these letters as part of a political struggle, in order to show that Röhm is not worthy of being the leader of German youths, it does not seem illegal."[112] The court thus declined to intervene, but this refusal did not stop Röhm from trying again. Röhm's repeatedly unsuccessful attempts to sue Klotz became a regular feature of the Hamburger Echo's political coverage that spring. The paper also published longer and more substantive critiques of the SA, such as an exposé of how much it cost the Party to keep its stormtroopers in what the SPD portrayed as a lavish lifestyle that revealed the Nazis' connections to big business.[113] The paper also ran a series challenging both Hitler's and Kaufmann's war records in the hope of deflating the heroic mythology the two had cultivated.[114] Röhm, however, continued to be the star during the pre-election period of March and April, and the frequency of the reporting eventually established homosexuality as a Nazi-associated vice, which opened up possibilities for more subjective attacks.[115] As the *Echo* eventually noted, Hitler himself had little to do with women; therefore, he too could well be homosexual.[116]

In May, another prominent voice entered the chorus against Röhm: Erich von Ludendorff, the quartermaster general of the Imperial Army, whom many considered to have been the real German monarch during the war's final years. After his key role in spreading the stab-in-the-back legend after the war, Ludendorff continued to degenerate into a full-throated advocate of racist, antisemitic, and mystic-supernatural theories of German nationalism. Even so, he still enjoyed a great deal of respect in many corners of the nationalist right. Ludendorff now attacked not only Röhm but Hitler, whom Ludendorff accused of having known since 1927 of Röhm's attempt to seduce a member of the Hitler Youth. Ludendorff published his own account of the case in a book called *Out of the Brown Swamp*—an allusion to Roman historian Tacitus' claim that the ancient Germanic peoples, in a sign of their superior morality, drowned homosexuals in bogs. Although the SPD hardly supported such brutal punishments, many antifascist papers could not resist reporting favorably on Ludendorff's campaign.

As the year progressed, stories in opposition papers about Röhm's homosexuality continued alongside warnings against SA violence. Many of the tales tied the two themes together, as did a *Hamburger Echo* report on the internal politics of the "Brown House" in Munich, where Röhm and his fellow stormtrooper elites gathered to, in the *Echo's* characterization, plot their acts of murder and depravity.[117] Other stories offered more creative accounts, such as one that told of a stormtrooper mother who refused to allow the SA to participate in her son's funeral. Her opposition came from the fact that Hitler and Röhm had declined to share information with her about the circumstances of the boy's death. Given the long context of homophobic propaganda, readers could not help but think of darkly salacious scenarios.[118]

The sinister nature of the SA's ersatz family became a consistent theme of SPD propaganda, which sometimes approached the issue through humor rather than fear mongering. A satire from October 1932 took the form of a letter written by a stormtrooper to his mother, whom he good-naturedly informed of how well he enjoyed living with the SA. Astute readers, how-ever, could see what the naïve stormtrooper could not: that the leader who cared so much about him was in fact a would-be paramour, whose gifts of chocolate, invitations to the movies, and even physical caresses in fact con-stituted homosexual propositions. The stormtrooper, failing to recognize these signs, thought instead that the SA cared for him as no other organiza-tion would:

> It is so nice here, and [we have] such a good understanding. You won't find that anywhere in any other group, that the officers and the men feel such harmony with each other. [Our leader] was for a long time in the Chief of Staff's Brown House, where this feeling between leaders and their men goes even deeper, something that comes all the way from Röhm at the top.[119]

The story ended with an appeal from the innocent stormtrooper that his mother send him a fresh pair of socks, because his feet were sweaty. The humor softened the scene and lent sympathy to the misguided protagonist, but otherwise the story mobilized homophobia in the traditional way: it portrayed a secretive clique that took advantage of innocent young men in order to seduce them into radical and militarist politics. In the end, satire was almost worse for the SA than a straightforward critical essay, since it made Ernst Röhm and his tough paramilitary warriors into punch lines. As all these news stories show, wider publicity concerning Röhm's sexuality became an arrow in the antifascist quiver. Humorous interpretations, how-ever, proved the sharpest arrow of all, one that threatened to strike at the heart of the SA's self-image.

After the series of revelations and failed lawsuits catapulted Röhm's sex-uality into the public consciousness, homophobic taunts became common against stormtroopers. One such insult included the catcall, "*SA, Hose runter!*" (SA, pants down!), which was almost guaranteed to start a fight. In one doc-umented case, *Reichsbanner* men mobbing a stormtrooper's laundromat used the taunt to goad him into drawing and firing his revolver, an act that caused the late-arriving police to arrest him. The Nazis, of course, considered the stormtrooper the injured party.[120] The KPD's *Volksblatt* reported enthusiastical-ly on other homophobic confrontations, which it claimed even took place between Nazi factions. In one alleged incident, a Party member returned a stormtrooper's "Heil Hitler" with a well-intentioned "Heil Röhm"—thus drawing outrage, accusations of slander, and a physical attack. "It seems to be dawning in the brains of SA men," wrote the *Volksblatt*, "that it is unworthy for a German man to be commanded by a Bolivian homosexual."[121]

The socialist mocking of stormtrooper sexuality may have served a short-term political purpose, but it also reinforced a lasting slanderous claim against homosexual men as a group. Maxim Gorky, the radical Russian writer, proclaimed, "If you just root out all the homosexuals—then fascism will vanish!"[122] More restrained voices on the left began to see that such broad attacks conflicted with socialism's proclaimed mission of liberation and modernization, which included homosexuals in theory if not always in practice. Kurt Tucholsky, a German-Jewish journalist and social critic, said that, while criticism of the Nazis' private lives was fair game for antifascist politics, in Röhm's case "it has gone too far." In his mind, socialists should raise the subject of stormtrooper homosexuality only when directly refuting the Nazis' own homophobic propaganda. If socialists truly opposed "the disgraceful Paragraph 175," he wrote, they must "not join voices with the chorus that would condemn a man because he is a homosexual."[123]

For too many antifascists, however, Röhm's sexuality posed a weapon too tempting not to deploy. Dr. Klotz denied that attacks against Röhm indicated animosity toward homosexuals generally, or that they strengthened social attitudes demonizing same-sex relations. As Klotz wrote in his pamphlet outing Röhm,

> By publishing the Röhm letters, I make no value judgment against homosexuals—neither a value judgment in the negative or positive sense—and if I am fully honest, when I consider the special feelings of these unhappy people, I will not deny my sympathy.
>
> I declare, however, with all resolution that this sympathy will not lead me to remain silent and stand aside, if—as is the case with Chief of Staff Röhm!—great numbers of German youths are to be delivered to the mercies of a homosexual.[124]

Klotz reminded readers that the Nazis "in their public programs seek 'punishments' against homosexuals, including forced castration," and that Nazi support of Röhm thereby indicated a vast hypocrisy. Klotz stated that he "feels a measure of sympathy for Röhm, whether he needs it or not." Despite his disclaimers, however, Klotz seemed not to know or care that his vilification campaign increased not only readers' opposition to Röhm personally but to homosexuals more generally. In the end, Klotz called his mobilization of homophobic panic an act of "reckless candor" in the service of "the highest moral duty." As Klotz said, to allow Röhm to continue in his leadership position would abet "crimes of having knowingly and intentionally furthered the seduction of German youths into becoming homosexual minions."[125]

Later historians of Weimar politics have called antifascist homophobia the "darker side of antifascist culture," a way of thinking that spread the alleged connection of fascism and homosexuality widely through space and far in time.[126] Klaus Mann lamented that homosexuals had become "the Jews of the antifascist left," and he asked how antifascist papers could demonize Nazis as "murderers and pederasts" with the same persecutory intensity as the Nazis decried "race-traitors and Jews."[127] The slander affixed itself into the public consciousness well after the Weimar era, when it would have far-reaching consequences for generations of gay men entirely innocent of the association.

The political and personal campaign against Röhm took legal forms as well. After Röhm's return to Germany, prosecutors tried at least five times to convict him under Paragraph 175. None of the charges stuck, partially because the evidence for such a private crime was difficult to obtain.[128] The constant drumbeat of scandal ignited further resistance to Röhm within the Party, but Hitler continually rejected any calls for his removal. Hitler dismissed any negative talk of Röhm's sexuality as "irrelevant and absurd," and he reminded subordinates of Röhm's professional competence and loyalty.[129] Hitler's defense of Röhm seems to have been based in personal affection, his practical recognition of the man's skills, and his defensiveness at his decisions as supreme leader being challenged.

Lower-ranking stormtroopers were not so lucky. As with Hamburg's stormtrooper Bisschopinck, whom Conn had attacked over his inappropriate closeness to their superior, lower-ranking SA men remained under constant threat from their own leadership, which often took great care in controlling the enlisted ranks and managing the public face of their local chapter. Accusations of homosexuality, even in Röhm's time as chief of staff, remained powerful weapons for Party members and SA officers to use against rivals, as long as the accusation remained within Party circles. One of Kaufmann's closest Nazi friends, a Party member named Brust, had come in conflict with the local SA in just this way. Brust's rivals began spreading rumors of his homosexuality in an attempt to force Kaufmann to ostracize him, lest the appearance of impropriety bring down a scandal reminiscent of the furor over Röhm. Fortunately for the Hamburg Nazis' public reputation, Brust died before the accusations came to light and the matter died with him.[130]

Although the SA's relationship to its stormtroopers' sexuality was complicated and contradictory, one message was clear: if a homosexual stormtrooper wanted to stay within the movement, he had to remain hidden—possibly from his comrades and always from the public eye. These men could, like Röhm, remain in the Party so long as they were useful and utterly loyal, but they must have wondered what would happen if that utility ever expired or if that loyalty came into question. Adolf Brand, whose militarized interpretation of homosexuality and scorn for all things feminine made him seem like someone likely to approve of a homoerotic SA, warned that the match of homosexuality and Nazism would not last. He wrote that homosexuals who joined the SA were "carrying their hangman's rope in their pockets."[131]

This psychological tension created a dangerous situation resolvable only through the SA's usual preferred solution: violence. Stormtroopers proved generally unwilling to analyze and conquer their psychological issues, preferring instead to act them out through increased physical and political conflict. Those who were homosexual hoped that their contributions to a Nazi victory would win them tolerance in the coming Nazi state. They believed that Röhm's place in the movement signaled that Hitler ultimately cared little for policing sexual morality, and they expected that a Nazi state would follow his supposed disinclination and allow them to remain, despite the Party's claim to favor conservative sexual morals and family life.

Heterosexual stormtroopers were no less conflicted. The disconnect between their same-sex lives of impoverished violence and their hopes for a more stable existence as responsible family men created psychological and political tension that demanded release. Many stormtroopers came to see their condition as a burden of suffering imposed by the collapse of Germany, the incompetence of the Republic, and the plots of Communists and Jews. So long as economic strife and political conflict prevented them from growing into responsible maturity, these men determined that the quickest way to become the "upstanding person" they envisioned was to end the political struggle as quickly and violently as possible.

FIGURE 5.4

Chair Fighter

Even as the stormtroopers joyfully increased the level of violence in German society and politics, they always claimed to be acting defensively. The original caption of this image of a stormtrooper battling in a meeting hall claimed that "terror from the left can be fought only with greater terror." The stormtrooper's brutish look in this drawing is unusual for Nazi media, which usually portrayed SA men as clean-cut heroes. The caption dispels the thuggish look, however, by blaming the Nazis' enemies for creating an environment in which this fighter was needed. In reality, the SA was no mere response to violence—it in fact continually injected violence into German political life, thus exacerbating the problems it claimed to decry.

Source: *Deutschland erwacht: Werden, Kampf und Sieg der NSDAP* (Germany, Awake! Origins, struggle, and victory of the NSDAP) (Hamburg-Bahrenfeld: Cigaretten-Bilderdienst, 1933). Personal collection, Geoffrey Giles.

NOTES

1   On the history and general contents of this type of document, called a *"Lebenslauf,"* see Bruce Campbell, "Autobiographies of Violence: The SA in Its Own Words," *Central European History* 46, no. 22 (2013): 217–237.

2   NARA A3341 SA Kartei: 046 Paul B.

3   NARA A3341 SA Kartei: 023 Karl B.

4   NARA A3341 SA Kartei: 023 Karl B.

5   StAHH, 614-2/5 *Nationalsozialistische Arbeiterpartei (NSDAP) und ihre Gliederung*, B16, unsigned letter to Amtsgericht Hamburg of October 14, 1930.

6   For the City of Hamburg's files of convicted SA men, before and after 1933, see StAHH, 241-1 *Justizanwaltung* I XXII Cb vols. 1–4. For the SA's own files, see StAHH, 614–2/5 *Nationalsozialistische Arbeiterpartei (NSDAP) und ihre Gliederung* B18, B77, and B103 Band 1–3.

7   NARA 3341 SA Kartei: 023 Karl B.

8   Karl Koch, *Das Ehrenbuch der SA* (Düsseldorf: Floeder, 1934), 69.

9   Koch, *Das Ehrenbuch der SA*, 69.

10 Koch, *Das Ehrenbuch der SA*, 71.

11 These examples include the film *SA Mann Brand*, as well as several SA novels: Julius Witthuhn, *Gotthard Kraft* (Hannover: NS-Kulturverlag, 1932); Heinz Lohmann, *SA räumt auf* (Hamburg: Hanseatische Verlaganstalt, 1935); Bernhard Voss, *Willi Dickkopp. Aus dem Tagebuch eines unbekannten SA Mannes* (Rostock: Bernhard Voss, n.d.); and the anonymously written *10 Jahre unbekannter SA Mann* (Oldenburg: Stalling, 1933).

12 Koch, *Das Ehrenbuch der SA*, 61.

13 Koch, *Das Ehrenbuch der SA*, 62.

14 Koch, *Das Ehrenbuch der SA*, 62.

15 Koch, *Das Ehrenbuch der SA*, 63.

16 Koch, *Das Ehrenbuch der SA*, 64–65.

17 NARA 3341 SA Kartei: Wackerfuss sample (N = 111).

18 StAHH, 614-2/5 *Nationalsozialistische Arbeiterpartei (NSDAP) und ihre Gliederung*, B16, unsigned letters to Amtsgericht Hamburg of October 14, 1930.

19 Karen Hagemann, "Wir hatten mehr Notjahre als reichliche Jahre . . . Lebenshaltung und Hausarbeit Hamburger Arbeiterfamilien in der Weimarer Republik," *Journal Geschichte* 2–3 (1991): 33.

20 StAHH, 213-3 *Staatsanwaltschaft Hamburg—Strafsachen* 4407/38, letter of Karl V. to Amtsgericht Hamburg of March 14, 1938.

21 StAHH, 213-3 *Staatsanwaltschaft Hamburg—Strafsachen* 4407/38.

22 StAHH, 213-3 *Staatsanwaltschaft Hamburg—Strafsachen* 4407/38.

23 StAHH, 213-3 *Staatsanwaltschaft Hamburg—Strafsachen* 4407/38.

24 StAHH, 213-3 *Staatsanwaltschaft Hamburg—Strafsachen* 4407/38.

25 StAHH, 213-3 *Staatsanwaltschaft Hamburg—Strafsachen* 4407/38.

26 StAHH, 213-3 *Staatsanwaltschaft Hamburg—Strafsachen* 4407/38.

27 Anne Nesbet, "Suicide as Literary Fact in the 1920s," *Slavic Review* 50, no. 4 (1991): 827–835.

28 StAHH, 614-2/5 *Nationalsozialistische Arbeiterpartei (NSDAP) und ihre Gliederung* B174, Anzeige by Meier of June 20, 1931.

29 StAHH, 614-2/5 *Nationalsozialistische Arbeiterpartei (NSDAP) und ihre Gliederung* B16, letter of Raeke to Böckenhauer, December 17, 1931.

30 StAHH, 614-2/5 *Nationalsozialistische Arbeiterpartei (NSDAP) und ihre Gliederung* B16, letter of Raeke to Böckenhauer.

31 StAHH, 614-2/5 *Nationalsozialistische Arbeiterpartei (NSDAP) und ihre Gliederung* B16, letter of Pawlowski to Raeke, December 17, 1931.

32 StAHH, 614-2/5 *Nationalsozialistische Arbeiterpartei (NSDAP) und ihre Gliederung* B24, Führerbesprechung of December 21, 1931.

33 Richard Hamilton, "The Rise of Nazism: A Case Study and Review of Interpretations: Kiel, 1928–1933," *German Studies Review* 26, no. 1 (2003): 58. Hamilton's works have generally challenged explanations of Nazism as the product of a middle class threatened with descent into the working class. That thesis is contested but affirmed in Hamburg's case in such works as Thomas Krause, *Hamburg wird Braun. Der Aufstieg der NSDAP von 1921–1933* (Hamburg: Ergebnisse Verlag, 1987), 57–66, 101–107.

34 StAHH, 614-2/5 *Nationalsozialistische Arbeiterpartei (NSDAP) und ihre Gliederung* B66, "Was viele noch nicht wissen!"

35 StAHH, 614-2/5 *Nationalsozialistische Arbeiterpartei (NSDAP) und ihre Gliederung* B66.

36 StAHH, 614-2/5 *Nationalsozialistische Arbeiterpartei (NSDAP) und ihre Gliederung* B66, letter of April 1, 1929 to Standarte II. For total Hamburg SA strength at this time, see Krause, *Hamburg wird Braun*, 97. He estimates the SA's strength that summer to be approximately 400 men.

37 StAHH, 614-2/5 *Nationalsozialistische Arbeiterpartei (NSDAP) und ihre Gliederung* B152, letter from Böckenhauer to Blücher, November 5, 1926.

38 Archiv FZH, 991 Opposition Gau Hamburg, letter of Kaufmann to the Organisationsabteilung der Reichsleitung der NSDAP, January 24, 1931.

39 Archiv FZH, 991 Opposition Gau Hamburg, letter of Kaufmann to the Organisationsabteilung der Reichsleitung der NSDAP.

40 StAHH, 614-2/5 *Nationalsozialistische Arbeiterpartei (NSDAP) und ihre Gliederung* B152, letter to the *Hanseatische Warte*, October 14, 1930.

41 StAHH, 614-2/5 *Nationalsozialistische Arbeiterpartei (NSDAP) und ihre Gliederung* B152, letter from Oberführer NM to Pg. Tesch, November 19, 1930.

42 StAHH, 614-2/5 *Nationalsozialistische Arbeiterpartei (NSDAP) und ihre Gliederung* B152, letter from Oberführer NM to Pg. Tesch.

43 Koch, *Das Ehrenbuch der SA*, 213.

44 "Bramfeld, Auch hier eine SA-Notküche," *Hamburger Tageblatt*, March 9, 1931.

45 Eve Rosenhaft, *Beating the Fascists: The German Communists and Political Violence 1929–1933* (Cambridge, England: Cambridge University Press, 1983), 53.

46 Sven Reichardt, *Faschistische Kampfbünde. Gewalt und Gemeinschaft im italienischen Squadrismus und in der deutschen SA* (Cologne: Böhlau Verlag, 2002), 468.

47 "Kampf dem Hunger in unseren Reihen," *Hamburger Tageblatt*, April 16, 1931.

48 "Kampf dem Hunger in unseren Reihen," *Hamburger Tageblatt*.

49 "Kampf dem Hunger in unseren Reihen," *Hamburger Tageblatt*.

50 Geoffrey Giles, *Students and National Socialism in Germany* (Princeton, NJ: Princeton University Press, 1985).

51 Giles, *Students and National Socialism*, 46–47, 93–96.

52 StAHH, 614–2/5 *Nationalsozialistische Arbeiterpartei (NSDAP) und ihre Gliederung* B184G, Monatsbericht des Sturmes 76, June 1931.

53 Article reproduced in Anthony McElligott's ". . . und so kame es zu einem schweren Schlägerei. Strassenschlachten in Altona und Hamburg am Ende der Weimarer Republik," in Maike Bruhns, ed., *Hier war doch alles nicht so schlimm. Wie die Nazis in Hamburg den Alltag eroberten* (Hamburg: VSA, 1984), 76–77.

54 Krause, *Hamburg wird Braun*, 192.

55 StAHH, 614-2/5 *Nationalsozialistische Arbeiterpartei (NSDAP) und ihre Gliederung* B152, letter of Möhring to Böckenhauer, July 4, 1932.

56 Koch, *Das Ehrenbuch der SA*, 214.

57 Koch, *Das Ehrenbuch der SA*, 214.

58 Koch, *Das Ehrenbuch der SA*, 214.

59 Heinrich Anacker, *Die Trommel. SA Gedichte*, 3rd ed. (Munich: Eher Verlag, 1935), 63.

60 Eleanor Hancock, *Ernst Röhm: Hitler's SA Chief of Staff* (New York: Palgrave Macmillan, 2008), 107.

61 Archiv FZG, 991 Opposition Gau Hamburg, letter of Kaufmann to the Organi-sationabteilung der Reichsleitung der NSDAP, January 24, 1931.

62 Archiv FZG, 991 Opposition Gau Hamburg, letter of Kaufmann to the Organi-sationabteilung der Reichsleitung der NSDAP.

63 Archiv FZG, 991 Opposition Gau Hamburg, letter of Kaufmann to the Organi-sationabteilung der Reichsleitung der NSDAP.

64 StAHH, 614-2/5 *Nationalsozialistische Arbeiterpartei (NSDAP) und ihre Gliederung* B184f, Tages-befehl, August 18, 1932.

65 StAHH, 614-2/5 *Nationalsozialistische Arbeiterpartei (NSDAP) und ihre Gliederung* B184f, Tages-befehl, August 6, 1932.

66 StAHH, 614-2/5 *Nationalsozialistische Arbeiterpartei (NSDAP) und ihre Gliederung* B184f, Tages-befehl.

67 StAHH, 614-2/5 *Nationalsozialistische Arbeiterpartei (NSDAP) und ihre Gliederung* B107, Böcken-hauer letter to Gau Hannover-Ost, December 4, 1931.

68 StAHH, 614-2/5 *Nationalsozialistische Arbeiterpartei (NSDAP) und ihre Gliederung* B107, Böcken-hauer letter to Standarte 15, September 14, 1932.

69 Dagmar Herzog, *Sex After Fascism: Memory and Morality in Twentieth-Century Germany* (Princeton, NJ: Princeton University Press, 2005), 5, 17.

70 Wilhelm Reich, "Politicizing the Sexual Problems of Youth," first published in *Der sexuelle Kampf der Jugend* (Vienna: Sexpol Verlag, 1932); English translation in Anton Katz, Martin Jay, and Edward Dimendberg, eds., *The Weimar Republic Sourcebook* (Berkeley: University of California Press, 1994), 323.

71   Reich, in *The Weimar Republic Sourcebook*, 323–324.

72   W. U. Eissler, *Arbeiterparteien und Homosexuellenfrage. Zur Sexualpolitik von SPD und KPD in der Weimarer Republik* (Berlin: Verlag Rosa Winkel, 1980).

73   StAHH, 614-2/5 *Nationalsozialistische Arbeiterpartei (NSDAP) und ihre Gliederung* B152, letter of Focking to Böckenhauer, September 14, 1932.

74   Koch, *Das Ehrenbuch der SA*, 212–213.

75   StAHH, 614-2/5 *Nationalsozialistische Arbeiterpartei (NSDAP) und ihre Gliederung* B184f, Rundschreiben Nr. 1, May 24, 1932.

76   StAHH, 614-2/5 *Nationalsozialistische Arbeiterpartei (NSDAP) und ihre Gliederung* B154, Böckenhauer letter to Frauenorden, September 15, 1931.

77   StAHH, 614-2/5 *Nationalsozialistische Arbeiterpartei (NSDAP) und ihre Gliederung* B124, letter to Standarte 45, September 8, 1933.

78   StAHH, 614-2/5 *Nationalsozialistische Arbeiterpartei (NSDAP) und ihre Gliederung* B152, letter of Böckenhauer to Paul Dorndorf, January 20, 1932.

79   See Reichardt, *Faschistische Kampfbünde*, 672–678.

80   William A. Pelz, *The Spartakusbund and the German Working-Class Movement, 1914–1919* (Lewiston, NY: Edwin Mellen Press, 1987), 42–47.

81   "Mudder kann allens," *Hamburger Tageblatt*, July 27, 1931.

82   "Mudder kann allens," *Hamburger Tageblatt*.

83   On the actual record of German wartime women, see Belinda Davis, "Food, Politics, and Women's Everyday Life During the First World War," in Karen Hagemann and Stefanie Schüler-Springorum, eds., *Home/Front: The Military, War, and Gender in Twentieth-Century Germany* (Oxford, England: Berg, 2002), 115–138.

84   "Die Familie als Kulturträgerin," *Hamburger Tageblatt*, June 3, 1932.

85   Koch, *Das Ehrenbuch der SA*, 215.

86   Gudrun Streiter, *Dem Tod so nah . . . Tagebuchblätter eines SA-Mannes Braut* (Munich: Self-published, 1932), 14.

87   Streiter, *Dem Tod so nah . . .*, 40.

88   "Das Fest der Fünftausend. Das jüngste Hamburg Gast der SA," *Hamburger Tageblatt*, September 8, 1931.

89   "Grosse Weihnachtsmesse der NS-Frauenschaft im Zoo," *Hamburger Tageblatt*, December 12, 1932.

90   Archiv FZH/WdE, 131.

91   Archiv FZH/WdE, 131.

92   "Hochzeit im Braunhemd," *Hamburger Tageblatt*, June 19, 1931.

93   "Doch sind unsere Gedanken bei Dir, Kamerad!" *Hamburger Tageblatt*, December 26, 1931.

94   "Doch sind unsere Gedanken bei Dir, Kamerad!" *Hamburger Tageblatt*.

95   "Doch sind unsere Gedanken bei Dir, Kamerad!" *Hamburger Tageblatt*.

96   Hancock, *Ernst Röhm*, 105.

97   Conan Fischer, "Ernst Röhm: Indispensable Outsider," in Ronald Smelser and Rainer Zitelmann, eds., *The Nazi Elite* (New York: Macmillan, 1993), 177.

98   Hancock, *Ernst Röhm*, 107.

99   Fischer, "Ernst Röhm," 177.

100 Eleanor Hancock, *Ernst Röhm*, 110.

101 Karl-Günter Heimsoth, "Freundesliebe oder Homosexualität. Ein Versuch einer anregenden und scheidenden Klarstelling," *Der Eigene*, 1925, 415–425.

102 Helmut Klotz, *Der Fall Röhm* (Berlin: Tempelhof, 1932), 7.

103 Klotz, *Der Fall Röhm*.

104 Klotz, *Der Fall Röhm*, 8–9.

105 Klotz, *Der Fall Röhm*, 9–10.

106 Klotz, *Der Fall Röhm*, 10.

107 Klotz, *Der Fall Röhm*, 10.

108 Klotz, *Der Fall Röhm*, 16.

109 Hancock, "Only the Real," 629.

110 "Sauberes Deutschland durch Nazi?" *Hamburger Echo*, September 24, 1931.

111 "Ein Führer der Hitlerjugend in Röhms Spuren. Schwere Vergehen an Schülern," *Hamburger Echo*, February 19, 1932.

112 Klotz, *Der Fall Röhm*, 1.

113 "Was kostet die SA?" *Das Echo der Woche*, March 6, 1932.

114 "Schluss mit der Heldenlegenden um Hitler!" *Hamburger Echo*, March 9, 1932.

115 "Die Liebesbriefe des Hauptmann Röhms," *Hamburger Echo*, March 9, 1932; "Das System Röhm entlarvt," *Hamburger Echo*, March 10, 1932; "Röhm will klagen? Denn man zu!" *Hamburger Echo*, March 11, 1932; "Röhm möchte einschuchtern," *Hamburger Echo*, April 5, 1932; "Bedeutsame Ausserung der Germania," *Hamburger Echo*, April 7, 1932; "Röhm zieht Klage zurück. Er weiss warum," *Hamburger Echo*, April 16, 1932.

116 "Hitlers Frauen," *Hamburger Echo*, April 16, 1932.

117 "Die Tschekla im Braunen Haus. Die Mordorganisation der NSDAP," *Hamburger Echo*, October 3, 1932; "Major Mayr setzt wieder ein. Wie Röhm unter Reichsbannersittiche flüchtete. Kopfscherzen im braunen Haus," *Hamburger Echo*, October 6, 1932.

118 "Hitler und Röhm wissen um nichts. Der Fememord in der Dresdener SA," *Hamburger Echo*, December 28, 1932.

119 "Brief aus der SA-Kaserne," *Das Echo der Woche*, October 2, 1932.

120 "Die Angegriffenen ins Gefängnis," *Hamburger Tageblatt*, January 9, 1932.

121 "Ist 'Heil Röhm' eine Beleidigung?" *Hamburger Volksblatt*, collected in StAHH, 614-2/5 *Nationalsozialistische Arbeiterpartei (NSDAP) und ihre Gliederung* B220.

122 Quoted in Klaus Mann's essay, "Homosexualität und Fascismus," in *Zahnärzte und Künztler. Aufsätze, Reden, Kritiken 1933–1936* (Hamburg: Rowohlt, 1993), 237.

123 Kurt Tucholsky, "Röhm," *Die Weltbühne*, April 26, 1932.

124 Klotz, *Der Fall Röhm*, 4.

125 Klotz, *Der Fall Röhm*, 4.

126 George Mosse, *Confronting History* (Madison: University of Wisconsin Press, 2000), 106. For the stereotype's propagation, see Jörn Meve, *"Homosexuelle Nazis". Ein Stereotyp in Politik und Litertur des Exils* (Hamburg: Männerschwarm, 1990), as well as Alexander Zinn, *Die soziale Konstruktion des homosexuellen Nationalsozialisten. Zu Genese und Etabierung eines Stereotyp* (Frankfurt am Main: Peter Lang, 1997).

127 Mann, "Homosexualität und Fascismus," 237.

128 Hancock, "Only the Real," 628.

129 Hancock, "Only the Real," 631–634.

130 Archiv FZH, 991 SA Opposition Gau Hamburg.

131 Adolf Brand, "Political Criminals: A Word About the Röhm Case," in Harry Oosterhuis and Hubert Kennedy, eds., *Homosexuality and Male Bonding in Pre-Nazi Germany* (New York: Haworth Press, 1992), 236.

BLOODY SUNDAYS

By September 1930, in the aftermath of the defeat at Sternschanze, Alfred Conn's focus on establishing systems of stormtrooper support in Hamburg cemented his status as the local group's most promising and effective leader—or so it seemed. His first month in power saw the start of the SA's Heim system and its significant addition to the Nazis' propaganda arsenal. Conn clearly recognized how to attract and retain stormtroopers, and he seemed to know how to integrate these men into a fighting force to prepare for the years to come. In November, however, the Nazis dismissed him from his post and expelled him from the Party.

As unified as the SA and the Nazi Party tried to appear from the outside, astute observers of their politics could detect significant rifts. The controversy over Röhm proved to be one continual source of strife, but stormtrooper institutions housed other fault lines as well, and they all became deeper as the organization attempted to keep the growing group under tighter central control. During this time, tolerance for intellectual diversity and idiosyncrasy faded, even for the SA leaders themselves. Conn's mistake had been to profess openly his adherence to a strain of German paganism that he called the German Faith Movement. He had written extensively on the topic, including several self-published books on subjects like the relevance of ancient Germanic myths to the present political situation.[1] To an extent, Conn's "Germanic" belief in mystical racist nationalism was common and popular on the radical right, and his profession of this belief even attracted adherents to the Nazi cause. Conn's old unit, Sturm 2, which had been among Hamburg's fastest-growing SA units, had called itself the deutschgläubiger Sturm (German faith Sturm).[2]

Whether or not Sturm 2's members converted to Conn's formal belief system, they did appreciate his preaching of heroic virtue as the main spiritual element of the stormtrooper struggle. Conn's ancient gods and warriors sought martyrdom, a holy death that would further the cause of good against evil. As Conn wrote in his first book, such heroes "will go consciously down into death, but through this self-sacrifice in the service of the light, they will redeem the universe, for in death they will drag the evil forces down with them."[3] A drive for holy martyrdom ran through all SA politics, as any successful SA leader instinctively understood.

Conn erred, however, in casting his belief system as exclusionary. While his outspoken paganism and emphasis on metaphysical struggle won him great affection among his own troopers, these positions caused tension between him and other SA leaders. Worse, they brought him into conflict with the Hamburg Party's political leaders: Klant, Krebs, and finally Kaufmann, who, through a quirk of fate, were all Catholic. It galled Conn that the Party's national leadership continually called adherents of this southern religion to lead in the great northern city. To him this action proved the disconnect between the Party's Bavarian central authority and the local traditions of other regions. He thus resented the Party's top leaders as the product of a "Catholic south" that often mocked "the Odin-seeking north."[4]

Phrased in this way, Conn's enmity for Catholicism was no radical statement in Protestant Hamburg, whose leading citizens for centuries had nurtured a low-key but persistent anti-Catholic sentiment. Party notables might therefore have ignored Conn's writings, if not for the fact that he also made the far broader accusation that any form of Christian belief was incompatible with *völkisch* politics. It was madness to think that Christianity and National Socialism could cooperate with one another, he wrote in a self-published book, *The Illusion of a National Socialist State on Christian Foundations.*[5] This work—along with another entitled *German Believers or Christian Marxists?*— accused Christianity of being an alien belief system of passivity and control, in contrast to German paganism's promotion of the heroic and ennobling values of individual will.[6] Although we cannot know how many people read Conn's vanity publications, most Hamburg stormtroopers and local Party members would have known his general political and religious views. Conn's writing thus posed a problem for the SA and the Party. Outside of his core of stormtrooper comrades, his constructions greatly risked offending Hamburg's majority Protestants, who did not appreciate the irony of their own long-standing critique of Catholic citizenship being turned against Christianity in general.

Given the content and tone of Conn's anti-Christian sentiments, Party leaders and SA rivals attempted to undermine him almost immediately when he inherited Ellerhusen's position as *Brigadeführer*. Conn's eventual expulsion from the SA showed the limits of "German faith" as a spiritual basis for the movement. Although he and his fellow pagan enthusiasts had been among the Party's most natural early constituents, they steadily became less appealing Party members as the SA transformed itself into a mass organization that was greatly concerned with integrating large numbers of people, and thus appealed to a broad segment of local society. Allowing pagan radicals to serve at the top of the SA risked offending and repelling potential Christian recruits. Moreover, Party leaders feared how Conn's iconoclastic belief system might influence the SA, which had always been unruly and was now growing at an unprecedented rate. Party leaders therefore sought spiritual leadership for the SA that would integrate new recruits as respectful followers of a hierarchy, rather than as independent and uncontrollable actors who followed their own interpretation of the movement's principles.

Not coincidentally, Hamburg's Nazi Party at this time was growing increasingly close to the right wing of the city's Lutheran church. Several of its bishops had already worked for some time to achieve greater cooperation between the two. Around the time Conn and his pagan rebels were being chased out of the SA, Lutheran pastor Franz Tügel and his flock were being lured in. Tügel's journey to his church's extreme right flank progressed steadily through the 1920s, as he looked with resentment on the Weimar era's decreasing respect for authority in the political, social, and familial realms. He particularly resented the movement for women's independence and equality, which he bitterly opposed in the church itself. As he had done while a chaplain during the war, Tügel saw his role as doing "service" in a "manly church of war" that bolstered combatants' fighting strength through spiritual confidence.[7] His frequent use of the word Dienst (service) for his own pastoral activities echoed the stormtroopers' preferred language, which Tügel reflected back to them in order to emphasize the unity between the SA and Lutheranism. In terms of stormtrooper violence, he preached that their war against socialism had God's seal of approval. According to Tügel, stormtroopers were the church's only defense against destruction by the godless forces of socialism and Communism, which had declared war on God in Germany just as they had in Russia. As proof, he cited a supposed attack on his own church during a time when the SA was banned:

When the defenders of the unjust and incomprehensible actions [against the church] say that without the SA we would once again have peace and order, one must respond that without it we would long ago have had Bolshevism in the land . . . I refer once again to the facts: immediately after the ban [on the SA], the red terror renewed and intensified, and it was to me a tangible sign of the times that on the next Sunday our house of god was again overrun by the unhindered Communist horde, which disturbed our church's tranquility.[8]

Such attacks were often more mythical than real. Many incidents claimed to have occurred reflected the Nazis' willingness to see any leftist demonstration in their neighborhood as an attack on them—for instance, when the noise of a Sunday street demonstration seeped into the church during services or meetings. Nazi pastors often interpreted these interactions as deliberate provocations, given the Communist Party's overt anti-church position. In practice, however, a large number of Communists still considered themselves Christians, and they had little desire to attack or provoke the church directly.[9] Tügel and the other Protestant Nazi leaders rarely acknowledged this fact, however, focusing instead on the KPD's larger ideological position against the church. Therefore, Tügel believed that any Communist who claimed to be a Christian still served the devil, whereas Christian stormtroopers served the forces of God. Tügel often made this latter link explicit by claiming that stormtroopers fought "not for the will to power, but rather for a belief in the good" that paralleled early Christian struggles to defend their persecuted community.[10]

As the political conflict intensified, Tügel's church became a spiritual and literal bastion for the SA. Its location in St. Pauli placed it at the center of some of the most violent warfare between stormtroopers and Communists. A heavy neo-Romanesque building meant to recall a Carolingian fortress-church, its central tower cast a heavy shadow over the Holy Ghost Field, a market and fairground that was a popular site for political battles, especially during its famous Christmas carnival. In this context, the church's name—the Gnadenkirche, or Church of Mercy—became darkly ironic, as Tügel fashioned it into a physical and ideological stronghold for stormtroopers fighting in a heavily contested area. Although no physical fighting took place in the church itself, it became a place of spiritual civil war. Local stormtroopers faithfully attended Tügel's services, they lingered after church to thank him for his sermons, and they visited him in his office to seek spiritual counsel (Figure 6.1). Tügel made the church and his parsonage available for Nazi events, particularly those the women's section held to provide social services.[11] Tügel's efforts each Sunday built bonds between the Nazi Party and the Lutheran church, so that the members of each community increasingly saw themselves as one community. Tügel was not the only pastor to pursue such efforts; he and other pastor colleagues who were sympathetic to National Socialism collectively arranged to increase the integration of stormtroopers and Lutheranism.

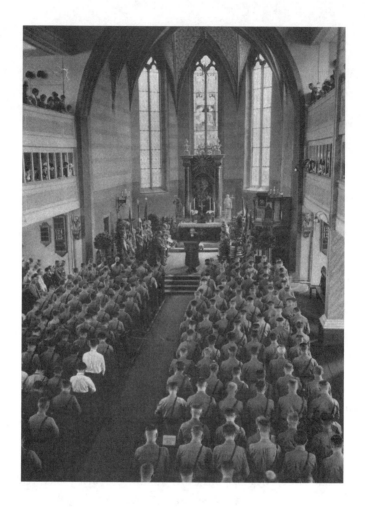

FIGURE 6.1

Stormtroopers in church

Stormtroopers attend church services in uniform.
In Hamburg and Berlin, a faction of conservative
Lutheran pastors came to see themselves as chaplains
to the stormtroopers, who in turn would provide
the foot soldiers needed to retake a state that had
departed from what the clergymen thought was its
divinely directed political path.

Source: Heinrich Hoffman, *Das braune Heer.*
100 Bilddokumente. Leben, Kampf, und Sieg der SA und SS
(Berlin: Zeitgeschichte, 1932).

The history of the stormtroopers' religious beliefs and influences is an important and understudied subject, one worthy of a book in its own right. The Hamburg SA's transition from Conn to Tügel as a source of spiritual inspiration provides one small illustration of the larger dynamic, in which the Nazi movement sought to bridge significant rifts within its community during the period that it neared its ultimate victory over the Republic. As the SA grew, it concentrated increasingly on building a unified identity out of the separate communities it comprised.

Every Sunday, Tügel and his allied pastors spoke in support of this shared identity, thus forming a ritual of allegiance that transcended any doubts that could develop during the week. The stormtroopers' daily interactions within SA living spaces also galvanized the stormtroopers into a unified mentality by giving them similar experiences, which they were encouraged to interpret in a like manner. Living systems thus became ideological systems that were teaching members to perceive the Party as upstanding, family oriented, socially responsible, and connected to the institutions of a strong society. Those living within this closed social loop ingested only the Party's preferred interpretations of local events, whether they read them in the official newspaper, heard them from a friend, or received them from the pulpit. This intellectual submersion into the Party's mental world effectively convinced stormtroopers and their allies that the constant violence they unleashed against enemies was in fact a work of good. Those who knew a stormtrooper personally could easily be convinced that a son, brother, coworker, or fellow churchgoer acted for pure motives, even when they behaved badly. For those outside the movement, the mediating institutions of the SA lifestyle and the Nazi media increasingly succeeded in recasting violent episodes into positive attractors. The Nazi share of the vote thus grew steadily from 1930 to 1933. It did so not in spite of this pro-family movement's reliance on violence but because of it.

The SA Subculture as School of Violence

Life in the SA meant spending as much time as possible with comrades, eating and living with them while sharing thoughts on politics, philosophy, life, and love. The unemployed stormtroopers spent essentially all of their time in places the movement had built for their political work, personal relaxation, and ideological edification. Even those with jobs often made the

SA taverns, and later the SA Heime, the first stop on their daily schedule. A working stormtrooper might visit his home tavern to greet his comrades at the beginning of the day and then travel with them to work, while unemployed stormtroopers also went in groups to social-insurance or food-stamp offices. Traveling together protected the stormtroopers from possible attack. These unemployed SA men then returned to the SA Heim and kept themselves busy throughout the day, as the Book of Honor described in mournfully paranoid fashion:

> Other comrades appear according to the time available, to ask about how the party work is going, or to learn bits of local news. Some find themselves together over a game of cards to pass the time. What else should they do? They're registered as seeking work, but since they're known as SA men they receive no assignments. That's all part of the system's resistance: it weakens the SA and the movement through unemployment. Hungry and miserable SA men might drop out.[12]

As much as the stormtroopers preferred to believe it, "the system" had no such plot to keep stormtroopers unemployed until they gave up on the movement. If it had such a phantom policy, it would have had the opposite effect, since economic distress strengthened rather than weakened the stormtrooper community. The Heime and taverns gave unemployed comrades a place to spend the day away from the guilt-inducing stares of any dependent family members who might be lurking at home, and they could pass the time in the company of similarly downtrodden comrades without feeling like failures.

After working hours, the taverns and Heime again became meeting points for all stormtroopers. In addition to social calls, SA men were required to appear twice a week: once for roll call, at which all members received orders from the commanding officer, and once for an informal social evening. Even these events ran in an organized and efficient manner, beginning with the hoisting of a swastika flag and posting guards against Communist attacks. Then the Sturmführer would inform the SA men of the week's pressing issues and give orders for coming assignments. Both roll call and social evenings could also provide formal ideological instruction from official Party speakers and experts invited to speak on national, military, and "racial" questions. Talks often combined ideological and practical elements, such as how to conduct oneself on watch duty or "how to keep the Commune and *Reichsbanner* off you in a street fight."[13]

Stormtroopers were forbidden to drink, at least while on official duty, and they had to "stay sharp" while on duty lest they receive demerits or be assigned to punishment duties. The prohibition against alcohol, however, often meant nothing in practice. Contemporary reports and letters from stormtroopers often mentioned comrades' extreme drunkenness, saying they had imbibed on the way to the tavern or that those eating supper in the back room drank with their meal, but in fact the line between being on or off duty rarely existed for men living such an all-encompassing lifestyle.[14] Whether drunk or not, tavern-dwelling stormtroopers entertained themselves with card games and conversation. Skat was the most popular game, as it had been with soldiers in the trenches during the war. The Party supplied newspapers, magazines, and books, which fueled conversation. The most important reading material was found in the *Tageblatt*'s special section for the SA and the SA newspaper, *Der SA Mann*. Each copy of a paper would be consumed by multiple stormtroopers, who shared articles and discussed issues while biding their time between official gatherings and sudden calls to alarm. The newspapers allowed them to teach one another and to take responsibility for cultivating their comrades' knowledge and abilities. The papers combined with formal SA service to teach stormtroopers "how to engage political opponents in discussion" and how to "become hard, disciplined, and able to meet violence with violence."[15]

Articles that taught stormtroopers new ways to justify their paranoia and define their violence as defensive action did so not only through overt claims, but also by describing a world in which they were under constant threat from international, national, and local enemies. Frequent reporting on such threats gave the stormtroopers a sense of being under siege in their own country and city. It encouraged them to embrace feelings of anxiety, of being encircled, and even of helplessness, which they could eliminate only by committing acts of violence against their enemies. On the international level, articles in the "Storm Column" highlighted the alleged inequality and unfairness of the Versailles system. Under the guise of technology reviews, articles reminded SA men of the latest military capabilities under development in Britain, France, and the United States—weapons and vehicles these countries could use to threaten Germany's borders and economy. New French bombers, for instance, could directly attack an undefended

Hamburg.[16] The hated treaty prevented stormtroopers from acquiring their own deadly toys, offensive or defensive, and it also banned them from ever receiving any kind of formal military training.

Articles in the SA section of the *Tageblatt* and *SA Mann* spoke of "future wars" as if they were already certain to occur, leading the untrained stormtroopers to fear for their safety when the inevitable war broke out.[17] SA media also played to the young male fascination with weapons, vehicles, and war-making technology to instill in the stormtroopers a fear of being unprepared for violence. SA media and regular quasi-military training then posed as the solution to this fear, offering the added allure of teaching banned knowledge. Stories on military technology and training along with articles describing the foreign-policy conflicts of the time reinforced the stormtroopers' sense that they were under threat from foreign powers, and that they had to be prepared as best they could to protect themselves, their comrades, and their nation.

Eleven Narratives of Everyday Violence

SA media also stoked stormtrooper paranoia at the local level, where coverage of urban political combat gave SA men a sense of being under constant threat in their own neighborhoods. Typical accounts included tales of stormtroopers being attacked while "on the way home" (*Nachhauseweg*) from meetings, robbed while on their way to work, or besieged in their hostels and taverns by Communist hordes. In some sense, the details of individual incidents proved less important than the pattern created by repetition, within which several recurring types of violent encounters emerged. These cases frightened and fascinated the SA men, who read them with special attention to learn the myriad ways that danger threatened their lives and families. The various types of violent encounters represented categories of knowledge or narrative frameworks that the stormtroopers absorbed and then used to shape their understanding of the persecution they claimed to face (see Table 6.1).

1. Generic Attacks

Most accounts of violent encounters took the form of short, generic descriptions, usually only a paragraph in length. Bereft of specific detail, the stories highlighted the wide variety of circumstances under which a stormtrooper

Generic attacks	113
Police persecution	44
Stormtroopers outnumbered	43
Attacks outside Hamburg	36
Attacks on SA spaces	36
Attacks on private homes	27
Attacks on Nachhauseweg	17
Destruction of property	14
SA protection of public order	11
Treacherous tactics	6
Attacks on women	5

TABLE 6.1

Types of violent incidents, 1931–1932

could come under threat: in the morning while on his way to work, while distributing fliers or hanging posters, or simply while walking the streets.[18] These stories used repetition to encourage the persecution mentality that fueled the Nazi mind-set.

The 568 issues of the *Hamburger Tageblatt* published in 1931 and 1932 included 352 reports of stormtrooper persecution at the hands of Reichsbanner, Communists, or the police.[19] This included all newspaper reports that stormtroopers, their family members, Party members, and SA private spaces had come under physical attack. The number of incidents would have been even higher had the *Tageblatt* been published every day during this period. It did not publish on Sundays, when stormtroopers received their political information in church, and it lost an additional 64 issues during the periods when the state banned publication as punishment for SA violence. Therefore, averaged out over the two peak years of the *Kampfzeit*, these 352 reports meant that stormtroopers learned of a comrade being attacked or otherwise persecuted in three of five issues, with the events themselves taking place every two days. The sheer number of incidents carried its own message.

2. Police Persecution

Stories of stormtroopers clashing with policemen appeared more often—44 times in 1931–1932—than any other conflict type. Specific cases included the arrest of SA men for peaceful political activities, the arrest or harassment of stormtroopers victimized by leftist violence, police refusal to stop attacks on stormtroopers, and police hindrance of SA reinforcements to assist their victimized comrades.[20] The police also frequently searched stormtroopers and their buildings for illegal weapons—a reasonable precaution, one might think, except that the *Tageblatt* also frequently claimed that local Communists got away without punishment for openly carrying firearms.[21] The paper also described how police, despite this blatant threat against the Nazis, refused to allow crippled war veterans to carry their canes.[22] Another paper might have observed that this seeming act of dishonor had a logical origin, as policemen often encountered supposedly crippled rightist veterans who somehow became quite spry when a fight broke out and used their canes as clubs. The *Tageblatt*, however, found it useful to stoke the persecution fantasies of rightist veterans, and to portray policemen loyal to the Republic as outright villains who attacked, arrested, and abused the unfortunate and innocent stormtroopers.[23]

Conflict between stormtroopers and the police came from a very real rivalry between the two groups, since both saw themselves as the rightful guardians of social order. In other circumstances, however, stormtroopers saw themselves as the policemen's natural allies. Many stormtroopers, including Böckenhauer and several other key early leaders, had in fact been policemen themselves. These men hated the fact that the bulk of the police force remained loyal to the state with its republican form of government, rather than to a not-yet-realized Nazi regime. SA media therefore walked a fine line when portraying the mutual antagonism between the two supposed forces of order. The stormtroopers, the paper claimed, committed overtly violent and criminal acts only because the revolutionaries had perverted German systems of authority into illegitimate forms. Nazis therefore saw the police as misguided agents of a false regime. This portrayal enhanced the stormtroopers' status as persecuted victims of a corrupt police force, which now worked hand in hand with the internal enemies who had taken over the state.[24]

Although images of cooperation between the Communists and the police seem hard to swallow, the police did coordinate with the Social Democratic militia at times. Lothar Danner, the Social Democratic chief of Hamburg's republican police force, admitted that police functions at the time had become more closely bound to protecting the state than they had previously been. During the imperial era, according to Danner, the police had been "an effective and reliable organ of the state, but no instrument of power."[25] Danner's formulation ignores the fact that the imperial police had actually been just such an instrument, spying on socialists, labor unions, and other political groups judged to threaten the imperial system or its major corporate concerns. The relationship did become more formal under the Weimar government, especially after the uprisings from right and left in its early years led the Hamburg Senate to mandate that the police focus on preventing putsches. Given these political alignments, the Social Democratic Reichsbanner did enjoy the official support of Hamburg's police captain when the SA and Red Front Fighting Brigade did not.[26] This real difference led to much of the conflict that the *Tageblatt* unfairly described.

Despite orders from on high, the lower ranks of the police force teemed with officers sympathetic to the parties of the far right. Policemen who were also former trench soldiers, *Freikorps* men, and members of all the various rightist paramilitaries and sporting groups increasingly drifted to the Nazi Party as it became the dominant rightist party.[27] As Danner later recalled, many of these men came from the neighborhoods most susceptible to the Party's rhetoric of responsibility, and they were therefore enmeshed in the social networks that fueled the Nazis' growth.[28] Joseph Goebbels even went so far as to claim "an absolute National Socialist majority in Hamburg's police barracks," although this assertion never approached reality.[29] Those who were openly Nazis could not stay in the police ranks, as Böckenhauer had discovered after the Battle of Sternschanze, when the Senate issued a statement: "Officers who support parties that seek the violent overthrow of the system of government violate their oath of loyalty to the state and transgress against service regulations."[30]

Rightist policemen therefore had to decline any formal association with Nazi groups, lest they lose their jobs. Even so, they retained a great degree of secret sympathy for the Party, a tendency frequently featured in stormtrooper literature that portrayed policemen as finding small ways to mitigate the persecution of the SA that they were allegedly required to carry out.[31] Family connections and appeals to common morality could apparently persuade these sympathetic officers to move past stereotypes and into cooperation, as happened in a pivotal scene in the book *Gotthard Kraft*, when a conversation between a stormtrooper and his sympathetic policeman in-law developed into one of the most extended intellectual debates in all of stormtrooper literature.[32] Stories like these taught stormtroopers that policemen were not the enemies they often appeared to be, and that if they could overcome the barriers the Republic had placed between them the two could in fact find common ground, form productive partnerships, and share a sense of family. Fictional portrayals of sympathetic policemen had to carry much of the weight of Nazi claims of police sympathy, since the *Tageblatt* generally avoided anything that could compromise the movement's hidden allies. The paper instead discussed the conflict in familial and generational terms. In the *Tageblatt*'s coverage, policemen and stormtroopers had the same worldview and the same goals, differing only in their methods. The police, older men who had grown up in a more responsible time, naively tried to enforce old laws and outmoded peaceful forms of political activity. The youths of the SA, however, recognized that the Communists had inaugurated a new era of political violence that only the SA's forceful resistance could overcome. Both groups therefore served the German state, if not the Republic, and the conflict between them only helped Communist provocateurs to weaken the nation. This conflict was therefore, in the stormtroopers' view, one of the era's great tragedies.

Stormtroopers constantly complained of their treatment at the hands of the police and were unable to fathom why the forces of order would oppose rather than assist them. As it was, the stormtroopers believed the police were all too willing to take action against the SA when tricked by leftist provocateurs. For instance, Communists allegedly sparked brawls near SA taverns in order to create patterns of violence that would lead the police to close the establishments. As the *Tageblatt* wrote when the Lokal Balzuweit on Eppendorfer Weg fell victim to this ploy, "Our people, even underage youths, are attacked and beaten down—and as a punishment for this, they close our taverns!"[33]

Stormtroopers summed up their view of this dynamic with the slogan, "The victims are guilty!"[34] The *Tageblatt* taught stormtroopers that they had been abandoned by the state and by the police—in other words, by their natural allies and by the structures of authority that their fathers and grandfathers had built. In this state of abandonment, the SA men could only protect themselves to the best of their ability. Their goal was to eventually reclaim the state as a moral agent of nationalist self-protection. Stories about the SA's conflicts with the police therefore appeared with particular frequency, not only because they actually took place regularly but because they built a psychological foundation on which stormtroopers could build their understanding of all other conflict types.

3. Stormtroopers Outnumbered

While the police allegedly continued their unfair persecution of would-be allies, stormtroopers came under attack by overwhelming hordes of other enemies. Although many of the *Tageblatt*'s stories of combat did not state the number of attackers, when reporters did give such information they almost always described overwhelming odds against the SA. Stormtroopers who believed these articles learned that Communists and socialists regularly outnumbered SA men in fights by 10, 20, 60, 100, or 150 to one.[35] In one instance, 500 Communists reportedly stormed a Nazi newsstand in broad daylight, destroyed it, attacked the proprietor, and battled SA reinforcements until the police arrived.[36] In a way, these reports did reflect the reality of street combat during the late Weimar era: everyday attacks occurred spontaneously when one side found itself with enough numerical superiority to minimize its risk. Alternately, perpetrators of planned attacks made sure in advance that they would enjoy the same advantage—a form of aggression that the Nazis themselves practiced, even if the *Tageblatt* never admitted it in print. The paper's penchant for reporting only incidents where the SA was in the minority boosted the stormtroopers' sense of righteous suffering. The image of the beleaguered stormtrooper had an ideological component as well, which tied into the masochistic tendencies and martyr complexes many stormtroopers had.[37] Stormtroopers considered themselves among the heroic few willing to stand up to a red tide, a role the Freikorps fighters had also proclaimed for themselves during the postwar border skirmishes.

Reports of outnumbered stormtroopers thus built on the standard tropes of right-wing persecution literature, which enabled stormtroopers to see connections between their local combat and national defense. This type of narrative also increased stormtroopers' confidence in their own abilities, since they usually fought off their attackers and escaped with only minor injuries. One SA man, the stormtroopers learned, could fight off 50

FIGURE 6.2

Jiu-jitsu illustration

An illustration for the SA jiu-jitsu newspaper course demonstrates how to defend
against multiple attackers. Stormtroopers
saw their enemies as a dark mass of armed
ambushers, in contrast to the heroic
bearing and honorable conduct of the
unarmed individual SA man.

Source: *Der SA Mann*, issue unknown.

or even 100 lesser men of the Communist party. The SA even promised to teach stormtroopers to fight with such skill through a recurring series in *Der SA Mann*, which presented a course on jiu-jitsu techniques illustrated by SA men punching, kicking, head-butting, and otherwise defending themselves from groups of shadowy figures in working-class attire (Figure 6.2). The Nazi emphasis on the Communists' numerical superiority matched the movement's insistence on its opponents' cowardice. The *Tageblatt* often commented sardonically, usually with sarcastic quotation marks, on the enemy's "heroism" or "courage."[38] A story about 100 Communists attacking a lone Nazi exclaimed, "What heroism!"[39] A similar pair of attacks later that year offered a chance for the Communists to "show their heroism" by attacking only when they greatly outnumbered the SA.[40] Ironically, the Social Democratic newspaper the *Echo* began to use similar language against the Nazis. By late 1932, the two papers' sarcastic coverage of their respective enemies sounded much alike, and this name-calling served to diminish the individual enemy while as a mass it remained a threat.

4. Attacks outside Hamburg

The *Tageblatt* increased stormtroopers' anxiety about being encircled by covering violent events outside the city as prominently as they did those within its borders. The headlines encouraged Hamburg stormtroopers to think they were the ones being targeted, even when the story concerned another place altogether. In the June 17, 1932, issue of the *Tageblatt*, for example, stormtroopers read the headline, "Warning! The Red Front is mobilizing! Through terror they plan to force a new ban on the SA!"[41]—but the article described events in Berlin, not Hamburg.

The *Tageblatt* particularly concentrated on incidents when stormtroopers outside Hamburg incurred serious or fatal wounds during political combat, as they did 36 times in 1931–1932.[42] The paper gave periodic updates of the national tally of SA "martyrs" and wounded. In May 1931 alone it told of 5 deaths, 134 seriously wounded, and 183 lightly wounded.[43] These statistics, however, often misled, as Nazi journalists tended to exaggerate their side's body count. A different article that month listed 5 dead, 369 seriously wounded, and "thousands" of others who received lesser wounds.[44] Raising the body count increased the level of persecution the SA men could decry, and it raised the stormtroopers' paranoia that "red terror across the Reich" would strike them next.[45] The frequency of the reporting on these events became as significant as the specific details. It created a constant sense of insecurity among the stormtroopers, who thus became more prone to resort to aggression as a form of preemptive self-defense.

5. Attacks on SA Spaces

As the drumbeat of frequent attacks on the SA sounded across the country, attacks nearer to home echoed most loudly in stormtroopers' ears. The *Tageblatt* reported 36 attacks against SA taverns and Heime during 1931–1932, making them the most targeted locations for political combat. In a sense, the emphasis on these locations continued the SA's self-image as tavern brawlers during the turbulent postwar years. Now that the SA had expanded its operations into a unified network of protected spaces, the need for defense seemed greater than ever.

Local members of the various political parties struggled to gain control over their neighborhood taverns. They sought to convert neutral or enemy pubs to their side by shifting the balance of the clientele. Once the Nazis represented the majority of customers in a tavern, it became first an unofficial then an official Party outpost, as occurred with the Lokal von Habermann at Schellingstrasse 17. For 25 years the pub had hosted SPD events, and its conversion to an SA tavern in March 1932 was a significant marker of Nazi Party success in the neighborhood.[46] Once its loyalty was secured, an SA tavern technically remained open to all comers but in effect functioned like a private club that welcomed only stormtroopers, Party members, and friends of the movement. Many stormtroopers spent more time in their chosen tavern than in their own home. These taverns thus held particular importance in the struggle over contested neighborhoods, as they served as strongholds that housed combat-ready stormtroopers.[47] Both Nazis and their opponents often called these spaces *Kaserne* (barracks), and Party members who came under attack in the area could call the tavern and summon stormtrooper reinforcements to sally forth.

The overtly military function of these taverns encouraged architectural features that echoed design elements of fortresses and trenches. Many taverns, including the Hotel Adler on Susannenstrasse and the Lokal Balzuweit at Eppendorfer Weg 175, sat on strategic corners that controlled vital cross streets. Both buildings faced the street at an angle, which made them more defensible and reduced the number of attackable windows and entryways. Other taverns, such as the *Sturmlokal* Struck on Fruchtallee 60, protected themselves with fences and other barricades reminiscent of the features soldiers had built to defend their territory during the Great War.[48] Although these defensive measures were less obviously deadly than the barbed wire and minefields of that conflict, the fortified front yards of the SA taverns encouraged a similar mind-set of entrenchment and paranoia.

These taverns gained local infamy as points of origin for ad hoc attacks on neighborhood rivals and thus came under assault themselves. Beginning in 1931, the SPD in Berlin, Hamburg, and other major cities launched an "assault on the taverns" to root out Nazi "invaders" of Communist neighborhoods. The vast majority of these attacks consisted of minor vandalism, such as smashed windows or stones thrown at a building. At times, however, carloads of Communists fired shots at a tavern from a moving vehicle.[49] In two incidents, political opponents threw homemade bombs at SS taverns in Altona.[50]

Taverns were both private and public spaces: private because they hosted the SA's intimate ersatz family life, and public because a party's control over specific locations and neighborhoods served as a measure of its political success. While the attacks on SA pubs and Heime posed a danger to and irritated the stormtroopers, they nevertheless played by the Nazis' own rules of the political game.

6. Attacks on Private Homes

The Communist threat to stormtroopers' private lives reached its apex in direct attacks against them in their homes, or against the homes themselves. The *Tageblatt* reported 27 such attacks, an average of two per month, from 1931 to 1932.[52] These assaults took many forms. Sometimes an attack began with stones thrown through a Party member's window; when he emerged to clean up the damage, the enemy attacked in force, beat him, and destroyed parts of the house.[53] On other occasions, Communists waited to attack inside a stairwell or in the shadows around a building.[54] One stormtrooper was ambushed while climbing his stairs, thrown over the railing, then kicked repeatedly and thrown through his neighbor's closed front door.[55] These stories portrayed Communist violence as particularly wild and untargeted, as not only the stormtroopers themselves came under attack—a conflict sometimes crashed without warning into neighboring homes. One incident in May 1932, if the *Tageblatt* can be believed, saw the Communists demolish an apartment belonging to a stormtrooper's neighbor.[56]

All these incidents created the impression that the Nazis' enemies did not limit political violence to the public realm and were carrying it into traditionally safe areas of German life. Other vulnerable realms included churches and religious celebrations. In novels and autobiographies written by SA men, the stormtroopers' enemies often attacked on Sundays, during the Christmas holiday, and while people were at church.[57] Franz Tügel claimed in his memoirs to have suffered several of these attacks. However, the fact that the *Tageblatt* never recorded any such incident casts doubt on his claim, since any attack by Communists against a church would have made for stellar propaganda. Newspapers of various stripes did report several Christmas Eve attacks, as well as many that took place at the Hamburger Dom, the Christmastime carnival held at the Heiligengeistfeld near Tügel's church. The roots of the event stretched back centuries as a Christmas celebration for all of Hamburg's citizens, but the Communists who had come to dominate the surrounding neighborhood now claimed the site as their home territory.[58] They therefore stalked the fairgrounds in search of political enemies, even when said enemies were there only to participate in a traditional Christmas event. In 1931, Communists attacked and wounded an out-of-town SA man visiting the festival, and fought a shootout with police that killed at least one officer.[59] As spontaneous conflicts between usually drunken gangs of young men, these attacks did not represent an organized political plan so much as local rivalries and social interactions. However, two similar attacks the next year provided evidence enough for stormtroopers to convince themselves that leftist criminals were attempting to appropriate for themselves what had been a universal Christmas celebration.[60]

7. Attacks on *Nachhauseweg*

Other narrative frames in Nazi media highlighted how the norms of political combat had changed. The *Tageblatt* blamed the Communists for this shift by featuring occasions when they committed acts of political violence beyond legitimate political locations. According to the *Tageblatt*, SA men on their way home from meetings, rallies, and evenings at the tavern faced special dangers once they separated from their comrades and went their way alone or in small groups. As an outraged Conn wrote in his memoirs, "What the Communists could not accomplish indoors against the united SA, they sought to inflict on single SA men on their way home."[51] Unlike most claims of stormtrooper persecution, the claim of heightened violence in these situations actually matched reality, although even here it misled by ignoring the fact that the stormtroopers themselves attacked their enemies in the same way. Hostage to their self-willed state of denial, stormtroopers read only about their own victimization during an attack while "on the way home"—*Nachhauseweg*—a situation so common it became its own category of narration.

The *Nachhauseweg* was a liminal space that represented a shadowy border between political and personal life, and thus proved especially dangerous for actual and symbolic reasons. The archetypical attack of this kind highlighted the particular dangers of the late evening, when the stormtroopers' official duties ended and they returned home to their families. Leaving the Lokal, perhaps slightly drunk, proved particularly dangerous if they lived in a contested or Communist-dominated area of the city. From early on, the SA organized its units west of the Alster into escort troops to protect men who lived in St. Pauli. The troops, who faced a winding route that started in the most dangerous streets, began in force so they could face these areas with the greatest numbers. As each man arrived home, the group diminished and its capacity for self-defense decreased, but so too did the danger as the neighborhoods became safer. By the time the escort troop reached Eimsbüttel, Hoheluft, and Eppendorf, which had long been among the Hamburg Nazis' upper-middle-class strongholds, the tiny group could safely walk the streets unmolested. By the time these last few reached their homes, it could be one or two o'clock in the morning.

Such a schedule exacerbated the tensions between Party and family life, because it meant stormtroopers spent even more time away from home than regular Party service required. But the *Tageblatt* chose to interpret the stormtroopers' sacrifice of sleep and security as evidence of the movement's caring side. It transformed accounts of these attacks into prominent testimonials to the sacrifices comrades and the SA leadership made to battle concrete problems of everyday life. The *Nachhauseweg* attacks also carried great symbolic importance, in that they represented a transition of violence from public political life into the private realm.

8. Destruction of Property

Communist attacks on stormtrooper homes and public accommodations threatened not only the domestic peace of the private sphere but also the sacred bourgeois notion of private property, which the Communists loudly and openly decried. The KPD had for years advocated "direct actions" to provide for the poor and unemployed, using methods that included "proletarian shopping trips" to rob welfare agencies and private food stores to secure provisions.[61] The *Tageblatt*'s reports emphasized these types of incidents, as well as attacks on National Socialists' property, which also experienced targeted assaults. At least once a month, stormtroopers read of Communists who destroyed windows and otherwise vandalized buildings, tore down swastika flags, robbed SA men and Party members of their backpacks and wallets, and pillaged newsstands that sold the *Tageblatt* and other Nazi papers (Figure 6.3).[62] Communists were thought to have attacked a Hitler Youth selling newspapers and stolen the boy's wares, money, and bicycle, and to have forced a Party member into his apartment at gunpoint and then looted the place of money, private papers, and Nazi paraphernalia.[63] These attacks represented political acts against the symbols of the Nazi movement, as seen in the high percentage that targeted flags, Party badges, newspapers, and other swastika-bearing items. They also reinforced Nazi narratives of Communist criminality and disdain for the hard-won rewards of individual industry.

9. SA Protection of Public Order

The waves of robberies by Communists that periodically swept across contested neighborhoods may have offered individual Communists short-term emotional satisfaction and helped fill the KPD's coffers, but they also allowed the Nazi Party to pose as protectors of order, property, and small businessmen.[64] Taken together, stories about public order cast SA men as forces of decency in dangerous neighborhoods, where they acted alongside policemen and firemen to serve the public. These stories featured stormtroopers who assisted in the aftermath of car accidents, chased down hit-and-run drivers, and helped firemen evacuate burning buildings.[65] Such stories proved particularly important for the stormtroopers' self-image as upstanding citizens who used violence only in service to the community. However, such incidents were not as common as the SA might have liked, and they were far fewer than acts of rivalry with the police.

FIGURE 6.3

A photo of a Nazi-affiliated newspaper shop's broken window claimed to demonstrate that their homes, businesses, and places of political business were under constant attack by the Communists. Nazi media frequently highlighted property damage against their spaces while ignoring their own attacks against rivals. *Source:* Collection of Archiv FZH.

10. Treacherous Tactics

Nazi media also created an image of the upstanding stormtrooper by showing his enemies using deceitful and treacherous tactics, which marked these
foes as having abandoned traditional modes of honorable masculine confrontation. According to the *Tageblatt*, one common trick in the Communist
arsenal was to steal Party badges and SA uniforms and use them to entrap
trusting stormtroopers.[66] Undercover Communists also asked stormtroopers for cigarettes, a ruse that used the stormtroopers' inherent generosity to
draw them into striking distance for an ambush or assault.[67] Given that this
tactic mirrored a common technique that male prostitutes used to approach
potential clients, it is possible that it also reflected the antifascist assumption
that stormtroopers were homosexuals whose unnatural attraction to men
could be used against them to set up an ambush.

The *Tageblatt* warned stormtroopers of another underhanded tactic the
Communists employed to harm the SA's reputation. Groups of Communists
would attack stormtroopers in the street, then flee to a Jewish home, turn
off the lights, and call the police. When the police arrived, they would interpret the scene as an SA attack against an innocent Jewish household.[68] These
stories became particularly important when they manipulated the supposed
link between Communists and Jews to portray a sort of inverse stereotype
of the stormtrooper. In contrast to the heroic, masculine, and appropriately
militarized stormtrooper, SA media presented Jews as weak and cowardly,
and thus needing to resort to underhanded tactics. These stories portray
stormtrooper antisemitism as different from the more biological and pseudoscientific racism that existed elsewhere in Nazi circles, and which later
came to dominate the Third Reich.

In the Kampfzeit years, Hamburg's SA eschewed the type of bloodthirsty
sexualized expressions of antisemitism popular in the central and southern
German cities, where Julius Streicher's *Der Stürmer* habitually showed Jewish
men savaging blonde women.[69] Instead, the *Tageblatt* and *SA Mann* charged
Jews and their supposed Communist agents with lacking the masculine virtues needed to win legitimate political power. Jews therefore appeared in
Nazi newspapers as shadowy figures who directed operations from the rear,
who used others to fight on their behalf, who shielded themselves behind
women and children, or who simply hid in their homes with the lights
turned out. Hamburg's SA media particularly hated one leader of the local

chapter of the Red Front Fighters, a Belgian Jew named Andre, who allegedly directed attacks on Nazi meetings from within a protective cordon of Communist minions. Andre had helped found the RFB in 1928 and had since become a member of the *Bürgerschaft*. This status brought him further immunity from SA retribution, leading stormtroopers to see the republican form of government as an underhanded socialist tactic to avoid physical confrontations with superior stormtrooper men.[70]

Stories about cowardly Jews and treacherous socialists resonated with rightist audiences because of their connections to long-standing discourse around German Jewish men as lacking martial masculinity.[71] In SA writings, Jews' pacifism and refusal to engage in honorable combat threatened to infect all of Germany with an "unmanly sense" or a "self-demasculinization."[72] The fact that Jewish men had in fact participated in the Great War in numbers far out of proportion to their percentage of the population had little impact on stormtroopers' beliefs, as they preferred to create simplistically clear categories for which types of men could wield legitimate political authority.

11. Attacks on Women

Whenever it could, SA media highlighted what it considered the ultimate violation of martial codes: attacks on women. Although there were not a large number of these attacks, each one that did take place sparked moral outrage and wider allegations that the SA's enemies had dark plans for the German gender order. Some of the chronicled attacks were more psychological than physical, such as when Communists targeted Nazi women for hateful graffiti, death threats, or threats against their families.[73] Communists told the mothers of SA men and Hitler Youths that they planned to target their sons for particular punishment, in the hopes that the mothers' fear would prompt them to convince their sons to quit political activity.[74]

Such tales stirred stormtrooper concerns that their actions could bring their families under threat, or at the very least would upset the women they sought to keep sheltered from the dark side of political conflict. In the worst cases, the *Tageblatt* warned, Communists might even attack women directly, perhaps after weekend events in outdoor areas of the city or as they walked through shopping districts.[75] Nazi media used these tales to teach women and their male protectors that, as long as the Nazis' enemies remained unchecked, women were not safe in public spaces. If they ventured into the wrong areas, they might face verbal or even physical abuse. The most common insult, "Nazi sow," could start brawls when stormtroopers in hearing distance felt compelled to protect a woman's honor.[76]

The gender trope that militant men must protect innocent women to ensure an orderly and upstanding society runs through many eras and places in history. In this time and place, however, it gained added currency because it matched stormtroopers' antagonism toward the socialist-led modernization of the gender order during the Republic. If women were to be equal to men in the political realm, then they too could become victims of political bloodshed. Killing of women had in fact already taken place. After the Great War, women had become not only political actors but also victims of riots, assaults, and even assassinations. In many cases, of course, the perpetrators of such misdeeds lived on the political right, as they had in the most famous case of the political murder of a woman: Rosa Luxembourg. Luxembourg was a socialist leader who had been captured during the Spartacist revolt in 1919 by a Freikorps unit. The group's leader ordered her roughed up, interrogated, and then executed. They dumped her body into a canal. Luxembourg's murder was hardly something the stormtroopers decried—in fact, they often celebrated the deed, and they eventually drew into the SA or Nazi Party many of the men who had participated in the execution.[77] When rightist women were attacked, however, the Nazis considered it an unprecedented and particularly evil violation of long-held norms. The more they believed that non-leftist women were under physical and psychological attack, the more justified the stormtroopers felt their own violence to be.

From Word to Deed: Nazi Murderers as Misguided Children

Stormtroopers' socialization toward violence was not an abstract issue. As the daily reports from all local newspapers showed, young stormtroopers who ingested messages of violence and paranoia while living in their barracks inevitably took this mentality into the streets, where they found themselves embroiled in frequent fights, regular ambushes, continual attacks and counter-attacks, and a range of general villainy. Most of these events were small-scale incidents that were soon forgotten, except by the participants and their direct social network, who treasured such negative memories as a source of self-justification when they then took the offensive.

This dynamic of attack, reprisal, and constant escalation predictably and perhaps inevitably caused serious injuries and even fatalities. In March 1931, two such incidents generated a year's worth of headlines for the stormtrooper perpetrators, publicity that brought an unwelcome focus on the SA's closed social world. In both cases, however, a significant strain of public opinion still found ways to view stormtrooper criminals as misguided and wayward youths whose crimes had come from—and to some extent could be excused by—their life experiences and social circumstances.

The Case of Friedrich Pohl

In March 1931, a young policeman named Friedrich Pohl found himself summoned to the offices of a state prosecutor named Lassally. Pohl, 28 years old and a member of Hamburg's bicycle police unit, had come under suspicion of anti-republican political activism as part of a far-reaching probe of such attitudes within police ranks. One of the chief pieces of evidence against Pohl consisted of antisemitic political statements he had made to a policeman comrade, which this man considered to be of such severity that he had lodged a complaint. During a hearing on March 4, Pohl denied being a member of the Nazi Party or SA, but after Lassally spoke with several witnesses, he summoned Pohl again on March 13. The appointment so unnerved Pohl that he drank himself into a stupor the night before.

Appearing early the next morning at Lassally's office, nervous and still drunk, Pohl stood before the inspector, who did not offer him a seat. As he stood, Pohl endured a series of questions regarding the statements of anonymous witnesses against him. He became increasingly agitated. At the close of the interview, Lassally, reading off a standard form, asked Pohl if he wanted to withdraw from police ranks. Pohl responded that "only socialists would be left" if nationalist policemen took that course of action. When Lassally wrote down the remark, Pohl took it as a sign that the deck was stacked against him. Lassally, who was Jewish, had obviously never been inclined to treat him fairly, and this Jewish inquisitor now had the evidence he needed to eject Pohl from the force and destroy his life. Pohl drew his service revolver and shot Lassally in the chest.

Lassally survived, but Pohl's trial later that year for attempted murder was just as sensational as if the bullet had been fatal. This crime by a Nazi-affiliated policeman created significant problems for the SA's claims of virtue. Along with other incidents that year, the case showed that SA men and their allies repeatedly acted in ways that mocked their claimed right of preemptive self-defense. Given that most violent incidents grew out of the stormtroopers' personal concerns and daily lives, the SA often lost control over when and how stormtrooper violence broke out. Impulsive choices stormtroopers made in the heat of the moment risked collapsing the Nazi Party's carefully constructed political narrative.

Pohl's attack on Lassally fit poorly with the image of a persecuted, down-trodden stormtrooper. Pohl was clearly the aggressor, having attacked a state official during a formal interview. He had instantly resorted to lethal force and had struck by surprise. As his personality became known over the course of his trial, he proved himself to be an arrogant and unsympathetic character whose exposure to the public would only discredit the SA. When Pohl stood before the court on September 28, he denied having any feelings of remorse for his actions, telling the judge, "I do not regret the deed. On the contrary, if it were up to me, Lassally and his spies would be the ones in jail."[78]

Given Pohl's unsympathetic personality, the *Tageblatt* sought to disclaim any connection with him. Indeed, he was no SA man—at least, not yet, although he did join several years later. During Pohl's trial, however, he was still formally unaligned. The *Tageblatt* claimed that Pohl's true political sympathy in fact lay with the Communists. The paper said he admired the Communists for their willingness "to disrupt the state with violence," in contrast to Hitler, who was "far too legal."[79] As for Pohl's alleged Nazi connections, the *Tageblatt* claimed, "We know no Party-comrade Pohl, we do not count ourselves among his friends, and we denounce his deed. He is a stranger to us. Our interest in this matter lies elsewhere—and that is the monstrous misdeeds of spying in the Hamburg police."[80]

While the *Tageblatt* denied having a common allegiance, the paper still felt it necessary to emphasize Pohl's reputation as an upstanding member of the community. His father was a doctor. Pohl himself had fought in the trenches (a logical impossibility, given his age). He had served seven years with the police and enjoyed, until now, a sterling record. He had even rented a room from two Jewish women, becoming quite close to one of them. Non-Nazi papers picked up on this strange fact as well.[81] In the *Tageblatt's* sympathetic reading, the events leading up to the shooting constituted a litany of offenses against Pohl's honor and indeed the honor of all police officers who merely sought to do their jobs in a politicized atmosphere. Police spies had been sent to find out where officers spent their evenings. They had searched private lockers for copies of the *Völkischer Beobachter* and *Tageblatt*. They had trailed off-duty officers and attempted to overhear their conversations. In the *Tageblatt*'s telling, Pohl's drunken state had been the result of his learning that Lassally was Jewish, a fact that he interpreted as ensuring the case's outcome. The drinking bout therefore reflected despair rather than degeneracy. Lassally, in contrast, had treated Pohl in a calculatingly insulting manner, as evidenced by his refusal to offer Pohl a seat. By the end of the interview, in the *Tageblatt*'s version:

> He [Pohl] felt as if he were already judged, and only the formalities remained. He knew therefore that he would not be allowed to defend himself. The "witnesses" were not made known to him. He fought against unknown forces. The only thing he knew is that formal expulsion would come. And then Lassally asked, per procedure, whether he wished to withdraw from the force.
>
> In this moment, the hatred and unjust suspicions were a thing of the past. The alcohol pulsed in his blood. Something must happen. He pulled out his pistol and shot. Just once, then the attack of rage was over. The states' attorney was lightly wounded. Pohl turned himself in immediately.[82]

The *Tageblatt* put its readers into Pohl's head and asked them to sympathize with how he had been persecuted, driven by "unknown forces" to a deed he immediately regretted. Even as the Party denied any formal association with him, it used his story to advance its complaints against the Republic and its guardians. The *Tageblatt* thus cast Pohl as one more dutiful, patriotic, and well-intentioned innocent whose life had been destroyed by the Republic's political persecution.

In the *Tageblatt*'s eyes, Pohl was not the only victim; the Nazi Party claimed itself among the injured parties as well. Pohl's deed had harmed the Party's image through false allegations, the paper argued, a slander that therefore illuminated the discrimination and persecution that Nazis supposedly faced within police ranks. The newspaper called one police witness a purveyor of "nasty denunciations," and it used such pejorative language against this government official that the police banned publication for eight days.[83] Krebs, Okrass, and another editor were charged with libel. These events only fed their sense of persecution. The ban and criminal charges helped the movement retain, as it had from the start of the affair, the language of victimhood and moral authority. As the *Tageblatt* had written in its very first story on the shooting, "We neither minimize the deed, nor do we want to take responsibility away from the perpetrator. But it appears to us that the main guilty parties can be found among those who promote denunciation within police ranks, and thereby laid the spiritual foundation for the deed."[84] This style of Nazi reporting on the Pohl case showed another pattern in the Party's narrative of violence: its press organs formally denounced acts of violence even as they defended the perpetrators. The reports sought above all to reverse the positions of victim and perpetrator, so the public would pity the aggressors for having no peaceful avenues of self-defense.

As with the Battle of Sternschanze, the Nazi narrative of the Pohl trial found surprising resonance outside Nazi circles. In this case, too, sympathy struck the judge: he found Pohl guilty of attempted murder but halved the prosecutor's recommended sentence. Pohl received only two years in jail. Danner complained later that the judge had felt inappropriately paternal sympathy with Pohl, whose "impudence" the judge chose to interpret as "a cry for attention." The judge found Pohl "at times short-tempered, but otherwise a pleasant, capable, and helpful person" whose sense of persecution was "understandable." The judge called Pohl a *Kindskopf* (mental child) whose fear of "appearing unmanly" had led him to commit more belligerent actions than he could rightly be blamed for, both during the shooting itself and throughout the trial.[85]

Bourgeois newspapers also melted with sympathy for this wayward youth. The *Fremdenblatt* agreed that the young Pohl was from an upstanding family and of heretofore good character.[86] While it could not condone his "senseless deed," the paper gave ample room for his sister to describe how hard his life had been. In the *Fremdenblatt*'s pages, she explained that Pohl's psychic distress originated in the loss of his merchant job. At that time, he had been truly fulfilled, not only in his work but also through the company of a male companion who "was a source of true friendship and support."[87] The paper made no comment as to whether the relationship crossed the line into sexual intimacy, and instead counted on readers to interpret it in light of time-honored traditions of German male friendship. The relationship was, in this description, of such emotional importance to Pohl that its loss drove him to drink. He also consequently developed a childlike desire for approval from acquaintances who spoke with mature authority on political matters. The *Fremdenblatt* reported that his landlady had called him "harmless, a good person . . . who was entirely trusting—like a big child."[88]

Nazi narratives of innocent and fundamentally goodhearted youths who fell into criminality resonated outside the Party because they appealed to middle-class values of respectability and family. Although Pohl himself was not (yet) a stormtrooper, the public coverage of the trial was often so confused on that point that most readers considered him a good representative of the type of young man the SA attracted. In any case, he was cast from the same mold as the stormtroopers, and thus both Nazi and non-Nazi papers defended him with the same narrative tropes they used for the SA men themselves. The more the Nazi-aligned newspapers could establish an image of wayward nationalist youths in the public mind, the more likely the public would be to forgive stormtroopers' misdeeds. When ingested by those already in the SA, the coverage taught that stormtroopers had the moral right to act violently so long as they chose the proper targets. In short, Nazi narratives often spoke of innocence, purity, and virtue, but they encouraged spiraling cycles of aggression, assault, and murder. Indeed, in the very month that Pohl shot Lassally, a second Nazi-inspired murder made headlines across the region and directly affected the city's governing institutions.

The Henning Assassination

In the darkness of an early Sunday morning, at half past midnight on March 15, 1931, the bus from Zollenspieker to Hamburg stopped to pick up three young passengers in Bergedorf, a leafy southeastern suburb whose general tranquility had of late come under threat, as urban political conflict expanded into surrounding locales. The three youths boarded the bus without attracting notice, and they took their seats in silence. But as the bus drove through the deserted small-town streets, the three suddenly stood, drew revolvers, and commanded the stunned passengers to put their hands in the air. One turned his gun on the driver and demanded that he stop the vehicle. The other two moved directly to a pair of middle-aged men and demanded of one, "Are you the Communist leader Andre?"

Andre, a Communist member of Hamburg's Citizens Council and leader of the RFB, had featured frequently in the *Tageblatt*'s pages as one of the SA's most hated enemies. He had recently led an attack on a Nazi meeting in Geesthacht, a town near Bergedorf that was a known socialist stronghold. These three youths apparently sought revenge.

"No," the man replied, "I'm Henning." Henning too was a Communist member of the Council, and local SA men thus knew of him as well. But neither Andre nor Henning would have been recognizable by sight to every stormtrooper, as Nazi media generally included only pictures of its allies, not its enemies.

"You're the one we're looking for," the gunman replied, rudely using the informal *du* to address the older city councilman. Henning clutched at his briefcase as he attempted to produce his papers and prove his identity. As he reached inside, shots rang out. They tore through Henning's briefcase and through his chest. Bullets hit another passenger, a schoolteacher, in the leg, and Henning's traveling companion was also wounded. Henning died in his seat.

The three youths fled from the bus and disappeared in the dark, but policemen caught them in time for the Monday papers to proclaim their arrest for a "cold-blooded political murder."[89] All three belonged to the SA. Yet again, stormtroopers had overstepped the bounds of self-defense. They had attacked a member of the Citizens Council, an older man who was a noncombatant, with no overt provocation, and with the intention of stealing his briefcase to make off with "important political materials" that might be inside.[90] Their wild actions had threatened another city employee, the bus driver, and had wounded an innocent female passenger. All political parties, including the Nazi Party, condemned this breach of decorum and law. This sympathetic reaction, however, was balanced by the Communists' retaliatory violence, a development that outraged Hamburg's citizens and created sympathy for the Nazis. When the Hamburg Bürgerschaft met on March 18 to discuss this most recent wave of violence, Communist members leapt from their seats and assaulted the two Nazi delegates before the debate had even begun. "Throw the murderers out!" they cried. As members of the bourgeois-nationalist DNVP tried to separate the combatants, Communist reinforcements stormed into the room and engulfed all on the right side of the council chamber in what the *Hamburger Echo* described as "senseless rage."[91] The Nazis received "bloody wounds," one DNVP delegate was trampled and his glasses shattered, and several members of other parties sustained light injuries. This assault on the National Socialists was not the only one that week—Communists besieged SA taverns across the city for days—but having taken place in council chambers it was an unprecedented violation of political norms.

Meanwhile, the police again banned the SA. Although SA men had of course set the match that ignited this most recent citywide conflagration, stormtroopers and even non-Nazi members of the middle class saw a ban as unfair during a time in which the Communists were attacking. Conservative publications urged sympathy for the stormtroopers, as did the *Fremdenblatt* when it reminded its readers that "it is essential that the deed [Henning's murder] be considered in light of a certain political context—specifically, the Communist attack on a National Socialist meeting in Geesthacht on January 28."[92] That event had taken place more than a month earlier, but the paper did not say how long it considered the right to retaliate to be valid.

Even the Social Democratic *Echo* agreed with putting the incident in context. Unlike the Nazi and the conservative-nationalist press, which accepted Nazi claims that they merely reacted to Communist violence, the *Echo's* writers presented the case as a problem of mutually escalating tactics by the KPD and the Nazi Party. As the paper observed shortly after the murder:

> The cold-blooded and premeditated assassinations of states' attorney Lassally and the Communist Henning are the consequences of a months-long mutual incitement of murderous hatred. And if the National Socialists have by now reached the high point of hatred, it must not be overlooked that the same hatred is also preached on the Communist press and from Communist speakers. Every act of bloodshed by one side is answered immediately by cries of revenge from the other side, and since cries of revenge soon lead to acts of revenge, the last weeks have seen ever-escalating conflict. Yesterday's articles in the *Hamburger Volkszeitung* were a singular call for unmeasured repayment for the deed against Henning: the shots on an Altona Nazi pub on Sunday night were obviously a down payment.[93]

As usual, the *Echo* correctly assessed a sad political situation. Both radical sides employed escalating violent rhetoric that prompted attacks on the opposing faction, which younger members committed in faith that they acted with the support of their party's father figures.

The Henning murder came to trial in November 1931, shortly after Pohl's conviction. The *Tageblatt* again tried to minimize the incident, but this time it had a harder task because all three defendants were formal SA members. The paper therefore emphasized passages from the trial that called to attention the three assassins' violation of the SA's own rules of conduct, which banned the carrying of weapons "either while on duty or while walking the streets," expulsion being the punishment.[94] Despite the paper's attempts to distance the SA from its wayward members, it could not resist emphasizing far more its usual array of exculpatory and apologetic details: The trio's judgment had been impaired by alcohol. Two came from good families. The third was an orphan and therefore to be pitied. As even the Echo conceded, the orphan lived in a men's home run by the Salvation Army and was so poor that he survived by begging or collecting clothes for resale. His own clothes had been tattered and dilapidated, until he joined the SA and received a sharp new uniform that he thereafter wore as street clothes.[95] All three assailants had endured years of Communist attacks, which the Tageblatt emphasized in order to justify their need to strike back. The murder, the paper claimed, resulted from the Communist slogan, "Smash the fascists wherever you find them."[96]

Other newspapers agreed with many elements of the Nazis' exculpatory narrative, but this time press coverage and public perception of the Hamburg SA remained generally negative. One reason may have been the SA's fresh provocations after Nazi victories in the September elections. This election broke for good the national power of the Weimar coalition of pro-democratic parties. The increasing number of National Socialist votes created a sense of inevitable victory within Nazi ranks—as long as the Party could keep the SA's violent dynamism productively harnessed. In 1932, the final year of the Weimar Republic, the SA kept its troops under tight control, lest it repeat the embarrassments, internal revolts, and public setbacks of 1931. Many stormtroopers continued to resent the political wing's control over the SA, but the arrangement proved successful as the year progressed.

"In public they play the innocents": The Deadly Easter Season of 1932

In the crucial April 1932 presidential elections, incumbent president Paul von Hindenburg faced a dual challenge from Hitler and the Communist Ernst Thälmann. During this crucial test of the Republic's stability, the Hamburg SA provoked Communist violence through supposedly peaceful marches and demonstrations. On February 14, Communists shot and killed Heinrich Heissinger, a stormtrooper who was distributing pamphlets on a street corner. It was 10:30 on a Sunday morning, and therefore the latest breach of public order on the Christian Sabbath by godless Communist thugs.[97] Two weeks later, only a few days after Heissinger's funeral, the police fatally shot SS man Henry Kobert during their attempt to break up a street fight. The Nazi press used the occasion to decry the Republic's lack of control of the streets and the police force's "unbelievable behavior" toward the Nazis.[98] Then, on election day itself—yet another violent Sunday—Communists killed two more stormtroopers.

As in 1930, martyrdom benefited the movement. The SA again held elaborate and highly publicized funerals that brought together the families of the deceased, prompted Tügel and other allied pastors to invoke God's blessings for the fighting stormtroopers, and allowed the Nazi press to vilify the Communists and decry the Republic's increasingly ineffective security agencies. In response to these attacks, and similar attacks across Germany that pushed state governments to appeal for Berlin's assistance, the *Reichstag* again banned the SA and SS via an emergency decree on April 13.[99] National Socialists reflexively decried the "illegal robbery of freedom" from SA leaders, whom police had arrested by bursting through the windows of the Party headquarters.[100] Other parties criticized the ban's one-sidedness as well. As the *Fremdenblatt* noted, the SA had already grown too strong to be crushed by simple prohibition. In that case, a ban against it would only generate more sympathy—especially since it had been prompted by a case in which stormtroopers had been direct victims of the Communists.[101]

The SPD tried to fight this sympathetic narrative by highlighting acts of SA aggression, such as a "planned Nazi-ambush on a Republican" that occurred the same day as Heissinger's death. The *Echo*'s story of this case spoke to the falsity of the stormtroopers' claims to innocence:

> The Nazis and their press still seek to create the impression, when reporting on fights and confrontations with political opponents, that the National Socialists are the most peaceful people in the world, and that it's always the other side that had provoked a confrontation. How little these claims speak to the facts is shown yet again by an incident last Friday on Stresemanstrasse, near the Nazi pub von Schulz.[102]

The *Echo* claimed that the attack in question, in which seven SA men ambushed a lone Republican in his apartment building, was "characteristic of National Socialist fighting methods. They plan in advance attacks against Republicans, but in public they play the innocents."[103] By the spring of 1932, the Echo featured as many stories of SA violence as the *Tageblatt* did of Nazi victimization. The Echo also attacked the image of prominent Nazi leaders like Kaufmann and Hitler for falsifying their war records, wearing unearned medals, and claiming illegitimate heroic status. Its series on Hitler's war record reproduced photos and documents from Hitler's regiment that showed a villa in which he and other members of the regimental staff lived, proving, the Echo hoped, that he lived a comfortable life while the enlisted men he now claimed to represent died in the misery of the trenches.[104] In specific detail, the Echo picked at the scabs of the Stennes revolt, which had broken out when Stennes and his followers concluded that Hitler's purchase of a Munich villa to serve as the Party headquarters made a mockery of the SA's sacrifices. Finally, the Echo also resurrected the attacks on Röhm's sexuality, digging up the embarrassing "Captain Röhm's love letters," which made the front page on March 9.

Stormtroopers, however, rarely succumbed to argument by evidence. They believed what they chose about themselves and their movement, and they worked constantly to manufacture violent confrontations that would fit their preferred self-image and thus make their beliefs a reality. Living within this pattern of rhetorical and real violence, they could dispute any attempt at reasoned discourse by referring to events that supposedly confirmed the SA view. In 1932, some stormtroopers' successful martyrdom ensured that their surviving comrades remained firm in their self-conceptions. As long as the most prominent incidents of political violence featured stormtrooper martyrs, not murderers, the SA's claims to victimhood remained viable. These deaths also helped convince an ever-greater share of Hamburg's bourgeois-conservative voters that the Nazis should receive a greater share of power in order to combat the threat of Communism.

In two rounds of presidential voting in March and April 1932, Hitler failed to unseat the iconic incumbent Hindenburg. He did, however, receive far more votes than Thälmann, and the Nazis thus continued to gain political momentum. In the state and local elections held on April 24, increasing radicalization and sympathy from voters traditionally aligned with the DNVP and other bourgeois-nationalist parties delivered a Nazi landslide.[105] The election dealt a major blow to the SPD, which until that point had held such a large share of the electorate as to be essential to any governing coalition.

Now other parties working together could theoretically form a coalition without it. The election also fatally damaged the integrity of the smaller bourgeois parties, whose voters increasingly seemed inclined toward the radical Nazi option. With the three major factions—Nazi, Communist, and Social Democratic—solidified against one another, and the ruined bourgeois parties unable to unite around any alternative, Hindenburg appointed the next chancellor. His choice, Franz von Papen, was a Catholic monarchist whom Hindenburg had chosen over the objections of Papen's own Center Party, and who governed with virtually no support. Hitler agreed to tolerate Papen's regime, but Hitler expected the new chancellor to pay the price, which he did: on June 15, Papen revoked the ban on the SA. He also dissolved the Reichstag, which triggered a new election at a time when the Nazis' most effective political tools were at their sharpest.

The Altona Bloody Sunday

After the SA returned to the streets in June, the *Tageblatt* quickly called for stormtroopers to rise in force, "to show the 'antifascists' how much work was cut out for them."[106] The Hamburg SA staged several large marches over the next few weeks, in both friendly and contested areas. One especially large march, on July 9, featured two thousand stormtroopers from Altona, Bahrenfeld, and Othmarschen, who strode through the streets of Altona. The *Tageblatt* claimed that they were greeted by the local residents with flowers, but with stones from antifascists who had infiltrated the area from outside. The rhetorical tactic was another common Nazi trope: that the residents of contested areas like Altona, which proved to be the Hamburg SA's prime target that summer, supported National Socialism and felt an organic connection to the Nazi community, whose help it sought in expelling outside agitators. Logically, of course, an Altona SA enhancing its ranks with stormtroopers from the greater Hamburg hinterlands was the true outside force, as it was imposing a Nazi claim on a territory that was either hostile or at best conflicted in its allegiance. The SA, as always, painted itself as a victim whose peaceful marchers had been attacked by Communists and persecuted by the police. At the march itself, "two SA men were arrested by [Altona police president Otto] Eggerstedt's police because they tried to defend themselves. SA men have to keep still when the reds come. If they are struck on one cheek, they have to turn the other."[107]

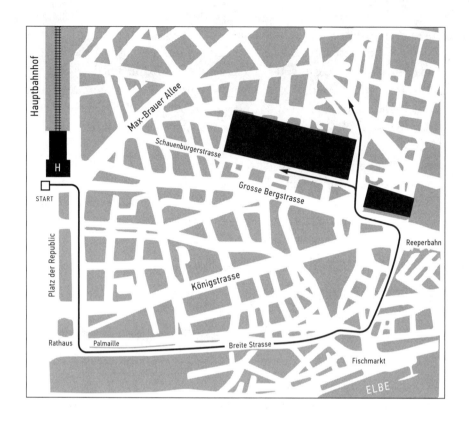

Communist ambush zones

FIGURE 6.4

Map of Altona Bloody Sunday march

Map of march route and battle zone,
Altona Bloody Sunday, July 17, 1932.
Source: Created by author

Such Christ-like language fit the stormtroopers' sense of themselves, as ridiculous as it must have sounded to others acquainted with SA violence. The *Echo* saw the march as one more event in a string of "daily terror," which included "daily attacks by SA men, daily arrests of and daily use of weapons by National Socialists." It mocked the SA's claims to victimhood as "impudence" and noted that each SA march left a neighborhood devastated: "Innumerable victims . . . the rubble of destroyed windows, attacks against police officers, a whole city in unrest—that is the experience of a single propaganda march, a single event of the National Socialists."[108]

SA marches in June and early July were but the prelude to the epic expedition it planned for July 17. Again stormtroopers targeted Altona as the most likely place where they could bait their enemies into attacking them, with a result that would continue to radicalize the conflict, encourage further attacks, and enhance the stormtroopers' sense of themselves as heroic martyrs. As the day of the march grew near, the *Tageblatt* gave its readers the impression that the Altona Nazis and their sympathizers were under constant attack from their political enemies. Incidents included random attacks, robberies and muggings, attacks against SA leafleters and newspaper stands, and—most threateningly—the "apartment terror" of home invasions and destruction of property by Communists.[109] By early July, the paper had focused stormtrooper alarmism on Altona in order to inspire the stormtroopers to retake this neighborhood by marching in force on July 17.

That morning, around seven thousand uniformed stormtroopers gathered at the Altona *Hauptbahnhof*, the main train station. The Party had driven them in from Hamburg's many neighborhoods and from a wide array of rural towns and cities in surrounding Schleswig-Holstein and Lower Saxony. The Communists massed their forces as well, combining their local fighting brigades with recruits from outside regions. The KPD armed these forces with truncheons and other melee weapons, massing them in back alleys and inner courtyards along the SA's march route (Figure 6.4). The SA set off around 1 PM, marching eastward along the broad avenues that led to the workers' neighborhoods, over which the Nazis and Communists had fought so intensely. Police officers controlled the situation throughout most of the day by closing streets and ordering residents to close their shutters and vacate their balconies. But as reports accumulated of minor confrontations and fights between stormtroopers, Communists, policemen, and onlookers, the forces of order steadily lost control.

By 4:55 PM, the first one thousand stormtroopers had passed into the smaller streets that housed numerous SA and KPD taverns. Onlookers who lined the sidewalks and loomed on balconies despite police warnings grew more numerous and aggressive, for this was the heart of red Altona. Stormtroopers from Sturm 2/31—a local unit led by Hubert Richter, one of the most aggressive and combative Nazis—began to taunt the other residents. These men for once enjoyed numerical superiority over their hated neighbors, and they now broke out singing their most provocative songs. These included several the Hamburg SA had banned as too bloodthirsty, with lyrics like "We'll hang Karl Liebknecht from a tree" and the infamous "When Jewish blood sprays from our knives."[110] Hearing these, the crowd surged against the police barrier and replied with taunts of its own, including the ever-reliable derision of stormtrooper masculinity—*Röhmlinge!* (Röhm boys).

At the corner of Grosse Johannisstrasse and Schauenburgerstrasse, the verbal confrontation turned physical. Later investigations could not establish what sparked the ensuing melee, but most reports, including contemporary police investigations, blamed sniper fire from Communists on rooftops.[111] These shots prompted the SA to break ranks and storm the apartment blocks, which in turn erupted with the Communist brigades that had been kept waiting in courtyards and alleys. Combat spread throughout the neighborhood. Newspaper reports of the melee, regardless of party loyalty, described images of horror. A young boy alongside the march route collapsed suddenly, shot through the neck.[112] "An ocean of blood and tears" filled the fatal intersection where the fight began.[113] Civilians fled directionless over shards of broken glass from shattered windows.[114] Policemen and firemen dragged their wounded comrades to safety in retreat.[115] Reports of the chaos reached as far as the United States, where *Time* magazine described how "the good citizens in Hamburg cafés looked up from their beer and ice cream" as armored police cars sped through the streets and bugles trumpeted a call to arms, summoning officers to restore order and doctors to treat hundreds of casualties.[116]

The peak of the battle raged for almost 30 minutes, after which the SA retreated to the relative safety of its taverns and the escape routes offered by local trains. The police, however, remained embroiled in efforts to pacify the neighborhood until well after midnight. As the night progressed, they set loose with escalating force against aggressive Communists and panicked residents alike. At first officers relied on nightsticks to keep combatants separated. When this method failed, a few fired warning shots to scare off the crowd. But the ongoing chaos convinced the officers that snipers, hiding on rooftops and in windows protected by the area's Communist residents, now were targeting police officers. The police responded by laying waste to a widening area of the neighborhood with rifles, armored cars, and tear gas. In the end, 18 people died—most of whom, aside from one stormtrooper and several policemen, were civilians killed by the police.[117] The dead included a female National Socialist. At least one hundred were wounded.

The riot the came to be known as the Altona Bloody Sunday, and the shockwave it sent across all of Germany had great national implications. Most significantly, the events fit the key narrative that the Nazis had worked for so long to establish: that the Republic and its guardians were unable to keep order in the face of Communist criminality, blood lust, "brother hate, and brother murder."[118] Although the SA march had provoked the violence, the main battle had taken place between police and Communists. Nationalist conservatives in Berlin saw an opportunity to blame the SPD for the lack of order, and on July 20 Papen deposed the SPD government in Prussia, the state that included Altona. This so-called "Prussian coup" dealt the Weimar Republic a mortal wound. In removing the SPD from power in Germany's largest state, Papen denied the most powerful and diligent defenders of democracy an important bulwark against nationalist radicalism. The lack of resistance to the coup itself injured the SPD's reputation, which demoralized Social Democrats nationwide and showed that not only the SPD but democracy itself had only a waning hold on the electorate and its leaders. With the coup, elite and bourgeois conservatives further signaled their willingness to cooperate with the Nazi Party, which they hoped would help smash the Communists before they themselves were "tamed" or otherwise neutralized.

The conservative acceptance of Nazism—a radical revolutionary movement with a self-admitted preference for violent political solutions and the eventual dissolution of the Republic—had grown over many years through the Nazis' repeated emphasis on family, spirituality, and defense of the nation against foreign and domestic enemies. Even if many traditionalists held the SA's methods to be brutal, they agreed that the stormtroopers fought for a noble cause. After Altona, Hamburg's conservatives tried to persuade Papen to repeat his coup in the Hansestadt. Although Papen refused, the Hamburg Senate lived in constant fear of it. For the rest of the era, it retreated into a

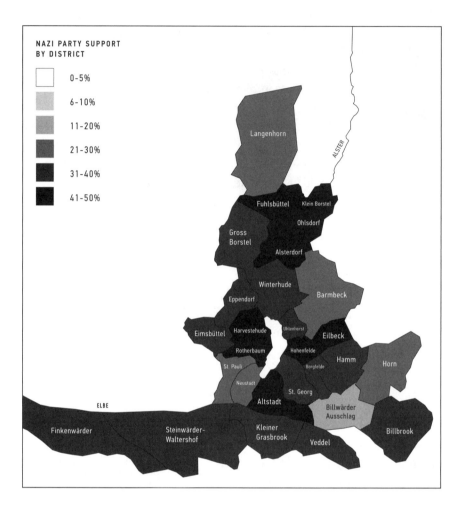

FIGURE 6.5

**Nazi Party support by electoral district,
July 31, 1932**

Source: Created by author. Data from Richard Hamilton,
Who Voted for Hitler? (Princeton, NJ: Princeton University Press, 1982).

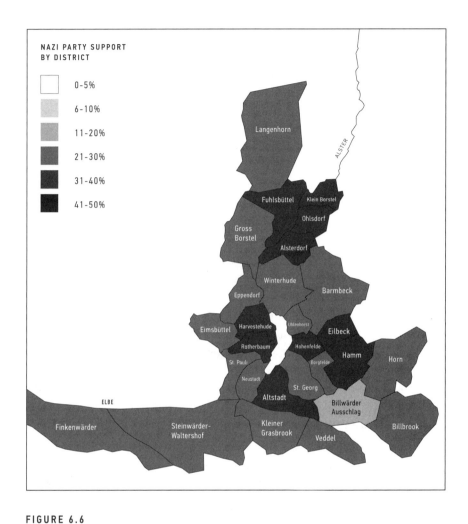

NAZI PARTY SUPPORT BY DISTRICT

	0–5%
	6–10%
	11–20%
	21–30%
	31–40%
	41–50%

Langenhorn

ALSTER

Fuhlsbüttel · Klein Borstel

Ohlsdorf

Gross Borstel

Alsterdorf

Winterhude

Eppendorf

Barmbeck

Eimsbüttel · Harvestehude · Uhlenhorst · Eilbeck

Rotherbaum · Hohenfelde

St. Pauli · Borgfelde · Hamm · Horn

Neustadt

St. Georg

Altstadt

ELBE

Billwärder Ausschlag

Finkenwärder

Steinwärder-Waltershof

Kleiner Grasbrook

Veddel

Billbrook

FIGURE 6.6

Nazi Party support by electoral district, November 6, 1932

Source: Created by author. Data from Richard Hamilton,

Who Voted for Hitler? (Princeton, NJ: Princeton University Press, 1982).

defensive posture of cautiously avoiding any measures that could provoke the radical right, lest it invite Berlin's wrath.[119] This attitude neutralized all efforts to control the SA. In a symbolically crucial concession, the Senate lifted its ban on state officials joining Nazi organizations, a barrier that had been in place since 1930. Hamburg's Nazi policemen now could form a Comrades' League of Nationalist Police Officers, a group whose very existence proved that the Nazis stood on the side of order.[120]

The July 31 Reichstag elections, held in the immediate aftermath of Bloody Sunday, brought the Nazis their greatest national success to date (Figure 6.5). Thereafter, some form of Hitler government seemed likely. The only questions were which coalition partners the Nazis could acquire and what the Party's relative power would be in that coalition. On August 13, Papen and Hindenburg offered Hitler the post of vice chancellor in a coalition with Papen's Center Party. Hitler refused, wanting nothing less than his own government.[121] His choice forced the Party to continue politicking through the rest of the year, a policy it followed with considerable tension between the political and paramilitary factions. Meanwhile, the stormtroopers were growing sick of restraint, and moderate members on the political side suspected that the Party's leaders had thrown away a realistic chance at governing in favor of a maximalist solution that might never come to pass.

To navigate between these opposite strains, the Nazi movement stuck to its tested formula of provoking conflict while blaming violence on the left. The tactic kept the Senate cowed and embarrassed at its lack of control, while also allowing an outlet for SA violence.[122]

Underneath this apparent success, however, the SA and the Nazi Party seemed about to fall into the widening rifts that existed within national socialist factions. In August, the *Echo* hyped reports of a mutiny brewing within Hamburg's SA.[123] It also revealed that a stormtrooper's death in September had resulted from his unwise decision to participate in SA duty while recovering from surgery, rather than the more straightforward tale of martyrdom the Party had pushed.[124] Stormtroopers across the Republic also committed a series of murders that fall—in Hamburg, of a Reichsbanner man during an otherwise normal street fight on October 31—that reflected badly on the movement's pretensions to legality.

Antifascists began to hope that Hitler's movement was falling apart. But in Hamburg, the continual deaths of stormtroopers gave the local SA renewed strength. Balzer's death, plus the martyrdom of two more SA men and one Nazi Youth before the year was out, reinforced stormtroopers' sense of being under constant threat, as well as their willingness to sacrifice for Hitler's power. If there had been an SA mutiny brewing, as the *Echo* reported, it would have been because the political leadership was not radical enough. The conditions of urban combat had only intensified since Bloody Sunday, and on November 8 the *Echo* featured an array of ominous headlines. One account, "Nazi terror in the streets," sardonically described "examples of National Socialist 'respectability.'"[125] Another story decried the desecration of Jewish graves that stormtroopers had committed across the city.[126] The third and largest reported that some 40 SA and SS men had been charged with a series of bombings in Altona and the Schleswig-Holstein hinterlands. The trial generated headlines for weeks, until the defendants' surprise acquittal on November 17.[127] The SA felt vindicated by the verdict, and it strained anew at its leash. The Party now faced the choice of conforming to the wishes of its most violent members, and thereby losing the votes of less radical citizens, or repudiating violence and losing its reason for existence.

The November 1932 elections brought this dilemma into focus. In Hamburg and nationally, the Nazi Party for the first time in years failed to gain votes—indeed, its percentage of the vote fell in every one of Hamburg's electoral districts (Figure 6.6). The setback could have been a crushing blow, and could have led to precisely the crackup that many believed was a likely outcome of the tension between the SA and the Party.[128] In some ways, Nazi factions seemed more antagonistic than ever, and at times they even attacked each other. That winter, as the *Echo* gleefully reported, stormtroopers and *Stahlhelmers* celebrating a Christmas festival came to blows, knives, and pistols, "beating each other up under the Christmas tree."[129] Five people had to be hospitalized.

The loss of Nazi votes, however, paradoxically brought the final victory. The Party's seeming weakness convinced conservatives in Berlin that the time had come to make a deal. Now that Hitler's movement had reached its high tide, they reasoned, he and his followers could be harnessed to the cause of methodical and legal anti-leftist government, as opposed to the radicalized and violent antisocialist warfare it had previously sought. Conservatives believed that Hitler's wilder tendencies could be contained in the long run. In the meantime, he had proven that he could keep relative control over his mass of paramilitary soldiers, whom he could keep in reserve as a threat against the forces of disorder.

This kind of thinking reflected the conservatives' nationalist and antisocialist bias, as well as the success of the Nazis' sustained work in developing narratives of violence that aligned them with more traditional nationalists and authoritarian traditions. Papen, Hindenburg, and their allies in Berlin therefore made a backroom deal with Hitler, naming him chancellor of a Nazi-led government, with Papen as vice chancellor. In return they expected Hitler to follow the governing advice of the non-Nazi members of his cabinet while keeping the SA on a tight leash. In short, these elites risked a bet that Hitler would exercise restraint so as not to lose what power his Party had acquired. They seriously miscalculated. Instead, as he had in the past, Hitler used small concessions to secure greater victories, using power to grab more power and unleashing the SA to secure, through intimidation and violence, total control over the increasingly authoritarian state he had always promised to create.

NOTES

1   Alfred Conn, *Die Mythen der Edda* (Hamburg: Self-published, 1924).

2   *Archiv der Forschungsstelle für Zeitgeschichte* (hereafter, *Archiv FZH*), 11C1 Alfred Conn, memoirs, 97; *Archiv FZH*, 922 SA, Gau Hamburg I. Sturm 2 grew from 52 men in May 1928 to 107 by July 1929.

3   Conn, *Die Mythen der Edda*, 23.

4   Conn, *Die Mythen der Edda*, 3.

5   Alfred Conn, *Der Wahn von völkischen Staat auf christlicher Grundlage* (Hamburg: Self-published, 1928).

6   Conn, *Der Wahn*, 49.

7   Franz Tügel, *Mein Weg, 1888–1946. Erinnerungen eines Hamburger Bischofs* (Hamburg: Wittig, 1972), 164, 135.

8   Franz Tügel, *Wer bist Du? Fragen der Kirche an den Nationalsozialismus* (Hamburg: Rauhes Haus, 1932), 33.

9   Eve Rosenhaft, *Beating the Fascists? The German Communists and Political Violence* (Cambridge, England, and New York: Cambridge University Press, 1983), 199.

10 Tügel, *Mein Weg*, 222.

11 Tügel, *Mein Weg*, 223.

12 Karl Koch, *Das Ehrenbuch der SA* (Düsseldorf: Floeder, 1934), 215.

13 Koch, *Das Ehrenbuch der SA*, 216.

14 Sven Reichardt, "Violence and Community: A Micro-Study on Nazi Storm Troopers," *Central European History* 46, no. 2 (2013): 291.

15 Koch, *Das Ehrenbuch der SA*, 216.

16 "Bomben auf Hamburg," *Hamburger Tageblatt*, July 6, 1932.

17 "Der Tank im Zukunftskriege," *Hamburger Tageblatt*, April 29, 1932.

18 *Hamburger Tageblatt* articles of August 31, 1931; March 7, 1932; April 6, 1932; April 8, 1932; May 9, 1932; July 17, 1932; October 6, 1932.

19 Wackerfuss fight sample 1931–1932 (N=352), *Hamburger Tageblatt*.

20 *Hamburger Tageblatt* articles of July 6, 1931; July 31, 1931; January 4, 1932; March 7, 1932; April 21, 1932; June 6, 1932; August 24, 1932; September 20, 1932; October 12, 1932.

21 *Hamburger Tageblatt* articles of March 6, 1932; April 20, 1932; September 15 and 20, 1932.

22 *Hamburger Tageblatt*, March 6, 1932; April 20, 1932.

23 *Hamburger Tageblatt* articles of May 11, 1931; January 14, 1932; April 25, 1932; August 2, 1932; October 11, 1932.

24 *Hamburger Tageblatt* articles of July 26, 1932; July 29, 1932; September 15, 1932.

25 Lother Danner, *Ordungspolizei Hamburg. Berichtungen zur ihrer Geschichte 1918–1933* (Hamburg: Verlag Deutsche Polizei, 1958), 195.

26 Danner, *Ordungspolizei Hamburg*, 206.

27 Danner, *Ordungspolizei Hamburg*, 213–214.

28 Danner, *Ordungspolizei Hamburg*, 222–223.

29 Danner, *Ordungspolizei Hamburg*, 223.

30 Danner, *Ordungspolizei Hamburg*, 217.

31 Heinz Lohmann, *SA räumt auf* (Hamburg: Hanseatische Verlagsanstalt, 1935), 238.

32 Julius Witthuhn, *Gotthard Kraft* (Hannover: NS Kulturverlag, 1932), 82.

33 *Hamburger Tageblatt*, May 19, 1932.

34 "Die Überfallenen haben Schuld!" *Hamburger Tageblatt*, October 20, 1931.

35 *Hamburger Tageblatt*, April 6, 1932; April 24, 1931; June 24, 1931; October 29, 1931; February 11, 1932; February 25, 1932; April 19, 1932; June 15, 1932; July 7, 1932; July 17, 1932 (one story that described two incidents); December 16, 1932.

36 *Hamburger Tageblatt*, September 28, 1932.

37 See Peter Merkl's conclusion based on the Abel collection of SA biographies, which he interpreted as showing a three-to-one ratio of masochists to sadists within the SA. *Political Violence under the Swastika: 581 Early Nazis* (Princeton, NJ: Princeton University Press, 1975), 591.

38 *Hamburger Tageblatt* articles of April 24, 1931; June 24, 1931; November 2, 1931.

39 *Hamburger Tageblatt*, July 17, 1932.

40 *Hamburger Tageblatt*, December 9, 1932.

41 "Achtung! Rot-Front mobilisiert!" *Hamburger Tageblatt*, June 17, 1932.

42 Wackerfuss fight sample, *Hamburger Tageblatt*.

43 *Hamburger Tageblatt*, June 10, 1931.

44 "Sie wagen an," *Hamburger Tageblatt*, May 22, 1931.

45 "Red terror across the Reich" was a frequent theme, with variations appearing in articles throughout the time period. See *Hamburger Tageblatt* articles of that title on September 7, 1931; February 22, 1932; May 24, 1932; June 17, 1932; July 11, 1932; July 14, 1932; and September 30, 1932.

46   *Hamburger Tageblatt*, March 14, 1932.

47   Anthony McElligott, *Contested City: Municipal Politics and the Rise of Nazism in Altona, 1917–1937*, Social History, Popular Culture, and Politics in Germany series (Ann Arbor: University of Michigan Press, 1998), 178-191.

48   See photo in Josef Schmid, ed., *Hamburg im "Dritten Reich"* (Göttingen: Wallstein, 2005), 43.

49   *Hamburger Tageblatt* articles of May 26, 1932; December 9, 1932

50   *Hamburger Tageblatt* articles of January 31, 1932; December 18, 1932.

51   Archiv FZH, 11C1 Alfred Conn, 55.

52   Wackerfuss fight sample, *Tageblatt*.

53   *Hamburger Tageblatt* articles of April 22, 1932; May 23, 1932.

54   *Hamburger Tageblatt*, November 24, 1932.

55   *Hamburger Tageblatt*, April 6, 1932.

56   *Hamburger Tageblatt*, May 1, 1932.

57   Anonymous, *10 Jahre unbekannter SA Mann*, 62; Lohmann, *SA räumt auf*, 55, 233.

58   After the Second World War, the Dom added summer and spring carnivals, making the festival more of a year-round occasion; see http://www.hamburg.de/dom/1475406/dom-geschichte.html.

59   *Hamburger Tageblatt* articles of November 19, 1931; December 14, 1931.

60   *Hamburger Tageblatt*, November 24, 1932.

61   Rosenhaft, *Beating the Fascists?* 53.

62   *Hamburger Tageblatt* articles of June 1, 1931; April 1, 1932; April 19, 1932; April 20, 1932; May 11, 1932; May 23, 1932; May 31, 1932; June 3, 1932; June 5, 1932; June 7, 1932; June 21, 1932; July 13, 1932; July 31, 1932; October 27, 1932.

63   *Hamburger Tageblatt*, September 4, 1932; June 22, 1932.

64   See also McElligott, *Contested City*, 174–176.

65   *Hamburger Tageblatt* articles of July 17, 1931; June 21, 1932.

66   "Wie die Schlägereien vorbeiführen," *Hamburger Tageblatt*, April 16, 1931. See also reports of May 11, 1931; January 12, 1932.

67   *Hamburger Tageblatt*, June 8, 1931.

68   *Hamburger Tageblatt* articles of January 26, 1931; July 4, 5, and 14, 1931; August 27, 1931.

69   Dennis Showalter, "Letters to *Der Stürmer*: The Mobilization of Hostility in the Weimar Republic," *Modern Judaism* 3, no. 2 (1983): 173–187, especially 179–181.

70   On Andre's background and eventual fate, see Gertrud Meyer, *Nacht uber Hamburg. Berichte und Dokumente* (Frankfurt/Main: Röderberg-Verlag, 1971), 46–48.

71   Greg Caplan, "Wicked Sons, German Heroes: Jewish Soldiers, Veterans, and Memories of World War I in Germany" (doctoral dissertation, Georgetown University, Washington, DC, 2001); Sander Gilman, *The Jew's Body* (New York and London: Routledge, 1991).

72   Gerhard L. Sinz, "Pazifismus als Feigheitslehre," *Der SA Mann*, January 12, 1932, 5; Ernst Röhm, "Tagesbefehl," *Der SA Mann*, March 23, 1932, p. 5.

73   *Hamburger Tageblatt*, March 13, 1932.

74   *Hamburger Tageblatt*, July 13, 1932.

75   *Hamburger Tageblatt* articles of October 13, 1931; August 15, 1932; October 11, 1932.

76   *Hamburger Tageblatt*, August 30, 1932.

77   On the influx of Freikorps men into the SA, including specific members of the

Garde-Kavallerie-Schutzen Division that had captured and killed Rosa Luxembourg, see Bruce Campbell, *The SA Generals and the Rise of Nazism* (Lexington: University of Kentucky Press, 2004), 57–62.

78   "Der Pohl-Prozess beginnt," *Hamburger Tageblatt*, September 28, 1931.

79   "Prozess Pohl-Lassally," *Hamburger Tageblatt*, September 29, 1931.

80   "Prozess Pohl-Lassally," *Hamburger Tageblatt*.

81   "We ist Oberwachtmeister Pohl?" *Hamburger Echo*, March 21, 1931.

82   "Wie es zu Tat kam," *Hamburger Tageblatt*, October 8, 1931.

83   "HT soll RM 20—Ordnungsstrafe bezahlen," *Hamburger Tageblatt*, June 9, 1932.

84   "Der Fall Pohl," *Hamburger Tageblatt*, March 15, 1931.

85   Danner, *Ordungspolizei Hamburg*, 218–220.

86   "Der Schuss auf den Regierungsrat," *Hamburger Fremdenblatt*, March 14, 1931.

87   "Das Attentat im Polizeipräsidium," *Hamburger Fremdenblatt*, September 29, 1931.

88   "Das Attentat im Polizeipräsidium," *Hamburger Fremdenblatt*.

89   "Kaltblütiger politischer Mord im Autobus," *Hamburger Echo*, March 16, 1931.

90   "Was der dritte Mörder aussagt," *Hamburger Echo*, March 17, 1931.

91   "Tumult in der Hamburger Bürgerschaft," *Hamburger Echo*, March 19, 1931. There were three Nazi delegates at the time, but one had not yet arrived when the attack commenced.

92   *Hamburger Fremdenblatt*, March 16, 1931.

93   "Staatsgewalt gegen Mordterror," *Hamburger Echo*, March 17, 1931.

94   "Der Henning-Prozess," *Hamburger Tageblatt*, November 4, 1931.

95   "Wer ist Hockmair?" *Hamburger Echo*, March 17, 1931.

96   "Die Schuesse auf Henning," *Hamburger Tageblatt*, November 4, 1931.

97   "Kommunistische Schiesserei," *Hamburger Echo*, February 15, 1932; "SA Mann in Hamburg auf offener Strasse niedergeschossen!" *Hamburger Tageblatt*, February 15, 1932.

98   "Die Erschiessung des SS-Mannes Kobert," *Hamburger Tageblatt*, March 1, 1932.

99   "Die Notverordnung zur Knebung des freiheitlichen Deutchlands," *Hamburger Tageblatt*, April 14, 1932. See also Hans Mommsen, *The Rise and Fall of Weimar Democracy* (Frankfurt am Main: Propyläen Verlag, 1989), 419.

100   "Verhaftungen im Hamburger Parteihaus," *Hamburger Tageblatt*, April 14, 1932.

101   Jürgen Fromme, *Zwischen Anpassung und Bewarnung. Das "Hamburger Fremdenblatt" im Übergang von der Weimarer Republik zum "Dritten Reich." Eine politische-historische Analyse*, Beiträge zur Geschichte Hamburgs, Band 17 (Hamburg: Chrisitans Verlag, 1981), 115–120. Pamela Swett agreed with this assessment in her study of Berlin. "If," she wrote, "the ban had been enacted earlier or had lasted longer, the SA might have experienced the same drop-off in participation that the RFB experienced after 1929." *Neighbors and Enemies: The Culture of Radicalism in Berlin, 1929–1933* (Cambridge, England: Cambridge University Press, 2004), 291.

102   "Planmässiger Naziüberfall auf einen Republikaner," *Hamburger Echo*, February 15, 1932.

103   "Planmässiger Naziüberfall auf einen Republikaner," *Hamburger Echo*.

104   "Hitlers Kameraden—Dokumenten Sprechen!" *Das Echo der Woche*, March 13, 1932. On the conditions of Hitler's trench service, see Thomas Weber, *Hitler's First World War: Adolf Hitler, the Men of the List Regiment, and the First World War* (New York: Oxford University Press, 2010).

105   Mommsen, *The Rise and Fall of Weimar*, 411.

106 *Hamburger Tageblatt*, July 10, 1932.

107 *Hamburger Tageblatt*, July 10, 1932.

108 "Neue Blutschuld der Nazis," *Hamburger Echo*, July 9, 1932.

109 *Hamburger Tageblatt* articles of June 3, 8, 12, 13, 15, 21, 22, and 23, 1932.

110 For these and other taunts delivered by the Richter Sturm, see McElligott's detailed account of the event in *Contested City*, 191–194.

111 Primary documents of the investigation can be found in the *Landesarchiv* Schleswig-Holstein (LAS 352). Witness reports in this file are contradictory and confused. Key secondary sources for the event can be found in Léon Schirmann's *Altonaer Blutsonntag 17 Juli 1932. Dichtungen und Wahrheit* (Hamburg: Ergebnisse Verlag, 1994), and *Justizmanipulation. Der Altonaer Blutsonntag und die Altonaer bzw. Hamburger Justiz 1932–1994* (Berlin: Typographica Mitte, 1995). See also McElligott, *Contested City*, 194; Ursula Büttner and Werner Jochmann, eds., *Hamburg auf dem Weg ins Dritte Reich* (Hamburg: Landeszentrale für politische Bildung, 1983), 30–31.

112 "Das Marsch durch Feuerhagel und Pistolfalven," *Hamburger Tageblatt*, July 18, 1932.

113 "Die Blutschuld," *Hamburger Echo*, July 18, 1932.

114 "Die Strassenkämpfe in Altona," *Hamburger Echo*, July 18, 1932.

115 "12 Tote über 60 Verletze in Altona," *Hamburger Fremdenblatt*, July 18, 1932.

116 "Bloody Sunday," *Time*, July 25, 1932.

117 McElligott, *Contested City*, 194, and Schirmann, *Altonaer Blutsonntag*, 116–123, 152–153.

118 *Hamburger Tageblatt*, July 25, 1932.

119 Büttner and Jochmann, *Hamburg auf dem Weg*, 31–32.

120 Büttner and Jochmann, *Hamburg auf dem Weg*, 32; Peter Longerich, *Geschichte der SA* (Munich: Verlag C. H. Beck, 2003), 155.

121 Ian Kershaw, *Hitler: Hubris, 1889–1936* (New York: W. W. Norton, 1999), 368–375.

122 Büttner, "Der Aufstieg der NSDAP," in Schmid, *Hamburg im "Dritten Reich,"* 58–59.

123 "Hamburger SA mutiert!" *Hamburger Echo*, August 24, 1932.

124 "Wie 'Reichsbanner' inszeniert werden," *Hamburger Echo*, September 4, 1932.

125 "Nazi Terror auf die Strasse / Beispiele für nationalsozialistische 'Anständigkeit,'" *Hamburger Echo*, November 8, 1932.

126 "Eindrucksvolle Demonstration der 'Aufbauwilligen.' Friedhofschädigung durch Nazis," *Hamburger Echo*, November 8, 1932.

127 "Was am Altonaer Sondergericht alles passieren kann," *Hamburger Echo*, November 18, 1932.

128 Thomas Grant, *Stormtroopers and Crisis in the Nazi Movement* (London: Routledge, 2004).

129 "'Deutsche Weihnacht' in Altona. Stahlhelmer and Nazis verprügeln sich unterm Weihnachtsbaunm," *Hamburger Echo*, November 8, 1932.

THE SA TAKES POWER

7

On January 31, 1933, the night that President Paul von Hindenburg appointed Hitler as Germany's new chancellor, thousands of stormtroopers marched through Berlin's Brandenburg Gate. The *Hamburger Tageblatt* described the procession as "an ocean of torchlight."[1] The newspaper depicted the march as a reunion of the youthful SA with its natural political family, the patriarchal elder statesmen of the nationalist movement. Foremost among these figures was Hindenburg, who supposedly allowed himself to be "surrounded with fiery celebration" by hero-worshipping young stormtroopers.[2] In Hamburg, SA men greeted news of Hitler's accession with an outpouring of pent-up emotion. Stormtrooper journalist Hermann Okrass described the scene as one that united the movement's disparate elements in the long-sought validation of their common purpose. "For a few hours," he wrote, stormtroopers "ran through the streets as if delirious; they screamed in the *Sturmlokalen* and bellowed their excitement. They all perched together at tables: SA, SS, and Party men. Women and girls join them, and Hitler Youths too."[3] Victory had united the Nazi factions, just as the Nazi Party claimed to unite German society.

The stormtroopers still had much work ahead of them to secure total power for the Party, but this task became easier because the parties of the socialist and democratic left proved unable to cooperate in opposing Nazi plans. On January 31, the police, still under Social Democratic authority, refused to allow a major Communist demonstration against Hitler's appointment. The KPD responded on February 5 with a reminder of the *Echo's* call during the April 1932 presidential election for voters to defeat the Nazi and Communist candidates by supporting Hindenburg, the hated militarist but lesser evil. In light of current events, the KPD argued, the article represented "a document of the SPD leadership's historical crimes" that had helped bring Hitler to power.[4] Two parties in such conflict could hardly form a united front against the fascist threat. Acts of resistance did indeed occur, but the Nazis and their supporters dismissed the resisters as an insignificant minority compared to the overwhelming number who allegedly supported the new regime. Boasts of Hitler's popularity in Nazi newspapers, history books, and other literature, however, obscured the actual mechanism of the Party's seizure of power in the early months of 1933: the brutal removal of its political enemies from public life. As a part of this process, the Nazis rewarded members of their community by seizing and transferring jobs, wealth, and political power away from those they defined as alien to a Nazi society. These seized resources then offered the means to solidify and enhance the families of the men who had invested their hopes in a Nazi community and had fought for its victory.

From Hansestadt to Führerstadt: The Nazi Takeover of Hamburg

In its broad outlines, the story of Nazi Party suppression of its political enemies after Hitler's appointment is well known. Both in Hamburg and nationally, SA and SS men rounded up Communist and Social Democratic leaders and held them in improvised jails. Some they simply attacked in the streets or in their homes. At first the actions were largely spontaneous, following patterns of local resentment and settling scores, as they had before the takeover of power. Now, however, these attacks became more frequent, as the stormtroopers realized that they could strike against their old enemies with little interference from either the police or the Party's political leadership. Stormtroopers across Germany now settled personal and political scores, sometimes committing acts of spontaneous antisemitism. While much of the SA's violence in early 1933 took place for personal and self-directed reasons, the Party and the SA also organized planned actions for public-political purposes, including many stormtrooper standbys such as marches, public demonstrations, and tavern invasions. The escalating violence helped intimidate opponents and discourage anti-Nazi political mobilization.[5]

Hamburg's Nazi media were of two minds concerning the Party's triumph. On the one hand, the *Tageblatt* and other press organs depicted the victory as the inevitable result of the Party's superior ideas, the SA's hard work, and the German people's unity in the service of National Socialism. On the other hand, Party propagandists had to keep the stormtroopers primed for battle. The *Tageblatt* thus highlighted the continuing physical danger to SA men, whose enemies it described as having grown more savage in defeat. The paper's early February issues featured stories of "Marxist terror-murders everywhere," "new murders by the Commune," and caches of weapons being hoarded by socialists in preparation for an uprising.[6] The SA responded to these rumors of terror with violent acts of its own.

As the month went on, the *Echo* reported increasingly numerous confrontations across the country between socialists and stormtroopers. The paper could have considered itself lucky to be able to report on these events at all—the Nazis had already shut down 28 Social Democratic papers on February 10.[7] On February 16 they closed around 30 more. On February 19, the *Reichsbanner* marched through Hamburg in one of its last public displays. The *Echo* reported "armed stormtroopers on every corner" who watched the march's progress "with provocative intent, approaching the column with visible weapons."[8] While the march went peacefully, smaller groups of Reichsbanner men afterward came under attack by SA men armed with pistols and daggers.

Yet the *Tageblatt* continued to insist that the stormtroopers were the ones under siege. Actual Communist attacks aided the paper in this effort. On February 21, a Communist assault on the Hotel Adler killed two people.[9] The SA responded on February 26 with a massive march through Hamburg and Altona, during which stormtroopers attacked political opponents and demolished at least one SPD tavern. That provocation, however, failed to catch public notice, as it was overshadowed by the fatal shooting that same day of a Hitler Youth outside the Nazi tavern Falkenburg, which was located on a quiet and leafy street in the wealthy neighborhood of Hoheluft. The next day, Communists shot and killed an SA man, the final stormtrooper martyr of the *Kampfzeit*. These murders, especially the killing of a child, once again allowed the Nazi Party to mask its own violence as being self-defensive and anti-criminal.

In Berlin that same day, February 27, 1933, the *Reichstag* went up in flames. Firemen and police responding to the blaze could not control it before large portions of the building, including the chamber of deputies that hosted parliamentary sessions, burned beyond recognition. In the ruins, policemen found Marinus van der Lubbe, a 24-year-old Dutchman who had recently arrived in Germany with a history of Communist activism and a newly developed habit for arson. Once arrested, the young pyromaniac immediately and proudly confessed to setting the blaze, saying that he wanted to light a beacon of resistance for the persecuted German working class. The event seemed to prove on a national level what the stormtroopers already believed on a local level: that Communists threatened the nation with terror and revolution. In response, Hitler persuaded Hindenburg to issue an emergency decree, the Law for the Protection of the People and State. Known as the Reichstag Fire Decree, it declared a series of measures "in defense against state-endangering acts of Communist violence," essentially suspending all constitutional rights of speech, assembly, and the press, as well as allowing unlimited police authority to search and seize private property. In states under Nazi control, which by now included Prussia, the decree in effect gave Hitler unchecked power to direct the police against his political enemies, to allow the SA to operate with impunity, and to summarily arrest members of the Communist Party.

As the political conflagrations resulting from the Reichstag fire began to die down, rumors and conspiracies still smoldered, like coals awaiting rekindling. The Nazis' official version of events cast van der Lubbe as an arsonist who worked on behalf of a broader Communist conspiracy. The lack of evidence for this alleged conspiracy, combined with the clear benefit the Party had gained from the event, convinced many observers that the Nazis had set the blaze themselves. Eventually, a group of German Communists living in exile in Paris published a sensational alternative account of the event, The Brown Book of the Reichstag Fire and Hitler Terror, in which they presented the case for Nazi complicity. Willi Münzenberg, a Communist member of the Reichstag and one of the party's master international propagandists, spearheaded the effort with his characteristic flair for drama, emphasis on scandal, and lack of concern for evidentiary standards. The work became a smash hit; it was translated into 24 languages, appeared in more than 55 authorized editions, and camouflaged copies spread across Nazi Germany. Its status as worldwide best seller cemented the conspiracy theory so solidly that it dominated public memory for generations.

Reputable professional historians accepted the Brown Book version of the story well into the 1960s, when the consensus shifted to accept van der Lubbe's claim to sole complicity. The debate continues today, although not as emotionally as in past decades, when accusations of personal malice raged alongside criticisms of historical methodology. At present, despite recent attempts at re-litigation, historical consensus remains that van der Lubbe lit the blaze alone.[10] At the time, however, Münzenberg's story that the young man acted as part of a Nazi plan became widely believed for three reasons. First, the Nazis had proven themselves quite capable of manufacturing violent crises in order to advance their agenda, thus it seemed likely that they had done so again in this greatly important case. The skill of presentation also contributed to public acceptance of the tale: Münzenberg's propaganda group included several of the Communist Party's most talented writers, editors, and graphic designers, whose combined efforts created a gripping, visceral tale that antifascists wanted to believe. Finally, the specifics of the conspiracy tale proved effective because they leveraged existing tropes of homosexual conspiracy and moral scandal. Members of all political factions had long believed that the heart of the Nazis' militant nationalist politics lay in the sinister schemes of decadent homosexual criminals, whose immoral personal lives encouraged them to collaborate in political crime. These three factors combined to create a new tale that gained wide currency: the Reichstag fire had not been set by a lone, misguided Communist, but was instead a premeditated conspiracy of homosexual stormtroopers.

In the Brown Book, van der Lubbe did not appear as the intelligent, engaged leftist that he had proven himself to be in his short but active political career. Instead the book portrayed him as an innocent and simpleminded fool who had been lured into service as one of several working-class sex slaves that Röhm's stormtrooper secretary had supposedly procured for the chief.[11] Münzenberg's propagandists described van der Lubbe as having feminine mannerisms and appearance, decidedly ignoring the fact that the youth was in fact so powerfully built as to be nicknamed "Dempsey," a reference to the American boxing champion, by his friends in the Dutch Communist movement. The new van der Lubbe of Communist invention became "in his whole essence homosexual."[12] He was fearful of women, shy and nervous, and obsessed with gaining the affection of older comrades to satiate a psychopathic need for male attention. Once ensnared in this psychosexual complex, the youth could easily be swayed by sinister stormtrooper leaders to homosexual servitude. Eventually, the SA leaders converted van der Lubbe's obedience from sexual to criminal favors, and the young man agreed to be the torch man for their plot. As the Brown Book declared, "van der Lubbe's homosexual connections with the National Socialist leaders and his material dependence on them made him obedient and willing to carry out the incendiary's part."[13] He therefore became, the Communists claimed, a designated scapegoat that the homosexual SA leader Edmund Heines led into the Reichstag via a secret underground tunnel, whose existence Göring had helpfully pointed out after discovering it in his capacity as president of the Reichstag. The gang set the building ablaze, then abandoned van der Lubbe to loyally claim the deed as his own, thus gaining the approval of the older homosexual seducers whose comfort he so craved.[14]

The tunnel's existence was real, as was Heines' homosexuality, but the rest of the tale was fantasy. Münzenberg's propagandists tried mightily to support their claims with documentary and eyewitness evidence, which they presented to the world in a spectacular mock trial that was held in London at the same time the Nazis' own legal process took place in Leipzig. The Münzenberg group's efforts, however, in fact assembled only the appearance of evidence, rather than actual documentation that would stand up to scrutiny. A series of masked witnesses appeared, ostensibly to protect them from Nazi reprisal but actually to facilitate their utter lies to the mock court. One who testified to being among the stormtrooper arsonists was himself a member of the Münzenberg group. Alleged witnesses to van der Lubbe's homosexuality could not back up their statements, while multiple witnesses from van der Lubbe's Dutch activist days tried to speak out on his behalf. Judges running the show trial refused to allow these inconvenient witnesses to testify, so they instead published a *Red Book* of their own to dispute both the homophobic and political claims Münzenberg had made. Even these efforts, however, still reinforced antifascist homophobia, since they merely denied that van der Lubbe himself took part in the "pestilential atmosphere among Nazi homosexuals" whose existence these Dutch Communists took as a given.[15] In the end, the Münzenberg show trial reached its intended conclusion that van der Lubbe had set the fire without being part of a Communist conspiracy.

All told, the mock trial represented a spectacular success for Communist propaganda. The narrative frame that Münzenberg imposed on the fire and its aftermath proved so strong as to require the Nazis' own trial in Leipzig to address its claims directly. At several points, Nazi lawyers and witnesses struggled to reconcile their claims with the evidence. One defendant so trounced Göring in their verbal duel that the Communists rushed into print a *Second Brown Book*, which offered that section of the trial's transcript as additional evidence of Nazi scheming. The court, which still functioned under Weimar era rules of jurisprudence, agreed with the Nazis' claims of Communist responsibility for the fire, but it decided that the conspiracy charges did not meet evidentiary standards. It found guilty only van der Lubbe himself, who had attended the trial in a state of apathy and indifference, possibly dragged there by his captors. The Nazis so resented the court's lack of Party obedience that they swiftly moved to subordinate the justice system by creating the infamous People's Court. In the future, this new Nazi court would make sure that facts did not prevent convictions.

The Nazis beheaded van der Lubbe in 1934, but the Communists' connection of his alleged sexuality to Nazi terror-politics lived on long after he died. Throughout both the mock trial in London and the actual trial in Leipzig, antifascist journalists and those simply seeking scandal happily broadcast the Münzenberg group's claims without a critical eye, eager to connect a Nazi political crime to moral scandal. The results then echoed across the years. One historian of the events described the theory's popular appeal as originating in its skillful use of preexisting elements of the political thriller genre. The Brown Book's scandalous contents therefore reflected the image on the most famous of its many covers, a photo montage that depicted Göring as a bloody executioner in front of the burning building. Just as the graphic designer had stitched together various photos to compose the illustration, so too did the editors assemble the interior story as "an artful suture of investigative journalism, communist tract, and modern polit-thriller."[16] The resulting tale "brought together disparate elements of terror, capitalist conspiracy, sexual anomaly and degeneracy, morphine addiction," and other sins akin to the pulp detective stories that dominated print media.[17] The irresistible tale proved so popular that many still believe it today, despite long-standing refutation. But these debates over van der Lubbe's sexuality and complicity, as high profile and riveting as they are, in fact were but a sideshow to the main events of political importance that took place in the immediate aftermath of the fire.

In Hamburg, rumors of further Communist criminality and impending terroristic rebellion dominated the local mood in the week after the fire. These fears seemed plausible when members of the KPD killed a policeman during a street fight, a killing that even non-Nazi audiences thought justified extreme measures in the context of the sudden national emergency.[18] Over the next several days, SPD senator and police president Adolph Schönfelder banned all Communist demonstrations, occupied KPD headquarters, and arrested as many as one hundred leading Communists.[19] The SA leadership concluded that Communists who escaped these raids would continue such acts of resistance from their hiding places, and it issued orders warning about Communist "preparations for bomb attacks" on stormtrooper homes.[20]

The SPD and the Reichsbanner meanwhile tried to keep a public presence without provoking the new regime, but the latter goal neutered its efforts to do the former. The Echo moved its editorial office to Schleswig-Holstein in the futile hope of protecting itself from persecution. The SPD cancelled a large rally it had scheduled for March 3 so as not to conflict with an appearance by Hitler on that same day.[21] These conciliatory efforts, however, did nothing to save the paper. The same day Hitler spoke in Hamburg, a joint order of the national government and the Hamburg Senate banned the *Echo*. Its final issue warned against the "lying propaganda" circulated by the National Socialists against the Republic's leading supporters.

After the *Echo* was banned, no paper in Hamburg remained to counter Nazi lies. Aside from its own media, the Party allowed to survive only those conservative and national-liberal papers whose acceptance of key Nazi narratives had long compromised their coverage of the political scene. Almost every day, the remaining newspapers reported tales of an ongoing threat to the nation or the Party, often failing to distinguish between the two. Such stories primed the SA men to suppress their political opponents in preparation for a national election to be held on March 5, which Hitler had called in the hope of gaining enough support to push through a second law that would grant him dictatorial powers.

During this new election, the Nazis had a variety of legal and extralegal methods available to remove their enemies from the streets and prevent them from casting their votes. Using the police in the legal realm and the SA in the illegal, the Nazis arrested Communist leaders, closed their party offices, banned and confiscated their newspapers, tore down their posters, and effectively squashed any means the KPD had of rallying its despairing supporters. While SPD delegates were not arrested en masse like the Communists, the loss of their own news media, their canceling of public demonstrations, and their refusal to engage in violent resistance left the socialists with few options. Even under these conditions, the SPD and KPD together garnered more than 30 percent of the vote, an impressive total under the circumstances, which indicated a deep reservoir of opposition to the Nazi state.[22] The Party failed to win a majority as Hitler had hoped, but the Nazis and their coalition partner, the Catholic Center Party, held steady, which allowed the government to continue under a fascist-conservative alliance.

For the next several weeks, Nazi elites in Berlin plotted how to use this majority to achieve Hitler's long-held goal of passing an Enabling Act that would allow the government—that is, Hitler acting alone in his role as chancellor—to pass laws directly. The coalition needed a two-thirds majority to pass such a sweeping and ultimately final change to the structure of government, but it had little hope of achieving this total honestly. It had only gained a majority in the first place because 81 Communist representatives had been arrested or had gone into hiding to escape Nazi violence and thus could not vote. Wilhelm Frick, the Nazi's interior minister, determined that the Party could now subtract the absent Communists, as well as any other representatives absent without permission, from the total number of delegates needed to pass a law. Hermann Göring, speaking as president of the Reichstag, suggested that any further shortfall of votes could be made up by ejecting on the spot as many SPD deputies as would be needed to achieve a Nazi supermajority.[23]

When the Reichstag met on March 23 to decide on the Enabling Act, the very appearance of the room predicted how the vote would go. The Nazis had decorated the meeting hall with a large swastika flag, surrounded the building with guards, and posted SA, SS, and *Stahlhelmers* at every exit from the chamber of deputies. The fearful but defiant Social Democrats were literally surrounded by armed enemies, while empty seats marked the places of the Social Democratic and Communist delegates whom the Nazis had prevented from attending. Members of the Catholic Center Party and other conservative parties' shrinking ranks, dressed in high bourgeois finery, sat in a reluctant and ultimately submissive posture. They feared the results of an Enabling Act, but they feared even more what wrathful reaction the Nazis would have if opposed. Most of the Nazi members wore their Party uniforms and functioned as an enthusiastic cheering section for Hitler's 2½-hour speech, in which he declared grand plans for fascist national renewal while falsely promising respect for the rule of law.

When time for the vote arrived, members of the Catholic Center Party accepted Hitler's assurances that he would not attack the church, as long as he got his way. They consequently sided with the Nazis, as did the other representatives of the vanishing old-line conservative parties. Their votes represented a final act of willful blindness to Nazi radicalism. For years these parties had increasingly accommodated and appeased the Party in the hope that the Nazis would protect them from social and economic reforms the left had sought. In doing so, the conservative parties ignored the fact that the Nazis were themselves a radical and revolutionary faction that also hated traditional conservatives, whom they would allow to remain among Germany's economic and political elites only as utter subordinates to Hitler.[24] Even if some members of the non-Nazi conservative-nationalist factions realized that their partnership would not be equal, they pushed aside their doubts and voted to allow the cabinet to pass laws. They ignored or did not realize that, in this context, rule by cabinet meant rule by personal legislation.

In the end, only the Social Democrats resisted, voting bravely against granting Hitler dictatorial power. Their opposition could not, however, overcome the Nazis' parliamentary manipulation. The Act for the Removal of Distress from People and Reich received 441 votes, enough to pass, given the deduction of "absent" votes from the total needed. Thus on March 23, 1933, the Reichstag surrendered its power to Hitler's personal will and subordinated the functions of government to the Nazi Party's bureaucratic imperatives. In the coming years, the Party would from time to time return to the Kroll Opera House for Reichstag meetings, but these future sessions represented only a sham version of the democracy that had once existed. During the Third Reich, the Reichstag instead offered only a venue for the Nazis to conduct pseudo-legal rituals that were managed public performances of support for policies they had already chosen.

In Hamburg, the Nazis' rise to power followed a similar path of pseudo-legality and close partnership with traditional elements of the center right's "national front."[25] The Nazis even nominated a non-Nazi candidate for mayor, Carl Vincent Krogmann, whose venerable merchant lineage granted him instant respectability among Hamburg's elite bourgeois circles. The Nazis' choice for deputy mayor, Wilhelm Burchard-Motz, came from the same class; his father had been a patrician candidate for mayor during the imperial years. Neither man belonged to the Party. Their promotion as the leading candidates of the "national front" helped the Nazis secure a new alliance with their old collaborator, the DNVP, as well as the smaller nationalist DVP and *Deutsche Staatspartei* (German State Party). The March 5 elections gave these four parties 79 out of 160 seats (Table 7.1) on the Bürgerschaft. As they did in Berlin, the Nazis decided that the 26 Communist deputies either under arrest or in hiding could simply be subtracted from the body's total numbers, giving the Nazi coalition a bare majority of the remaining delegates. Hamburg's republican form of government, among Germany's oldest and most respected political institutions, thus perished. The Free and Hanseatic City became a Führerstadt.[26]

The mood inside the *Rathaus* on March 8, the day the new government was sworn in, was subdued and cautious among these new coalition partners, who were hopeful but wary of the scale of political change about to be unleashed. Outside the Rathaus, however, thousands of Nazi supporters gathered: uniformed stormtroopers, members of the Stahlhelm and other

PARTY	VOTES	PERCENTAGE	COMPARISON TO 11.6.32 ELECTION	NATIONAL PERCENTAGE
NDSP	317,783	38.9	+11.7%	43.9%
SPD	220,570	26.9	-1.7%	18.3%
KPD	144,095	17.6	-4.3%	12.3%
DNVP	65,365	8.0	-1.3%	8.0%
DStP	28,450	3.5	-1.9%	0.9%
DVP	25,199	2.4	-0.9%	1.1%
Center	15,665	1.9	+0.1%	11.2%
Other parties		0.8		4.4%

TABLE 7.1

**Election results by political party,
March 5, 1933**

Shaded rows represent members of the Nazi
governing coalition.
Source: Created by author, based on data in Maike
Bruhns, Claudia Preuschoft, and Werner Skrentny, eds.,
Als Hamburg "erwachte" 1933—Alltag im Nationalsozialismus
(Hamburg: Museumspädogogischer Dienst der
Kulturbehörde Hamburg, 1983).

rightist paramilitary and veterans groups, nationalist policemen and civil servants, and thousands of citizens who claimed to be fed up with the economic misery, political strife, and public chaos that they blamed on the Republic. As supporters raised a giant swastika flag over the Rathausmarkt, which they soon renamed Adolf Hitler Platz, thousands of stormtroopers cheered their moment of victory. It was, they believed, the result of a long, hard slog through years of continual violence and persecution. But just as the soldiers in the Great War's trenches had been ignorant of the diplomatic negotiations surrounding the 1918 ceasefire, so too were stormtroopers ignorant of political calculations made in 1933. Unaware of the discussions behind closed doors, they dwelled instead on the daily struggles and personal concerns they had experienced, and they thought now of the reward they would gain for their years of sacrifice.

"Coordinating" the Community

During the Kampfzeit, SA writers and speakers generally avoided discussing individual stormtroopers' demands. Their rhetoric focused instead on the stormtroopers' collective sacrifice, self-denial, and willingness to martyr themselves for national renewal. Befitting their communitarian pretensions, stormtroopers claimed not to struggle for personal gain but for the good of the *Volk*. Böckenhauer's orders of the day for March 7, 1933, employed the SA's rhetoric of self-denial when it described the group as having operated

> always in the mind-set: nothing for ourselves, but everything for our poor, persecuted people and nation. The only thanks we enjoy for our fighting operations is the consciousness to have faithfully executed our duty and to have made the way clear for our *Führer* Adolf Hitler to rebuild Germany.[27]

Common as that rhetoric may have been to the SA, the group had also famously agitated within the Party for a variety of benefits: financial support for individual stormtroopers, programs to benefit the SA as a whole, and even systemic changes to German economic life that many interpreted as a demand for social revolution. Indeed, SA pressure for its members' material gain had been at the heart of the most major schism within the party, the Stennes revolt. Given this dynamic, once the SA had helped the Party into power it expected that the newly ascendant regime would give priority to its key foot soldiers when distributing the spoils of victory.

Stormtrooper demands on the new Nazi state fell into three broad categories: public displays of appreciation for the SA's role in victory, access to jobs and other economic advantages, and establishing SA men as agents of authority in both public and private life. These demands overlapped in many ways, especially given the common thread that stormtroopers now be elevated to positions of patriarchal authority within their communities. The demands also corresponded fairly well, at least in theory, with the Party's goal of securing a new political order. Insofar as SA men asked to be rewarded with jobs, state positions, and public acclaim, the Party found it easy in principle to satisfy them. As 1933 wore on, however, the stormtroopers grew increasingly confident, more demanding, and even more numerous. They needed constant validation and frequent economic assistance, they resented compromises intended to placate them, and they refused to rein in their often violent assertions of authority in both the political and private realms. These character traits sowed the seeds of future conflict between the SA and the Nazi Party, even while they improved many stormtroopers' personal economic position.

The Party found it relatively easy to fulfill the stormtroopers' demand for recognition. Party politics already featured mass public gatherings centered around the SA and its supposed heroism. Now that the Party controlled the state, the SA could assemble whenever it chose. Its gatherings now included symbolic takeovers of key public spaces, such as the rallies outside the Rathaus in Hamburg and Altona in early March, and the subsequent occupation of trade union buildings. These gatherings, while similar in form and appearance to those held before the takeover, now had the advantage of demonstrating that the new regime enjoyed the protection of a paramilitary army. In return, public demonstrations enshrined the stormtrooper as the new iconic figure of the state, a model of heroism and public service.

In addition to the Party's efforts, elements of German society interested in supporting the new regime also heaped public veneration upon the SA. Nazi publications and books by friendly or profit-seeking presses published a series of novels and memorial books dedicated to local, national, and mythical SA heroes.[28] Similar efforts, both earnest and money chasing, produced newspaper articles, films, memorabilia, and even assignments in academic courses, all of which played to stormtroopers' desire for an honored and respected public image.[29] In the religious realm, Tügel and the other members of Hamburg's faction of conservative Lutheran pastors waxed poetic during the Easter season, when Christian images of blood sacrifice and spiritual renewal held special meaning. Tügel's sermon during that year's ceremonies for the Great War's fallen soldiers linked national martyrdom to Jesus' sacrifice and God's plan for Germany, which the stormtroopers now furthered through their own martyrdom. Tügel thus preached the National Socialist revolution as God's work, and the stormtroopers as His agents.[30]

In preparation for Holy Week services in April, Tügel worked closely with SA leaders to ensure that stormtroopers filled Lutheran churches throughout the city. He held special Sunday ceremonies in the Michaeliskirche, named for the archangel commander of God's armies who was the patron saint of soldiers, police officers, and Germany itself. Visitors to the church, Hamburg's most prominent point of navigation and the center of its religious life, passed under a bronze statue that depicted Michael's victory over the devil. Tügel welcomed the stormtroopers to this key symbolic site, where they celebrated the Führer's birthday and promoted a drive to help needy children in the German borderlands.[31] The SA cleared its schedule of Sunday activities so the stormtroopers could rejuvenate their strength by participating in religious services.[32] The leadership felt that the stormtroopers should, like the Apostles receiving the Holy Spirit at Pentecost, prepare for a new phase of missionary activity in which they would spread the gospel of National Socialism. The *Tageblatt* made similar words and deeds known throughout the city. Its stories about Easter exhorted readers to lower their egos and bask in the glory of unity with God and the state—which, one of Tügel's pastoral allies reminded the *Tageblatt*'s readers, was created by God and was thus owed a similar level of allegiance.[33] These stories and images certified the SA's sanction by Hamburg's religious powers, who in turn lionized the stormtroopers as agents of God.

Stormtrooper commemorations were not just symbolic. Having already named the Rathausmarkt for Hitler, the Hamburg Party established several additional memorials to fallen stormtroopers. The most prominent, to mark the place where Dreckmann died during the Battle of Sternschanze, met with some delay after internal debate on how to commemorate this premier stormtrooper leader. Eventually, a plaque was dedicated on the fatal corner in an elaborate ceremony that transformed Susannenstrasse into Heinrich

Dreckmannstrasse.[34] For a time, an SA honor guard kept watch over the site. The Party planned to rebury Dreckmann and his fellow martyrs from the SA, SS, and Hitler Youth in a common grave at the Ohlsdorf Cemetery. But the scheme came to naught, due to objections from Hitler Youth Otto Blöcker's parents, who wanted their son to remain in the family plot.[35] At the same time, however, three fallen stormtroopers—Dreckmann, Brands, and Hahn—had ships named after them, one of the greatest honors a citizen of Hamburg could hope to receive.[36]

In addition to these memorials to the fallen, living stormtroopers saw their institutions spread across the city. On April 1, the Marine SA opened a new Heim in a former school on Mühlenstrasse. Kaufmann dedicated it that July, naming it the Heinrich Heissinger House in honor of the Marine SA's fallen comrade.[37] Sturm 21/45 also dedicated a new hostel on the prominent Wandsbeker Chaussee, laying claim to the historic location near where the march to Sternschanze had begun. Not only did the number of SA Heime increase, the facilities also became more elaborate. Sturm 21/45's new Heim featured several bedrooms, two kitchens, an office, and a lounge.[38] SA taverns also spread across Hamburg in the months following the takeover.[39] Impetus for this expansion came from the Party, which wanted to establish outposts of stormtroopers to monitor the neighborhoods; from the SA, which hoped to provide better for its fighters; and from Nazi sympathizers and sycophants who wanted to curry favor with the ascendant movement. Tavern keepers who offered their pubs to the SA also pursued their own economic interests; as had been true during the Kampfzeit, hosting an SA unit could provide a stable base of customers, many of them heavy drinkers prone to spending large amounts on beer. Tavern and hotel keepers could also use the SA presence as an advertisement of Party loyalty to attract other customers, as the new proprietor of the Hotel Voss did in May. Upon assuming management of the building, he offered to rent rooms and common areas as "a comfortable home" for SA and SS men.[40] With this offer, the Party could offer haven to an additional 300–350 of its soldiers. In many cases, Party members and private citizens offered discounts to stormtroopers, and they sometimes turned public accommodations over to SA use. These alliances aided the Party in raising the SA's profile throughout the city, giving the stormtroopers a firmer foothold in neighborhoods recently contested. This tactic also served a more practical purpose in solving one of the SA's most long-standing problems: how to keep its masses of young, unemployed recruits fed, clothed, and housed.

Stormtroopers' individual financial problems had long created and exacerbated tensions between the Party and the SA, between the SA and its men, and among the stormtroopers themselves. In April 1933, stormtrooper unemployment and poverty were still so high that Böckenhauer feared sending the Marine SA on a collection drive. The Party had offered the SA 20,000–30,000 copies of its latest pamphlet, "The Jew as Enemy of the State," but Böckenhauer lacked confidence that the SA could make any profit. Even when selling the fliers at twice the cost of their purchase from the Party, Böckenhauer feared that, "as seen in previous experiences with pamphleting," too many impoverished stormtroopers would embezzle much of the money.[41] The experience showed how the SA and the Party alike recognized during the takeover that the stormtroopers did not just seek public acclaim, cultural validation, and the extension of their institutional centers—they also sought to convert public triumph into private gain.

As the events of spring 1933 cemented the Party's reign over Hamburg, many locals eager to curry favor with Nazi enforcers presented the stormtroopers with free goods and services. In some cases, single women and mothers offered free Sunday meals to neighborhood SA men.[42] The Party encouraged private citizens and public buildings with cafeterias to open their doors to unemployed stormtroopers, as did the Lohmühlen Hospital, which supplied local SA work units with free lunches through much of 1933.[43] Other individuals and firms donated trinkets and supplies, such as packets of assorted dried fruits, powdered milk, cigarettes, and socks, as well as gasoline, furniture, light bulbs, meat, beer, and coffee beans from Hamburg's many overseas trading firms. Stormtroopers also received free tickets to cultural events that would otherwise have been out of their price range. The Stadt Theater offered a row of free tickets to uniformed stormtroopers for its performance of Wagner's *Meistersinger* on Hitler's birthday.[44] In this case, the theater had allied with the SA to celebrate its leader's birthday with a free performance of his favorite opera. Such events in the regime's early months helped the theater demonstrate allegiance to the new state by exploiting existing cultural similarities, rather than by directly supporting the new Nazi culture. Later, during the general radicalization of the regime in 1935, theaters offered stormtroopers tickets to explicitly ideological titles that Nazi-aligned theater groups had developed to teach the Party's ever more extreme stance on the German homeland, the pseudoscience of race, and the necessity of eugenics and euthanasia.[45]

In other cultural spheres, stormtroopers scooped up tickets to soccer matches, festivals, and screenings of both movement films and popular features. Some of these prizes came with strings attached. Free library cards, for instance, were given only to SA men whose terms of service and good standing marked them as men who could be trusted to read only ideologically appropriate material.[46] These service-connected offers tended to be spontaneous, one time only, and limited to a set number of men. On April 5, 1933, for instance, a "camaraderie hour" offered by the pub Tirol could host only 180 men. Marine SA leadership therefore limited the evening of free food and beer to "especially needy, worthy, and deserving SA men."[47] Other free offers stayed open to all stormtroopers regardless of rank or length of service. Some of the private businesses that participated in these thinly veiled schemes of bribery and patronage had been in the Nazi movement for years. Yet even businesses that had not previously cooperated with the SA saw that donating free or discounted goods would serve them well in the post-1933 German marketplace.[48]

Many SA leaders felt wary of accepting too many gifts, especially items like cigars, cigarettes, and alcohol.[49] That is not to say that they did not desire them; these materials had long been associated with Hamburg's international trading houses and hence served as markers of the Hanseatic mercantile respectability that stormtroopers simultaneously sought and derided. As time went on, imported items such as cigars and coffee increasingly found their way directly to high-ranking officers. A student leader's young wife was seen flaunting a new fur coat around town.[50] A gift of imported coffee beans eventually made its way to the highest ranks of the brigade, where *Sturmführer* Behrens sent it in March 1934 with wishes of *"guten Apetit"* to his superior officer.[51] SA leaders who passed donations upward in this way hoped to strengthen their relationships with superior officers. A well-chosen present demonstrated the giver's attention to detail and his knowledge of a comrade's tastes, reaffirmed the SA's social ethic of sharing and camaraderie, and confirmed the elite local identities of both giver and recipient by equipping them with items of Hanseatic prestige.

Such schemes, however, risked creating an impression of graft and favoritism, thus exacerbating tensions between officers and members of the lower ranks, who still suffered from the economic crisis. High-ranking SA officers who flaunted imported cigars and other luxury goods also strained relationships between stormtroopers and civilians—both the civilian leadership of the Party and the public at large. Aware of the potential problems that arose when SA commanders chased gifts and donations, the Party's civilian leadership instructed Böckenhauer to forbid his officers from soliciting goods from firms.[52] SA leaders also sought to keep newspapers from mentioning specific goods in SA requests for supplies—especially when those requests included sinful items like cigarettes and beer, or when writers used "Marxist" language portraying the stormtroopers as "the poorest of the poor."[53] As the Third Reich became more established, the SA needed to show less and less initiative in this regard. Businesses knew that to donate to the SA, or to its leaders directly, curried favor with the largest and most publicly impressive of the Nazi Party's sub-organizations. SA leaders exerted pressure behind the scenes on both businessmen and bureaucrats. By 1934, even public agencies felt dragooned into supplying the SA. In February, for example, police barracks received orders to turn over spare bicycle wheels for SA use, while other SA units requisitioned trucks from the Hamburg Gasworks for an expedition to the Baltic Sea.[54]

In many cases, businesses provided items without specifying whether the materials were for official use. After all, stormtroopers had long integrated consumption of food and beverages into their political rituals, just as they had done with sports, trips to the countryside, theater performances, film screenings, and a wide variety of other activities that could attract otherwise apolitical young men. However, the SA's pursuit of these activities after the takeover carried different associations. No longer a private club, the SA now formed an essential part of an aggressive ruling party, and its requests for support took on the implicit character of extortion.

Ironically, the SA's encouragement of financial support from local businesses also threatened the SA itself. By pressing for funding, the stormtroopers risked confirming negative perceptions about them, above all that they did indeed fight for their own gain rather than for communal renewal. Their enemies had accused them of self-interest and greed before, calling the stormtroopers a gang of corrupt, parasitical beggars who backed their demands with threats. After the takeover, some Party and SA leaders lived in fear that these charges would prove true.

Hamburg's SA leadership therefore tried to restrain suspicious contact not only between businesses and the SA as institutions, but also between individuals on either side. Eventually, SA leaders expelled a number of stormtroopers who had sought personal financial advantage. Georg F., a troop leader who had been involved in the SA since 1929, had long leaned on the SA for financial support. Having lost his mother and never known his father, he typified the orphaned and drifting young stormtrooper who had made the SA an ersatz family. He borrowed from comrades and used the money to buy jewelry for his girlfriend. The last straw came when he was caught begging in uniform "for a little lunch or something to eat; I'm doing terribly."[55] Begging in uniform was a grave offense against the SA; it either deceived people into thinking they were donating to the SA itself or gave the impression the SA could not take care of its own. The SA finally expelled Georg for "repeated attempts to further his own personal advantage."[56]

Neither the Party nor the SA opposed stormtroopers gaining "personal advantage" per se. They did, however, greatly worry that stormtroopers might pursue their ambitions through corrupt arrangements that would upset the Party's control of society during the Reich's fragile first year. However, they also knew that, if done properly, stabilizing stormtrooper finances could help stabilize the regime. Party and SA leaders therefore preferred to help stormtroopers line their pockets through more sustained and productive means of support—specifically, by helping them secure steady employment. Jobs would not only reward individual stormtroopers for their service, they would also place loyal SA men in key positions in private businesses, public utilities, and police agencies. Such positioning would, Party officials hoped, secure Hamburg's businesses, bureaucracies, and law-enforcement agencies for the Party's long-term purposes without alienating the public.[57]

The Party itself at first sought to employ SA men. In the first half of 1933, it offered stormtroopers a variety of positions based on their skills. It sought painters, masons, and carpenters to build a new headquarters, and it asked multilingual SA men to work as interpreters.[58] The plan continued the pre-takeover tradition of mobilizing skilled stormtroopers whenever possible and demonstrated the self-help elements of the SA lifestyle, but it never amounted to much; when last reckoned at the end of 1932, over half the Hamburg stormtroopers had no work.[59] The SA thus pressured the Party for more comprehensive assistance, which the newly empowered Party could now provide. Starting in 1933, the Nazi Party worked with state employment agencies to place SA men in organizations essential to big city life, such as the gas works, the railroad, and the cemetery. The total number of Hamburg stormtroopers benefitting from these policies numbered in the hundreds, and perhaps thousands.[60]

The Party especially sought to place stormtroopers as public school teachers, where they would be invaluable in educating the rising generation in Party-approved "virtues," such as racism, militarism, and obedience.[61] Stormtrooper teachers could make sure that their non-stormtrooper colleagues adhered to ideologically correct materials, and they could also enforce National Socialist standards of behavior among school faculty, staff, and students. Strangely, however, oral histories conducted after the war suggest that not all stormtrooper teachers lived up to this role. A surprising number of accounts by Jewish students describe SA teachers who treated them nicely, or who at least did not single them out for persecution, as they had expected. One such teacher expressed regret for having to wear the uniform in class, while another professed that he cared little for teaching Nazi ideology and really just felt nostalgia for the now-vanished Kampfzeit camaraderie. Sympathetic accounts in oral histories, however, most likely represent anomalous incidents that stood out in the memories of Jewish students because they played against type.

Because they are counterintuitive cases, sympathetic stormtrooper teachers appear in postwar interviews with frequency that is likely out of proportion to their actual numbers.[62] Teaching was an ideologically key profession that provided many stormtroopers with a job, but no public position was too small to fill with a stormtrooper. The SA pressured managers of Hamburg's public pools to replace even lifeguards with SA men. One social democrat and licensed lifeguard who lost his job in this way described his position as a "coveted place" that the stormtroopers eagerly sought.[63] Being a lifeguard presented a chance to pose heroically, show off a fit body, and attract the attention of young women—or young men. It was also a natural ideological fit, for stormtroopers saw themselves as protectors and guardians—in effect, as Germany's "lifeguards" against the red tide of socialism. The size of Hamburg's public bureaucracy meant that it could absorb a large number of job-seeking stormtroopers, but also that it could in some sense resist change through inertia. One scholar noted that Hamburg's public agencies "showed nearly unbroken continuity through all political breaches of the 20th century," including through the Nazi *Gleichschaltung*—the "coordination" of the various parts of German society into unified obedience to the Nazi Party. Yet the new Nazi office holders often occupied key positions in the topmost ranks of the civil service, as well as jobs of immense symbolic importance that, like the lifeguard jobs, enabled stormtroopers to stand as agents of state authority whose vigilance and physical prowess protected the community's life and well-being. Stormtrooper firemen carried great weight in this respect, but they were in fact few in number because the profession required considerable time and skill.[64] The main focus of SA job placement was instead the police.

Unifying the Police and SA Families

SA *Standartenführer* Richter, who had long functioned as a Nazi spy within police ranks, replaced social democratic police president Schönfelder on March 5, 1933. Richter immediately began his department's political coordination by naming a fellow Nazi policeman as head of the *Ordnungspolizei*, the division of the police that enforced regular law.[65] On March 15, the Hamburg Senate ordered the police to take on 310 stormtroopers as *Hilfspolizei* (auxiliary police). This innovation, like so many changes made to Hamburg's police agencies over the years, came from Prussia. On February 15, Hermann Göring, in his capacity as Prussian interior minister, had empowered the Hilfspolizei to supplement police forces that the Nazis claimed were insufficient to maintain order.[66] In doing so, he used a little known 1921 law that allowed for temporary officers to be invested with police powers during a state of emergency.[67] Nationally, these new officers comprised 25,000 stormtroopers, 15,000 SS men, and 10,000 Stahlhelmers whose organizations had chosen them as appropriate candidates.

As the innovation spread beyond Prussia after March 5, the SA encouraged applications from all stormtroopers between ages 21 and 45 who had a firearms permit and could qualify as regular police officers. The Nazis left the use of these helpers to the discretion of regular police agencies, but the distinction between police and Party became increasingly meaningless as National Socialists coordinated the police bureaucracy.[68] Hilfspolizei tasks resembled those the SA had long carried out: to protect political meetings and marches; to secure pubs, taverns, and other social spaces; and to put down "unrest" and other "states of emergency" caused by political opponents.[69] But the stormtroopers had gained new powers through their official status: they could blockade streets, "assume responsibility for the protection of important operations," and, above all, carry firearms.[70] SA hostels, taverns, and other places of operation could now stockpile weapons without limit.[71] Stormtrooper Hilfspolizei could also monitor the police units in which they worked for "red" officers, who when discovered would be expelled.[72] In exchange for their self-interested services, these men received food and provisions, equipment and arms, and health-care benefits at public expense. Indeed, these benefits were as important to the SA as the duty itself. Nearly half the paragraphs in Röhm's initial orders to the Hilfspolizei concerned not the stormtroopers' responsibility to the justice system they joined but the police departments' obligations to support the stormtrooper officers.[73]

The Senate's initial order deployed 310 of these officers to police stations, the Rathaus, and other prominent state buildings, post offices, and the harbor.[74] The number had increased to 358 by the end of April.[75] SA units in Hamburg's suburbs furnished another 196 men, who guarded their home areas and the Elbe River bridges, which the Nazis insisted were particular targets for Communist bombings.[76] The number of SA Hilfspolizei in Hamburg peaked at around 600 that June.[77] This put the number of officers there at around the same level as in Germany's other big cities, as well as some smaller ones, like Nuremberg, that had added stormtrooper officers at an unusually high rate.[78] The emphasis on stormtrooper police across Germany shows the immense symbolic importance the position held for the movement. By linking regular policemen with stormtrooper "helpers," the Party sought to demonstrate two paradoxical qualities. On the one hand, an SA presence would show that the police now functioned as a partisan force that would protect and serve the Nazi Party, and which would be more ready to resort to violence than Hamburg's police traditionally had been. SA presence therefore sought to make the police force a feared agent of National Socialism. On the other hand, the experiment sought to impart an opposite set of associations to the stormtroopers themselves. Even as the Party intended this public display of cooperation to make the police more fearsome, it also hoped it would make the SA more trusted. By securing stormtroopers a legal presence in the streets alongside regular police officers, the Party hoped to confirm the SA's long-sought association with the forces of public order, to extend the credibility of the police force to the SA, and to encourage Hamburg's inhabitants to think of stormtroopers as upright citizens and vectors of legitimate authority. In short, the Party hoped to prove that stormtroopers could command not only fear but respect.

The Hilfspolizei experiment, however, failed on almost all levels. Its only success came in its negative goal—to impress upon citizens the new regime's lethal intent. For the Party's enemies, stormtrooper police remained figures who used their knowledge of neighbors and neighborhoods to identify targets for persecution, lead house-to-house searches, and otherwise root out and remove from local life anyone who opposed Nazi plans.[79] The special threat of the SA-police alliance came in the ways stormtroopers reminded potential victims that state authority now knew no moral or legal limits. Stories swept the city of residents being rounded up and held in "protective custody" in the basement of the police headquarters at Stadthausbrücke, where they were abused by the police and stormtroopers alike.[80]

Citizens' fear of the SA reached a new level at the end of March, when the Party and its new agencies established its first *Konzentrationslager* (KZ)— the concentration camps—which were run by the SA. Konzentrationslager Wittmoor, a jail hastily established in a peat factory north of Hamburg, was among the earliest of the so-called "wild camps." Within its walls, 36 SA guards oversaw 140 prisoners, mostly Communists.[81] Guards judged the facilities to be inadequate and too small. Kaufmann, however, deemed the conditions too humane when he visited in August. He ordered that the Fuhlsbüttel prison be remade as the main concentration camp for Hamburg's metropolitan area, and he named his trusted friend Paul Ellerhusen as its commander. Kaufmann's choice of Ellerhusen, with SS leader Willi Dusenschön as commander of the guards, spoke volumes about how Kaufmann intended "Ko-la-Fu" (Konzentrationslager Fuhlsbüttel) to function. Ellerhusen's loyalty and long-standing service to the Party and the SA had never come into question, despite his inability to manage an organization or even to keep discipline among his men. His failure at both had cost him his position as Hamburg's highest SA leader after the disaster at Sternschanze; now, however, these faults became virtues. Who better to oversee the lawless territory of a KZ than one who could not be bothered to take a firm hand with his underlings? Dusenschön seemed to have been chosen to ensure that acts of cruelty would be the order of the day. The 24-year-old had joined the Party and the SA in 1928 and transferred quickly to the SS. Most of the SS leaders who eventually came to run Hamburg's concentration camps fit this profile. Men such as Dusenschön, Max Pauly, Martin Weiss, and Bruno Streckenbach differed in significant ways from stormtroopers who did not become SS men, most prominently in their affinity for large-scale bureaucratic persecution of political and "racial" enemies.[82] After 1934, these men led the systemization and extension of the camp system in a way the disorganized and neighborhood-dwelling SA could not.[83] In the regime's first year, however, the SA Hilfspolizei still ruled the wild camps, which cast the stormtroopers' shadow over the entire justice system.

The police program's other two goals—to furnish SA men with lucrative positions and to lend the stormtrooper the policeman's aura of authority and respect—met with less success. Financially, stormtroopers complained that they generally found their positions as Hilfspolizei unrewarding, despite the care taken to provide them with room, board, health care, and weapons. They groused about their rate of pay, even when they received bonuses for their dependents.[84] A failure to meet basic needs also reduced morale. Many stormtroopers complained that they had to train in their own uniforms and boots, which the police declined to replace when they became worn out and unusable.[85] These complaints about uniforms persisted for months and proved a particular sticking point, because recently unemployed stormtroopers resented having to spend their own scarce resources on items the job required them to have.[86] Guards at Wittmoor complained that they received only bread and coffee for breakfast, little for lunch, and dry fried potatoes for supper, with nothing to drink.[87] They did not record what the prisoners received, but it must have been even less. Stormtroopers expected that prisoners would not receive medical care, but at Wittmoor, neither did the guards. In fact, no doctors worked at Wittmoor, and stormtroopers who got sick or were wounded while abusing their prisoners had to travel to Wandsbek for medical treatment.[88] Before the end of April, both the police and the SA had to deal with increasing complaints from stormtrooper policemen about these shortfalls.

The experience of one young stormtrooper–police helper at Wittmoor encapsulated the problems that police encountered in working with stormtroopers. Stormtrooper Sartory, who was "very well regarded by his Sturm, and despite his youth a service-ready and conscientious SA man," felt dissatisfied with the conditions of service at Wittmoor.[89] His father also disapproved of his service there—not because of the camp's deserved reputation for brutality but because it placed his son too far from the family. Sartory lived with his parents in the old Nazi bastion of Beim Schlump, not far from Sternschanze, and both father and son preferred that the younger Sartory serve with the Hilfspolizei in that area. The SA dragged its feet on the matter and advised Sartory to submit a transfer application, which he failed to do. Instead, he simply vanished. One Sunday morning, according to the SA, he "left his equipment, weapons, munitions, and armband neatly laid out on his bed, and made off without notification."[90] When the SA caught up with him in Hamburg a month later, he admitted deserting his post. He claimed, of course, that he was in fact the wronged party; when he arrived at Wittmoor for a weekend shift, he said, he had been promised he could return to the city "to pick up important items of clothing from my parents' house."[91] When his superior then denied him this leave and posted him on a 24-hour watch that overlapped with the May 1 holiday, he decided to return home without permission and to pursue his case directly at the local police barracks. Neither the police nor the SA took sympathy with him, and they quickly relieved Sartory of his Hilfspolizei duties.

Sartory's story shows the difficulty the police had in retaining SA Hilfspolizei, who proved sensitive to the location, conditions, and rewards of their work. Wandsbeker stormtroopers who had responded to an Altona police unit's request for 70 Hilfspolizei lodged similar complaints.[92] The Altona SA not only failed to appreciate these stormtroopers' service, it also treated them in ways they considered combative, insulting, and even threatening. Stormtroopers posted away from their families and neighborhoods proved unhappy, ineffective, and difficult to integrate into the new communities. Even when SA Hilfspolizei worked locally, many showed up late to training sessions, failed to appear for duty, or disappeared before the end of their shift. The problem loomed particularly large when Hilfspolizei duties conflicted with the stormtroopers' other priorities. On April 20, when most SA men raucously celebrated Hitler's birthday, dozens failed to report for duty. Dozens more stayed home the next day, most likely nursing hangovers.[93]

Formal SA obligations also took time away from Hilfspolizei duties, a problem exacerbated by SA leaders' tendency to issue conflicting orders. On one hand, they told their men that the police service was part of SA service, was mandatory for those who had been sworn in, and should not be treated as an extracurricular activity to be pursued at whim. However, many SA leaders also ordered their men to attend events at times they should have been training with the police. Böckenhauer reminded his sub-officers that they should not place rank-and-file members in a situation where they could not obey all orders given to them.[94] Nevertheless, by late April it seemed clear that many SA men lacked the interest or discipline to function as auxiliary policemen. Fifty-five were removed from the program on April 27, most because they had failed to report for duty, had missed the swearing-in, had been deemed unreliable by superiors, or had withdrawn due to lack of interest.[95] Although the SA could always find new recruits, including second and third waves in May and June, these men also failed to perform reliably. Generally, the police criticized "a notable lack of discipline" among their stormtrooper auxiliaries.[96]

The worst outcome of the attempt to link the SA and the police, however, came not from the behavior of stormtroopers who treated their positions flippantly but of those who embraced their positions. From the start of the experiment, the SA issued strongly worded orders that stormtroopers control their tempers—and their firearms. One early order decreed:

> The use of firearms must come only when they are actually attacked. The *Standarten* here have issued strong warnings that shoot-outs resulting from a certain need for attention, or from other reasons, are unconditionally banned. All groups are advised that, apart from conditions of emergency, firearms must be used only under orders and on the responsibility of the leader in question. Lack of fire discipline hurts the reputation of the SA and damages its operations. Every SA man must be clear that unauthorized use of firearms will call down disciplinary penalties. We owe it to the state power that now finds itself in our hands that our conduct does not counter the regime's laws and orders.[97]

These orders seem to have accomplished little, especially since the SA proved inconsistent in following through on its threat to deploy "all disciplinary penalties" against the overzealous.

SA Hilfspolizei thus quickly became known around town as a source of trouble. They demanded free rides on public transportation even when not on duty, "arranging" their transit by flaunting their weapons.[98] Some drew their revolvers on train conductors who requested fares ("Either you drive or we will. There'll be no paying today"[99]). In fact, access to firearms had been one of the great attractors to police service for stormtroopers. They had always claimed they needed guns to protect themselves and their families from Communist violence, but many stormtroopers proved unrestrained with their weapons as soon as they acquired them. The SA as an organization contributed to the problem by exercising little moral oversight in choosing stormtroopers for the positions, picking men on the basis of loyalty or financial position rather than discipline or reliability. Many of those chosen had long criminal records, with one particularly seedy specimen boasting 33 separate criminal convictions spanning 35 years.[100]

Before 1933, the SA had been relatively uninterested in assessing its members' criminal pasts. Stormtroopers' recklessness nevertheless carried dangerous consequences. In January 1932, an SA man named Küppers, having sat in the SA tavern long enough to consume "five grogs and some beer," had gotten the sudden urge to pick up his motorcycle from a repair shop. His comrade described this unwise plan with the uniquely German phrase of a *Schnappsidee*—something that sounds like a great idea when drunk but in fact is so impractical or foolhardy it should not be acted on.[101] Küppers, who had a reputation as a fast and dangerous driver, ordered two other stormtroopers to accompany him in a borrowed truck. He drove so recklessly that his two comrades clasped hold of one another for safety.[102] The younger one pleaded to get out of the vehicle. Küppers responded by stepping on the gas, waving both hands out the window, and asking, "You guys are soldiers? Are you afraid?"[103] At that point the truck crashed, killing the young stormtrooper who had pleaded for caution. Küppers fled and vanished into a nearby pub. He later turned himself in to the police and withdrew from the SA. Küppers' own SA leader called him a man of "unbounded ignorance and recklessness."[104] In 1933, the SA made him a police auxiliary.

Men like Küppers inevitably abused their powers. They burst unannounced into taverns and declared them closed, using the threat of violence.[105] They appeared on the doorsteps of private homes and extorted money.[106] Many considered their badges to be weapons with which they could manipulate and rob their fellow citizens. An SA man named Blab regretted selling two motorcycles to a dealer on Grindelallee, which was near the university and the humble cigar store where Josef Klant had founded the Party over ten years earlier. Having changed his mind about the sale, Blab returned to the store with a group of uniformed stormtrooper comrades, two of them Hilfspolizei. Upon being asked for identification, they responded, "We don't need identification." They demanded the motorcycles, and when the girl at the register asked for a receipt for the bikes, they told her to "shut up."[107] They took the bikes and left. The owner complained to the SA that Blab took the machines "through base robbery, under the protection of the brown uniform, the Hilfspolizei officers' uniform, and the open carrying of weapons."[108] Worst of all, from the Nazis' perspective, this shopkeeper had himself for years been a loyal member whose store had been one of the anchors of Party growth in its earliest neighborhood stronghold.

Incidents like these posed an unacceptable threat to the Party. They undermined propaganda efforts to paint the SA and the Nazi Party as bulwarks of order, calm, and bourgeois prosperity. By August, the national SA leadership, the interior ministry, and the police decided to end the failed experiment with stormtrooper auxiliaries.[109] They still needed stormtroopers to guard the concentration camps, which that same month were consolidated locally in the new facility at Fuhlsbüttel, but they decided to cut short the disruptive potential of stormtrooper policemen in public places. By August 14, only 110 Hilfspolizei remained,[110] and at the end of September, Richter instructed the SA to prepare for the Hilfspolizei's total dissolution.[111] This pleased the police, who claimed that "members of the Nazi Party" had overstepped the bounds of law and caused conflict with the true guarantors of order, the police. The police directed SA leaders to remind their men that they no longer enjoyed any official or unofficial police powers:

> Without police presence and permission, anyone who conducts house searches, orders arrests, uses firearms (when not in an emergency), threatens others with firearms, or takes advantage of people in any way will be charged without reservation with impersonating an officer, unlawful entry and breach of the peace, kidnapping, and coercion.[112]

The change in policy signaled that stormtroopers who wished to exercise public power had to join regular agencies as normal members. The SA in any case had long held this goal, and it now stepped up its efforts to place stormtroopers in permanent positions with the police, the army, and the navy.[113] These permanent posts, however, required traditional qualifications that many stormtroopers did not meet. The police mandated that all applicants be unemployed, between 18 and 20 years old, at least 1.68 meters tall, single, without children, and able to prove their "Aryan descent." They had to be members of a nationalist organization, which limited the applicant pool in ways favorable to stormtroopers, but they also had to possess a "spotless" criminal record, which obviously had the opposite effect.[114] In theory, SA Hilfspolizei had needed to qualify as regular officers to receive their posts, but the high number later discovered to have a criminal record suggests that the police did not conduct their own investigation of the men the SA sent. Provisions against criminal records thus became a new problem for many stormtroopers, including Friedrich Pohl, whose conviction for shooting Lasally had caused his expulsion from the police two years earlier. He had joined the SA after his release from prison, and in March 1933 he applied to the police for reinstatement. For this purpose he employed his old defense attorney, the longtime Nazi lawyer Dr. Raeke, who noted that "Pohl is certainly no church mouse, but he is a very useful soldier who was hacked to pieces for the sake of his National Socialist leaders."[115] Böckenhauer supported the request. After all, Pohl seemed the perfect candidate for a newly Nazified police force. Yet Richter responded, "to my regret," that he could not help Pohl. "The reappointment must be denied," he wrote, "due to requirements of law that I cannot overcome."[116] Pohl's conviction, even if it had been in service to the Nazi cause, remained on the books.

The injustice of this situation in Nazi eyes soon led to a general amnesty for political crimes—at least those committed by the right.[117] Pohl's rejection showed how the Party and its appointed bureaucrats became less willing over time to ignore criminality within the SA. Police officials also sought to increase their isolation from the SA in general, as Richter did in June when he ordered that all members of the Ordnungspolizei had to withdraw from the SA and SS.[118] Henceforth, policemen could be policemen only. Many SA men who had joined the police, like Richter himself, had already come to identify more with that respectable agency than with their former comrades, whom they now increasingly considered a threat to public order and a source of interference in practical matters. Some SA-men-turned-policemen eventually denied their identity as stormtroopers altogether. "We aren't SA men anymore," said one during a dispute with SA leaders who had been "snuffing around" his patrol area near the docks. "We are now policemen."[119]

Although historians continue to disagree about the overall effectiveness of SA job-placement programs, it seems that by 1934 the project had begun to make a significant dent in the number of unemployed stormtroopers, many of whom had been out of work for years.[120] These efforts dovetailed with attempts to help stormtroopers find and furnish their own apartments and start their own families. As seen with the identity conflict within police ranks, however, the SA's success in these realms only caused further problems. The more stormtroopers enjoyed access to permanent jobs, private housing, and stable nuclear families, the more distant they grew from the SA subculture that had formerly provided an alternate family during their troubled years.

Old Fighters and Opportunists: The SA's Identity Crisis

SA men had always defined themselves in opposition to their foes—primarily Communists, Social Democrats, Jews, and effeminate homosexual men. They had also embraced a collective, cliquish lifestyle that focused on small groups, close friendships, and proximity to their comrades. This identity contained many paradoxes and contradictions. Stormtroopers claimed to oppose the Communists, yet they recruited within the Communist realm. They agitated against homosexuality in public yet embraced same-sex affection in private. They proclaimed their strength but welcomed a martyr's victimization. They claimed to stand for responsibility, propriety, and order, but used illegal and violent means to promote these ideals. As long as the Party represented the political opposition, stormtroopers could overcome these paradoxes through ostentatious self-sacrifice, a quest for martyrdom, and an unthinking brand of constant activity and following orders. In early 1933, they hoped that political victory would bring psychological resolution, but by the middle of the year they feared that victory would only fracture what unified sense of community they had been able to build.

In the minds of the "old fighters," the greatest danger the SA now faced was internal in the form of the legions of new SA men who flooded into the party and its sub-organizations following the takeover of power. The old comrades called them Märzgefallene, an ironic reference to the "March casualties" or fallen heroes of the failed but famous 1848 revolution. The name marked these new recruits as lacking the self-sacrificing heroism of great revolutionaries working to renew the nation. They were instead in it for themselves: egoistic, reward seeking, weakly committed, and more emotionally distant than the zealous and chummy types the SA had earlier attracted.[121] There had been approximately 500,000 stormtroopers nationwide when Hindenburg appointed Hitler as chancellor on January 30. By August, the opportunistic latecomers had swelled this number to 2,500,000.[122]

New SA men came from three categories, none of which fit well with the organization. The first comprised former members who had quit, been expelled, or otherwise drifted away from the movement in previous years. The second and by far the largest group was composed of men who lacked any paramilitary allegiance but now flocked to the SA as a vehicle to advance their careers in a new Nazi state. The third and last group to join did so against their will, as members of other rightist paramilitaries that the SA now forcibly absorbed. All three groups offered some advantage to the SA, if they could be properly integrated, but the problems encountered in doing so posed a great risk of damaging the SA's social cohesion and sense of identity.

Throughout the Kampfzeit, stormtroopers joined and quit the group as their personal circumstances changed. Now that national circumstances had changed too, many of those who had left before 1933 wrote plaintive, self-pitying applications to return to the fold. A typical plea asked:

> *Brigadeführer* Schormann, be a *Mensch* [good guy]. Turn off your suspi-
> cion for a moment and place yourself in my situation. By everything
> that is holy to me, for the sake of the Führer and our *Vaterland*, I ask
> you if I have deserved all this—to be still branded a traitor at our
> moment of victory. Help me please . . . rehabilitate me and let me
> again be an SA man.[123]

The writer's use in this letter of the servile *Sie* to address his superior broke with SA tradition, which generally favored the informal, soldierly *du* even between comrades of different ranks. This grammatical tic in the letter shows how far from a proper SA mentality its old members could drift, once their ties had been severed. Nevertheless, the SA welcomed some of these men back with open arms. Those who had left to perform other duties for National Socialism, like Okrass and several of his fellow journalists at the *Tageblatt*, had little trouble returning to the fold.[124] Other stormtroopers pleaded a variety of employment and family conflicts that had led them away from the SA during the difficult Depression years. The SA often accepted them back as well, in some cases "with the warmest support."[125] Many of these re-joiners climbed to still higher ranks in the following years.

Other re-applicants met with a cooler reception. The SA rejected many, especially those whose reputation within the close-knit community had come into question. The tone of correspondence in these cases showed that the SA still clung to its self-image as a network of small groups and cliques. Almost all former SA men who sought reentry appealed to a shared sense of membership in a common nationalist community, and they expressed fear that their continued detachment from the SA would harm their standing in their neighborhoods and with their families.

One former SA man named Henke described both his exit and return to the SA in familial terms. He had left, he claimed, because his father was "otherwise aligned politically."[126] The two had argued unceasingly, until eventually the elder Henke persuaded his son to leave the SA for the KPD, which he did in 1932.[127] But the father had since died, and Henke now pleaded for reentry as a way to reestablish ties with the rest of his family. "My mother, brother, and entire family are nationally oriented people," he wrote, "and I would like to ask you again to take me into the SA so that I can get my life in order again, and not run around anymore as a pariah rejected by my family and everyone else."[128] In this case, SA leaders felt torn between a son's filial piety and the Communistic path it had caused him to follow. In the end, however, they judged the youth's political and familial wanderings to be "downright psychopathic" in their frequency.[129] Böckenhauer himself suggested that the young man seek medical attention for "his psychopathic qualities."[130]

In evaluating applicants for reentry, officials combed the movement for relatives, comrades, and others who had dealt with the former storm-troopers, and they judged the applications based on what witnesses testified about the men's relationships. Many applicants came up lacking, especially those who had ill-treated National Socialist women. One former storm-trooper was revealed to have taken 125 RM from Dreckmann's wife a few days before the famous martyr's death.[131] Not even eight-plus years of ser-vice and a personal friendship with Böckenhauer could offset this moral failing. Several other former stormtroopers had committed acts of fraud against their comrades, their comrades' wives or girlfriends, or against the SA itself.[132] Another met with rejection when his wife revealed that the man had avoided street actions out of doubt that his comrades would protect him—words that, to the SA, proved he had been "instinctively avoided" by his comrades and therefore should continue to be shunned.[133] In all these cases, the SA judged loyalty on the basis of the applicant's interactions with the officers, comrades, relatives, and other members of the extended local network that made up the SA family.

Men trying to rejoin the SA, however, represented but a small fraction of the massive number of new applicants who now sought entry for the first time. This group of opportunistic job-seekers swelled as the SA's success in providing for its members became established in the public mind.[134] The new stormtroopers caused significant problems for the SA because of their sheer number, their lack of grounding in the SA's traditional neighborhoods and associational networks, and their uncertain ideological commitment. Old fighters resented having to compete with the new recruits for jobs and favors that they felt they had already earned through their sacrifices in darker times.

A typical complaint came from Truppführer Preuss, who fought a "paper war" for over a year trying to distinguish himself from the crowd of late-comers. He had watched several new members gain promotions before he did, and in 1934 he made a final plea to the brigade:

> Since 1928 I have not asked what am I going to get out of this, but instead entered the ranks out of pure idealism for the idea of our Führer. I was ready for action at any time, whether day or night. Wherever there was dicke Luft [thick air, a favored SA phrase for a brawl], you knew where to find me. But today I must sadly conclude that I am no longer needed.
>
> I know what I have borne for the movement as a National Socialist and as an SA man, and I need neither recognition nor commendation for myself personally—in contrast to new comrades who today are more highly esteemed than we old ones. We are the ones who lost work because of our membership in the Party, who now after $4\frac{1}{2}$ years of unemployment are not in the position to do as others do.[135]

Many other longtime stormtroopers lodged similar complaints, and they tried, like Preuss, to appeal directly to the top of the local SA leadership. Their complaints, however, were often drowned in the tide of new recruits that were swelling the SA wave.

Challenges of social integration among stormtroopers became more difficult, due to the loss of one of the SA's most proven methods: violence against outsiders. One stormtrooper carped that, "after the takeover of power, a special means for evaluating a man and judging his leadership qualities has disappeared—namely, the trial and judgment of combat [emphasis in original]."[136] While the SA remained a bombastic group and a significant minority of stormtroopers continued to lash out against their enemies and neutral civilians alike, the meaning of violence for the group had already begun to change. The days in which the SA pursued violent confrontation in the streets as a means of creating emotional bonds between comrades had ended. Violence had also been the basis for determining individual talent, granting promotions, and generally measuring the men. With it no longer available, and with thousands of newcomers flocking to the banner, leaders had lost their main tool for assessing who deserved to receive the benefits of jobs, housing, and support payments. Increasing numbers of old fighters complained that new comrades seemed more like competitors. One wrote that he was "very disappointed" with the behavior of a new recruit whom he had helped establish in a part-time job. "I must assume," he told the SA, "that he did not become a National Socialist out of true conviction, but rather for material advantage; the expectation of gain moved him to join the movement and the SA."[137] The letter writer advised caution in meeting new-comers' demands before those of trusted old comrades. Forward-looking stormtrooper leaders, however, likely feared that placing the old guard first would injure the SA's ability to integrate vast numbers of German men into the Nazi movement, and thus the situation remained unchanged.

The problems of expansion intensified throughout the year as the SA absorbed the other nationalist paramilitaries en masse.[138] The process began in April, prompted by one of the Stahlhelm's co-leaders who hoped to gain favor with the Nazis by bringing over his men. By July, the Party had decided that the SA should be the Reich's only paramilitary. Other nationalist groups thus received orders that they were to be transferred into the SA—a forcible arrangement, but one with favorable terms. While these men had the fighting spirit, nationalist ideology, and paramilitary experience that stormtroopers valued, they also came with different backgrounds, age groups, and outlooks on the nationalist struggle. Stormtroopers considered many of them, especially the older Stahlhelmers, to be the "reactionaries" that Wessel's SA anthem accused of having shot stormtroopers in earlier times.

Together, these three types of new stormtroopers—returned exiles, op-portunistic joiners, and forcibly assimilated rivals—bloated the SA into a form almost unrecognizable to the old fighters. In the summer of 1933, Röhm and the other national SA leaders restructured the SA to take into account the already unwieldy membership. Above all they sought to cre-ate a structure that would quickly integrate younger members of other paramilitaries, whom they rewarded with high ranks. Röhm shunted most Stahlhelmers off into an SA reserve consisting of mostly older men, but he also had to increase the size and number of brigades, Standarten, and other smaller units, thus weakening the emphasis on small groups and personal connections that had always nourished the SA on the local level. While the restructuring solved some of the organizational problems of increased membership, it failed to counteract the more pressing social and psychological problems the SA faced.

At its height in the summer of 1934, the SA numbered around 4.5 million men nationwide.[139] About 30,000 of these came from Hamburg. The rapid and incomplete absorption of so many new members created an existential crisis in many stormtroopers' minds, as they had long lived in a subculture where they knew their comrades closely. Although they had experienced some problems with police and Communist spies, in general they assured themselves that their comrades were sincere. After all, the movement supported the opposition and the cost of wearing the brown shirt could still be high. Now, however, membership was so attractive that it drew friend and foe alike, and stormtroopers no longer knew how to tell the difference.

SA leaders thus had to deal with increasing verbal and physical confrontations between old fighters and new recruits. By the 1934 holiday season, a song that had gained popularity in SA taverns exhorted stormtroopers, "when the Stahlhelmer comes into the room / hit him again!"[140] Stormtroopers continued to greet their new comrades with this verse, even after repeated warnings that it was, in the words of a Stahlhelmer's complaint, "unsoldierly and uncomradely conduct in full opposition to the clear and unambiguous will of the Führer and the Chief of Staff."[141] Such insults, however, were mutual. Stahlhelmers made "mean jokes" about Göring, "stupid pronouncements" about the fallen Dreckmann, and general insults against the SA itself.[142] One stormtrooper took offense when a Stahlhelmer claimed, "If somebody hung Hitler from a tree we'd have political peace in Germany."[143] Generally, the older and more traditionalist Stahlhelmers considered the stormtroopers "stupid boys," and at times they tossed out the types of homophobic insults long levied against the SA.[144] Stormtroopers in turn considered the Stahlhelmers "monocle fops," "cursed Stahlhelmers," and even "shitty Stahlhelmers."[145]

To groups that placed great emphasis on proper forms of address, proper etiquette meant more than avoiding "stupid pronouncements" and overt insults. A large number of confrontations began with disputes over the formal greeting, in which the lower-ranking member raised his arm in the Party salute and cried "*Heil Hitler*" or, in the Stahlhelm version, "*Frontheil Hitler*" or simply "*Frontheil!*" The higher-ranking officer then returned a matching Heil. Sometimes, however, a man who wished to insult a would-be comrade either ignored his presence or simply refused to greet him according to the formula. Conflicts over greetings became rife in late 1933 and early 1934, after those who had formerly been in competition with the stormtroopers had been absorbed into their ranks. Refusing to offer a greeting to such new members showed that a stormtrooper refused to recognize these other groups' equality with the SA. One outraged Stahlhelmer complained to the SA that a stormtrooper "passed on the street with his right hand in his pocket, without finding it necessary to stop and greet."[146] The honor- and status-conscious men of the nationalist milieu defined these slights as mortal insults that often demanded a violent response. Stormtroopers flew into a rage when Stahlhelmers pronounced "Heil Hitler" in what they perceived as "a taunting and provocative tone."[147]

By March 1934, the violence within the SA prompted a reaction: Hamburg's SA leadership banned Stahlhelmers from SA taverns after 1 AM.[148] The ban curbed fighting to some extent but did little to mitigate the underlying conflict. The SA's growth had destroyed its sense of community, and it now seemed to undermine the group's long-standing purpose of helping comrades build better lives. Now that so many German men had joined the stormtroopers, efforts to help them find jobs became most effective through national and general measures that affected all workers, not just SA men. Stormtroopers who had served longest had little patience with programs seeking to improve the long-term structural problems of the German economy, and they took this shift in approach as their abandonment by the SA. As if to compensate, these men redoubled their insistence on obtaining the remaining reward they had sought: recognition of their personal authority over neighbors, family members, and potential spouses. Long-standing SA men felt that the authority of the Party and the state now backed their claims over those around them. The problems inherent in this authoritarian relational style appeared almost immediately after the Nazis took power.

Coercive Community: The Backlash against the Triumphant SA

Just one week after the Nazi takeover of Hamburg, Professor Gustaf Deuchler wrote to the SA to report a disturbing incident. He had been sitting with other patrons on the patio of a local tavern, enjoying the spring weather and a glass of beer. The guests had risen to sing the *Deutschlandlied* (national anthem). After they had sat back down, the "Horst Wessel Lied" began and the stormtroopers in the crowd rose again. One became angry that the other guests remained seated. He barked at them to "Stand up!"—an order Deuchler described as being gradually and reluctantly obeyed by the cowed crowd. Deuchler and the other patrons took offense at the public recognition demanded in this incident. Some even left the tavern—and "they weren't wrong to do so," Deuchler said. Yet these café patrons were not angry Communists, resentful Social Democrats, effete bourgeois liberals, or retrograde monarchists. Deuchler himself was an ardent National Socialist, one of the few professors who ingratiated himself with his radical students by wearing the brown shirt and fraternizing with stormtroopers. His letter in this case spoke eloquently about the importance of the movement's larger projects.[149] He felt that communal singing of the Party anthem should be "greeted with the highest regard," and that "it cannot be overlooked as a factor in building a true *Volksgemeinschaft* [people's community]." But he felt that such singing must arise from custom and conviction, not coercion:

> It is not conducive to building a community, but rather the opposite, when SA people believe they have the obligation to stand up as in the barracks yards . . . and command the guests to sing the "Horst Wessel Lied."

Deuchler suggested how things should have gone:

> [The SA man should have said,] "To honor our heroic fore-fighter Horst Wessel, let us all rise!" and then the whole problem would have been solved. It wouldn't have ruined the mood—quite the opposite, the majority of the good and worthy *Bürger* would have caught the sense of it and been glad; they would have experienced in that moment an aspect of Volksgemeinschaft. This is how one works through the ideas of the Führer and the leadership, and thus builds Volksgemeinschaft.

In the end, even if Deuchler granted that the stormtrooper in question had acted with the best of intentions, the whole affair "made an embarrassing impression on many members of the National Socialist movement" who sat in the tavern that day. Deuchler specifically criticized the stormtroopers' adherence to their old "barracks-yard" mentality, which was "absolutely sure to destroy the rising feeling of Volksgemeinschaft, and thus do unholy damage to the NS-movement and its great tasks."[150]

SA leaders did not need Deuchler's warning to predict these dire consequences. Disputes had already occurred in which the SA's taste in songs came into conflict with Hamburg's staid public norms. In February, a stormtrooper had seized the baton from a dance hall's bandleader and directed his comrades in the Party anthem, while the musicians stalked out. When, after 15 minutes of disruption, the conductor and musicians attempted to resume playing, the SA man grabbed their music sheets and threw them to the ground.[151] As for the stormtroopers' choice of songs, Böckenhauer had already banned "bloodthirsty songs" like the ones that had started the Altona riots, but stormtroopers continued to sing them anyway.[152] The SA itself opposed singing both the Deutschlandlied and "Horst Wessel Lied" in public—although less for Deuchler's reasons than for a desire to keep sacred songs in the private realm, lest they lose their power through repetition.[153] The SA made several other attempts to clean up its public reputation, including monitoring the SA taverns more closely. These efforts, however, seemed more concerned with overseeing a pub's political history and reliability than with any moral issues, and the SA's problems in controlling its men remained.

As 1933 progressed, most citizens of Hamburg believed that they had earned a respite from political terror. The Nazis themselves often presented this hope—the restoration of public order—as a reason to vote for them. For this reason, once the initial violence associated with the takeover of power had ended, and with exceptions for orchestrated terror campaigns such as the anti-Jewish boycott in April, SA men became least dangerous in public spaces when massed in large numbers, where discipline largely prevailed, their leaders could control their behavior, and their self-interest encouraged them to project calm. When in private settings or in smaller groups, however, stormtroopers knew that their uniforms commanded obedience backed by threat. Many used this effect to coerce authority in quotidian personal interactions that leaders could never fully monitor.

One of the most politically and sociologically fraught areas of stormtrooper abuse concerned their attempts to claim an almost patriarchal power over women's sexuality. Stormtroopers monitored the streets for couples whom they interpreted as mixed Jewish-Aryan pairs, assaulting the Jewish men involved whenever they felt they could get away with it.[154] Such behavior by itself posed problems for the Party's efforts to reduce public violence, now that it held governing responsibility. Even worse, stormtroopers targeted Aryan women as well—not with violence but to attempt to claim them for themselves. Empowered by their enhanced political and economic status, SA men pursued girls with such zeal that they risked becoming the predatory stereotypes they had long decried. They stalked women after dances and pressured them for favors. They asked on dates girls who worked in cafés, bars, and other public places, where the women might hesitate to refuse stormtroopers' advances out of fear for what they would do if rejected. SA men saw increased access to women as one of the rewards of battle. Nazi ideology had long emphasized the idea that stormtroopers could attract mates by being a warrior for the movement. A stormtrooper's performance would prove his commitment to the Volk and make him an appealing candidate to pure German girls who hoped to start Aryan families.[155] In pursuing women after the takeover, stormtroopers hoped to make good on the Party's promise that the Nazi order would allow them to found their own families, but their abuse of the uniform to force their attention on women risked reversing the stereotypes that had propelled them to power. It also humiliated the Party when such interactions turned sour. One encounter had a comedic finale: the girl in question was "so mighty" that she lifted the SA man up and hung him on a fence by his jacket, causing his comrades to "run away in fright."[156] Other encounters, however, turned violent. Stormtroopers sometimes also inserted themselves into verbal arguments between women. One SA man publicly struck a female Party member who had quarreled with his girlfriend. He defended himself in an SA inquiry by calling the woman a prostitute, implying that she lacked the integrity needed to undermine his authority.[157]

Citizens flooded the SA with complaints as the stormtroopers raged increasingly out of control in personal encounters. SA men tried to arrest motorists on their own authority while flouting traffic laws themselves.[158] They abused drugs, drunkenly disrupted church services, and littered the streets with garbage.[159] They attacked foreigners with little provocation other than that their victims "looked Jewish"—the injured parties usually turned out to be Greek, Turkish, and even Danish or British.[160] In a less violent but still offensive incident, residents near the Sturmlokal at Grevenweg

10 were awakened at 1:30 AM by a group of drunken stormtroopers making their way home, stopping here and there along the street to urinate on houses, garden walls, and even a children's playground. The "celebration," as the complainant called it, lasted an hour and reinforced the resident's resentment of local SA rowdies, who he claimed began such behavior "punctually" at 10:30 every night.[161]

As constant yet unpredictable threats, these incidents threatened the SA and the Party's grip on power by harming their reputation among supporters and neutral citizens. The Party allowed and even encouraged SA violence against the regime's enemies, but it knew that its pose as a protector of Hamburg's "responsible people" became weaker every time a stormtrooper abused his power or forced his will on fellow citizens. The stormtroopers' imposition on their neighbors thus placed the Party in a difficult situation: it still needed to bolster the SA's reputation as one of the regime's most important founding forces, but any attempt to do so seemed to encourage the thuggish behavior perfected during the Kampfzeit. That era was fading into the past, but many stormtroopers refused to change their ways. Such stubbornness risked turning people against the regime during the very time the SA was trying to build public loyalty.

A particularly embarrassing episode took place outside the Passage Theater in March 1934.[162] The incident, a dangerous brawl in the middle of Hamburg's poshest shopping street, transformed an event designed to increase support for the Party into a public relations disaster. The Party had produced a film, *Hans Westmar*, that honored the SA. It presented a powerful heroic adventure story based on Horst Wessel's life and death. The film peaked with the protagonist's martyrdom and a victory for the movement, after which, as they had in reality, SA men marched through the Brandenburg Gate accompanied by Wessel's "Die Fahne Hoch." In the film, the slain Westmar's ghostly form materialized alongside the stormtroopers, embodying the song's promise that fallen comrades would march with them in spirit. Stormtroopers and civilians alike had received the film with great acclaim, but the emotions it unleashed whenever it played generated some difficulty. The screening in Hamburg's Passage Theater proved this when a violent melee erupted, initiated by SA Truppführer Böhl, who had taken offense that some members of the crowd had not risen in salute when the Party anthem played at the end. Böhl centered his rage on a fellow moviegoer wearing the badge of the NSKK, a Nazi organization for motor vehicle enthusiasts. After an argument in the balcony that drew in other patrons, the two men left the theater accompanied by a large number of onlookers. As the crowd emptied into the upscale shopping street, the NSKK man, named Böger, lost track of his girlfriend and slowed down to wait for her. Böhl took this as a sign of resistance. He grabbed Böger, tore off his NSKK badge, and beat him about the head before dragging him off to a nearby police station.

Böhl later complained, "Too bad I didn't give that guy a few more in the face." But he took a more demure stance once SA leaders began investigating the incident. To them he justified his actions in terms he thought they would understand:

> I noticed a very clear movement, as when a man intends to free himself from a group through the application of force. But I prevented this and gave him several (2 to 3) blows on the chin. After that, he followed me without further incident to the police station.

Böhl had learned through many street battles how to recognize signs that an opponent was making a move. The SA had even taught its stormtroopers the techniques and language of unarmed combat, through the *Tageblatt*'s jiu-jitsu course and in-person training sessions with knowledgeable comrades. Böhl had learned how useful violence could be in preventing "further incident," especially when asserting that he was defending the law. In this case, he alleged his enemy to be resisting arrest—an arrest that was only lawful based on his self-assumed powers. However, the era had passed when stormtroopers could seize on an enemy's violation of social codes as a way to justify their violence.

Böhl's conduct embarrassed the SA. He had caused a scene during the film, created a public spectacle, and had broken the unified front that members of the movement sought to maintain in the presence of civilians. Several other stormtroopers, all of them doctors or medics with the SA and with the local hospital at St. Georg, had tried to de-escalate the situation, but Böhl rejected their intervention with an attitude that one described as "confrontational." Even after police arrived, Böhl insisted that his authority as an "old fighter" trumped their judgment. Neutral observers found Böhl's interpretation of the scene questionable at best; one of the medics pointed out that Böhl's insistence on standing for the Wessel anthem in fact violated the Party's recent orders. This medic told the SA that he himself had not stood because a Jan. 1 notice in the paper had made known that one shouldn't stand up in theatres when the "Horst Wessel Lied" is played—for example in the newsreels, where the "Horst Wessel Lied" is often played multiple times—because this would disturb others.

Böhl's aggression caused a disturbance even greater than the kind these orders had envisioned. Given the bevy of insults he hurled at Böger, at other comrades, and at the NSKK as an organization, Böhl's attitude encapsulated many old stormtroopers' belief that the SA reigned as the superior organization in the Nazi state. Furthermore, they believed that within the SA the oldest and most violent members reigned supreme, and they would not hesitate to impulsively and violently enforce their conceptions of honor and Party patriotism. These attitudes contradicted the regime's message that citizens could prosper if they gave up resistance and joined the movement. In the end, a film screening intended to bolster public respect for the Party, the SA, and its old fighters instead made any show of esteem seem forced. As the medic said, "Truppführer Böhl, through his undisciplined behavior, ruined any good feelings within the theater." The SA allowed Böhl to quit of his own accord, an option available only to old fighters. The film itself also left the movement, as Propaganda Minister Joseph Goebbels eventually ordered it withdrawn from circulation. His reasons remain unclear and seem connected less to specific incidents like this one than to his greater concern with the SA's role in the Nazi state.[163]

Böhl's punishment notwithstanding, the SA's efforts to restrain its leaders often proved ineffective. The group's insistence that SA men be treated with respect—even when they flouted the law—exacerbated disciplinary problems. After an episode in which a stormtrooper had tried to start a fight with a Jewish man walking arm in arm with an Aryan girl, Böckenhauer wrote that the stormtrooper should not have allowed himself to be taken to the police station with the eyes of the public upon him. The police, Böckenhauer insisted, should handle stormtroopers more discreetly, "with consideration of the stormtroopers' place in the state, their backgrounds, their sacrifices, and their work in service to the Volk and the movement."[164] Such an attitude signaled that ordinary actions of regular state agencies could never hope to constrain SA misdeeds. Nazi politics, however, had already proved willing to oscillate rapidly between legal and extralegal means of resolving problems considered a threat to the regime. Leaders of agencies that competed or conflicted with the SA took increasing note of public pressure against the stormtroopers, and eventually felt that public pressure had built to the point where they could take action. True to Nazi form, they chose a sudden and murderous solution.

NOTES

1   "Nation im Aufbruch," *Hamburger Tageblatt*, January 31, 1933.

2   "Nation im Aufbruch," *Hamburger Tageblatt*.

3   Hermann Okrass, *Hamburg bleibt Rot: Das Ende einer Parole* (Hamburg: Hanseatische Verlaganstalt, 1934), 301.

4   Maike Bruhns, Claudia Preuschoft, and Werner Skrentny, eds., *Als Hamburg "erwachte" 1933 —Alltag im Nationalsozialismus* (Hamburg: Museumspädogogischer Dienst der Kulturbehörde Hamburg, 1983), 10.

5   Peter Longerich, *Geschichte der SA* (Munich: Verlag C. H. Beck, 2003), 169–179.

6   "Marxistische Terrormord überall," *Hamburger Tageblatt*, February 2, 1933; "Neue Mordtatender Kommune," *Hamburger Tageblatt*, February 2, 1933; "Sozialdemokratische Maschining-ewehr-Depot entdeckt," *Hamburger Tageblatt*, February 2, 1933.

7   "28 sozialdemokratische Zeitungen verboten," *Hamburger Echo*, February 11, 1933.

8   "Bewaffnete SA-Leute an allen Ecken," *Hamburger Echo*, February 20, 1933.

9   "Kommunistische Feuerüberfall—Sturm auf das Hotel-Adler," *Hamburger Tageblatt*, February 22, 1933.

10   Readers interested in an overview of Reichstag fire conspiracy historiography can find it in Anson Rabinbach's "Staging Antifascism: The Brown Book of the Reichstag Fire and Hitler Terror," *New German Critique* 35, no. 1 (Spring 2008): 97–126. The latest major entry on the side of Nazi complicity, Benjamin Hett's *Burning the Reichstag: An Investigation into the Third Reich's Enduring Mystery* (Oxford, England: Oxford University Press, 2014), has persuaded the generalist media far more than it has convinced specialist historians. See Richard Evans, "The Conspirators," *London Review of Books* 36, no. 9 (2014): 3–9. The online version includes an exchange of responses between Hett and Evans, available at www.lrb.co.uk/v36/n09/richard-j-evans/the-conspirators.

11   Anson Rabinbach, "Van der Lubbe—ein Lustknabe Röhms?" in Susanne zur Neiden, ed., *Homosexualität und Staatsräson* (Frankfurt am Main: Campus Verlag, 2005), 193–213.

12   World Committee for the Victims of German Fascism, *Brown Book of the Hitler Terror and the Burning of the Reichstag* (New York: Alfred A. Knopf, 1933), 52.

13   World Committee, *Brown Book*, 52.

14   World Committee, *Brown Book*, 46–58.

15   *Roodboek. Marinus van der Lubbe en de Reijksdagbrand* (Amsterdam: International Uitgeversbedrijf, 1933), 69. See also the lengthy defense of van der Lubbe by current Dutch leftists, available at www.left-dis.nl/uk/marinus.htm.

16   Rabinbach, "Staging Antifascism," 111.

17   Rabinbach, "Staging Antifascism," 111.

18   Ursula Büttner, "Der Aufsteig der NSDAP," in Josef Schmid, ed., *Hamburg im "Dritten Reich"* (Göttingen: Wallstein, 2005), 59.

19   Bruhns et al., *Als Hamburg "erwachte,"* 24; Detlef Grabe, "Institutionen des Terrors und der Widerstand der Wenigen," in Schmid, *Hamburg im "Dritten Reich,"* 519.

20   StAHH, 614-2/5 *Nationalsozialistische Arbeiterpartei (NSDAP) und ihre Gliederung* B262, Gruppen-befehl Nr. 2 of March 1, 1933.

21   Büttner, "Der Aufsteig der NSDAP," 61.

22   Ian Kershaw, *Hitler: Hubris* (New York: W. W. Norton & Company, 1999), 463.

23   Kershaw, *Hitler: Hubris,* 466–467.

24   Hermann Beck, *Fateful Alliance: German Conservatism and National Socialism* (New York: Berghahn Books, 2009).

25   Büttner, "Der Aufsteig der NSDAP," 60–64.

26   For the early details of this process, see Frank Bajohr's "Die Zustimmungsdiktatur. Grundzüge nationalsozialistischer Herrschaft in Hamburg," in Schmid, *Hamburg im "Dritten Reich,"* 69–77; also for the later period, see Uwe Lohalm, "'Modell Hamburg.' Vom Stadtstaat zum Reichsgau," in Schmid, *Hamburg im "Dritten Reich,"* 122–153.

27   "Tagesbefehl," *Hamburger Tageblatt,* March 7, 1933.

28   Andrew Wackerfuss, "The Myth of the Unknown Stormtrooper: Selling SA Stories in the Third Reich," *Central European History* 46, no. 2 (2013): 298–324.

29   Jay Baird, *Hitler's War Poets: Literature and Politics in the Third Reich* (Cambridge, England: Cambridge University Press, 2008), 98, and Wackerfuss, "The Myth of the Unknown Stormtrooper," 299–300.

30   "Das graue Herr," *Das evangelische Hamburg* 27, no. 7 (April 1, 1933): 93–94.

31   StAHH, 614-2/5 *Nationalsozialistische Arbeiterpartei (NSDAP) und ihre Gliederung* B184f, Tages-befehl, April 21, 1933.

32   StAHH, 614-2/5 *Nationalsozialistische Arbeiterpartei (NSDAP) und ihre Gliederung* B184b, Gruppen-führer Nordsee to Böckenhauer, May 1, 1933.

33   "Ostern" and "Deutscher Osterglaube," *Hamburger Tageblatt,* April 16, 1933.

34   StAHH, 614-2/5 *Nationalsozialistische Arbeiterpartei (NSDAP) und ihre Gliederung* B172, letter of Sturmführer 1/76 to the Hamburg Senat, May 29, 1933; Sturmhauptbahnführer 1/464, letters of January 1, 1934.

35   StAHH, 614-2/5 *Nationalsozialistische Arbeiterpartei (NSDAP) und ihre Gliederung* B175, letter of Präses der Baubehörde to Untergruppe Hamburg, August 22, 1933; letter of Stand-artenführer Schormann to Baubehörde, September 19, 1933; letter of HJ Oberbann Hamburg to Schormann, October 7, 1933.

36   StAHH, 614-2/5 *Nationalsozialistische Arbeiterpartei (NSDAP) und ihre Gliederung* B172, letter of Standartenführer Schormann to Hochbahn Aktionengesellschaft, August 3, 1933; letter of Hochbahn to Schormann, August 7, 1933.

37   StAHH, 614-2/5 *Nationalsozialistische Arbeiterpartei (NSDAP) und ihre Gliederung* B189, undated notes on the history of the Marine-SA, 3.

38   "Sturm 21/45 weihte sein Heim," *Hamburger Tageblatt,* April 4, 1933.

39   StAHH, 614-2/5 *Nationalsozialistische Arbeiterpartei (NSDAP) und ihre Gliederung* B5, especially:

letter of Winkler to Untergruppe Hamburg, April 18, 1933; Boschmann to Untergruppe Hamburg, April 6, 1933; Böckenhauer to Ortsgruppe Billwärder, March 18, 1933.

40 StAHH, 614-2/5 *Nationalsozialistische Arbeiterpartei (NSDAP) und ihre Gliederung* B5, letter of Böckenhauer to 28 SS Standarte, May 22, 1933.

41 StAHH, 614-2/5 *Nationalsozialistische Arbeiterpartei (NSDAP) und ihre Gliederung* B220, letter of Böckenhauer to Gaupropagandaabteilung, April 7, 1933.

42 StAHH, 614-2/5 *Nationalsozialistische Arbeiterpartei (NSDAP) und ihre Gliederung* B124, letter of September 8, 1933.

43 StAHH, 614-2/5 *Nationalsozialistische Arbeiterpartei (NSDAP) und ihre Gliederung* B124, letter of Brigade 12 to Verwaltung des Lohmühlenkrankenhause, October 6, 1933.

44 StAHH, 614-2/5 *Nationalsozialistische Arbeiterpartei (NSDAP) und ihre Gliederung* B213.2, Böckenhauer letter of April 13, 1933.

45 StAHH, 614-2/5 *Nationalsozialistische Arbeiterpartei (NSDAP) und ihre Gliederung* B213.2, Führer des Sturmes 3/R 76 letter of January 10, 1936.

46 StAHH, 614-2/5 *Nationalsozialistische Arbeiterpartei (NSDAP) und ihre Gliederung* 614-1-38, Hamburger Öffentliche Bücherhallen 12, Band 1, Document 120.

47 StAHH, 614-2/5 *Nationalsozialistische Arbeiterpartei (NSDAP) und ihre Gliederung* B164, Tagesbefehl of April 4, 1933.

48 StAHH, 614-2/5 *Nationalsozialistische Arbeiterpartei (NSDAP) und ihre Gliederung* B132, letter of AÖHG to Brigade 12, 1934.

49 StAHH, 614-2/5 *Nationalsozialistische Arbeiterpartei (NSDAP) und ihre Gliederung* B262, Führer der Standarte 76 to SA Untergruppe Hamburg letter of May 19, 1933.

50 Geoffrey Giles, *Students and National Socialism in Germany* (Princeton, NJ: Princeton University Press, 1985), 144.

51 StAHH, 614-2/5 *Nationalsozialistische Arbeiterpartei (NSDAP) und ihre Gliederung* B132, Standarte 76 to Brigade 12 letter of March 24, 1934.

52 StAHH, 614-2/5 *Nationalsozialistische Arbeiterpartei (NSDAP) und ihre Gliederung* B231, Böckenhauer to Gau Hamburg, letter of June 12, 1933.

53 StAHH, 614-2/5 *Nationalsozialistische Arbeiterpartei (NSDAP) und ihre Gliederung* B262, Führer der Standarte 76 to SA Untergruppe Hamburg letter of May 19, 1933.

54 StAHH, 614-2/5 *Nationalsozialistische Arbeiterpartei (NSDAP) und ihre Gliederung* B44, letter of Standarte 464 to Brigade 12, February 15, 1934; StASH B132 Standarte 464 to Brigade 12, letter of July 26, 1934.

55 NARA A3341 SA Kartei: 143 Georg F.

56 NARA A3341 SA Kartei: 143 Georg F.

57 Uwe Lohalm, "Garant nationalsozialistischer Herrschaft: Der öffentliche Dienst," in Schmid, *Hamburg im "Dritten Reich,"* 154–186.

58 StAHH, 614-2/5 *Nationalsozialistische Arbeiterpartei (NSDAP) und ihre Gliederung* B139, letter of Arbeitsamt Hamburg to Brigade 12, October 7, 1933. StAH B140, which tracks both the initial call for interpreters and the results of individual experiences.

59 Lohalm, "Garant nationalsozialistischer Herrschaft," 165.

60 From 1933 to 1934, the Party placed over 1,000 Nazi-affiliated applicants with the railroad alone, although it is difficult to tell how many of these were stormtroopers. See

Lohalm, "Garant nationalsozialistischer Herrschaft," 165, as well as StAHH, 614-2/5 *Nationalsozialistische Arbeiterpartei (NSDAP) und ihre Gliederung* B49 and B64.

61 Giles, *Students and National Socialism*, as well as Uwe Schmidt and Paul Weidemann, "Modernisierung als Mittel zur Indoktrination des Schulwesen" in Schmid, *Hamburg im "Dritten Reich*," 305–335.

62 Archiv FZH/WdE 10, 163T, 207T, 365, 414, 453T.

63 Archiv FZH/WdE 330T.

64 StAHH, 614-2/5 *Nationalsozialistische Arbeiterpartei (NSDAP) und ihre Gliederung* B166. There were 190 stormtrooper firemen in Hamburg in 1935.

65 See his reports on political debates within the police department, StAHH, 614-2/5 *Nationalsozialistische Arbeiterpartei (NSDAP) und ihre Gliederung* B260.

66 Robert Lewis Koehl, *Black Corps: Structure and Power Struggles of the Nazi SS* (Madison: University of Wisconsin Press, 1983), 64–67.

67 StAHH, 614-2/5 *Nationalsozialistische Arbeiterpartei (NSDAP) und ihre Gliederung* B262, Chef der Ordnungspolizei letter of March 17, 1933.

68 StAHH, 614-2/5 *Nationalsozialistische Arbeiterpartei (NSDAP) und ihre Gliederung* B262, Chef der Ordnungspolizei letter of March 17, 1933.

69 StAHH, 614-2/5 *Nationalsozialistische Arbeiterpartei (NSDAP) und ihre Gliederung* B262, Röhm orders of February 27, 1933; Chef der Ordnungspolizei letter of March 17, 1933.

70 StAHH, 614-2/5 *Nationalsozialistische Arbeiterpartei (NSDAP) und ihre Gliederung* B262, Röhm orders of February 27, 1933; Chef der Ordnungspolizei letter of March 17, 1933.

71 StAHH, 614-2/5 *Nationalsozialistische Arbeiterpartei (NSDAP) und ihre Gliederung* B24, SA-Führerbesprechung, March 27, 1933.

72 StAHH, 614-2/5 *Nationalsozialistische Arbeiterpartei (NSDAP) und ihre Gliederung* B24, SA-Führerbesprechung, March 27, 1933.

73 StAHH, 614-2/5 *Nationalsozialistische Arbeiterpartei (NSDAP) und ihre Gliederung* B262, Standartenführer J9 to Untergruppe Hamburg, March 24, 1933.

74 StAHH, 614-2/5 *Nationalsozialistische Arbeiterpartei (NSDAP) und ihre Gliederung* B262, *Chef der Ordnungspolizei*, March 17, 1933.

75 StAHH, 614-2/5 *Nationalsozialistische Arbeiterpartei (NSDAP) und ihre Gliederung* B262, order of April 27, 1933.

76 StAHH, 614-2/5 *Nationalsozialistische Arbeiterpartei (NSDAP) und ihre Gliederung* B262, Standartenführer J9 to Untergruppe Hamburg, March 24, 1933.

77 StAHH, 614-2/5 *Nationalsozialistische Arbeiterpartei (NSDAP) und ihre Gliederung* B262, April 27, 1933.

78 Eric Reiche, *The Development of the SA in Nurnberg, 1922–1934* (Cambridge, England: Cambridge University Press, 1986), 179, 185.

79 For examples of this type of historical memory, see oral histories in Archiv FZH/WdE 330T and 99T.

80 On the coordination of Hamburg's police, see Detlef Garbe, "Institutionen des Terrors und der Widerstand der Wenigen," in Schmid, *Hamburg im "Dritten Reich*," 520–521.

81 Garbe, "Institutionen des Terrors und der Widerstand der Wenigen," 526.

82 Garbe, "Institutionen des Terrors und der Widerstand der Wenigen," 522–523, 538–539.

83 Pierre Aycoberry labeled the difference between the two organizations as a contrast between "brute violence" and "systematic terror." *The Social History of the Third Reich, 1933– 1945* (New York: The New Press, 1999), 17–36. See also Longerich, *Geschichte der SA*, 172.

84 StAHH, 614-2/5 *Nationalsozialistische Arbeiterpartei* (NSDAP) *und ihre Gliederung* B262, Polizeibehörde Hamburg to Untergruppe Hamburg, May 27, 1933.

85 StAHH, 614-2/5 *Nationalsozialistische Arbeiterpartei* (NSDAP) *und ihre Gliederung* B262, Sturmbannführer der Standarte 45 to Untergruppe Hamburg, April 28, 1933.

86 StAHH, 614-2/5 *Nationalsozialistische Arbeiterpartei* (NSDAP) *und ihre Gliederung* B262, Böckenhauer to Richter, May 8, 1933; Richter to Untergruppe Hamburg, May 13, 1933.

87 StAHH, 614-2/5 *Nationalsozialistische Arbeiterpartei* (NSDAP) *und ihre Gliederung* B262, document 26.

88 StAHH, 614-2/5 *Nationalsozialistische Arbeiterpartei* (NSDAP) *und ihre Gliederung* B262, Römpnagel report of May 15, 1933.

89 StAHH, 614-2/5 *Nationalsozialistische Arbeiterpartei* (NSDAP) *und ihre Gliederung* B262, Schormann to Untergruppe Hamburg, June 15, 1933. Several documents concerning him misspell his name as Satory, but all discuss the same man, Sartory.

90 StAHH, 614-2/5 *Nationalsozialistische Arbeiterpartei* (NSDAP) *und ihre Gliederung* B262, Kissemer report of April 30, 1933.

91 StAHH, 614-2/5 *Nationalsozialistische Arbeiterpartei* (NSDAP) *und ihre Gliederung* B262, Sartory testimony of June 13, 1933.

92 StAHH, 614-2/5 *Nationalsozialistische Arbeiterpartei* (NSDAP) *und ihre Gliederung* B262, Polizeipräsident Hinkler to Untergruppe SA-Hamburg, May 29, 1933.

93 StAHH, 614-2/5 *Nationalsozialistische Arbeiterpartei* (NSDAP) *und ihre Gliederung* B262, Böckenhauer circular of April 21, 1933.

94 StAHH, 614-2/5 *Nationalsozialistische Arbeiterpartei* (NSDAP) *und ihre Gliederung* B262, Böckenhauer circular of April 21, 1933.

95 StAHH, 614-2/5 *Nationalsozialistische Arbeiterpartei* (NSDAP) *und ihre Gliederung* B262, April 27, 1933.

96 StAHH, 614-2/5 *Nationalsozialistische Arbeiterpartei* (NSDAP) *und ihre Gliederung* B262, Truppführer K. to Untergruppe Hamburg, April 21, 1933.

97 StAHH, 614-2/5 *Nationalsozialistische Arbeiterpartei* (NSDAP) *und ihre Gliederung* B262, Gruppenbefehl Nr. 2, March 1, 1933.

98 StAHH, 614-2/5 *Nationalsozialistische Arbeiterpartei* (NSDAP) *und ihre Gliederung* B112, Hamburger Hochbahn to Untergruppe Hamburg, July 17, 1933.

99 StAHH, 614-2/5 *Nationalsozialistische Arbeiterpartei* (NSDAP) *und ihre Gliederung* B112, Hamburger Hochbahn reports of March 5, 1933.

100 StAHH, 614-2/5 *Nationalsozialistische Arbeiterpartei* (NSDAP) *und ihre Gliederung* 241-1, Justizverwalting I.XII Cb 3 vol. 1: Carl Franz Josef M.

101 StAHH, 614-2/5 *Nationalsozialistische Arbeiterpartei* (NSDAP) *und ihre Gliederung* B170, undated statement by Schäfer.

102 StAHH, 614-2/5 *Nationalsozialistische Arbeiterpartei* (NSDAP) *und ihre Gliederung* B170, Schäfer statement of February 17, 1932.

103 StAHH, 614-2/5 *Nationalsozialistische Arbeiterpartei* (NSDAP) *und ihre Gliederung* B170, Bericht des Sturmbannes IV/45, January 1932; Schäfer statement of February 19, 1932.

104 StAHH, 614-2/5 Nationalsozialistische Arbeiterpartei (NSDAP) und ihre Gliederung B170, Bericht des Sturmbannes IV/45 January 1932.

105 StAHH, 614-2/5 Nationalsozialistische Arbeiterpartei (NSDAP) und ihre Gliederung B112, Sturmführer 2/76 to Sturmbann I/76, March 22, 1933.

106 StAHH, 614-2/5 Nationalsozialistische Arbeiterpartei (NSDAP) und ihre Gliederung 241-1, Justizverwaltung I. XII Cb 3 vol. 1: Carl Franz Josef M.

107 NARA A3341 SA Kartei: 050 Blab.

108 NARA A3341 SA Kartei: 050 Blab.

109 Longerich, Geschichte der SA, 83.

110 StAHH, 614-2/5 Nationalsozialistische Arbeiterpartei (NSDAP) und ihre Gliederung B262, Polizeibehörde Hamburg to Reichsminister des Innern, July 19, 1933; Chef der Ordnungspolizei orders of August 7, 1933.

111 StAHH, 614-2/5 Nationalsozialistische Arbeiterpartei (NSDAP) und ihre Gliederung B262, Richter to Fust, September 27, 1933.

112 StAHH, 614-2/5 Nationalsozialistische Arbeiterpartei (NSDAP) und ihre Gliederung B262, Schormann brief of November 10, 1933.

113 StAHH, 614-2/5 Nationalsozialistische Arbeiterpartei (NSDAP) und ihre Gliederung B260, Röhm Abschrift, January 12, 1933, StAHH, B24, SA-Führerbesprechung, March 27, 1933.

114 StAHH, 614-2/5 Nationalsozialistische Arbeiterpartei (NSDAP) und ihre Gliederung B260, Merkblatt für den Eintritt in die Ordungspolizei Hamburg. [No date, likely late January or early February 1933.]

115 StAHH, 614-2/5 Nationalsozialistische Arbeiterpartei (NSDAP) und ihre Gliederung B260 Raeke to Böckenhauer, March 15, 1933.

116 StAHH, 614-2/5 Nationalsozialistische Arbeiterpartei (NSDAP) und ihre Gliederung B260, Richter to Raeke, May 8, 1933.

117 Kershaw, Hitler: Hubris, 383.

118 StAHH, 614-2/5 Nationalsozialistische Arbeiterpartei (NSDAP) und ihre Gliederung B260, Böckenhauer circular of June 17, 1933.

119 NARA A3341 SA Kartei: 074 Hermann B.

120 Longerich, Geschichte der SA, 88. Historians on various sides of the debate over job program effectiveness include Mason, who found that 40–60 percent of unemployed stormtroopers had found work by October 1933; Tim Mason, Arbeiterklasse und Volksgemeinschaft. Dokumente und Materialien zur Deutscher Arbeiterpolitik 1936–1939 (Opladen: Westdeutscher Verlag, 1975), 53. Kater came to a more pessimistic conclusion, describing the SA as having the weakest record in job creation among the Nazi sub-organizations; Michael Kater, "Zum gegensitigen Verhältnis von SA und SS in der Sozialgeschichte des Nationalsozialismus von 1925 bis 1939," Vierteljahresschrift für Sozial- und Wirtschaftsgeschichte 62, no. 3 (1975): 364–372. Fischer presented a mixed report: while SA job placement programs largely failed, in his view, individual SA men and small groups of stormtroopers found effective relief by using their contacts in the SA. Conan Fischer, Stormtroopers: A Social, Economic, and Ideological Analysis (London: Allen and Unwin, 1983), 82–102.

121 For the term's full etymology, see Cornelia Schmitz-Berning, Vokabular des Nationalsozialismus (Berlin and New York: Walter de Gruyter, 2000), 399. Several studies discuss, but do not

agree on, the differing backgrounds of the old and new fighters. See Herbert Andrew, "The Social Composition of the NSDAP: Problems and Possible Solutions," *German Studies Review* 9, no. 2 (1986): 293–318, which includes a useful literature review on the subject.

122 Bruce Campbell, *The SA Generals and the Rise of Nazism* (Lexington: University of Kentucky Press, 1998), 120.

123 StAHH, 614-2/5 *Nationalsozialistische Arbeiterpartei (NSDAP) und ihre Gliederung* B73, Zagst to Schormann, September 17, 1933.

124 StAHH, 614-2/5 *Nationalsozialistische Arbeiterpartei (NSDAP) und ihre Gliederung* B73, Schormann to Gruppe Hanse, November 1, 1933.

125 StAHH, 614-2/5 *Nationalsozialistische Arbeiterpartei (NSDAP) und ihre Gliederung* B73, Sturmführer Biedermann to Scharführer Lampe, March 23, 1933. See also the cases of stormtroopers Henze, Hoyer, Krüger, and Wesel in B73.

126 StAHH, 614-2/5 *Nationalsozialistische Arbeiterpartei (NSDAP) und ihre Gliederung* B73, Henke to Oberführer [sic] der SA Hamburg, March 8, 1933.

127 StAHH, 614-2/5 *Nationalsozialistische Arbeiterpartei (NSDAP) und ihre Gliederung* B73, Sturmbannführer Loff to Sturmbann I/76, March 14, 1933.

128 StAHH, 614-2/5 *Nationalsozialistische Arbeiterpartei (NSDAP) und ihre Gliederung* B73, Henke to Oberführer [sic] der SA Hamburg, March 8, 1933.

129 StAHH, 614-2/5 *Nationalsozialistische Arbeiterpartei (NSDAP) und ihre Gliederung*, B73, Sturmbannführer Loff to Sturmbann I/76, March 14, 1933.

130 StAHH, 614-2/5 *Nationalsozialistische Arbeiterpartei (NSDAP) und ihre Gliederung* B73, Böckenhauer to Sturm 2/76, Mach 18, 1933.

131 StAHH, 614-2/5 *Nationalsozialistische Arbeiterpartei (NSDAP) und ihre Gliederung* B73, Böckenhauer to Paschke, March 25, 1933.

132 See the cases of SA men Meyer, Pfob, and Preibe found in StAHH, 614-2/5 *Nationalsozialistische Arbeiterpartei (NSDAP) und ihre Gliederung* B73.

133 StAHH, 614-2/5 *Nationalsozialistische Arbeiterpartei (NSDAP) und ihre Gliederung* B73, Obersturmbannführer Meyer to SA-Brigade 12, June 15, 1933.

134 Peter Longerich: "Every success in the sphere of securing work must only have raised the attractiveness of the SA for further numbers of unemployed"; *Geschichte der SA*, 188.

135 StAHH, 614-2/5 *Nationalsozialistische Arbeiterpartei (NSDAP) und ihre Gliederung* B91, Truppführer Preuss to Brigade 12, June 13, 1934. See also the cases of SA-men Lüders and Raddass in StAHH, 614-2/5 *Nationalsozialistische Arbeiterpartei (NSDAP) und ihre Gliederung* B91.

136 StAHH, 614-2/5 *Nationalsozialistische Arbeiterpartei (NSDAP) und ihre Gliederung* B94, Bearbeitung von Personalfällen, February 28, 1933.

137 StAHH, 614-2/5 *Nationalsozialistische Arbeiterpartei (NSDAP) und ihre Gliederung* B103 Band 2. Hassenkamp to Untergruppe Hamburg, April 21, 1933.

138 Longerich, *Geschichte der SA*, 171, and Campbell, *The SA Generals*, 125–126.

139 Campbell, *The SA Generals*, 120, and Michael Kater, "Ansätze zu einer Soziologie der SA bis zur Röhm-Krise," in Ulrich Engelhardt, Volker Sellin, and Horst Stuke, eds., *Soziale Bewegung und politische Verfassung. Beiträge zur Geschichte der modernen Welt* (Stuttgart: Klett, 1976), 799.

140 StAHH, 614-2/5 *Nationalsozialistische Arbeiterpartei (NSDAP) und ihre Gliederung* B197, Sturmführer Lüssenhop letter of November 18, 1933.

141 StAHH, 614-2/5 *Nationalsozialistische Arbeiterpartei* (NSDAP) *und ihre Gliederung* B197, Kriegsverbandführer to SA-Brigade 12, January 6, 1934.

142 StAHH, 614-2/5 *Nationalsozialistische Arbeiterpartei* (NSDAP) *und ihre Gliederung* B37, Sturmbannführer Meier Abschrift, undated.

143 StAHH, 614-2/5 *Nationalsozialistische Arbeiterpartei* (NSDAP) *und ihre Gliederung* B37, Pfefferkorn to Standarte 15, September 20, 1933.

144 StAHH, 614-2/5 *Nationalsozialistische Arbeiterpartei* (NSDAP) *und ihre Gliederung* B37, Brigade 12 to Marinestandarte 1, June 21, 1934. Homophobic insults, such as the old standard "Röhmlinge," grew more numerous after June 1934. StAHH, 614-2/5 *Nationalsozialistische Arbeiterpartei* (NSDAP) *und ihre Gliederung* B37. Pol.Mstr 6269 report of September 14, 1934.

145 StAHH, 614-2/5 *Nationalsozialistische Arbeiterpartei* (NSDAP) *und ihre Gliederung* B37, Brigade 12 to Marinestandarte 1, June 21, 1934.

146 StAHH, 614-2/5 *Nationalsozialistische Arbeiterpartei* (NSDAP) *und ihre Gliederung* B37, Obersturmführer S to NS Frontkämpferbund, May 22, 1923. See also the case against Rottenführer Meyer.

147 StAHH, 614-2/5 *Nationalsozialistische Arbeiterpartei* (NSDAP) *und ihre Gliederung* B37, Obergruppenführer M. to Brigade 12, December 10, 1933.

148 StAHH, 614-2/5 *Nationalsozialistische Arbeiterpartei* (NSDAP) *und ihre Gliederung* Polizeistunde für Angehörige des "Stahlhelms," March 29, 1934.

149 Giles, *Students and National Socialism*, 123.

150 StAHH, 614-2/5 *Nationalsozialistische Arbeiterpartei* (NSDAP) *und ihre Gliederung* B197, Deuchler to NSDAP Hamburg, March 11, 1933.

151 StAHH, 614-2/5 *Nationalsozialistische Arbeiterpartei* (NSDAP) *und ihre Gliederung* B109, February 20, 1933.

152 StAHH, 614-2/5 *Nationalsozialistische Arbeiterpartei* (NSDAP) *und ihre Gliederung* B197, Böckenhauer to Standarte 31, February 8, 1933.

153 StAHH, 614-2/5 *Nationalsozialistische Arbeiterpartei* (NSDAP) *und ihre Gliederung* B197, Böckenhauer to Deuchler, March 29, 1933.

154 Maike Bruhns, "'Deutsche und Juden': Antisemitismus im Hamburg," in Maike Bruhns, ed., *Hier war doch alles nicht so schlimm. Wie die Nazis in Hamburg den Alltag eroberten* (Hamburg: VSA, 1984), 122–123.

155 See, for example, "Will und das Mädchen," *Hamburger Tageblatt*, December 28, 1933.

156 Archiv FZH/WdE 269T.

157 StAHH, 614-2/5 *Nationalsozialistische Arbeiterpartei* (NSDAP) *und ihre Gliederung* B103 Band 2, Meldung an die Untergruppe Hamburg, February 9, 1933.

158 StAHH, 614-2/5 *Nationalsozialistische Arbeiterpartei* (NSDAP) *und ihre Gliederung* B114, Chef der Ordnungspolizei letter of June 22, 1933.

159 StAHH, 614-2/5 *Nationalsozialistische Arbeiterpartei* (NSDAP) *und ihre Gliederung* B112 contains several examples of these public embarrassments.

160 StAHH, 614-2/5 *Nationalsozialistische Arbeiterpartei* (NSDAP) *und ihre Gliederung* B112 contains almost a dozen such incidents.

161 StAHH, 614-2/5 *Nationalsozialistische Arbeiterpartei* (NSDAP) *und ihre Gliederung* B109, Wilhelm Kremer to SA-Kommando, May 19, 1933.

162 All accounts of this incident are taken from NARA A3341 SA Kartei: 036 Johann Friedrich B. The victim's version of the story seems more trustworthy, as it was corroborated by five other SA men present, all of them doctors or medics at the nearby St. Georg Hospital.

163 Robert Herzstein, "'No Second Revolution': Joseph Goebbels and the Röhm Crisis, 1933–1934: The Cinematic Evidence," *Proceedings of the South Carolina Historical Association* (1984); 52–66. Herzstein claims that the film "was suppressed for good" after December 1933, "though a special screening may have taken place in Munich in March 1934" (54). Evidence of the Hamburg screening, also in March 1934, calls this assessment into question, at least regarding the speed and efficacy of Goebbels' ban.

164 NARA A3341 SA Kartei: 036 Johann Friedrich B.

LONG KNIVES

As the stormtroopers continued to cause trouble in everyday situations across Hamburg, larger political tensions brewed elsewhere between their leaders and other high-ranking Nazis. The conflict between the SA and the Party had broken into open revolt several times in the past, but Röhm had kept the organization closely tied to Hitler even as his own personality cult within the SA grew.[1] In addition, fissures between the SA and the Party had been bridged by the SA's reliance on Party finances, the individual storm-troopers' loyalty to Hitler, and the hope that at any moment the Party would turn them loose against their enemies. These centripetal forces kept storm-troopers in line politically, even if they still acted out as individuals. After the takeover of power, however, Röhm's plans for the SA—actual or alleged—brought the group into conflict with institutional rivals who did not wish to see their authority usurped by the Party's pet thugs. High-ranking Nazis and influential members of key non-Nazi institutions therefore found common cause with the ordinary citizens so plagued by stormtrooper threats.

In the growing consensus for the need to tame the SA, the military and industrial establishments proved to be its two most powerful institutional enemies outside the Party. The general staff and military officers generally distrusted Röhm, who had often said that the SA should be built up to be more than a mere paramilitary group. In his vision, the SA would refash-ion itself into a more formal and better equipped fighting force that would first supplement, then replace the army with a younger, more dynamic, and ideologically pure SA corps.[2] This naturally raised suspicion in traditional army ranks. In practice, the SA and the army actually cooperated well in the regime's first year. The SA assumed responsibility for light military training and "military sport" as a way of re-militarizing German men at a time the army could not, given the restrictions of the Versailles Treaty.[3] In February 1934, during a meeting with Hitler and military officers, Röhm even signed an agreement giving up his military ambitions. Despite these arrangements, military officers continued to watch the SA carefully, especially General von Blomberg, who strongly encouraged Röhm's Nazi rivals to plot against him.[4] Röhm's loud advocacy of the stormtroopers' economic demands also played a role in the growing conspiracy.

The stormtroopers' economic activism represented the left or socialist wing of National Socialism, a part of the movement that had long appealed to the working and lower classes so devastated by the Depression. In this re-gard, Nazi and Communist economic demands often seemed quite similar, using a shared love of violence to compete for the same base of impoverished underclass and threatened middle class. Although historians continue to debate the true nature of National Socialism's class base, those who have studied the SA in other German regions have observed a significant back-and-forth migration of members between the two enemies' fighting organizations. By 1934, now that the SA had crushed the Communist Party, stormtroopers sought to entice their former enemies into cooperating with a second economic revolution against "bosses," finance capital, big banks, heavy industry, and department stores.[5]

These earnest and appealing hopes never matched well with the Nazi Party's governing plans. To allow them would only encourage the underground Communist Party's attempts to infiltrate and convert the "proletarian SA," thus compromising stormtrooper loyalty and weakening the regime's support among its shock troops. Moreover, stormtroopers had already shown a desire to take matters into their own hands—not only small-scale actions like those the *Hilfspolizei* had performed in Hamburg but also large riots that took place in other German cities, where stormtroopers were seen to occupy and destroy buildings belonging to their economic enemies. In May 1934, stormtroopers in the Hanseatic city of Bremen sallied forth from their headquarters to attack the Karstadt department store, smashing its windows and raising 15 giant swastika flags from the roof—an act that brought out the police, who battled stormtroopers in the streets for several hours.[6]

These words and deeds unnerved the population at large, but they positively terrified business and industrial leaders, whose cooperation Hitler would need to fight the war he already planned to begin. Unease among economic elites thus combined with the distrust many high-ranking Nazis held for the SA's role in the state, as well as their distaste for Röhm personally—for his ambition and for his millions of wild followers. Hermann Göring and Heinrich Himmler became the main conspirators against Röhm and the SA, along with Himmler's deputy, Reinhard Heydrich, and interior minister Wilhelm Frick. All these individuals and institutions were key players in the Nazis' internal and external security policy, and none of them wished to see the SA gain influence in these areas.

By the summer of 1934, these factions had convinced Hitler to tame the SA. Hitler's own thoughts on the matter are difficult to divine, but he seems to have long considered the SA a barely controllable mob in comparison to the elite guard of the SS. In one famous anecdote, Hitler drew a bold line across a map of Germany, bisecting the country into northeastern and south-western halves. He claimed that the SA's popularity in the northern Protestant area signified its rebelliousness and iconoclasm, while the SS spread in Catholic areas because of a common attitude of obedience and servility to a sole ruler.[7] Hitler's speech in this possibly apocryphal story served to lionize both groups, each of which had played a role in the Nazis' rise. Hitler had embraced the SA in an earlier period when he preached revolution. Now, however, he needed servants. In the end, whatever his personal beliefs may have been about Röhm and the SA's loyalty, Hitler allowed Göring, Himmler, and Heydrich to convince him that Röhm planned an SA coup and a radical second revolution that would overturn the German economic order.[8]

Historians generally agree that Röhm had no concrete plans for such an action. However, his articulation of the stormtroopers' broader concerns over economic and organizational policy did challenge Hitler's leadership and strain the nascent Nazi state.[9] In the words of Hitler biographer Ian Kershaw, the SA's inclination toward social revolution was "the greatest threat to Hitler in the early phase of the dictatorship."[10] This threat embodied itself less in organized plans than in daily disruptions, less in formal bureaucratic maneuvers than in spontaneous personal conflicts and rash local actions, as in Bremen. These incidents were local corollaries to the national tensions that bred resentment and distrust of the SA. As citizen complaints resonated up through the Nazi hierarchy, a growing number of military, economic, and political elites joined forces to convince Hitler to put an end to the SA's independence and arrogance. As long as the SA continued to rage unchecked through the streets, cafés, and public spaces of German cities, their actions would negate Hitler's claims after July 1933 that the revolution had ended and order had been restored to the German state. Hitler thus needed one last act of violence to secure his claim to order.

June 30, 1934: The Night of the Long Knives

True to form, Hitler's eventual decision about the SA settled upon a dramatically violent solution. In June 1934, Hitler directed Röhm to order the SA on a monthlong vacation and promised to attend an SA leadership conference set for June 30 in Bad Wiessee, a Bavarian resort town. The SA vacation distracted SA men and leaders from politics and reduced the chances that they could compare notes and thus uncover the growing plot against them.

Röhm's decision to disperse the stormtroopers to whatever individual destinations pleased them, scattering them across the country and isolating
them from their leadership, indicated that the chief of staff had no plans
for a putsch.

Röhm's personal circle of high-ranking SA commanders spent the
weekend of June 30 at a drunken party at the Pension Hanselbrauer in the
Bavarian countryside. A great deal of beer flowed all that Saturday evening,
and at least two SA men paired off to enjoy each other's company in private.[11] Around 6:30 AM, however, Hitler and a column of SS men arrived at
the hotel. According to the diaries and memoirs of several men who were
either present at the event or who heard Hitler's version of the tale firsthand,
the *Führer* and his SS vanguard quietly approached Röhm's hotel room. Hitler
knocked on the door and said in a disguised voice, "Message from Munich."
Röhm, lying in bed undressed, replied that the door was open and the mes-
senger should come in. Hitler then burst through the door, flew into the
room, and grabbed Röhm by the throat, screaming, "You are under arrest,
you pig." An SS guard threw Röhm's clothes into his face and ordered him to
get dressed. They then led him out of the hotel at gunpoint, dressed only in
his pajama bottoms. Meanwhile, the attackers stormed another room to find
Edmund Heines, the SA leader of Breslau, in bed with his 18-year-old driver.
Later legends told that the SS men, on Hitler's personal orders, summarily
shot both Heines and his young companion.[12] In reality, they took Heines to
a prison in Munich and shot him there. The identity and fate of the young
stormtrooper remains unknown.[13]

As for Röhm, Himmler's SS minions left him in a cell for several days
while Hitler vacillated on how to punish him. Röhm passed the time mournfully, still half-dressed and despondent. When visited by Hans Frank, the
Nazi lawyer who would go on to become the brutal governor of occupied
Poland, Röhm complained that "all revolutions devour their own children."
Whether or not Frank understood the reference to a famous statement made
by a French revolutionary who lost his head in that revolution's persecution
of its own supporters, he likely displayed little sympathy. Several days later,
at around 2:30 PM on July 2, two SS officers appeared at Röhm's cell. Both
Theodor Eicke and Michael Lippert later became infamous leaders of the SS's
military and concentration camp projects, but now they carried out a much
more focused plan of murder. They handed Röhm a pistol, loaded with a
single bullet, as well as a copy of the *Volkischer Beobachter* that announced to

the nation Röhm's downfall and disgrace. One of the SS men told Röhm, "You have ruined your life, but the Führer has not forgotten his old comrade in arms. He is giving you a chance to draw the necessary conclusions. You have ten minutes."[14] The SS men left and waited for the pistol's sound. Fifteen minutes passed. Finally, their patience expired, the two returned to Röhm's cell, where he stood with the newspaper in hand. "If I am to be killed," he said, "let Adolf do it himself!"[15] Lippert then drew his own pistol and fired twice into Röhm's naked chest at point-blank range. Röhm fell to the ground, moaning, "Mein Führer, mein Führer!"[16] Eicke stepped forward and fired again, ending the life of one of Hitler's closest friends and most important revolutionary comrades.

In the coming hours, similar scenes were repeated across Germany. The storming of Röhm's hotel inaugurated a three-day massacre across the Reich, conducted by the SS with the assistance of the army and Himmler's security forces. In addition to organizationally decapitating the SA, SS assassins also settled scores with a variety of other adversaries who, over the past decade, had crossed Hitler, Himmler, or the Party's interests generally. These victims included Gregor Strasser, Hitler's old rival for the affections of the Party's populist northern faction, to which many of Hamburg's stormtroopers had belonged and which had argued strongly for the economic demands that the regime now wished to downplay. General and former chancellor von Schleicher was shot in his home, along with his wife, in revenge for his failure to aid Hitler's backroom scheming in Berlin's halls of power. Gustav von Kahr, the right-wing Bavarian politician whose refusal to participate in Hitler's Beerhall Putsch helped doom it to failure, now died for his lack of vision. Papen, Hitler's predecessor and now vice chancellor, was put under house arrest but somehow survived, although several of his close associates did not. The plotters arrested over one thousand people, and killed dozens.[17] All told, at least 85 people, and possibly as many as several hundred, died in the purge, only half of them stormtroopers. The bloodshed caused onlookers to give the event a suitably sinister name: the Night of the Long Knives. The actual number of victims cannot be calculated because Göring and Himmler ordered all records of the operation to be burned on July 2, the day of Röhm's murder.[18]

Because of this deliberate obfuscation, the course of the purge in Hamburg and the number of its victims there are difficult to determine. The killings were most numerous in and near Munich, Berlin, and Silesia—the oldest party strongholds, and where Himmler and Heydrich had nurtured many rivalries.[19] But some measure of violence came to Hamburg as well, where at least 11 people were reportedly killed.[20] Several high-ranking SA leaders and police officials were arrested and sent to Berlin, including Ellerhusen. His friendships with Kaufmann (Heydrich's old rival) and Bisschopinck (whom Conn had driven from Hamburg over the man's homosexuality) seem to have made Ellerhusen a target.[21] But he and most others were soon released at the urging of Kaufmann and Krogmann, who went to Berlin to argue their cases. Some stormtroopers fled the city in fear for their lives, including Plasberg, Jaworski, and several other homosexual stormtroopers who disappeared from the SA's sight during the purge.[22] These men were later expelled from the SA, but they did survive. Bisschopinck, being isolated from the centers of violence in his new position in Goslar, seems to have been miraculously passed over by the SS angel of death.[23] Aside from the unknown 11 victims, the purge in Hamburg does not seem to have shed much blood. It did send a clear and threatening message to the city's stormtroopers, who began to realize what it was like to face Nazi persecution rather than to dish it out.

Justifying the Purge through Homophobic Panic

The greatest significance of the Night of the Long Knives did not lie in the number of stormtroopers killed or arrested, which after all represented only a small fraction of the huge group. The SA's decapitation was a targeted action that killed Röhm's immediate circle, as well as those who had openly caused trouble or otherwise crossed the architects of the purge. The vast majority of stormtroopers could not be simply murdered, both because of their numbers and because of their symbolic importance to the Party. The purge's larger meaning thus lay in the rhetoric Hitler used to justify the killings, which he explained as an executive action to defend the state and restore the Party's moral standing in penance for the stormtroopers' vice, decadence, and homosexuality. By deploying public panic against homosexuality, Hitler and the Nazi media won support for their illegal murders and laid further foundations for unchecked state violence.

Goebbels set the tone in his radio address the following Monday morning, in which he painted the SA's supposed threat to the state in moral terms. Röhm, Goebbels claimed, had planned a coup against Hitler, a second revolution, and an SA state. These of course provided enough reason for his elimination. But Goebbels also added harsh words about SA leaders' immorality, mobilizing the language of moral outrage to paint the killings as an act to protect the Party and the nation:

> [Röhm and the SA leaders] have discredited the honor and prestige of our *Sturmabteilung*. By a life of unparalleled debauchery, by their parade of high living, by their feasting and carousing, they have damaged the principles of simplicity and personal decency that our Party supports. They were close to tainting the entire leadership with their shameful and disgusting sexual aberrations.[24]

This clear reference to stormtrooper homosexuality fit Goebbels' portrayal of the action as a "storm of purification," which he said the Party needed to unleash in order to cleanse itself of degenerate elements. "The Führer," he said in his radio address, "has decided to act without pity when the principles of decency, simplicity, and public propriety are at stake, and the punishment must be all the greater when the persons concerned occupy the highest positions."[25]

The *Hamburger Tageblatt* reported these remarks, along with Göring's "statement on the cleansing."[26] The paper prominently displayed 12 orders for the new SA given by Hitler and the new chief of staff, Victor Lutze. The seventh point on this list addressed homosexuality in the SA more directly and openly than SA leaders had ever done. Hitler made clear that any tolerance of homosexuality in the SA had ended:

> I expect from all SA leaders that they assist in keeping the SA a pure and clean institution. I wish especially that every mother be able to give her son to the SA, the Party, and the Hitler Youth without fear that he could be ethically or morally ruined. I therefore wish that all SA leaders exactingly punish all offenses against P175 with immediate expulsion from the SA and the Party. I want men as SA leaders, not ridiculous apes.[27]

Hitler's public address to the *Reichstag* followed up on these themes. The July 13 speech was long awaited. Hitler had uncharacteristically kept himself from the public eye since the murders, and he had not addressed the

Nazi faithful outside of a few minor appearances. The mood in the Kroll Opera House, where the Reichstag had met since the fire, was uneasy. The parliament was missing 13 members who had just been killed by the very SS that now guarded the hall. The event was, in Kershaw's words, "a vital speech, one of the most difficult [Hitler] had ever given."[28]

Hitler addressed his remarks not only to National Socialists but to "members of our leading bourgeois circles," particularly women.[29] He claimed that women had built the Nazi state, having believed in its moral values. "Millions of women love our new state," he said. "They sacrifice, work, and pray for it. They discover its mission to be their natural instincts: the preservation of our people, which they themselves have given a living pledge in the form of their children." The "crimes of high SA leaders" thus threatened to undermine both Hitler's own position and the Party's larger base of support. "One thing is clear," he declared. "The work to renew our *Volk* . . . is only possible if the German people follow their leaders with calmness, order, and discipline—and above all, when they can trust in their leadership." Accordingly, Hitler's speech moved quickly from a description of the SA leaders' supposed ambitions to cataloguing their alleged moral failings. Chief of Staff Röhm, Hitler claimed, had "distanced himself from the Party" through the lifestyle "he and his circle" pursued, which was "unbearable to all conceptions of National Socialism." He said that Röhm's homosexuality and his propensity for promoting his own men had bred a conspiracy to overthrow the state for the benefit of a secretive homosexual clique:

> It was not only terrible that [Röhm] himself and his circle around him broke all laws of decent conduct, or that—even worse—this poison began to spread itself into larger circles. The worst was that a sect grew within the SA, sharing a common orientation, who formed the kernel of a conspiracy not only against the moral conceptions of a healthy Volk, but also against state security. A review of promotions carried out in May led to the terrible discovery that, within certain SA groups, men were being promoted without regard to National Socialist and SA service, *but only because they belonged to the circle of this orientation.*[30]

The *Tageblatt* printed this italicized final phrase in bold type. Hitler's message, dutifully magnified by his local press, presented the sexual transgressions of Röhm and his "circle" as the full explanation for their alleged political conspiracy. "A small group of similarly disposed elements," said Hitler, placed themselves "blindly" in the hands of their conspiratorial, homosexual leader Röhm, who then began plans for his cult to take over the state. In the face of this alleged moral decay and its consequent political threat, Hitler claimed, he acted in defense of German morality. In the speech's most famous passage, he claimed:

> In this hour I was responsible for the fate of the German people, and thereby I became the supreme judge of the German people. I gave the order to shoot the ringleaders in this treason, and I further gave the order to cauterize down to the raw flesh the ulcers poisoning the wells of our domestic life.[31]

The speech succeeded wildly. Kershaw judged it "if not one of [Hitler's] best rhetorical performances" then "certainly one of the most remarkable, and most effective, that he was ever to deliver."[32]

Many historians have called attention to the speech as one of the clearest elaborations of the Third Reich's guiding legal principle—that Hitler was the "supreme judge of the German nation" and could by definition decree what was law. On July 3, Hitler's puppet Reichstag retroactively declared his actions legal. In this respect, the massacre became one more step in a larger process of reversing long-standing legal principles. As an American lawyer described it at the time, "the judge is freed from positive law whenever the criminal code offers no basis for conviction," a situation representing a "revolutionary departure from the well-established principles of criminal law in civilized communities."[33] In retrospective agreement with this interpretation, historian Geoffrey Giles describes the regime as moving from the legal norm of "no punishment without law" to a standard of "no crime without punishment."[34] Under this doctrine of pseudo-legality, Hitler and the Nazi security agencies could define crimes and punish criminals as they saw fit, and only later concern themselves with covering their actions with a legal veneer.

Following the Night of the Long Knives, a large number of political elites and the common masses alike accepted these quasi-legal justifications. Both groups were seemingly won over by the alleged plot's double crime of political and moral corruption. Apologists from Hitler to Lutze justified the regime's actions through code words that shamed and sexualized internal enemies. Thus a secretive "sect" or "circle of conspirators" with a common "orientation" acted "against the Volk's healthy instincts" with their *"Treiben"*—a word meaning "carryings on," but whose use as a verb links it to sabotage and fornication (*die Sabotage treiben* or *die Unzucht treiben*).[35] Hitler and his allies thereby won the public over to the view that state actions, no matter how violent or illegal, could be considered moral so long as they claimed to promote private morality and eliminate homosexuality, which together would supposedly strengthen society and the state.

Astute observers of the German political scene saw through Hitler's characterization of his actions. The Social Democratic Party in exile, the SOPADE, reminded readers that Hitler had never before found fault with the SA's moral, political, or sexual crimes:

> Hitler accuses his closest collaborators, the very men who brought him to power, of the most shameless and moral depravities . . . But it is he who required of them terror and assassinations . . . He tolerated and approved of their atrocities, called them his comrades . . . Today he allows them to be assassinated, not because of their crimes, but to save himself.[36]

Many people still in Germany also saw through the justification, as did one SA doctor who incurred punishment for saying, "It's all a show, and Hitler's just a big actor."[37] In general, however, Hitler's explanation resonated with the public. As the SOPADE report admitted, "Our comrades report that Hitler has won strong approval and sympathy from that part of the population which still places its hopes in him. To these people, his action is proof that he wants order and decency."[38] The SOPADE concluded that charges of personal immorality against SA leaders "diverts the attention of the great mass of the population from the political background of the action, and at the same time elevates Hitler's standing as the cleanser of the movement."[39]

Hitler's mobilization of moral panic against SA leaders worked to a great extent because it tapped into existing opinions about homosexuals' purported tendency to form conniving cliques at the highest levels of government, as had most famously been charged back in the imperial years during the Eulenburg affair. Drawing inspiration from this established pattern, rumors around Hamburg in early 1934 anticipated the purge before it even took place, complete with details of uncanny similarity to the events that eventually took place. In one such story, SA leaders and an entourage of "questionable women" held a champagne party in the Hotel Atlantic, the ritzy hotel where Röhm had stayed before his departure for South America.[40]

Hitler also stayed there when visiting the city. According to the story, news of the party reached Hitler in Berlin. He flew to Hamburg, appeared in the Atlantic's dining hall, overturned the SA table, and ground the champagne glasses underfoot. The tale lacked plausibility—not least because Hitler's speedy appearance all the way from Berlin defied the laws of physics. But the rumor still featured several key elements of the moral accusations against SA leaders: their high-rolling lifestyle, corruption, sexual depravity (although heterosexual in this version), and public flouting of propriety and dignity. Hitler's rage upon hearing of these events and his personal intervention to correct the situation featured prominently in this precognitive rumor, as well as in the Nazis' official narrative of the purge after it had taken place.

Stories like this one laid the groundwork for a variety of Germans to greet Hitler as a heroic defender of national morality. Hindenburg sent Hitler and Göring telegrams of congratulations.[41] General von Blomberg and other army leaders also praised the "military determination" the assassins had displayed.[42] In Hamburg, Mayor Krogmann needed little convincing, due to his long-standing dislike of Röhm, which stemmed from the SA leader's homosexuality. Krogmann usually covered this prejudice, however, in coded language referring to decadence and appetite. Describing an official reception in the *Rathaus* in April 1933, Krogmann related that Röhm's large entourage had supposedly eaten 4,000 sandwiches and drunk over 1,000 liters of beer, then retired to a St. Pauli bar infamous for its male homosexual clientele.[43] In the weeks after the purge, Krogmann and other Nazi leaders received visits from high-ranking SS officers who shared manufactured evidence of Röhm's crimes and emphasized his homosexuality as a danger to the state. Krogmann later admitted that the proof, in retrospect, seemed thin. He said, however, that at the time he had faith that Hitler "must have had" harder evidence against Röhm.[44] Hitler's justifications resonated even within the SA, where late-joining members often resented the homoerotic old guard. One Marine stormtrooper smugly declared at the time that "the entire SA is made up of *Röhmlinge* (Röhm boys) and that these corrupt perverts "will be cleaned out soon."[45]

Even the Nazis' enemies portrayed homosexuality as a central reason for the purge. After all, they had long used the stereotype of homosexual Nazis as a propaganda image, and they now took Hitler's words as an admission that the Party had indeed been infested all along with immoral elements. Willi Münzenberg continued his recent career of linking SA homosexuality to the Third Reich's crimes, now claiming that the Night of the Long Knives' true purpose had been to eliminate the clique of homosexual Nazis who had burned the Reichstag.[46] Münzenberg had long claimed that Heines had led the puppet van der Lubbe through the underground tunnel to burn the Reichstag, and he now interpreted Heines' execution as proof that the Nazis wanted him silenced. Other antifascists invented still further sexualized justifications for the purge, including the unfortunate idea that Hitler had Röhm killed to protect the secret of his own homosexuality.[47] These tales of conspiracy were based on even less evidence than those of the Reichstag fire, but they too retained currency over the decades. Ironically, in the aftermath of the purge, antifascist links between homosexuality and Nazism for once worked to Hitler's advantage. He and his apologists now turned the socialist parties' own narrative against them: the "homosexual enemy of the state" that had lurked within Nazism had been eliminated, leaving the Party a trustworthy and moral political agent.[48]

Hitler's use of homophobic panic against the SA must be read as a political tactic rather than an honest expression of his opinions or morals. He himself had no personal discomfort with homosexuality, but in this case he found it politically useful to portray discomfort. Seen systemically, the Night of the Long Knives stands as the final settlement of homosexuality's troubled place in the SA and the Nazi movement. During the *Kampfzeit*, men of any sexual orientation who cultivated homoerotic ties with comrades saw themselves as the elite core of the SA's all-male "fighting community." They did so with the consciousness that they followed a long tradition of homoerotic military leadership in Germany—even if this tradition had come under threat in the later imperial period, and had in fact brought them much public grief during the Weimar Republic. Hitler had allowed and implicitly blessed the situation, despite growing discontent among homophobic Party members, because he knew these men to be loyal to the comrades with whom they shared political and erotic ties.

After the takeover, however, as the SA's lawlessness and criminality grew along with its numbers, Hitler reassessed the significance of its homosexual minority, whom he would now use as a scapegoat for the excesses of the movement as a whole. The strategy worked because it built on an existing discursive framework that associated male homosexuality with selfish and elite cliques that were lurking within militaristic governments, where these cliques allegedly sought to pervert state and society to their own ends while seducing new comrades into their circle. The strength of this framework nurtured genuine homophobia among such key figures as Himmler, whose unbounded loathing of homosexual men proved lethal, immediately after the takeover and in the future.[49] It also allowed the Nazis to appear resistant to corrupt and militaristic trends that they in fact indulged. The mobilization of homophobic panic therefore represented a crass and calculated act of political "instrumentation" by Hitler himself, one that succeeded wildly by tapping into honestly held, if misguided, moral concerns.[50]

Whereas the Nazis' public rhetoric concerning homosexuality in their own ranks had previously dismissed or minimized homosexuality, it highlighted stormtrooper homosexuality in the immediate aftermath of the purge. Focusing on the homosexuality of some victims, even if only through the coded and euphemistic language of the time, allowed the remaining stormtroopers and the general public to retain pride in the SA, now supposedly cleansed of depraved influences. This largely cosmetic redemption of the SA succeeded because it encouraged the belief that stormtrooper lawlessness came from sources other than its members' economic ambitions and lust for personal power. Almost all SA men had traits of greed and authoritarianism in some measure, and most of them abused power to achieve these ends whenever given the chance. Hitler, however, encouraged the public to overlook this behavior in favor of blaming a small, secretive sexual minority who could be easily purged. In this formulation, eliminating the minority solved the problem for the entire group. The new leader, Lutze, could then claim that "the simple and unknown SA man and his leaders knew nothing about" the supposed plots of "the high leadership clique," and that the SA as a whole "really has nothing to be ashamed of."[51] Instead "they were to have been misused by a small circle of their former leaders, but they stand today without blemish. I can say with pride, that the whole SA is clean and may now again wear the brown shirt with heads held high."[52] In the future, Lutze meant "to make of the brown formation an unquestionably clean and—this is of special importance—a politically reliable instrument of the movement."[53] The dynamic surrounding the purge and its aftermath thus portrayed the SA's unreliability, unpredictability, and disorganized use of violence as problems easily resolved by the expulsion of homosexual "elements."

Cleansing the SA

The Night of the Long Knives inaugurated a new era of persecution across Germany. This persecution did not yet target homosexuals as a whole group; that persecution began later in varying times and places according to the circumstances of local politics. In Hamburg it did not take place for two more years.[54] The witch-hunt of mid- to late 1934 focused instead on the stormtroopers. Adolf Brand's prediction that homosexual stormtroopers had been "carrying their hangman's rope in their pockets" had finally come to pass.[55] Yet Brand's warning had far broader implications. Once the inquisition had begun, all stormtroopers found their private lives under scrutiny by an increasingly invasive Party apparatus.

The SA had already been trying to reform itself before July 1934. These efforts, however, consisted mostly of small-scale programs to monitor members' physical health, fitness, and citizenship status.[56] After the Night of the Long Knives, a purge conducted on the basis of political loyalty could not have occurred, since the lack of any real plot meant that no SA traitors could be found.[57] Instead, expulsion took the form of a cleansing that cast out any stormtroopers found to have moral failings. These men included those who were suspected of being homosexuals, convicted criminals, poor husbands, fickle brothers, rude to women, or unreliable comrades. Stormtroopers had always argued that their private lives carried political import and their personal choices reflected political virtues. Now they found that the Party would for the first time hold them to the standards they claimed to promote. Given this dynamic, evidentiary standards for successful accusations of homosexuality were predictably lax, especially in the denunciatory atmosphere that reigned in the late summer and early fall. SA man Friedhelm S. was expelled on July 4 for "offenses against P175."[58] The incident in question, however, involved no allegations of sexual contact. The young accuser, whom Friedhelm S. had met at a café the previous March, claimed only that the stormtrooper had propositioned him. This proved enough for the police and the SA. When the SA investigated the incident in July, Friedhelm defended himself by noting his nonconformity to the stereotypes about effeminate homosexual men. His objections, however, failed to win the day. He had fatally weakened his case by signing a protocol that admitted to the accusation, a statement he recanted once he realized the seriousness of the charge. He then said he had signed the statement only because he had misinterpreted it, being hard of hearing and in a state of agitation. No other evidence against him existed. Nevertheless, the arresting officer said he "would make sure he was sent to a work camp."[59] The SA itself, which had done nothing for or against Friedhelm's case before the purge, now easily fit him into its new crusade against stormtrooper homosexuality. It expelled him on July 4, along with three other men whose cases the SA seems to have placed in the same category.[60] The Hitler Youth also came under scrutiny at this time. One historical review of Hitler Youth files found that 25 percent of those expelled between 1934 and 1939 were dismissed for suspected homosexuality.[61]

In the weeks following the purge, innuendo and rumor were enough to mark a stormtrooper as an unwanted outsider, no matter the actual evidence. One sport leader "suspected of unnatural fornication" was forced to leave "on his own wish," even though not enough evidence existed to convict him of any crime.[62] The SA then investigated every witness in the case for clues to their own possible "participation" in homosexual deeds. This type of investigative chain existed as a reaction to public beliefs about homosexual conspiracies, and it now became of enduring relevance for the later persecution of German homosexual men.[63] The Hamburg SA also monitored arrest records in other German states in order to catch stormtroopers convicted in other jurisdictions. Not content with merely expelling homosexual stormtroopers from the SA, the group forwarded this scandalous information to the men's employers, as it did with a stormtrooper university professor and *Hilfspolizist* whom police in East Prussia had arrested for crimes against P175.[64]

Many homosexual stormtroopers who had been accepted or lived under cover now met with expulsion.[65] This had not been the case as recently as the previous summer, when a stormtrooper had been caught in the woods with an underage boy whose father "intended to have him investigated for signs of sexual misuse."[66] This stormtrooper went undisciplined, despite far more detailed and reliable accusations than those levied against, for instance, Friedhelm S. Now, however, denunciations and expulsions became so frequent that after a few weeks Lutze and deputy Führer Rudolf Hess warned that they were growing out of control.[67] In a series of articles published not in the *Tageblatt* but in the bourgeois-conservative *Fremdenblatt*, these two influential figures cautioned against "rumor mongering" and "anonymous denunciations."[68] The public had taken heed of the call to drive homosexual Nazis out of the Party, but the Party preferred to do so behind closed doors. In 1935, the regime chose the anniversary of the purge to publish its extended version of P175, which expanded the category of the crime far beyond "actions resembling coitus," the previous standard. Now, Nazi judges could decree any act—even a simple touch or look—as evidence of homosexuality.[69] The situation had become so inflamed that denouncers even began to consider negative interest in homosexuality as evidence of same-sex orientation. One *Scharführer* M., who had been in the SA since 1932, was expelled in this way soon after the enhanced law was passed. Despite the fact that he had a wife and child, the SA began to take his unusually strong interest in rooting out homosexuality in his neighborhood of St. Georg as a sign of his own hidden inclinations. During a coffee break with a stormtrooper colleague at his office, Scharführer M. said that he knew of several local bars frequented by male homosexuals, and suggested that they visit these establishments to identify the patrons and expose them to the police. On the one hand, the plan fit with the regime's ever-escalating rhetorical and legal persecution of homosexual men, but the intensity of M.'s interest struck his comrades as odd. As *Standartenführer* Trzebiatowsky, one of the oldest and most accomplished SA leaders in Hamburg, wrote in his report on M.:

> The mere knowledge of these bars that M. displays supports the suspicion that he himself has similar inclinations. His further suggestion to [his stormtrooper workmate] that they should visit these bars and report their observances to the police appears as nothing other than a cloak under which M. hides in order to pursue his inclination without danger.[70]

As this case showed, determining which stormtroopers were actually homosexual proved as vexing as ever. The SA had responded to the problem in the past by ignoring the issue, but it could no longer use that solution. It therefore decided to err on the side of expulsion. M.'s case came to a head when a series of letters from July 1935 emerged, in which he openly discussed "committing unnatural fornication" with a young coal handler who worked in the area.[71] M. claimed that he had not actually done the deed but had written about it as part of a sting operation to cleanse his neighborhood of the young man, who M. claimed had propositioned him many times. The SA found his excuses unbelievable: "Each isolated case for suspicion against M. may not suffice as a reason for action. In their totality, however, they show that M. undoubtedly must have more than a criminological interest in these matters, and that he is himself same-sex inclined."[72] Despite his impeccable record of military and Freikorps service, despite his long tenure in the SA, despite the testimony of several other old fighters whose lives he had saved during Kampfzeit battles, despite there being no evidence that he had ever actually had sex with a man, and despite his having a wife and child, the SA found M. guilty of homosexuality and expelled him. He appealed the decision three times without success.

As with individuals in most historical eras, there is insufficient evidence to determine M.'s actual sexuality, or that of the other stormtroopers expelled after the Night of the Long Knives. It is possible that M.'s elaborate plan to spy on and entrap the patrons of local bars came from a genuine hatred of homosexuality, which one of his comrades implied had originated in his capture and rape by Bolsheviks behind the lines during the Freikorps' border wars in 1920.[73] Many members of the Nazi movement certainly had a similar drive to act on their homophobia—especially younger members of the SA and Hitler Youth. Some of these youths even posed as "bait" in sting operations to root out homosexual men across the city, attempts the police eventually put a halt to for being "impudent" actions of "amateur criminologists."[74] M.'s alibi therefore contained potential links to a real phenomenon. Ironically, however, his actual experience of undercover operations, both during the Freikorps years and with the SA itself, made the SA less inclined to believe him. The SA concluded that an experienced agent like M. would not have conducted such a clumsy and obvious sting, and would instead have known how to entrap a suspect "without putting himself in legal jeopardy."[75]

Besides these considerations, the SA's conclusion that M. masked his own desires through homophobic posturing rang true, given the stormtroopers' history of using homophobic violence to distract from their own sexuality—a form of psychological compensation that specialists in the field were already beginning to refer to as "reaction formation." But one need not know M.'s orientation, nor that of any other individual Nazi homophobe, to recognize that, after June 1934, the movement as a whole practiced a large-scale political equivalent of reaction formation. The SA resolved to prevent any association between itself and homosexuality in the public mind. It did so first by hunting down its own homosexual members, no matter how valuable their service had been. All the factors that had sheltered homosexual stormtroopers— Röhm's personal example, Hitler's purposeful ignorance, the traditional lauding of homoerotic ties between fighting comrades, and even homophobic self-positioning—had now vanished. Instead, Lutze followed Hitler's orders to cleanse the SA of any association with homosexuality, whether proven or alleged. His resolve did not fade over time. One young stormtrooper wrote him in 1937, hoping in vain that he would be welcomed back into the SA after his release from jail on charges of homosexuality. Lutze replied:

> To your complaint I have little to remark. You yourself admit that you have earned your punishment. The foundational principles of the SA that your misconduct violates are widely known. The Führer himself spoke of a pestilence that must be rooted out with all necessary means and brutal measures, so that a healthy German youth can be raised. Every SA man knows this, and every SA man must be guided by it. He who makes himself guilty of unnatural fornication must expect only the most ignominious expulsion from the SA.[76]

It may seem strange that after the June 1934 massacre even a young and naïve stormtrooper could believe that homosexuals had any place in the Nazi movement. Yet heterosexual men now discovered that the Party and the SA intended to monitor their sexual lives and their family relationships as well.

Stormtroopers accused of molesting girls fell first under the Party's new scrutiny. The SA had already vigorously pursued such allegations before the purge, but afterward its standards of evidence relaxed even further.[77] It seems that the Hamburg SA at this time came to consider heterosexual men from rural areas to be a particular threat to children, similar to the threat allegedly posed by urban homosexuals.[78] But the most important implications for the Party's monitoring of stormtrooper heterosexuality came when a stormtrooper's neighbors and relatives realized that the Party's new scrutiny gave them a powerful means to influence, threaten, or take revenge against stormtroopers who had wronged them.

Women proved particularly proficient with this new weapon. One stormtrooper found himself reported to the SA for supposedly hitting a local woman in the face. The stormtrooper and the woman had waged long-running arguments over their sons' interactions and other neighborhood matters, which the stormtrooper had been accustomed to resolving by grabbing her arm and "giving her a talking to."[79] She now accused him of battery—not to the police but to the SA directly. A stormtrooper wife who was living apart from her husband reported him to the SA for his failure to pay alimony and child support.[80] Other denouncers reported stormtroopers for beating their wives, living in sin with unmarried girls or with girls whose fathers did not approve, conducting affairs with married women, and interfering in their comrades' marriages.[81] Many of these cases involved acts that were not illegal, but which violated the sense of honor the SA claimed to promote.

In some cases, SA leaders displayed far more sympathy for the wives than for the stormtroopers. One member of the SA equestrian group had so offended his unit by the way he treated his wife that the SA took the unusual step of appealing to the political wing. The Party determined, despite a lack of cooperation from the victim, that the offender had "lived a life unbecoming an SA man." He had left his wife "to pursue his own pleasures" and he beat her when she asked for money. When her despair reached such a level that she tried to gas herself, the stormtrooper allegedly told a comrade, "Hopefully the cow is dead."[82] In the end, the Party's and the SA's efforts to expel this man came to naught because of his wife's refusal to cooperate and an array of positive testimonials from other comrades. Even so, the organizations' willingness to investigate in such an intense manner showed the lengths to which they would now go to ensure that members' marriages and personal relationships matched the exacting standards they claimed to uphold. Even Jewish women could accuse, and if the charge was severe enough—child molestation, for instance—the SA felt forced to investigate.[83] Jewish women could thus settle scores against stormtroopers who had attacked their male relatives. Accusations from women in the wake of the purge thus proved a significant source of annoyance to stormtroopers, who had grown used to having the Party's backing in their private disputes. Now, they faced its scrutiny.

Even within the SA, a sense grew that the insular, cliquish, and self-protective lifestyle the organization had long fostered had now become a danger. SA leaders admitted, at least to one another, that their embrace of "young and immature people" had brought on the SA's downfall.[84] The SA had taken young men under its wing with little oversight or guidance, and it had promised them material reward, emotional security, and political protection with few conditions other than loyalty to their comrades. This combination of reward without oversight, authority without responsibility, and power without control ill served the movement and the SA alike. The SA had given youths of limited experience "sudden and almost uncontrolled access" to economic and social power, a rash act that bred corruption, crime, and debauchery, and in the end revealed the group's moral posturing as a lie. After July 1934, even other Nazi agencies had come to see the SA as a corrupt and suspect institution. One judge, in his sentencing of a stormtrooper who had embezzled money in order to "succumb to the alleged pleasures of the big city," proclaimed that the SA leadership "bears official co-responsibility" for the misled youth's "mistakes."[85] In this case and many others, the judge said, "the building of a life has been put in danger" by the SA's failures.

Under these circumstances, the SA would and could no longer provide cover for its members. As Lutze wrote concerning the case of an old fighter who had "brought open resentment against the SA" because of his poor conduct:

> It is not the duty of SA offices to make good the excesses of single insubordinate SA men, nor to ask government agencies for lenience on their behalf. This must finally stop. The Führer made this unmistakably clear in his 12 points. The SA must now act accordingly.[86]

The so-called moral cleansing of the SA took several years to accomplish, but it became clear very quickly that the lifestyle the group had carefully cultivated during the Kampfzeit, and that had drawn millions into the Nazi movement, had ended for good. In the first year after the purge, the SA lost over a million men.[87] More were expelled in the following years, and many others abandoned the now-purposeless organization. By 1937, only about 1.2 million remained, from a high of almost three million.[88] The purge of June 1934 thus ended the SA's power and influence in the Nazi state, and it destroyed for good many of the essential communal elements of the original national socialist movement.

On the Night of the Long Knives and its yearlong aftermath, many of the oldest and most influential stormtroopers had been driven from the organization they had created. Some had lost their lives. In so doing, they unwillingly performed one last act of martyrdom for the Nazi movement.

Their violent exclusion from the *Volksgemeinschaft* had ended an immediate threat (if not the one that Hitler claimed), and it provided a lasting template for future extralegal actions against institutions powerful enough to resist the Nazi state. The stormtroopers' final blood sacrifice—this time of their own prominence in the state they had created—was the most painful one of all. The Party, however, had decided that it was a necessary one, as the stormtroopers had proven how difficult it would be to integrate them into an ordered and regulated post-revolutionary state. The SA's time had passed, and stormtroopers now had to move on with their lives.

NOTES

1   Peter Longerich, *Geschichte der SA* (Munich: Verlag C. H. Beck, 2003), 200.

2   Longerich, *Geschichte der SA*, 183–188.

3   Michael B. Barrett, "The Army and SA Partnership, 1933–1934," *Proceedings of the South Carolina Historical Association* (1984): 67.

4   See Ian Kershaw's account of the purge in *Hitler: Hubris* (New York: W. W. Norton & Company, 1999), 499–524, which places a great deal of weight on the army-SA rivalry.

5   Timothy Scott Brown, "The SA in the Radical Imagination of the Weimar Republic," *Central European History* 49, no. 2 (2013): 261. Brown's scholarship generally sees strong commonality between the SA and its left-wing enemy, as presented in *Weimar Radicals: Nazis and Communists Between Authenticity and Performance* (New York: Berghahn Books, 2009).

6   Brown, "The SA in the Radical Imagination," 261.

7   Otto Wagener, *Memoirs of a Confidant* (New Haven, CT: Yale University Press, 1985), 19–21.

8   For a gripping but fictionalized account of the deliberations among this circle in the weeks leading up to the purge, see Max Gallo, *The Night of the Long Knives* (New York: Harper & Row, 1972), 11–107.

9   See, for example, William Shirer, *Rise and Fall of the Third Reich* (New York: Simon & Schuster, 1990/1960), 213–226. More recent works, such as Kershaw's *Hitler: Hubris*, have followed this line as well, as have several specific studies of the purge itself. See Karl Martin Grass, "Edgar Jung. Papenkreis und Röhmkrise 1933/34," doctoral dissertation, Rupprecht-Karl Universität zu Heidelberg, 1966; Heinz Höhne, *Mordsache Röhm. Hitlers Durchbruch zur Alleinherrschaft 1933–1934* (Hamburg: Rowohlt Verlag, 1984).

10 Ian Kershaw, *The Nazi Dictatorship: Problems and Perspectives of Interpretation*, 4th ed. (London: Hodder Arnold, 2000), 82.

11 Kershaw, *Hitler: Hubris*, 514; Paul R. Maracin, *The Night of the Long Knives: Forty-Eight Hours That Changed the History of the World* (Guilford, CT: Globe Pequot, 2007), 120.

12 Hans-Günther Seraphim, ed., *Das politische Tagebuch Alfred Rosenberg* (Göttingen and Berlin: Musterschmidt, 1956), 33–34. See also interview with Erich Kempka (Library of Congress Hitler Collection, C-89, 9376-88A-B, 1971).

13 Otto Gritschneder, "*Der Führer hat sie zum Tode verurteilt . . .*": Hitlers "Röhm-Putsch"—Morde vor Gericht (Munich: Beck 1993), 60–62.

14 Martin Allen, *Himmler's Secret War* (London: Robson Books, 2005), 39.

15 Laura Ward and Robert Allen, *Famous Last Words* (London: Robson Books, 2004), 68.

16 Allen, *Himmler's Secret War*, 39.

17 Richard Evans, *The Third Reich in Power: 1933–1939* (New York: Penguin Press, 2005), 39, and Kershaw, *Hitler: Hubris*, 517.

18 Gallo, *The Night of the Long Knives*, 275, and Kershaw, *Hitler: Hubris*, 517.

19 Robert Lewis Koehl, *Black Corps: Structure and Power Struggles of the Nazi SS* (Madison: University of Wisconsin Press, 1983), 99–100.

20 NARA 3341 086 Georg C. This man claims to have shot "the 11" Hamburg victims of the purge. SA leaders investigating this claim determined him to be a "habitual criminal" and a liar. Regardless of his claim to responsibility, the statement demonstrates that it was common knowledge at the time that the number of victims in Hamburg had totaled 11.

21 Carl Vincent Krogmann, *Es ging um Deutschlands Zukunft, 1932–1939* (Leoni am Starnberger See: Druffel-Verlag, 1977), 147–152.

22 NARA 3341 104b and 108b.

23 NARA 3341 104b.

24 Gallo, *The Night of the Long Knives*, 264. See also Eleanor Hancock, *Ernst Röhm: Hitler's SA Chief of Staff* (Basingstoke, England: Palgrave Macmillan, 2008), 162–163.

25 Gallo, *The Night of the Long Knives*, 265.

26 "Göring spricht über die Säuberung," *Hamburger Tageblatt*, July 1, 1934.

27 "Befehl des Obersten SA-Führers," *Hamburger Tageblatt*, July 1, 1934.

28 Kershaw, *Hitler: Hubris*, 519.

29 "Der Führer der Nation gibt seinem Volke Rechenschaft," *Hamburger Tageblatt*, July 13, 1934.

30 "Der Führer der Nation," *Hamburger Tageblatt*.

31 "Der Führer der Nation," *Hamburger Tageblatt*.

32 "Der Führer der Nation," *Hamburger Tageblatt*; Kershaw, *Hitler: Hubris*, 519.

33 Karl Loewenstein, "Law in the Third Reich," *Yale Law Journal* 45, no. 5 (1936): 791.

34 Geoffrey Giles, "Legislating Homophobia in the Third Reich: The Radicalization of Prosecution against Homosexuality by the Legal Profession," *German History* 23, no. 3 (2005): 340.

35 "Was wird aus der SA?" *Hamburger Tageblatt*, July 7, 1934; "Der Führer der Nation," *Hamburger Tageblatt*.

36 Quoted in Gallo, *The Night of the Long Knives*, 274.

37 StAHH, 614-2/5 *Nationalsozialistische Arbeiterpartei (NSDAP) und ihre Gliederung B201*, Truppführer D to Brigade 12, September 1934.

38 Quoted in Detlev Peukert, *Inside Nazi Germany: Conformity, Opposition, and Racism in Everyday Life* (New Haven, CT: Yale University Press, 1987), 71. Ian Kershaw affirms this conclusion in his *The "Hitler Myth": Image and Reality in the Third Reich* (Oxford, England: Oxford University Press, 1987), 87.

39 Quoted in Kershaw, *Hitler: Hubris*, 520.

40 StAHH, 614-2/5 *Nationalsozialistische Arbeiterpartei (NSDAP) und ihre Gliederung B201*, Brigade 12 to Staatspolizei Hamburg, February 22, 1934.

41 Gallo, *The Night of the Long Knives*, 276.

42 Gallo, *The Night of the Long Knives*, 266.

43 Krogmann, *Es ging um Deutschlands Zukunft*, 149. Even Krogmann had to admit that Röhm's eloquent Spanish had impressed the Latin American guests. In general, however, his memoir reliably vilifies Nazi enemies in order to advance the apologist and exculpatory agenda typical of the right-wing Drüffel-Verlag, which printed the memoirs of unrepentant ex-Nazis.

44 Krogmann, *Es ging um Deutschlands Zukunft*, 150–152.

45 StAHH, 614-2/5 Nationalsozialistische Arbeiterpartei (NSDAP) und ihre Gliederung B241-1 vol. 4, Edgar H.

46 See Willi Münzenberg, *Weissbuch über die Erschiessungen des 30 Juni* (Paris: Editions de Carrefour, 1934), which some credit to Otto Strasser. See also Gert Hekma, Harry Oosterhuis, and James Steakley, *Gay Men and the Sexual History of the Political Left* (New York: Haworth Press, 1995), 234.

47 Lothar Machtan, *Hitlers Geheimnis. Das Doppelleben eines Diktaturs* (Frankfurt: Fischer, 2001), as well as the outright homophobic charges in Scott Lively and Kevin Abrams, *The Pink Swastika: Homosexuality in the Nazi Party* (Keizer, OR: Founders Publishing, 1995).

48 On the term *homosexuallen Staatsfeind*, see Susanne zur Neiden, "Aufstieg und Fall des virilen Männerhelden. Der Skandal um Ernst Röhm und seine Ermordung," in Susanne zur Neiden, ed., *Homosexualität und Staatsräson* (Frankfurt am Main: Campus Verlag, 2005), 147–192.

49 Geoffrey Giles shows in detail Himmler's practical solutions to this political problem. The SS leader loathed male homosexuality and wanted to exterminate it, yet was often confused when discovering homosexuals among those he considered his best men. "The Denial of Homosexuality: Same-Sex Incidents in Himmler's SS and Police," *Journal of the History of Sexuality* 11, nos. 1/2 (2002): 256–290.

50 See Susanne zur Neiden's plea in this vein, which claims that pure political calculation is "insufficient" as an explanation for homophobic persecution. Instead, scholars must examine "a closely woven discursive net" that links homosexuality to masculinity, politics, and reasons of state. "Homophobia und Staatsräson," in zur Neiden, *Homosexualität und Staatsräson*, 45.

51 "Was wird aus der SA," *Hamburger Tageblatt*, July 7, 1934.

52 "Was wird aus der SA," *Hamburger Tageblatt*.

53 "Was wird aus der SA," *Hamburger Tageblatt*.

54 Stefan Micheler, "Homophobic Propaganda and the Persecution of Same-Sex Desiring Men," in Dagmar Herzog, ed., *Sexuality and German Fascism* (New York: Berghahn Books, 2002), 109.

55 Quoted in Harry Oosterhuis and Hubert Kennedy, eds., *Homosexuality and Male Bonding in Pre-Nazi Germany* (New York: Haworth Press, 1991), 236.

56 StAHH, 614-2/5 Nationalsozialistische Arbeiterpartei (NSDAP) und ihre Gliederung B64 (physical fitness and health issues) and B72 (citizenship status).

57 Bruce Campbell, "The SA After the Röhm Purge," *Journal of Contemporary History* 28, no. 4 (1993): 660.

58 StAHH, 614-2/5 Nationalsozialistische Arbeiterpartei (NSDAP) und ihre Gliederung B103, letter of Sturmbannführer P. to Brigade R11, July 4, 1934.

59 StAHH, 614-2/5 *Nationalsozialistische Arbeiterpartei (NSDAP) und ihre Gliederung* B103, letter of Sturmbannführer P to Brigade R11, July 4, 1934.

60 StAHH, 614-2/5 *Nationalsozialistische Arbeiterpartei (NSDAP) und ihre Gliederung* B103, letter of SA-Mann Friedhelm S. to SA Gruppe Hansa, July 26, 1934.

61 Geoffrey Giles, "Straight Talk for Nazi Youths: The Attempt to Transmit Heterosexual Norms," in *Education and Cultural Transmission: Historical Studies of Continuity and Change in Families, Schooling, and Youth Cultures* (Ghent, Belgium: CSHP, 1996), 308–309.

62 StAHH 241-1 Justizverwaltung I:XXII Cb3 vol. 4: Adolf S.

63 Giles, "Legislating Homophobia," 345.

64 StAHH 361-6 Hochschulwesen—Dozenten und Personalakten IV 248.

65 StAHH 241-1 Justizverwaltung I: XXII Cb3 vol. 2: Friedrich M., as well as NARA A3341 SA Kartei: 104b, 069b, 037.

66 StAHH, 614-2/5 *Nationalsozialistische Arbeiterpartei (NSDAP) und ihre Gliederung* B109, files of May 27, 1933, June 24, 1933, and June 27, 1933.

67 "Chef des Stabes Lutze warnt die Denunzianten, "*Hamburger Fremdenblatt,* July 19, 1934; "Rudolf Hess gegen die Denunzianten," *Hamburger Fremdenblatt,* July 24, 1934.

68 "Gegen Gerüchtemacher und anonyme Denunzianten," *Hamburger Fremdenblatt,* July 31, 1934.

69 Giles, "Legislating Homophobia," 339, and Richard Plant, *The Pink Triangle:The Nazi Persecution of Homosexuals* (New York: Henry Holt & Co., 1986), 108–110.

70 NARA A3341 SA Kartei: B022 Heinrich M.

71 NARA A3341 SA Kartei: B022 Heinrich M.

72 NARA A3341 SA Kartei: B022 Heinrich M.

73 NARA A3341 SA Kartei: B022 Heinrich M.

74 Stefan Micheler, "Homophobic Propaganda," 125.

75 NARA A3341 SA Kartei: B022 Heinrich M.

76 NARA A3341 SA Kartei: 022 Johannes B.

77 StAHH 241-1 Justizverwaltung I: XXII Cb3 vol. 2: docs. 141, 404, and 405.

78 StAHH 241-1 Justizverwaltung I: XXII Cb3 vol. 4: doc. 34.

79 StAHH, 614-2/5 *Nationalsozialistische Arbeiterpartei (NSDAP) und ihre Gliederung* B109, Obertruppführer Heinsen to Nachrichtensturm 12, November 23, 1934.

80 StAHH 241-1 Justizverwaltung I:XXII Cb3: vol. 1: doc. 155.

81 All these and other examples can be found in StAHH, 614-2/5 *Nationalsozialistische Arbeiterpartei (NSDAP) und ihre Gliederung* B166, which includes dozens of cases of family problems reported to the SA.

82 StAHH, 614-2/5 *Nationalsozialistische Arbeiterpartei (NSDAP) und ihre Gliederung* B166, Ortsgrupper Winterhude-Jarrestadt, November 6, 1934.

83 See, for example, NARA A3341 SA Kartei: 051 Arthur B. case of November 1935.

84 NARA A3341 SA Kartei: 078 Fritz B. The phrase comes from court documents, but was underlined in agreement by the SA leader in charge of the file.

85 NARA A3341 SA Kartei: 078 Fritz B.

86 NARA A3341 SA Kartei: 020 Emil B.

87 Campbell, "The SA After the Röhm Purge," 671.

88 Campbell, "The SA After the Röhm Purge," 671.

FROM SODOM
TO GOMORRAH:
HAMBURG IN RUINS

In October 1934, as the aftereffects of the Röhm purge continued to reverberate, the *Hamburger Tageblatt* published a series of semi-fictionalized stories on "the Old Storm Tavern," the SA pub scene of the now-vanished *Kampfzeit*, the time of struggle. These places, the *Tageblatt* told its readers, encapsulated the honor and trust that existed among members of the movement, a quality of emotional connection that was enhanced by the stormtroopers' humble abodes. The writer described the titular tavern as a meager space: "Only a group of close-set walls, raw wooden tables and benches, and for an inventory just a counter with a few wretched bottles and glasses. Yet still these walls enclosed a world full of joy and song."[1] Here the stormtroopers gathered, day after day, listening for the alarm that would summon them to protect their comrades from danger, or waiting for word from the hospital regarding the health of fallen friends.

As the series continued through the month of October, it told of a tavern keeper who had bought his establishment just before the economic crash of late 1929, and thus faced ruin until the local SA's patronage and friendship saved his business. The stormtroopers, still disguising themselves as a sporting club while suffering under one of the state's periodic bans, drew thick curtains over the windows to hide their political meetings, which they conducted quietly under low lights. Great danger and constant threat lay like a shadow over these brave few as they faced down the powerful interests controlling German life, knowing they risked retaliation. Indeed, readers learned, the stormtroopers suffered regular attacks by Communist thugs, as well as legal persecution by police and republican authorities. But through all the violence and victimization, the stories said, the stormtroopers did their best to protect the tavern and its guests. In return, the tavern keeper, now a stormtrooper himself, treated the men like family. He took care always to provide these younger brothers and sons with food and drink to keep them strong, "and when one had nothing at all to offer, then the poor devil was his son, and needed pay nothing."[2]

This warm feeling had suffused the SA during the Kampfzeit, the *Tageblatt* explained. Although the newspaper hoped to soften readers' hearts toward the disruptive and dangerous stormtroopers, stories like these described a vanished world, a stormtrooper community that the Nazi state had now destroyed in order to consolidate power. Instead of minority opposition to supposedly powerful forces, the Nazis now constituted the most powerful and aggressively controlling political movement Germany had ever seen.

Instead of receiving official duties and great influence in this powerful state, the stormtroopers no longer had a meaningful organization. Instead of having a close-knit ersatz family of political comrades, the stormtroopers had drifted toward more traditional families, whose existence now distracted them from politics. As the *Tageblatt's* lionization of a now-mythical SA world revealed, the Nazi movement had moved far beyond the need for its stormtroopers. Stormtroopers could retain a place of cultural importance, but only as relics. In many ways, the dynamic resembled that seen in other states that had defeated opposing warrior bands; in 18th-century Britain, for example, tartans and bagpipes became popular symbols of rugged masculinity after the Scottish opponents of unification had been quashed. In the United States of the 1890s, Wild West shows featuring aged Indian warriors traveled the country, showing off defeated yet noble savages whom spectators could gape at as representatives of a thrilling but safely vanished past.

The Night of the Long Knives and its organizational aftermath reconciled once and for all the tension between the stormtroopers' male-bonding form of political activity and their simultaneous grounding in local family life. Hitler had never named this goal as an intention of the purge, and indeed the event's other instigators clearly declared different reasons. Nevertheless, the massacre had an effect on family: it destroyed the homoerotic family in favor of the heteronormative one. By eliminating the leading representatives of a separate and insular stormtrooper community, Himmler and the other assassins enshrined for good their concept of a Nazi state grounded in a racist conception of the biological family unit. Many stormtroopers had difficulty navigating such a decisive change, and so for the next 11 years the contrast between the stormtroopers' two families continued to resonate in their own lives, if not in the larger politics of the state. Retreating to their private families after 1934, many stormtroopers lost their connection to their political community.

The SA after the Purge

After the Night of the Long Knives, the SA's few remaining organizational responsibilities became largely unofficial and ceremonial. Many of the men continued to gather at taverns for regular bar nights, although these evenings were now almost entirely social and nostalgic, rather than opportunities for immersive and direct political action. Organizationally, the SA conducted pre- and post-military training, which the Party found useful while the German armed forces still languished under the restrictions of the Versailles Treaty. The function fit well with the SA's traditional conception of itself as an alternative option for German men unable to serve in an army to learn the secrets of military masculinity.

On the surface, these training programs in some small ways matched Röhm's plan to involve the SA more closely in German military affairs. In actuality, however, SA paramilitary training was a poor substitute for what its members had hoped to accomplish. The programs were purely voluntary, and over time other state agencies eclipsed them with more formal programs.[3] SA leadership and sporting schools continued to teach first aid and Morse code, and they offered a still-prestigious award for sports achievement. Here, too, the SA seemed to return to its early roots as a men's movement centered on teaching skills of physical self-improvement. However, while the early SA had advocated its sporting activities as preparation for taking political power, its efforts now had no political meaning other than as one element in the Nazis' broader project to militarize the German public and prepare for a new war. SA sport schools and paramilitary training were now, in two senses, pastimes: they helped stormtroopers fill the hours with unthreatening activity, and they let the men feel they could still live in their lost glory days.

Given the SA's loss of place, many stormtroopers concluded that the Party no longer cared about them. Most left the SA, but many "old fighters" who remained in the group out of dedication resented their new lower status. Many grew depressed. Some even killed themselves. The SA's internal reporting and investigations of stormtrooper deaths had traditionally been among the movement's most developed areas of recordkeeping. The Kampfzeit SA felt it politically vital to know the circumstances and context of a stormtrooper's death. Its reporting mechanisms allowed leaders to determine if the SA could be held responsible for a man's death, either in the courts or in the media, or whether the Nazis could blame their enemies for his demise. SA reports typically included a wealth of detail on the cause of death, the man's history in the Party and the SA, his place of employment and work life, and his marital status and family relationships. Even if the reports most often concluded that the deaths originated in "not official" or "purely private" matters (a designation that would allow them to decline making insurance payments), they also indicated the attention, interest, and respect that the organization paid its dead and their families. These reports ended in late 1934. The SA stopped tracking stormtrooper suicides by the end of that year, and by mid-1935 reports of deceased SA men became so terse as to include only the man's name, rank, and Sturm.[4]

A short time later, Hamburg's SA leadership also stopped soliciting morale reports, which it had traditionally ordered its neighborhood leaders to produce for the local and national leadership. The reason for terminating the reports may be that they had become depressing. The last group of them, from the second quarter of 1935, expressed dissatisfaction on a variety of fronts and overflowed with resentment for the SA's lost role and prestige. Although the reporting officers tried to put the best face on the situation, citing recent sporting events as having improved morale, they could not hide their overall complaints. The leader of Sturm 16/15, named in honor of the fallen Heinz Brands, admitted that within his group "the will and spirit of sacrifice seems to have lost all worth and meaning."[5] In this atmosphere, SA leadership decreed an end to what it now called "unnecessary works of writing." In the future, it expected that local leaders would contain sour moods on their own, "working together in camaraderie" to resolve problems without having to trouble the organization.[6] In other words, the SA's top leadership no longer cared to hear their men's complaints, which they in any case now lacked the power to resolve.

What then became of the men who were once stormtroopers? Of the million-plus who left the organization, some sensed that better opportunities lay in other Nazi agencies. Most SA men who went on to develop their political careers did so as members of other Nazi organizations. Many others retreated from public life.

The years after the purge saw a marked increase in stormtrooper marriages. Many stormtroopers had always claimed that their unusually intense political lifestyle, which often kept them from contact with potential mates, had been a temporary measure that they would abandon as soon as they could overthrow the Republic. Now they had reached that point, and the employment and welfare benefits stormtroopers received made marriage more possible than it had been since the brief period immediately after the Great War. This state of affairs proved to them that their authoritarian politics had brought economic recovery.[7] Now, for the first time, the number of SA men getting married rose steadily to ten times the rate during the Kampfzeit. Thus did many of the most committed and the most casual stormtroopers leave the organization after 1934 to pursue their own lives. Even in this organizationally degraded state, stormtroopers still remained the most visible and pervasive symbol of the Nazi regime. Despite setbacks, 1.5 million brown shirts still walked the streets, worked in offices, and remained an ominous presence in public spaces. The uniform's continued ubiquity reminded every neighborhood that the Party's thugs still existed among them, and that the Party could reactivate them any time it chose. Indeed, it did so at several critical junctures.

In the spring and summer of 1935, the Party allowed the SA to carry out a series of supposedly spontaneous antisemitic actions. Partly an attempt to dissipate the continued alienation and disaffection within the SA, the attacks also helped to resolve the regime's internal tensions and to pave the way for its later offensives against German Jews. After allowing the SA to demonstrate its chaotic, physically violent approach to antisemitic oppression, the state then stepped in with more bureaucratic techniques that again won the loyalties of citizens turned off by overt violence. It was the same approach the Nazis had used to win power in the first place: display stormtrooper violence to increase panic about problems of public order that the Party could then claim to resolve through pseudo-legal means.[8] In September, Hitler announced the Nuremberg Laws, which banned intermarriage between Jews and Aryans and introduced a new distinction between "*Reich* citizens" of "Aryan blood" and "nationals" who did not possess full rights. Too many Germans now found this solution both pragmatic and moderate, given the alternative of stormtrooper pogroms. Hitler's speech on the Nuremberg Laws insisted that they made it possible "that the nation itself does not depart from the rule of law."[9] The stormtroopers had proved themselves useful one more time—even if, to an astute observer, the targeted re-activation of the SA revealed that the group had lost a leading role even in the persecution of National Socialism's enemies.

To fit into the new regime, the old stormtrooper mentality had to be adjusted. This meant surrendering many of the stormtroopers' independent sources of ideology and opinion. During the campaign to prepare public sentiment for the Nuremberg Laws, and possibly to prepare the stormtroopers for planned violence even further down the road, the Party and the SA made a conscious effort to replace *Der SA Mann* with Julius Streicher's *Der Stürmer* as the stormtroopers' reading material of choice. The SA leader in charge of the drive, an *Oberführer* Schwäble of the southern town of Ulm, claimed that it would "put a real antisemitic newspaper in the hands of SA leaders and educational officers." The transition would also serve "to deepen the public's antisemitic feelings and to further the struggle against Jews and their servants."[10] Apparently many local SA units lacked such a spirit. Schwäble bemoaned the number of SA leaders "who do not value *Der Stürmer* and have not pursued its distribution energetically."[11] While an average stormtrooper might exist within the movement without any special antisemitic fervor, Schwäble claimed, SA leaders should seek to encourage such sentiments at every turn. Throughout 1935, southern stormtrooper leaders working for the goals of the national Party leadership steadily undermined *Der SA Mann* by encouraging the ordinary stormtrooper to read *Der Stürmer* instead. In 1936, the Party ceased publishing *Der SA Mann* altogether, replacing it with *Der SA Führer*, a much smaller newsletter for leaders only.

Thus did the SA's own newspaper, written by and for the average stormtrooper, cease publication in favor of an elite newsletter and an infamous, primitive, and bloodthirsty tabloid that targeted the lowest common denominator with hateful messages useful to the high leadership's coordinated plan. This period coincided with the Party's major ideological push to train SA men in active antisemitism according to the Party's new racial and pseudoscientific spin on the old prejudice. In January and February, SA officers lectured their men on such topics as "the Jewish character," "culture and race," and "racial lawmaking."[12] While stormtrooper units had certainly hosted antisemitic lectures during the Kampfzeit, these talks now took on the overtly pseudoscientific tone favored by the SS. Thus the SA had not only lost its power, it had lost its voice. It could play no further organizational role in the Nazi state.

Stormtroopers could instead only await a call to action. The most spectacular of these, along the model of 1935, came in 1938 when the Party organized stormtroopers to attack Jewish property during the one-night pogrom of *Kristallnacht*, on November 9–10, during which Nazis across Germany attacked Jewish shops, homes, and temples.[13] Once again the SA proved itself a key agent of the Nazi state by actively planning and perpetrating coordinated attacks on Jewish property and individuals. Hamburg's stormtroopers performed this role in typical fashion, and several dozen of them faced prosecution after the war for their role in the atrocities committed that night.[14] Other than these spectacular but relatively few outbursts of violence, stormtroopers in the late 1930s mainly served only to help the

Party further its public relations goals, particularly by presenting the illusion of mass support for authoritarian policies. The Nazis and other totalitarian regimes favored pro forma elections and plebiscites as a way to place a veneer of legality and public approval on radical changes to the rule of law. At these times, the stormtroopers publicly staged a degraded democratic charade, where their concrete examples of approved behavior would model proper participation and strengthen the people's resolve. As SA leadership ordered in February 1936:

> The SA man must be able to give a positive answer to all questions of worldview. As a member of the National Socialist movement's core troop, the SA man stands always in the public eye. His outer bearing must be a model—just as in the Kampfzeit, our best advertisement is the personal example of the individual man, whether in public, in office, or in the family.[15]

Goebbels also hoped that the stormtroopers would represent the new Germany well to foreigners attending the Olympic games that year. The SA excused from duty any stormtroopers who had a chance of making the German team, which Goebbels hoped would display to the world that the Nazis had "raised a new race, hard and unyielding," in contrast to the old image of Germans as poets and thinkers.[16] In public spectacles such as the Olympics, memorably filmed by Leni Riefenstahl, the Nazis hoped to depict a clean, disciplined, and energetic youth whose controlled power promised to reclaim for Germany a place in the sun. But a comparison of Riefenstahl's Olympia to her earlier Triumph of the Will reveals how the stormtroopers had lost their former pride of place in such propaganda efforts. Triumph of the Will, filmed at the 1934 Party congress, still used stormtroopers as some of the most prominent visual tropes of Nazi purity. Scenes of the healthy young stormtroopers washing up, shaving, dressing in their uniforms, and helping one another prepare for their moment in the sun literally embodied Nazi claims to promote a healthy community. Although the film conveniently ignored the missing murdered leaders, the stormtrooper rank and file still served this essential function. By the time Riefenstahl made Olympia, however, her eye had moved on to a more detached, mythic gaze on depoliticized athletic bodies. These two films of course had different audiences and purposes, but the contrast still illuminates how the SA steadily lost its place as the regime's preeminent representative.

FIGURE E.1

**A lone stormtrooper looks back as his marching
column moves forward on the eve of war.**

Source: Rolf Lennar, *Kamerad, auch Du! Ernstes und Heiteres um das
SA-Sportabzeichnen* (Munich: Eher Verlag, 1939).

Even so, the brown shirt continued to mark a certain type of Party man. Its implicit threat kept the public in line and provided cover for legal radicalization by reminding citizens that the Nazis now preferred less overtly violent solutions to the problems they claimed to face. The uniform thus carried a retrograde connotation, worn by men who were stuck in the past, resistant to progress and rationality even when they would further the men's goals, and more concerned with living (or reliving) their exciting youth than with mature and responsible participation in present-day governance. Eventually, most stormtroopers traded in their brown shirts altogether, exchanging them for field-gray military uniforms (Figure E.1). Through their participation in the coming war, both as individuals and as a group, stormtroopers briefly regained a sense of purpose and connection to the community. But the war soon rent this connection asunder as well.

At first it appeared that the preparations for and outbreak of war would again grant the SA a meaningful role in the Nazi state. The organization played some key logistical roles for the *Wehrmacht* (German armed forces). It provided equipment and guarded supplies, inspected vehicles and controlled traffic, built facilities, guarded prisoners of war, and at times interrogated captives.[17] Behind the lines of the eastern front, individual stormtroopers, particularly the older ones who would not serve with regular troops, participated in paramilitary and anti-partisan operations, including the infamous death squads who murdered Jewish communities behind the front lines. Most stormtroopers of fighting age leapt at the long-denied chance to play soldier. Both at home and near the front, SA men also retained their role as the local embodiment of Nazi authority. Their ideological trustworthiness and local outlook made them ideal administrators in the captured eastern territories that the Nazis targeted for German colonization.

SA man Walter A. was one who embodied this trend. He was of the SA's first generation, an old fighter and veteran of both world wars, married with two young children.[18] At 41 years old, he had been working for years in his father's firm selling house and kitchen wares, but he now saw his chance to have a shop of his own. In March 1940 he applied for an opportunity in Zichenau, a rural administrative district in occupied Poland. After his SA references confirmed his competence (as well as his taste in interior decorating), he joined thousands of German colonists who hoped to transform the east into a region of small German farmers and shopkeepers. One recent scholar called the project "a drive . . . to create model communities and a model domestic culture as the bedrock of the future German nation."[19] Many stormtroopers had begun their careers in the Third Reich through a type of local imperialism that confiscated Jewish property and transferred it to loyalists, a way of establishing ready-made businesses for stormtroopers and other Nazis who had long struggled to found firms of their own.[20] Stormtroopers who had been too young to benefit or had otherwise missed out on that chance to seize assets now turned their eyes to the east and joined what they hoped would be a German vanguard to reshape the fertile but wild plains into a domesticated, utopian landscape of nuclear family farmers and small shopkeepers. In this way, stormtrooper conceptions of family and masculine roles still motivated their political lives.

This plan may have looked possible in the war's early stages, but by 1942 the realities of its execution began to set in. Stormtroopers had always claimed a connection between their personal lives and the life of the Nazi movement, and they now found themselves literally on the front lines of an overt war against Germany's alleged enemies. The meaning of stormtrooper deaths, however, changed. While the state still issued public pronouncements in the old tone, which lauded violent death as a blood sacrifice to renew the German nation and fulfill a mission of Christlike redemption, the Party decreed that during wartime it would no longer laud individual stormtrooper deaths. The *Oberste SA Führung* (OSAF), the central SA leadership, ordered instead that names of stormtroopers killed in action be held back from the public "until the war's end," which at that point it arrogantly believed would come quickly.[21] As the fortunes of war turned against the Third Reich, the OSAF continued to shield the public from the names of the fallen, lest such knowledge reveal how dramatically the tide had turned against Germany. During the fighting in the east, SA men suffered casualties at a rate normal for German men of their age—in other words, at a rate so high as to kill almost all who fought. The ultimate destiny of the unknown stormtrooper, the figure whom Nazi media had lauded as a local warrior for German renewal, was therefore to die far from home in the frozen eastern wastelands. But while stormtrooper martyrs of the Kampfzeit had become the movement's heroes, the wartime Nazi state took a different approach to death, a change that reflected the regime's general concern over how to attach meaning to an increasingly unmanageable number of soldier and civilian casualties.[22]

Even as the front lines drew ominously close to German territory, the Nazi state never returned to its reliance on the SA as a key organization. However, in the war's last years, the stormtroopers who had not joined the military—that is, men who had been pugnacious during their Weimar youth but now had other priorities or were simply too old to fight—saw themselves as key players in maintaining morale on the home front. Here they hoped to "train the *Volk* in the will to defend" through word-of-mouth propaganda passed among family, friends, and neighbors. SA leaders ordered their few remaining men to "seek every opportunity to present positive thoughts" during conversations with friends and neighbors, suggesting such messages as "The Führer is always right!" and "The German people will victoriously end this struggle!" A stormtrooper wife also had to be "as good a propagandist as the man himself."[23] Together the pair would ensure that Hamburg's citizens remained personally invested in the war and confident of a victorious conclusion.

But the war soon came to Hamburg in a way that none could ignore. On the night of July 24, 1943, air-raid sirens sounded across the city, an alarming but not unprecedented event. This time, however, the bombing turned out to be more intense and destructive than any Hamburg had yet endured. Almost eight hundred aircraft, guided by clear weather and protected by the Allies' new radar-deceiving chaff launchers, attacked Altona, Eimsbüttel, Hoheluft, and other areas in the central and northwestern districts that had been among the SA's and the Party's earliest loyal neighborhoods. The devastation killed around 1,500 people and also destroyed the Nikolaikirche, the central police station, and the famous Hagenbeck Zoo.

As bad as the blow was, it proved only the first in the series of attacks ominously named Operation Gomorrah. Each day and night for the next week, Allied bombers returned. Sometimes smaller bomber flights simply feinted an attack, harassing and retreating to keep the public awake at night and in a state of terror during the day. On the night of July 27, the 800-strong fleet returned. Thirty minutes of concentrated bombing incinerated the southeastern harbor districts of Hamm, Hammerbrook, and Rothenburgsort. British pilots reported seeing the fire's glow from 200 miles away. Smoke, pulled upwards by the combined heat of the many fires, mushroomed over the city to a height of 23,000 feet. The heated column of rising air drew in more oxygen at ground level, increasing wind speeds and creating a new and terrible phenomenon: the firestorm.[24] While firestorms had taken place in several major cities during the great fires of the 19th century, including in Chicago (1871) and in Hamburg itself (1842), the 1943 firestorm was the first to be recognized and studied as a discrete meteorological phenomenon. Winds of up to 150 mph drove flames across roofs and over canals. Temperatures reached 1,500 degrees Fahrenheit. Tens of thousands of people suffocated in underground shelters as the firestorm's flue-like effect sucked all oxygen into the inferno. Those not in shelters ran over burning asphalt or jumped into canals for refuge, where many drowned or were crushed by burning buildings that collapsed across streets and canals alike. On that night alone, 40,000 people died and more than a million more fled the city.[25] Allied bombers returned each day and night until August 3, and another 69 times before the war's end.

The firestorm burned the stormtroopers' homes, killed their family members, and destroyed their city. It also marked for some their final alienation from the communities they claimed always to serve. While many embraced their role as defenders of the public and therefore leapt into action as volunteer firemen and other local air-defense forces, others prioritized their long-professed identity as domestic guardians. During the attacks, these men tried to save their wives and children, even at the expense of their public duties.

Sturmführer Werner B., although older than many stormtroopers, had been one of the late joiners who came to the movement in the wake of its takeover of the state. In 1934, as the SA died in the purge, he married, had a child, and moved to the northeastern suburb of Volksdorf. For a time he continued to serve as *Standarte* 15's medic and dentist, but he seems to have steadily drifted away from his comrades once the war began. The July firebombing inflicted its damage even as far as Volksdorf, where his house caught fire and the local authorities began mobilizing to help those closer to the city center. The local Senate representative chose Werner B., a stormtrooper medic, to receive a supply of gasoline and drive into town to rescue as many refugees as possible. At first he did so. During the night, however, his wife began having heart problems, at which point he dropped his other duties and went to rescue her. Having rescued her from danger, he later claimed, he could not return to the city because of a general blockade against inbound traffic, which authorities feared would hamper evacuation. Stormtrooper medic Werner B. therefore chose to take his wife to Bad Salzuflen, a spa town in the Rhineland where the two had planned a vacation to treat his rheumatism, which he now claimed had become so acute as to prevent his further participation in SA firefighting and rescue efforts.

The OSAF flew into a bureaucratic rage at Werner B.'s choices. It accused him of abandoning his responsibilities as a stormtrooper and as a representative of the Nazi community:

> And so during the catastrophe he apparently laid aside all thought of enlisting his own person to assist the SA in its difficult operations. Even if it is not incomprehensible that he would want to bring his sick wife out of Hamburg, it must count as the most severe accusation against him that he did not return to Hamburg and again apply himself. Even without orders, he must admit that as a dentist his skills would be useful in rendering medical assistance. He has therefore shown that he lacks every proper SA spirit, and every spirit of self-sacrifice, that one expects SA leaders to display for the benefit of the *Volksgemeinshaft*.[26]

As a defense, Werner B. claimed that for some time "I had no real function as an SA medic, and since the outbreak of the war have lost touch with the SA. I was therefore completely unaware that I should [during the firebombing] offer my services to the SA or contact SA Standarte 15."[27] Predictably, SA leaders found this statement less than exculpatory; indeed, it only inflamed their anger all the more. The SA expelled Werner B. in November, concluding that he had damaged the entire group by his actions. "As an SA leader," the OSAF concluded, "he is the kind of man at which the populace points a finger and says that the SA cannot be relied upon."[28] Indeed, stormtroopers who prioritized their family's needs over the needs of the community during these times of crisis came under particular scrutiny from the Party, perhaps because the dilemmas they faced laid bare that the Party's long claim to unite families under a monolithic Volk identity had always been a lie. To the extent that German families now had a common destiny, it lay only in the common ruin caused by the Nazis' war.

As a growing number of Hamburg's citizens came to see the war as lost, stormtroopers who still remained in the city looked increasingly alien. Some stood in the streets trying to rally the remaining populace to ridiculously useless defensive measures. One witness described "an angry old Nazi, who to the last ran around in his SA uniform, and right at the end he hauled people out of their apartments to build tank barriers in the streets. They had to rip up the cobblestones and pile them up. You could laugh yourself to death."[29] Other stormtroopers slowly realized that the war was lost, and that its pursuit had estranged the very families whose protection had supposedly justified the conflict. One girl later recalled her best friend's brother, a "steadfast SA man" who nonetheless was "no *Dummkopf*," and therefore realized "that what they had created was completely backwards."[30] Rather than a system in which "the little guy" could secure his economic prosperity and familial stability, the SA had created a monstrous leviathan that made war in order to enrich the powerful and persecute the powerless. Most stormtroopers did not realize this truth until the end, since they had long entrenched themselves within a closed intellectual and social circle of fellow true believers. By the end, however, even this closed community's loyalty cracked. The girl who recalled her "firm SA man" noted that by the wartime his relatives and friends had come to fear and isolate him:

> He had no contact with anyone else. Anyone who was aware of how involved he was as an SA man was somehow wary of getting too close to him. Anyone with different opinions. Because everyone still felt tangible fear. To knowingly put oneself in danger [by speaking honestly to him] would have been dumb, and nobody did it.[31]

By the end of the war, stormtroopers realized that even their closest associates distrusted and feared them. Perhaps many also realized that this situation had in fact been true for some time.

Some of the oldest stormtroopers, generally those too old for combat, survived long enough to see Hamburg surrender to the British without mounting a defense. British forces then imprisoned them in some of the very camps they had run. Ellerhusen, who had overseen the Fuhlsbüttel concentration camp with characteristic apathy, became a prisoner there until his eventual conviction for crimes against humanity. Abandoned by his network of male associates, who were all now either dead or disgraced, he had to mobilize his wife to beg on his behalf. She wrote to the new mayor and, in English, to the British that her ill health and lack of ability to support a family argued for her husband's release. Her pleas fell on deaf ears.[32]

"SA pastor" Franz Tügel suffered a series of personal disasters that mirrored his city's fate. In the early phases of the fight against Russia he had retained a great commitment to the "final battle" that would bring "final victory."[33] He still called Hitler "a man sent to us by God" and "a tool of divine providence," as he wrote in his birthday wishes to Hitler in 1941.[34] But as Germany's war fortunes turned, Tügel retreated ever more into doubt and reassessment. National Socialism had at first seemed the virtuous political partner he had hoped his church would find, and though he had held true to the Führer through an array of setbacks and policy conflicts, the firestorm had now shown Tügel on which side "history's judgment" lay. He therefore accepted the end of the war and the defeat of National Socialism as the closing episode of a terrible mistake.[35] While his expressed rejection came only after the Nazis had lost, it still contained a grain of honesty. Whatever his politics may have been, he now clearly regretted the terrible price they carried for his beloved Hamburg. As the war ended, Tügel's personal health mirrored that of his city: broken, crumbling, and gazing into the abyss. Although Hamburg recovered, Tügel did not. The lung disease that he had long fought continued to eat at him for a final year, during which he resigned his office, fought with other pastors, and exchanged bitter letters with his remaining contacts. He died on December 15, 1946.

Alfred Conn, Tügel's old theological enemy and the SA's influential leader who had been expelled early, passed the war's final years in the Schleswig-Holstein countryside. He had taught school in Hamburg before his dismissal as Hamburg's SA general, after which he drifted to Cuxhaven and several other small "East Frisian" coastal towns.[36] There he embraced his neo-pagan beliefs and presided over solstice festivals, marriages, and funerals. By 1935 he had already become a leader in the neo-pagan German Faith Movement, a position he held well into the 1960s.[37] He thus observed from a position of rural relative safety what he called "the German *Götterdämmerung*"—total destruction akin to the mythic cataclysm in Wagner's "Twilight of the Gods." Ever the keen observer and intellect, he recognized that Germany's political conditions might never again allow a movement based on nationalistic communalism. National Socialism had thus increased only its enemies' power; not only the Communists, who now occupied half of Europe and continued to spread throughout the world, but also liberal international actors like the European Community, the United Nations, and the forces of globalized capitalism. These villains, he believed, would now have a free hand because the Nazis' failure had discredited any resistance to them, making defense of German national interests "impossible in the future."[38]

The SA had been founded to protect the Party's own, and it had always considered itself a showcase for the Party's connection to its people. The SA sought to signal National Socialism's concern for its fighting men and its families, and it sought to enshrine its warriors as national heroes whose names would go down in memory. But as Conn wrote near the close of his bitter memoirs, "Men, because they are limited in time, cannot properly reckon the great and final consequences of an idea."[39] The stormtroopers' grand idea, National Socialism, in the end estranged them from their families, destroyed the city they claimed to protect, and led them largely to their own deaths and to their disgrace in historical memory. It harmed, perhaps irrevocably, the reputation of Germany and its people; rather than the previous vision of "poets and thinkers," scientists, and technicians without peer, the world now sees stereotypes of sadists and murderers. SA men naïvely believed that constant and brutal violence could protect the things they loved most and create the community whose comfort they craved. Their criminal tactics were, however, more destructive to the things they claimed to promote than anything their many enemies had done. From the SA's beginnings in 1922 to its final fate in 1945, the stormtroopers' worst enemies were themselves.

Images of Evil: Homosexual Stormtroopers after 1945

In the decades after 1945, stormtroopers continued to represent a prototypical image of National Socialism, a vision that loomed especially large in eras fascinated by a mix of sex and violence. Given the cultural sensitivities of the early postwar era, the topic of homosexuality was at first only on the margins of respectable historical works, an unfit subject for a scholar. On these margins, however, pop historians of the 1950s and 1960s alluded to dark deeds in order to titillate readers and vilify fascism. Many hinted that the presence of a homosexual faction in the SA leadership had determined the SA's particularly malignant influence on Nazi politics. Stormtrooper homosexuality, writers hinted but did not elaborate, had shaped organizational structure, set political goals, and enhanced an affinity for violence. While it is true that the SA embodied the most violent tendencies of the movement during its rise to power, the connection between homosexuality and violence remained unexplained, except as a reflection of old tropes of sinfulness and depravity. Fortunately, the era's distaste for the subject of homosexuality, which scholars judged as beneath serious study and unfit for much public discussion, prevented any emphasis on homosexual Nazism from taking hold.

Popular culture had no such qualms. Hollywood films focused particularly on fascist sexuality as an antithesis of American democratic values, arguing that family arrangements and sexual life that departed too far from approved heteronormative forms created warped masculinity in young men, who then lashed out in political violence and embraced fascist politics. Homosexual Nazis thus became a popular image of an "ideal nemesis" for democratic societies, part of a larger argument connecting the personal and the political in postwar America.[40]

As the scholarly prohibition on studying sexuality eroded in the 1970s, several published works did formally discuss Nazi sexuality, as well as the treatment of homosexuals under National Socialism. The latter category proved essential in documenting Nazi persecution of homosexuals that previously had been ignored or minimized, and it established the number of gay men who died in concentration camps as somewhere between 10,000 and 15,000. Through this work, gay and lesbian activists also reclaimed the pink triangle as a symbol of triumph over oppression, making fascist homophobia a powerful argument for why democratic societies should reject anti-gay attitudes.[41]

Other popular cultural depictions of fascist sexual history focused less on the victims and more on the perpetrators. Films and pulp books featuring Nazi sexuality often behaved irresponsibly, looking to history for titillation rather than liberation. Given the generally increased comfort in the 1970s with depictions of human sexuality, the figure of the gay Nazi returned with a vengeance, and the public became fixated on scandalous images of Nazi sexuality as never before. In the best-known example, 1974's *Ilsa, She-Wolf of the SS*, a sadistic concentration camp matron essentially raped to death her unfortunate inmates, until finally being tamed and overthrown by the prodigious sexual talents of an American prisoner. This low-budget Canadian film spawned many imitators and created a new sub-genre of "Nazisploitation" films that attracted great attention.

Ilsa had been inspired by the era's lesbian-chic "women in prison" sexploitation works, but it also owed a great debt to Lucino Visconte's *The Damned*. This Italian art-house film had portrayed the decline and fall of a German industrialist family of dark political and sexual urges. The sexploitation themes included cross-dressing, incest, and child molestation—a potent mix of decadent lusts meant to link the decline of Germany with that of ancient Rome, following the old moralist myth that Rome's collapse stemmed from sexual depravity. In *The Damned*, the death of the patriarch on the day of the Nazi takeover triggered a scramble for dynastic succession, which the stormtrooper uncle (an Ernst Röhm archetype) initially won. He soon met his end, however, in a 20-minute Night of the Long Knives sequence that showed the stormtrooper resort party of June 1934 as progressing from shooting to skinny dipping, drinking to drag shows, and implied gay orgy to machine-gun massacre. The extended scene was among the film's most famous aspects, and in the decades since, its images of SS assassins gunning down naked stormtroopers have come to be accepted as a realistic depiction of how the event transpired. We have no evidence that the original Night of the Long Knives proceeded in this way; contemporary accounts claimed only one pair of stormtroopers caught in flagrante behind closed doors, while nobody testified to the extreme level of open public decadence or immediate mass murder in which the film reveled.

However, just as with the 1934 urban legend of Hitler interrupting Ernst Röhm's champagne party in Hamburg's Hotel Atlantik, the lurid version of the massacre gained currency because it mythologized the massacre's underlying political meaning. The cliquish, overly emotional, and appetite-driven homosexuals who had supposedly made up the stormtroopers had grown too confident in their immunity to law and morality, and had thus brought on their own destruction by the Nazi beast they had helped to create. As with the Eulenberg affair in the imperial period, the homosexual militarist came to represent the internal dynamics of self-destructive nationalist politics in far more dramatic and compelling ways than the far larger number of heterosexual comrades ever could. The legend, not the reality, became remembered.

After *The Damned* and *Ilsa*, a veritable subculture of "Nazi chic" became popular, and "Nazisploitation" marked one way in which a culturally revolutionary generation began falling into its own dark side. Smashing norms and overturning tradition, which had begun with such hope in the 1960s, had curdled into a more aggressive and violent strain of resistance to authority. A new wave of anarchist youth rose, many of them inspired by the Sex Pistols, who wore swastikas along with their safety-pin earrings, and who warned against the British queen's "fascist regime." This was Nazism as costume, a shock tactic that the young used against older generations who still remembered what the Nazis were.

The shock value emerged in specifically sexual realms as well, as fetish subcultures donned Nazi outfits for their nighttime romps. Cultural theorist Susan Sontag attempted to explain this phenomenon in her influential 1974 essay, "Fascinating Fascism," in which she described an affinity for "playing with cultural horror." Noting specifically the titillating and exploitative aspects of fascism, Sontag believed that "a general fascination among the young with horror" combined with an eroticized view of Nazism to create "a reserve of sexual energy [that] can now be tapped."[42] In other words, later generations clung to Nazi imagery as a titillating, thrilling, and forbidden fruit that tastes of evil's pleasures, while avoiding actual evil through the subtle power of consent.

Sexualized Nazi costumes usually conveyed no sympathy with fascism. They instead carried a political meaning of vague yet aggressive generational protest, a dynamic that in some ways harkened back to the stormtroopers' original youthful outbursts against their fathers' generation. Neither the punk rockers wearing swastika earrings nor the gay men donning leather versions of Nazi uniforms did so to promote fascist politics. In both cases, however, homosexual stormtroopers again proved a key symbol to members of a new generation seeking to smash old values in both sexual and political realms. Conversely, the gleeful appropriation of fascist symbols to non-fascist ends often caused older observers to harden their assumptions about the connections between homosexuality and fascism, which new research on Nazi homophobic persecution did little to revise.

Although Sontag's essay may at times seem like a relic of the 1970s and early 1980s, when youthful anti-establishment protest saw strong links between sexual and political revolution, casual observers can see that this pattern has persisted. Sontag saw that sexualized symbols of Nazism offered a "reserve of sexual energy" that the young sought to employ and the media sought to manipulate. The endurance of this energy even today also comes from the incessant sex scandals that seem to surround politicians of the extreme right.

Alongside Ernst Röhm and his fellow original homosexual Nazis, a long line of neo-Nazi leaders over the decades have repeatedly been "outed" as gay. Frank Collin, the leader of the National Socialist Party of America whose proposed march in Skokie, Illinois, became a national issue, was not only gay but also a pedophile. Fellow Nazis turned him over to the police during an internal power struggle, and he was eventually sent to prison. It is probably his case that inspired one of the "Illinois Nazi" antagonists in *The Blues Brothers* to suddenly turn to a comrade and admit, just before their demise, "I've always loved you."

Other important European neo-Nazi leaders of the early 1980s—including the German Michael Kühnen and Englishman Nicky Crane—came out as gay during their political careers. Kühnen, who came out while in prison, explicitly modeled himself on Ernst Röhm and worked to justify a place for gays in Nazi movements. Crane—a literal poster boy for fascism due to his appearance on the cover for an album called *Strength through Oi!*— had long lived a double life in London gay clubs. He admitted as much in 1992. Two years later, Bela Ewald Althans, a follower of Kühnen and a neo-Nazi youth leader with international reach, came out while on trial for distributing a Holocaust denial video. He seems to have thought thereby to prove that he had renounced neo-Nazism, although the jury did not find this tactic persuasive. Overall, these men represented only a small minority of neo-Nazi activists, and their political and personal downfalls were only blips on the larger cultural radar screen. However, the revelations did lend continued energy to the stereotype that something innately connected gay men and fascism, an association strongest in the most muscular and violent strains adhering to the stormtroopers' all-male street gang style.

Outings of gay neo-Nazis combined with the culture wars of the early 1990s to create a lasting smear that in its most extreme form tried to rebrand the brown shirt as a pink swastika. The 1995 book of this name by a pair of anti-gay political activists claimed openly that the Nazis' occult homosexual nature had caused the regime's crimes.[43] Despite numerous and persuasive criticisms of their misuse of the historical method, the authors have stuck to their guns. One of them, Scott Lively, has traveled the world spreading warnings of supposed gay fascism. His efforts have gained wide popularity on the American right, and he has been particularly active in Russia and Uganda, where his speeches have encouraged local efforts to enact harsh anti-gay laws.[44]

In 2008, Lively spoke at a Ugandan seminar that compared gay activists to the Nazis and to the perpetrators of the Rwandan genocide. Afterwards, organizers circulated petitions that prompted the government to propose a law imposing the death penalty for same-sex acts. The proposal was later mitigated to provide for life imprisonment rather than execution, and later withdrawn altogether. It threatens, however, to return.[45] Ugandan gays thus still exist under sustained assault from a toxic mix of anti-Western sentiment (which judges homosexuality to be a form of European decadence) and American evangelical homophobia. Lively denied that he supported the punishments the law proposed, claiming instead that he recommends conversion therapy for gays and lesbians. But Ugandan gay-rights activists have described his role in spreading visions of gay fascism as having such a pernicious effect that they have sued him in a U.S. federal court, accusing him of inciting violence against gays.[46] The case remains open as of this writing. Meanwhile, in Russia, Lively has also served as a Typhoid Mary of gay fascist conspiracy theories. When Russia passed sweeping homophobic legislation in 2013, he called it "one of the proudest achievements of my career," grandiosely taking credit for helping inspire persecution with his multicity speaking tour.[47] Many Russian politicians have echoed Lively's mixture of Christianist and antifascist homophobia, claiming that their persecutory efforts somehow serve the cause of democracy and morality. When the separatist crisis in Ukraine burst into open violence in 2014, the Russianbacked separatists gladly connected traditional Soviet antifascist posturing with Russia's more recent homophobic campaigns.[48] Lively even claimed that "the Obama state department and the homosexualist leaders of the EU" had caused the crisis by trying to impose homosexual fascism on the Ukrainian people.[49] An alliance with Russia, he claimed, would defeat both sides of this sinister political conspiracy.

While gay-rights activists and neo-fascist nationalist activists did coexist within the vast and multifaceted spectrum of the Ukrainian anti-Russian movement—along with Muslims, Jews, neoliberals, and all manner of other anti-Russian Ukrainians—in reality their collaboration represented a movement with many strange bedfellows rather than a conspiracy of homosexual fascism. Nevertheless, the popularity of the Russophiles' gay-fascist propaganda adhered to long-standing stereotypes so effectively that reporters documenting attitudes in separatist areas regularly found locals eager to proclaim their homophobia as justification for rebellion.[50] According to some sources, accusations of supposed Ukrainian "gay fascism" have come directly from Russian president Vladimir Putin himself.[51]

The image of the gay Nazi therefore has very real consequences for modern politics, in America and abroad, and it persists as a political and cultural stereotype despite the relatively few men who embody it. The myth's persistence comes in part because of the regularity with which these atypical specimens appear. It seems that in every generation, some percentage of gay men growing up within a dominant social group experience a push toward political extremism, due to the conflict between their social allegiance and their sexual identity. These men may begin as conservatives of a common and easily recognizable type: comfortable with conformity, hierarchy, and authority; resistant to changing a system that has benefited their group; suspicious of outsiders seeking such change; and comfortable with the idea that a group must defend itself against those who would do it harm. However, even more so than heterosexual men of this socio-political outlook, gay men loyal to conservative communities exist in an inherently threatened state. Revelation of their sexuality would mark them as outsiders, causing the family, social, or political system that they otherwise feel in harmony with to cast them out. Rather than allowing their sexual differences to lead them to a different understanding of society, as many gay men and lesbians do, they instead seek to reaffirm their place in the community by embracing its most authoritarian interpretation. Comfort with authority becomes worship of power. Resistance to change becomes violence against reform. Suspicion of outsiders becomes demonization of anyone not in full conformity with the dictates of authority, and comfort with defense becomes an eagerness to use violence against rivals. Men experiencing this psychological dynamic seek to prove their worth to a system by posing as its strongest and most aggressive defenders, eagerly using violence against designated enemies as a way of confirming who does and does not belong. They then gravitate to extremist political parties as a way of expressing publicly their inner social conflict.

This does not mean that fascism is homosexual, or that homosexuality is fascist. The vast majority of homosexuals have been antifascist, while the vast majority of fascists have been heterosexuals. Additionally, the majority of people experiencing the dynamic just described are also heterosexuals. In fact, the pattern holds true for many other types of identities, and can be particularly prevalent among men threatened with loss of economic status. But whether the origins of their political inclinations are economic, ethnic, or sexual, their attempt to ensure a place in their community by violently oppressing its supposed enemies rarely ends well for them, or for the systems they serve. Gay men, and today some gay women, who participate in these styles of authoritarian politics do court a special danger, since these systems tend to turn on them first. But as the stormtroopers discovered, violent authoritarian political systems invariably spawn an array of hazards, to their enemies and to their own people, against which heterosexuality offers no defense.

Those who consider claims of gay fascism should therefore consider the historical record, and they should avoid the temptation to link homosexuality and fascism too closely as exclusive partners in political crime. This book has considered the story of homosexuality within the Hamburg SA not as the sinister, scheming cult that Hitler and Lively would have us believe to be responsible for fascism's excesses. Instead, it has located homosexual stormtroopers in the broader context of community, family, and local social relationships that include far more heterosexuals than homosexuals. This book has sought not only to illuminate the lived experiences of the small but fascinating sample of homosexual Nazis, but also to allow a proper focus on how political movements are shaped by their relationship with homosexuality as a concept, just as much as by their relationship to homosexual men and women as individuals. In this light, Nazism's mobilization of homophobia, and its alternating use and abuse of homosexual loyalists, shows how the importance of homosexuality in political systems does not come from the actions of a homosexual minority. It comes instead from the way political movements use the concept of homosexuality to manipulate loyalties among heterosexuals. In other words, although homosexual stormtroopers have often been among this book's main subjects, heterosexual readers should pay equally close attention to its lessons.

Other works exploring the history of homosexual Nazis have paired the two in order to titillate readers with the story of a strange evil. Whether they paint this evil as defeated or still threatening, they give the homosexual stormtrooper the critical role in shaping Nazism, and they define the most negative elements of Nazism as resulting from its gay members. This approach, however, risks erecting a moral blockade between the "normal," putatively heterosexual reader and the Nazis. By equating sexual deviance and political deviance, audiences can distance themselves from the causes of fascism and rest comfortably in a naïve belief that their societies, their social circles, and they themselves can never fall into fascist temptations. This is exactly the mistake of recent political writers who have misused versions of this history in the service of political campaigns. They have admitted to setting out to create a vision of fascism to which their own politics have no connection, while their enemies' politics assume the entire blame. This stance, however, reduces the Nazis merely to moral Others. They become simplistic bad guys whose actions can be scorned in order to preserve innocence of similar tendencies in the self.

Such "Othering" was in fact the very project in which the Nazis themselves engaged. It retains great popularity in America, not just in the homophobic conspiracies already discussed but in a broader tendency among Anglo-American audiences to readily cast Germany as a national Other whose special pathologies naturally made it home to such a dark ideology, which could never happen in the United States.

I recommend the opposite approach: to understand how people like us could become Nazis. Rather than studying National Socialism to gain ammunition to use against political enemies, we should understand the Nazis so we can understand ourselves. I hope that readers who are interested in Hamburg's descent into Nazism will grapple with it not as the product of a German pathology, or a homosexual conspiracy, or the result of an otherwise already authoritarian population, but as the outcome of a deteriorating democratic and economic system that had previously been a model of success. The men who became stormtroopers did not always come to the movement through their existing ideological stance as militarists, nationalists, or antisemites. Instead they often followed brothers, neighbors, friends, and co-workers along a social path to political destinations. Men joined the stormtroopers in order to live among like-minded comrades, to help care for one another in the context of economic devastation, and to try to rebuild family lives that the economy and their own mistakes had shattered. Unfortunately for all who encountered them, however, the positive impulses that stormtroopers claimed lay at the heart of their political life served mostly to justify their worst excesses. Competing tribal elements in their political style, as well as their own inherently combative personalities and narcissism, bred increasingly violent attempts to resolve social differences. As this study's examination of the stormtroopers' two dueling families has shown, the dynamic unleashed an astonishing level of violence, death, and tragedy.

The only positive thing that can come from a story like this is its warning to readers. Unless readers see their own societies, their own families, and their own selves in the stormtroopers, similar tragedies can occur.

NOTES

1   "Das alte Sturmlokal," *Hamburger Tageblatt*, October 6, 1934.

2   "Das alte Sturmlokal," *Hamburger Tageblatt*.

3   Bruce Campbell, "The SA After the Röhm Purge," *Journal of Contemporary History* 28, no. 4 (1993), 662, and Peter Longerich, *Geschichte der SA* (Munich: Verlag C. H. Beck, 2003), 223–224.

4   StAHH, 614-2/5 *Nationalsozialistische Arbeiterpartei (NSDAP) und ihre Gliederung* B174, and B177.

5   StAHH, 614-2/5 *Nationalsozialistische Arbeiterpartei (NSDAP) und ihre Gliederung* B186, Standarten 15 second quarter report.

6   StAHH, 614-2/5 *Nationalsozialistische Arbeiterpartei (NSDAP) und ihre Gliederung* B186 Fust letter of December 10, 1935.

7   Götz Aly, *Hitler's Beneficiaries: Plunder, Racial War, and the Nazi Welfare State* (New York: Henry Holt & Co., 2006), 36.

8   Ian Kershaw, *Hitler: Hubris* (New York: W. W. Norton & Company, 1999), 562, and Longerich, *Geschichte der SA*, 227–230.

9   Kershaw, *Hitler: Hubris*, 569–571.

10   StAHH, 614-2/5 *Nationalsozialistische Arbeiterpartei (NSDAP) und ihre Gliederung* B220, Oberführer Schwäble to sämtliche Standarten und Sturmbanne, January 4, 1935.

11   StAHH, 614-2/5 *Nationalsozialistische Arbeiterpartei (NSDAP) und ihre Gliederung* B220, Oberführer Schwäble to Julius Streicher, January 4, 1935.

12   StAHH, 614-2/5 *Nationalsozialistische Arbeiterpartei (NSDAP) und ihre Gliederung* B223 Band 1, documents spanning January 11, 1935, to February 28, 1935.

13   Campbell, "The SA After the Röhm Purge," 665.

14   Alan E. Steinweis, *Kristallnacht 1938* (Cambridge, MA: Harvard University Press, 2009), 150. Steinweis references files in the Wiener Library, London, that contain more details on these and other attacks, the importance of which to the SA could merit a separate study.

15   StAHH, 614-2/5 *Nationalsozialistische Arbeiterpartei (NSDAP) und ihre Gliederung* B200, Fust orders of February 1, 1936.

16   StAHH, 614-2/5 *Nationalsozialistische Arbeiterpartei (NSDAP) und ihre Gliederung* B246, Joseph Goebbels, "Aufruf zur deutschen olympischen Schulung."

17   Campbell, "The SA After the Röhm Purge," 666–669.

18   NARA A3341 SA Kartei 005: Walter A.

19   Elizabeth Harvey, *Women and the Nazi East: Agents and Witnesses of Germanization* (New Haven, CT: Yale University Press, 2003), 10.

20   Frank Bajohr, *"Aryanisation" in Hamburg: The Economic Exclusion of Jews and the Confiscation of Their Property in Nazi Germany* (New York: Berghahn Books, 2002).

21   StAHH, 614-2/5 *Nationalsozialistische Arbeiterpartei (NSDAP) und ihre Gliederung* B178, Jüttner letter of February 7, 1940.

22   Monica Black, *Death in Berlin: From Weimar to Divided Germany*, Publications of the German Historical Institute (Cambridge, England: Cambridge University Press, 2010).

23   StAHH, 614-2/5 *Nationalsozialistische Arbeiterpartei (NSDAP) und ihre Gliederung* B184b, undated document.

24 On the mechanics of a firestorm, see Gordon Musgrove, *Operation Gomorrah: The Hamburg Firestorm Raids* (London: Jane's, 1981), 102–116.

25 Jan Heitmann, *Das Ende des Zweiten Weltkrieges in Hamburg* (Frankfurt am Main: Peter Lang, 1990), 21–22, and 162–170. Hans Erich Nossack has written a gripping first-person account of his experiences in the firestorm: *The End: Hamburg 1943* (Chicago: University of Chicago Press, 2004).

26 NARA A3341 SA Kartei 048: Werner B.

27 NARA A3341 SA Kartei 048: Werner B.

28 NARA A3341 SA Kartei 048: Werner B.

29 Archiv FZH/WdE – 88 CZ.

30 Archiv FZH/WdE – 348 T.

31 Archiv FZH/WdE – 348 T.

32 StAHH 131-15 Senatskanzlei – Personalakten C608.

33 Rainer Hering, *Die Bischöpfe. Simon Schöffel, Franz Tügel. Hamburger Lebensbilder*, Band 10 (Hamburg: Verlag Verein für Hamburgische Geschichte, 1995), 271.

34 Hering, *Die Bischöpfe*, 271 and 272.

35 Hering, *Die Bischöpfe*, 280–281.

36 Archiv FZH, 11C1 Alfred Conn, memoirs 148–149.

37 Archiv FZH, 11C1 Alfred Conn, 148–149, and *Widar: Deutschglaubiges Kampfblatt* 26, no. 6 (1935/1936), and *Ring der Treue* 7 (1963), both found in Archiv FZH, 662-8.

38 Archiv FZH, 11C1 Alfred Conn, 161.

39 Archiv FZH, 11C1 Alfred Conn, 189.

40 Andrea Slade, *A Not So Foreign Affair: Fascism, Sexuality, and the Cultural Rhetoric of American Democracy* (Durham, NC: Duke University Press, 2001), 4.

41 For the history of the triangle's reclamation in this way—as well as the problems and criticisms of the approach—see Erik Jensen, "The Pink Triangle and Political Consciousness: Gays, Lesbians, and the Memory of Nazi Persecution," *Journal of the History of Sexuality* 11, nos. 1–2 (January/April 2002): 319–349.

42 Susan Sontag, "Fascinating Fascism," *New York Review of Books*, February 6, 1975.

43 Scott Lively and Kevin Abrams, *The Pink Swastika: Homosexuality in the Nazi Party* (Keizer, OR: Founders Publishing Corporation, 1995), iv. A useful guide to the errors and inaccuracies can be found in "The Annotated Pink Swastika," in which the text is deconstructed page by page in order to reveal its many flaws. Available at http://www.qrd.org/qrd/religion/anti/annotated.pink.swastika.

44 Mariah Blake, "Meet the American Pastor behind Uganda's Anti-Gay Crackdown," *Mother Jones*, March 10, 2014. Available at http://www.motherjones.com/politics/2014/03/scott-lively-anti-gay-law-uganda.

45 "Uganda plans to introduce a new anti-gay law that will withstand any legal challenge, a government minister has told the BBC. It will not explicitly refer to homosexuality, but will rely on the penal code which prescribes a life sentence for 'unnatural acts' . . . Activists say the plan is more draconian than anti-gay legislation annulled by the courts in August. The minister . . . said the proposed legislation will be a streamlined version of the annulled Anti-Homosexuality Act." "Uganda Planning New Anti-Gay Law Despite

Opposition," BBC *News Africa*, November 10, 2014. Available at http://www.bbc.com/news/world-africa-29994678.

46 Laurie Goodstein, "Ugandan Gay Rights Group Sues U.S. Evangelist," *New York Times*, March 14, 2012.

47 *Huffington Post*, "Russia's Anti-Gay Law Is 'One of My Proudest Achievements' Claims Pastor Scott Lively," September 24, 2013. Available at http://www.huffingtonpost.com/2013/09/24/russia-scott-lively-_n_3982608.html. Last accessed October 5, 2014.

48 Timothy Snyder, "Russia, Fascism, and the Ukraine," *New York Review of Books*, March 20, 2014.

49 Brian Tashman, "Scott Lively Blames Gays for Ukrainian Crisis, Lauds Russia as Human Rights Leader of the World," *Right Wing Watch*, March 11, 2014. Available at http://www.rightwingwatch.org/content/scott-lively-blames-gays-ukraine-crisis-lauds-russia-human-rights-leader-world. Last accessed October 5, 2014.

50 Oleg Shynkarenko, "Ukraine Separatists' Pro-Putin Raps," *The Daily Beast*, June 23, 2014. Available at http://www.thedailybeast.com/articles/2014/06/23/ukraine-separatists-dj-pro-putin-raps.html.

51 Paul Wesley Sullivan, "'Gay Nazis' Fueling Ukraine Uprising, Putin Says," WTVM, May 13, 2014. Available at http://www.wtvm.com/story/25509513/gay-nazis-fueling-ukraine-uprising-putin-says.

ACKNOWLEDGMENTS

This study of the stormtroopers' social relationships and support networks would not have been possible had I not enjoyed such strong systems of support myself. I therefore take great pleasure in thanking the many family members, friends, colleagues, and institutions that helped bring this project from idea to reality.

I have been fortunate to have studied under a number of inspiring scholars of European history. At Georgetown, my dissertation advisor, Roger Chickering, guided my research and writing with a wise eye, a firm editorial hand, and at times a gentle and necessary foot to the backside. Richard Stites, dearly missed by all who knew him, intuitively understood my interest in totalitarian culture and gave me the confidence to push through when challenged by historians who did not share my interest. Katrin Sieg introduced me to a level of theoretical rigor I had not expected to apply. The final member of my dissertation committee, Geoffrey Giles of the University of Florida, has long been a fierce supporter and a trenchant, detail-oriented critic whose efforts greatly improved both my dissertation and my book manuscript. Other scholars at Georgetown, including Amy Leonard, Richard Kuisel, John McNiel, and Aviel Roshwald, offered consistent intellectual, professional, and personal advice, for which I am grateful. In Germany, my fellow SA specialists Sven Reichardt and Daniel Siemens both provided key counsel and critique, contributing to the earliest and latest stages of this work, respectively. Finally, I must thank Peter Hayes of Northwestern University, who first taught a very young me about the stormtroopers, and whose continuing mentorship gave me a model to follow in life. This book would not have been possible without the support of these and countless other scholars.

Many institutions have supported my work, including Georgetown University's BMW Center for German and European Studies, which supported summer research and language study in Germany. The Fulbright Commission provided funds for my major archival research in Hamburg, where I benefited from the knowledge and assistance of professionals in the Staatsarchiv Hamburg, Forschungsstelle für Zeitgeschichte, and Geschichtswerkstatt Eimsbüttel. Heino Rose of the Staatsarchiv proved a tireless investigator of police and judicial records, successfully finding many of the names on the seemingly endless lists I regularly sent him. The

Staatsarchiv's Rainer Hering and Helga Wunderlich also provided significant reference assistance. At the Forschungsstelle, Axel Schildt hosted my research abroad, while Angelika Voss-Louis provided both local and long-distance reference assistance. I am fortunate to have studied in a city that provides so many avenues of support to historians.

But historians cannot live on financial support alone.

While in Hamburg, I enjoyed the hospitality and encouragement of several friends, whose warmth and generosity should put to rest any lingering stereotypes of cold north Germans. Gunnar, Heidi, and Boris Brunst welcomed a stranger into their home during my first weeks in the city, and afterward continued to prove friendly hosts. Katrin Johnson, Dennis Beier, Heiko Rabenalt, and Marcel Werth proved great friends who opened their homes to me on many occasions, which allowed me to return to do further research even when grant money ran its course.

I have also been fortunate to benefit from the local presence of the German Historical Institute (GHI) of Washington, D.C., an invaluable resource just minutes from home. Within the GHI, Richard Wetzell's tireless organization of the Transatlantic Doctoral Seminar (TDS) and Young Scholars' Forum introduced me to peers on both sides of the Atlantic. Special thanks must go to the participants of the 2006 TDS in Freiburg, who pushed me to explore my work in new and challenging ways. Similarly, the 2007 conference "Reading Hamburg," jointly sponsored by the GHI and Forschungsstelle, enabled me to meet many Anglo-American scholars of the Hansestadt whose work I had long admired. Their warm engagement and trenchant commentary greatly improved my work.

In a work about families, I must thank mine. My parents, Tom and Dorene Wackerfuss, have from my first moments given me the love, support, and encouragement that make possible everything I have done or will yet do. My brothers, Eric and Phil Wackerfuss, my first comrades, have always inspired me to excel. My partner, Eric Spears, provided encouragement for my work from our first conversation, and over the ensuing years he has proven a bastion of support on the long road to publication. I must also thank the friends who became my comrades through young adulthood and early professional trials: Eric Kleiman, Nathan Kreps, Joe Hickerson, Chris Wiley, and Adam Kaplan, who left us too soon. Their support and friendship during my adventure through this history has profoundly shaped my outlook on both the present and the past.

Finally, I must thank the group of professionals at Harrington Park Press, whose enthusiasm and work ethic have put this project over the top and given it physical form. Bill Cohen earns my everlasting gratitude for choosing me to help relaunch his press. His fatherly concern and professional advice have been invaluable. Richard Koffler, Steven Rigolosi, and Dody Riggs provided a level of editorial support that both thrilled and humbled its recipient. Any author would be lucky for his or her work to receive such sustained and skilled attention. Irina Oryshkevich did yeoman's work preparing the glossary. Patrick Ciano as designer and Ann Twombly as production editor have both exerted their skilled influence on the final product. This abundance of intellectual, financial, and personal support have given me immeasurable strength through this long process. I take great pride in the final result, and I hope that those listed here are proud as well. One of the few points of agreement I have with my subjects is that heroic accomplishment is made possible only through the steadfast support of family, friends, and colleagues. Their energies have sustained me as I have worked to produce this book, which itself shows how these important support systems can be horribly misused.

GLOSSARY

Alexander the Great (356–323 BCE): King of ancient Macedon, who, through brilliant military conquests, created an empire stretching from Egypt to India.

Alldeutscher Verband (Pan-German League): Nationalist organization founded in 1891 to promote German nationalism, expand German territory in Europe and the colonies, and strengthen German economic and imperial might. Its antisemitism, social Darwinism, and expansionistic policy goals had great influence among the wealthy urban middle class and elite, especially in northern Germany. Its connections to these groups, as well as to the imperial government and military, gave it an important role in German politics despite its relatively small membership.

Aryan: A concept of 19th-century anthropology that theorized an "Aryan race" of Caucasians, who traced their descent from an influential prehistorical people of the western Himalayas. German nationalists, including most famously the Nazis, traced a mythic legacy to this ancient supposed master race. They used it to justify their ideology of white supremacism, within which the so-called Nordic race reigned above even the other branches of the Aryans' supposed descendants. Nazi abuse of the term caused it to fall out of use in academic study.

Bismarck, Otto von (1815–1898): The Prussian statesman who was instrumental in unifying the states of Germany (save Austria) into an empire. He became its most famous chancellor.

Bolsheviks: Faction of the Marxist Russian Social Democratic Labor Party under the leadership of Vladimir Lenin and Alexander Bogdanov, which rose to power in Russia during the October Revolution of 1917. Founders of the Russian Soviet Federative Socialist Republic, they eventually became the Communist Party of the USSR.

Bolshevism: A popular way, usually derogatory in Germany and Britain, to refer to the communist system and its worldwide political movement.

Brandenburger Tor (Brandenburg Gate): Neoclassical triumphal arch built at the beginning of Unter den Linden, one of Berlin's most magnificent boulevards, by King Frederick William II in Berlin in 1788–1791 as a symbol of peace.

Braunes Haus (Brown House): Munich headquarters of the Nazi Party, nicknamed for the Party's official color scheme, located at 45 Brienner Straße.

Brigade, Brigadeführer: "Brigade," "brigade leader." The SA's organizational and rank structure changed several times. For most of the period this story covers, the brigade level matched the SA's regional organization, in this case for the city of Hamburg.

Bürger: "Citizen," "member of the middle class." A German term historically describing a member of an urban middle class distinct from both farmers and nobles.

Bürgerschaft: "City council" or "citizens' council." The lower house of parliament in the Hanseatic cities of Hamburg and Bremen.

Bürgertum: "Bourgeoisie," "middle class," "citizenry." A German term historically related to the urban, mercantile middle class.

Bürgerverein: "Club" or "assembly of middle-class citizens." A term used for the wide variety of political associations, hobbyists' clubs, intellectual societies, and myriad other groups that many middle-class Germans belonged to in 19th- and early 20th–century Germany.

Carolingian: Early medieval style of architecture and art dating back to the Carolingian Empire (800–880 CE), which occupied much of present-day France and Germany.

Charlemagne (742?–814): King of the Franks who united much of northern Europe, laid the foundations of present-day Germany and France, and was crowned the first emperor of western Europe following the demise of the Roman Empire in the fifth century.

Communism: Socioeconomic system based on the political theory of Karl Marx (1818–1893), which advocated the common ownership of property, collective control of the means of production, and the absence of social classes. Although based on the same principles as socialism, Communism is more comfortable with violent political action, and it has generally been put into practice by a totalitarian state.

Czarism: Autocratic system of government ruled by a czar, a Slavic term for Caesar, or supreme ruler.

Danzig Corridor (Polish Corridor): Running through what was formerly Prussia, the Danzig corridor was a strip of land granted to the Second Republic of Poland (1920–1939) by the Treaty of Versailles (1919) to give Poland access to the Baltic Sea.

Deutsche Demokratische Partei, DDP (German Democratic Party): Party founded in 1918 by members of the former Progressive People's Party (Fortschrittliche Volkspartei) and the left wing of the National Liberal Party (Nazionalliberale Partei). Like the SPD and Zentrum, the DDP was committed to maintaining a republican form of government and protecting ethnic and religious minorities. Though initially popular and influential among the governing classes, it steadily lost votes throughout the Weimar period.

Deutsche Staatspartei, DStP (German State Party): A short-lived political party formed in 1930 as a sort of fusion party for liberal nationalists. It never gained much traction and dissolved itself after supporting the Enabling Act that ended the Republic.

Deutsche Volkspartei, DVP (German People's Party): Party formed in 1918 to represent the center and right-wing factions of the prewar National Liberal Party. As the National Liberals had done in the imperial period, it represented the business interests of major German industrialists, promoted free trade and economic expansion, and opposed socialism. For a time the DVP wielded influence in both opposition to and eventual cooperation with SPD governments, but it lost many seats after 1930. Like most non-Nazi parties, it was abolished after Hitler's rise to power in 1933.

Deutsche Zentrumspartei, Zentrum (Catholic Center Party): A lay Catholic party established in 1870 to prove and uphold the much-contested loyalty of Catholics to the German state. Politically pragmatic, it acknowledged both monarchy and democracy as acceptable forms of state and was thus willing to enter into various coalitions with governing parties. During the Weimar Republic its left-wing faction initially cooperated with the socialists, but shortly before the Republic's fall its right-wing faction participated in the deal that led to Hitler's assumption of absolute power.

Deutschlandlied: The German anthem since 1922, set to music by Joseph Haydn. It is more commonly known as "Deutschland, Deutschland, über Alles" ("Germany, Germany, above Everything").

Deutschnationaler Handlungsgehilfenverband, DHV (German Nationalist Workers Association): White-collar workers' union of the Weimar Republic.

Deutschnationale Volkspartei, DNVP (German National People's Party): Most important conservative and nationalist party of the Weimar Republic before the emergence of the Nazi Party. Formed in 1918 from a coalition of monarchists, wealthy capitalists, and landowners, it combined nationalist, antisemitic, and reactionary elements in opposition to both liberal democracy and socialism. Though generally made up of older and less radical members, it eventually cooperated with the Nazi Party.

Deutschvölkischer Schutz und Trutzbund (German Nationalist Protection and Defiance Federation): Radical, active, and influential antisemitic league in the Weimar Republic, many of whose members eventually joined the Nazi Party.

Dienst: "Service." The SA's most favored term for its political activities.

Dolchstoss: "Thrust of a dagger," "stab in the back." A legend popular in nationalist circles was that Germany had lost the Great War because of a lack of support on the home front and traitorous actions by pacifists, socialists, and Jews—what they referred to as the Dolchstoss.

Einwohnerwehr: "Citizens' militia."

Enabling Act: The act was added to the Weimar Constitution in 1933 with an amendment granting the German cabinet the right to pass laws without the approval of the Reichstag. Since the chancellor controlled the cabinet, this law essentially granted Adolf Hitler dictatorial power and ended the Weimar Republic.

Die Fahne Hoch ("Raise the Flag High"): The anthem of the Nazi Party, also known as the "Horst Wessel Lied." After 1930, it became, along with the Deutschlandlied, the co-national anthem of Germany. Its lyrics were composed by Horst Wessel, an SA commander who was killed by a Communist in 1930, thereby becoming the SA's most prominent national martyr.

Fascism: A notoriously difficult term to define that sees widespread but sloppy use, fascism in its basic definition can be considered an ideology of authoritarian ethnic nationalism. Fascism stands in opposition to liberalism, democracy, socialism, and communism. Although often allied with conservative parties, fascists share none of conservatism's respect for moderation, tradition, and restraint. Fascist parties instead preach revolutionary violent action, which they justify as the only way to defend a nation and state threatened by enemies. Fascist systems typically prize a sense of wounded nationhood, which they seek to redeem by purging designated enemies. The original fascist states grew in the aftermath of World War I, took power during the Great Depression, and were defeated in World War II. Since the war, few movements openly call themselves fascist, although the combination of radical ethnic nationalism and a belief in the redeeming power of violence continue to motivate political movements.

Frankfurt School: A school of neo-Marxist social scientists associated with the Institute of Social Science at Goethe University in Frankfurt, then organized in exile around the New School in New York.

Frederick the Great (1712–1786): One of the greatest Prussian kings, known for his military exploits, patronage of art and culture, advocacy of enlightened absolutism, and reputed homosexuality.

Freikorps: Literally "free corps," or voluntary militia. Taking their name from a historic term for volunteer militias in early modern German history, Free Corps units of nationalist veterans formed after World War I to defend German borders, resist attempts at revolution, and attack leftist political movements. Many of their members later drifted to Nazism and the SA.

Frontheil: Greeting common to nationalist war veterans, especially popular in Austria.

Führerstadt: Title given by Hitler to five cities (Berlin, Hamburg, Linz, Munich, and Nuremberg), which he intended to reconstruct and modernize.

Gau: A medieval term for a region analogous to an English shire, revived by the Nazi Party as the basis of its geographic organization. By 1938, all of Germany was divided into 30 Gaue, which became the de facto administrative units of the government.

Gauleiter: The governor of a Gau, or the leader of a regional branch of the Nazi Party. Appointed directly by Hitler, the Gauleiter enjoyed the highest political rank in the Nazi Party, subordinate only to the Reichsleiter and the Führer.

German Faith Movement: A religious movement of the Nazi period that combined German paganism and Nazi ideology. Associated with Jakob Wilhelm Hauer, a professor of religious studies at the University of Tübingen, it promoted Hitler's concept of "blood and soil" (the idea that ethnicity was rooted in blood and territory), the replacement of Christianity with pagan rituals and practices, and the cult of the Führer.

Gleichschaltung: "Synchronization" or "forcible coordination." Literally, "shifting into the same gear," a term used for the process of forcing all individuals and organizations to work in accordance with Nazi policies.

Gnadenkirche: "Church of Holy Mercy." A church in Hamburg's St. Pauli neighborhood.

Götterdämmerung: The last of Richard Wagner's four operas in the Ring Cycle (*Der Ring des Nibelungen*).

Grail Legend: Arthurian legend about medieval knights who attempted to retrieve the vessel (Holy Grail) that Christ used during the Last Supper.

Great Depression: Most severe worldwide economic recession of the 20th century. It began with the U.S. stock market crash of 1929, then spread across the globe with devastating economic and political effects, often strengthening authoritarian political movements.

Great War (World War I): Global war fought between 1914 and 1918, primarily in Europe. The aftermath of this legendarily deadly war saw the fall of several monarchies, the creation of new nation-states, and a general destruction of value systems that created an uncertain future for European nations and set the stage for future conflicts.

Hammonia: Patron goddess of Hamburg who first appeared in the 18th century.

Hanseatic League: A commercial league established in the 14th century by northern European coastal cities to protect their economic interests and diplomatic privileges.

Hansestadt: A city belonging to the Hanseatic League.

Heil Hitler: Literally "Hail Hitler," this was a greeting and salute used by the Nazis.

Heim: "Home" or "hostel." The SA's term for a system of barracks it established to house stormtroopers.

Hilfspolizei: A short-lived auxiliary police force created by the Nazis in February 1933 to supplement police ranks, consolidate the Nazi takeover of the German state, and punish Nazi enemies. The project also functioned as a jobs program for SA men, whose poor behavior in uniform led to its early end.

Hitlerjugend, HJ (Hitler Youth): A Nazi youth organization intended to mobilize and indoctrinate young people into the Party's militaristic and racist ideology. It was eventually composed of three groups: Hitlerjugend for boys ages 14 to 18; Deutsches Jungvolk for younger boys; and Bund Deutscher Mädel for girls ages 10 to 18. After 1936, membership was mandatory for all "Aryan" youth.

Hohenzollern: Dynastic family that ruled the Duchy of Brandenburg-Prussia under the Holy Roman Empire, eventually becoming rulers of the Kingdom of Prussia after much dynastic conflict in the 18th century.

Holy Roman Empire: Christian empire established in western Europe with the coronation of Charlemagne as emperor by the Catholic pope in 800. At its height in the 12th century, the empire's borders encompassed much of modern Germany, Austria, Belgium, the Czech Republic, Italy, and the Netherlands.

Honoratiorenpolitik: Loosely, "government of notables." A political style found in many transatlantic cities in which a republican oligarchy of mercantile elite leverage social and economic power into political authority.

Jungstahlhelm: Youth division of the Stahlhelm (Steel Helmets).

Kaiser: A German derivative of "Caesar," and the term applied to emperors of the German, Austrian, and Austro-Hungarian Empires.

Kameradschaft: "Camaraderie," "fellowship."

Kampfzeit: Literally "time of struggle," a term used by the Nazi Party to describe the period in which Hitler rose to power (1919–1933).

Kaserne: "Barracks."

Kindskopf: "Overgrown child."

Kommunistiche Partei Deutschlands, KPD (Communist Party of Germany): Party founded in 1917 by antiwar members of the SPD. One of the chief political parties in Germany between 1918 and 1933, it embodied the radical left of the German socialist movement. Its members drew inspiration and support from the Bolsheviks in Moscow and sought to replace the Republic with a Communist state along Soviet lines. Hitler banned it shortly after his appointment as chancellor, after which Communists who escaped imprisonment continued as an underground organization.

Konzentrationslager, KZ: "Concentration camp." A camp in which people are interned under inhumane conditions with no recourse to a fair trial. Although they existed before World War II, they are most commonly associated with the Nazi regime, of which they were an integral feature for incarcerating Jews, political opponents, homosexuals, and other designated enemies of the Nazi Party.

Kristallnacht: "Crystal Night" or "Night of Broken Glass." A series of coordinated attacks perpetrated by stormtroopers and other Nazis on Jewish synagogues, stores, and other property throughout Germany and Austria on the night of November 9–10, 1938. The term arose from the shattered glass that filled the streets the next day.

Langemarck: Small village in Belgium and site of the First Battle of Ypres, in October and November 1914. Around 2,000 German soldiers died in this early battle, many of them young volunteers who marched into battle singing patriotic songs.

Lenin, Vladimir Ilich (1870–1924): Marxist theorist and leading figure of the Bolsheviks during the Russian Revolution of 1917. Upon creation of the USSR in 1918, he became its first premier, serving until his death in 1924.

Liberalism: Political philosophy focused on personal and economic liberty and freedom. Through the 19th and early 20th centuries, liberalism became the governing ideology of big business, progress, and civil liberties. In Imperial Germany, the National Liberal Party allied itself with the crown to support nationalism, militarism, and expansionist foreign policy based on the successful models of the United Kingdom and United States. The party's demise with Germany's defeat in 1918 led to the formation of two new liberal parties in the country, the DVP (German People's Party) and the DDP (German Democratic Party), both of which supported the republican form of government during the Weimar era.

Lutheranism: A branch of Protestant Christianity based on the teachings and doctrine of the 16th-century German ecclesiastical reformer Martin Luther.

Luxembourg, Rosa (1871–1919): Marxist philosopher and economist of Polish-Jewish descent who immigrated to Germany and cofounded the Spartacus League, a revolutionary group that became the German Communist Party. During the failed Spartacus uprising in 1919, Luxembourg was captured by a Freikorps unit involved in suppressing the uprising; the troop beat her, killed her, and threw her body in a canal.

Männerbund: "Male society."

Marine SA: An SA unit composed of sailors who, without a permanent address on land, did not fall under normal SA geographic organization. It was headquartered in Hamburg, where SA Heime housed the men between assignments at sea.

Marxism: A method of social and economic analysis that focuses on the relations and conflict among social classes. The German philosophers Karl Marx and Friedrich Engels developed this view in the mid-19th century, based on theories of dialectical materialism: the idea that economic relationships produce social and political outcomes that determine the course of human history.

Märzgefallene: "March casualties." An epithet originally given to the heroic martyrs of the liberal March Revolution of 1848, who perished while fighting Prussian troops in the streets of Vienna and Berlin. After the Nazi rise to power in 1933, stormtroopers who had long fought with the movement applied this term ironically to latecomers, whom the old guard accused of joining the movement only for reasons of self-interest.

Nachhauseweg: "On the way home." For paramilitary organizations in the Weimar Republic, an attack *Nachhauseweg* was one that occurred while members walked home from political meetings, when they could potentially be caught alone or by surprise.

Nationalsozialistische Kraftfahrkorps, NSKK (National Socialist Motor Corps or National Socialist Drivers Corps): Nazi paramilitary organization whose main function was to train men to operate and maintain high-performance vehicles. Originally part of the SA (Motor SA), it became a separate organization after the purge of the SA in July 1934.

Nationalsozialistischer Deutscher Studentenbund, NSDStB (National Socialist Student Union): A branch of the NSDAP founded in 1926 as a student organization for Nazis.

Nazionalsozialismus (National Socialism): A right-wing reinterpretation of socialist ideology in which race or ethnicity replaced class as the defining basis of political conflict and loyalty. Though many different parties and organizations promoted this ideology, the National Socialist German Workers Party (see NSDAP) eventually came to dominate the field.

Nazionalsozialistische Deutsche Arbeiterpartei, NSDAP (Nationalist Socialist German Workers' Party): Commonly known as the Nazi Party, the NSDAP was a German political party formed to promote militaristic, racist, antisemitic, and nationalist political goals under the leadership of its Führer, Adolf Hitler (see Fascism). In 1933, after obtaining enough votes to form a coalition government in the Reichstag, the NSDAP engineered its total takeover the German state.

Nazionalsozialistische Freiheitsbewegung, NSFB (National Socialist Freedom Movement): Short-lived political party in Hamburg created by Nazi Party members in 1924 to continue their activities after authorities banned the NSDAP in the wake of Hitler's failed coup. The NSFB was absorbed into the Nazi Party when the ban was lifted in February 1925.

Neo-Romanesque: An architectural style modeled loosely on western European architecture of the 12th and 13th centuries, which gained popularity in both Germany and the United States in the 19th century.

Nietzsche, Friedrich Wilhelm (1844–1900): German philosopher, cultural critic, and poet whose philosophy and concepts (especially that of the Übermensch, or superman) were selectively adopted and exploited by the Nazis.

NS: Nazis often used this as a shorthand adjective to identify members of the movement: "NS women" would thus mean "Nazi women," or "women who are associated with the Nazi movement."

Nuremberg Laws: A series of antisemitic laws established by the Nazi Party in 1935 that classified Germans according to race. Those with four Aryan grandparents were deemed Germans with full citizens' rights; those with three or four Jewish, Roma, or black grandparents were deprived of German citizenship; those with two or three Aryan grandparents were classified as "Mischlingen" (of mixed race) and placed in an ambiguous category, but they could occasionally be raised to full citizens. The laws also banned intermarriage and sexual relations between members of these different groups, as well as display of the German flag by Jews.

Oberführer: "Senior leader." Roughly equivalent to that of senior colonel in the military. After 1926, it was the official rank granted to an SA leader in charge of a group of paramilitary units.

Oberste SA-Führung, OSAF (Supreme SA Leadership): Headquarters office of the SA as a whole, based in Stuttgart.

Odin: Major god in Norse and Germanic mythology.

Operation Gomorrah: A weeklong strategic bombing campaign over Hamburg carried out by the Royal Air Force and the U.S. Army Air Forces in July 1943. Unusually dry weather conditions and the concentrated heat of the bombs created a firestorm—a vortex of flames that devastated the city, killed 42,600 civilians, and destroyed hundreds of thousands of homes.

Ordnungspolizei: "Order police." The regular law-keeping arm of the police forces in Imperial and Weimar Germany. After 1933, it eventually came under SS control, replacing local police forces and extending itself into occupied territories.

Ortsgruppe: Local Nazi Party group or chapter, a territorial unit encompassing no more than 1,500 households.

Paragraph 175: Provision in Imperial German criminal code that forbade homosexual acts between men but did not apply to women. The Nazis broadened the law in 1935 to apply to any "lewd act" between men, even those without physical contact. The law remained on the books for decades in both postwar German states. The term was often used as a euphemism or shorthand for referring to homosexuality itself.

Parliamentarism: A democratic system of government in which the head of state is not the same as the head of government, who is instead chosen from the ranks of the political party with a majority in the legislature.

Proletarian/Proletariat: Members of the working class in Marxist theory, who work for wages rather than having capital.

Prussia: Originally a small kingdom on the Baltic Sea, Prussia became a major European power in the 18th century, with territories throughout central Europe. The Prussian-led unification of Germany in 1871 made it the center of the new German Empire, and the Prussian king became the German Kaiser. With the empire's fall in 1918, Prussia became the largest state of the Weimar Republic.

Rathaus: Literally, "council house." These town halls were particularly prominent in Hanseatic cities, where they served as centers of democratic governance and economic policy making.

Rathausmarkt: The central square in front of Hamburg's town hall. The Nazis renamed it Adolf-Hitler-Platz from 1933 to 1945.

Reichsbanner: "Flag of the Reich" was the centrist, republican paramilitary in the Weimar era. It was founded by the SPD, the DDP, and the Catholic Center Party (Zentrum) to defend democracy from the extremist paramilitaries of the left (Communist RFB) and right (Nazi SA). Although its members were from all three parties, it became most closely associated with the SPD.

Reichstagsbrandverordnung (Reichstag Fire Decree): Abbreviated term for the Decree of the Reich President for the Protection of People and State, a series of measures passed in the wake of the Reichstag fire of February 27, 1933. These measures severely curtailed German civil liberties, in effect granting Hitler unchecked power to direct the police against political enemies.

Reichmarks, RM: German currency from 1924 to 1948, also used in Austria from 1938 to 1945. Replaced the Papiermark after German inflation hit a peak in 1923.

Der Ring des Nibelungen (Ring Cycle): A cycle of four operas (*Das Rheingold, Die Walküre, Siegfried, and Götterdämmerung*) based on Norse legend and composed by Richard Wagner. Like other Wagner operas, they became strongly connected to German nationalist politics.

Röhmlinge: "Röhm boys." A derisive term used to mock the sexuality of members of the SA, based on chief of staff Ernst Röhm's known homosexuality.

Rotfrontkämpferbund, RFB (Red Front Fighting Brigade): The German Communist Party's paramilitary fighting organization during the Weimar era. It claimed to be a nonpartisan defense mechanism for the working class, though in practice it functioned to protect Communist political gatherings, stage public protests, attack symbols of capitalism, and engage in violent exchanges with the SA and other paramilitary organizations.

SA Heime: Group homes or hostels for members of the SA, catering to young, poor, and unemployed stormtroopers whose economic condition during the Great Depression made them targets of Nazi recruitment.

SA Mann: Literally "SA man," the term was both a specific rank and a general way to refer to stormtroopers.

Schar: "Squad" or "troop." The SA's smallest organizational unit.

Scharführer: "Squad leader." The title and later the rank were used by paramilitary organizations in the Third Reich, most notably the SA and the SS. In the SA, the Scharführer was the first noncommissioned officer.

Schlageter Bund: Nazi club founded in 1928, named after Leo Schlageter, a member of the resistance to French occupation of the Rhineland after World War I. Schlageter was arrested and executed in 1923, after which he became a martyr to German nationalist movements.

Schutzstaffel, SS (Protection Squadron): A Nazi Party paramilitary unit originally formed in 1923 as an elite guard for Party speakers at political meetings. Under its leader Heinrich Himmler, it became one of the most powerful Nazi institutions, expanding its portfolio to control police and security across Germany and the conquered territories, where it took a leading role in the worst crimes of the Nazi state.

Schwul: "Gay." Like the English term, this did not see widespread use before the later part of the 20th century, when it replaced the earlier term "homosexual" as a less stigmatizing way to refer to gay men and women.

Social Democrats: See Sozialdemokratische Partei Deutschlands.

Socialism: A socioeconomic ideology concerned with the inequalities of private property and capitalism, which it hopes to solve through greater government control over business and industry.

Soldatentum: "Soldierhood." The lifestyle of being a soldier.

SOPADE: Name of the SPD while in exile after Hitler's takeover in 1933. It operated in Prague, Paris, and London, continually escaping Nazi conquests in hopes of preserving the legacy and influence of German Social Democracy until the war could be won.

Sozialdemokratische Partei Deutschlands, SPD (Social Democratic Party of Germany): German political party blending democratic and socialist approaches to government. It was founded in 1875, and though outlawed for many years it became Germany's largest party by 1912. It led the Weimar Republic upon its creation in 1918, and throughout the Weimar period was the strongest proponent of the republican form of government. The Nazis banned the SPD after the takeover in 1933. Since its return after the war, it has remained among Germany's most important political parties.

Stahlhelm: Literally "the Steel Helmets," the Stahlhelm or Bund der Front-soldaten (League of Front Soldiers) was the largest political paramilitary organization in Weimar Germany. It functioned as a social and political veterans group, officially independent of political parties but mainly in support of nationalist and anti-republican forces. After the Nazi takeover of power, it was largely and reluctantly absorbed into the SA.

Standarte: An SA organizational unit roughly equivalent to a regiment (300–500 men).

Standartenführer: A paramilitary rank in various Nazi organizations, including the SA and SS, matching the organizational level of the Standarten.

Sturmabteilung, SA (Storm/Assault Division): Paramilitary wing of the Nazis whose violent tactics became the face of the Nazi Party during its drive for power. Through street battles and propaganda marches that often turned violent, they radicalized political conflict and undermined the stability of the Republic. Its members, the stormtroopers, were also known as Brownshirts owing to the color of their uniforms, and they are generally seen to represent the Nazi movement's socially and economically revolutionary wing.

Stürme/Sturmbanne: Smaller SA units roughly equivalent to a company, they were generally associated with specific neighborhoods.

Sturmführer: "Storm leader" or "assault leader." A paramilitary rank in the SA, inspired by a military specialty title in World War I. In the SA, it matched the organizational level of the Sturm.

Sturmlokale: Taverns associated with the SA, where stormtroopers held political meetings, enjoyed social gatherings, and planned paramilitary operations. Many taverns in the Weimar era were officially associated with political parties. The Lokale became key sites of violent conflict.

Swastika: This symbol, a cross with bent legs known in German as the twisted cross or *Hackenkreuz*, was originally a sacred symbol of Eastern religions, where it appears as an auspicious symbol on buildings and sacred sites. German mystic nationalists became fascinated with the symbol as a legacy of the Aryan people, which they misconstrued as progenitors of the Germans (see Aryan). Hitler appropriated the swastika symbol for Nazi use, twisting it 45 degrees to create a new image, which in the West is now mistakenly considered its main symbolic importance.

Tacitus (56–after 117 AD): Publius (or Gaius) Cornelius Tacitus was a Roman senator and historian.

Teutonic Knights: A medieval military order established during the Crusades but transformed in the 13th century to a force to spread Christianity in northeastern Europe.

Thermopylae and the 300: Reference to the famous ancient battle fought in 480 BCE between the Persian imperial army of Xerxes I and an alliance of Greek city-states led by King Leonidas of Sparta.

Third Reich: A term popularly used to describe Nazi Germany, whose official name was either the German Reich (1933–1943) or Greater German Reich (1943–1945). The Nazis favored this term for their own state because it legitimized their regime as a successor state to the Holy Roman Empire (the first Reich) and the German Empire of 1871–1818 (the second Reich).

Three-Kaiser Year: The year 1888, when three different German Kaisers occupied the throne. When the long-reigning Wilhelm I died in March, his son and successor, Frederick III, had already developed terminal cancer. He died in June, leaving his son to assume the throne as Wilhelm II.

Treaty of Versailles: The peace treaty between Germany and the Allied powers, signed on June 28, 1919, seven months after the armistice of November 11, 1918, which had brought the end to World War I. The treaty imposed a variety of punitive terms on Germany, including disarmament, territorial concessions, massive war reparations, and a "War Guilt Clause" that required Germany to accept moral and financial responsibility for the war. The extent of the punishment created lasting resentment among many Germans and encouraged the growth of right-wing political movements, which pledged to repeal them.

Truppführer: "Troop leader." A paramilitary rank in the SA above a Scharführer and comparable to senior (or first-class) sergeant.

Universum-Film Aktiengesellschaft, UFA: A German film-production company established in 1917 and purchased by the right-wing press baron Alfred Hugenberg in 1933, who transferred it to the Nazi Party.

Valhalla: Mythical land in Norse mythology where the souls of distinguished warriors dwell while they wait to fight alongside Odin in the final battles of the apocalypse.

Vaterstadt: "Hometown," literally "father-city."

Verband: "Association," "club."

Volk: "People." Term used by German nationalists to refer to the people of the German race (Germans, Scandinavians, the Dutch, and the English).

Völkisch: "Folkish" or "folkloric." Cultural and political movement beginning in 19th-century Germany that began as an embrace of the German language and literature for purposes of national unity. Over time, its increasingly extremist advocates combined folklore, history, and mysticism into a political project in the hope of establishing a militant and authoritarian racial state.

Völkisch-Sozialer Block, VSB: A cooperative party list, that is, a list comprising members of different political parties who by joining together in the 1927 parliamentary election hoped to garner more votes.

Volksgemeinschaft: "People's (or folk) community." Term for solidarity and community that became popular in Germany during World War I, when it had the connotation of a common purpose and equality among different members of the German nation. The Nazis transformed its associations into a more formal concept of social organization based on codified racial lines.

Wagner, Richard (1813–1883): German Romantic composer and theater producer whose popular and influential operas combined music, drama, poetry, and the visual arts into a "total work of art." Hitler and other leading Nazis admired Wagner's music for both its musical and political messages.

Weber, Max (1864–1920): German social scientist often considered one of the most important figures in creating the discipline of sociology.

Wehrverband: "Combat league."

Weimar Republic: When the Imperial German government fell at the end of World War I, it was replaced by a representative democracy featuring an elected president, an executive cabinet, and a legislature. Although the name of the state technically remained the German Reich, the new Republic was and is most often referred to by the city in which it was founded, Weimar. The Republic lasted until 1933, when Adolf Hitler's appointment as chancellor began a series of events that eventually ended in his dictatorship.

Wilhelm II (1859–1941): King of Prussia and last emperor of the German Empire, who ruled from 1888 to 1918. Fairly or unfairly, his personal character and idiosyncrasies often are blamed for causing World War I. In the war's final stage, when German defeat became clear, he abdicated the throne and spent the rest of his life in exile in the Netherlands.

Young Plan: A revised war reparations payment plan, one of several that sought to preserve the punitive terms of the Versailles Treaty by making them less harsh. The Young Plan of 1929, named after the American industrialist who chaired the Reparations Committee, eventually collapsed when the Great Depression made it impossible to expect any further payments from Germany.

INDEX